This book presents the most complete picture to date of faculty of color in elite HWCUs (historically white colleges and universities). It shows how higher education institutions promote unwelcoming climates that adversely affect their career trajectories and health and well-being. A fascinating read with both frustrating and triumphant moments, the book provides a necessary analysis of the professional lives of an important intellectual group in the academy.

—Eduardo Bonilla-Silva, author of *White Out:*
*The Continuing Significance of Racism*

In *Toxic Ivory Towers*, Ruth Zambrana deftly and painfully explores the life experiences of underrepresented minority faculty of color in the academy. The author demonstrates how hegemonic white cultures and structures create and sustain systems of exclusion and discrimination that result in extensive workplace psychological stress for many minority scholars. She goes further than most, locating these academic inequities in the broader and historical contexts of racial and economic injustice in the academy and the society at large.

—Mark Chesler, Professor Emeritus, University of Michigan,
coeditor of *Faculty Identities and the Challenge of Diversity*

*Toxic Ivory Towers* is a thorough review of relevant literature and critical analysis. It contributes to the literature a unique and nuanced examination of workplace stress and the health issues faced by minority faculty. A robust collection of survey and interview data, this book is an important read for educators leading the way toward intentional inclusion within the professoriate.

—Caroline Turner, author of *Diversifying the Faculty:*
*A Guidebook for Search Committees*

Through an insightful examination of relevant literature and original research, Ruth Zambrana offers a unique and compelling perspective on the entry, retention, and advancement of diverse professionals in science- and health-related careers from a historical and contemporary viewpoint. These are individuals who often find themselves in systems where they are marginalized and/or undervalued because of intersections related to race, ethnicity, gender, and being "other." *Toxic Ivory Towers* moves the dialogue and the strategic action-agenda and as such contributes significantly to understanding knowledge gaps and illuminating intervention points to advance diversity in the scientific workforce.

—Joan Y. Reede, Harvard Medical School,
Dean for Diversity and Community Partnership

# TOXIC IVORY TOWERS

# TOXIC IVORY TOWERS

## The Consequences of Work Stress on Underrepresented Minority Faculty

RUTH ENID ZAMBRANA

RUTGERS UNIVERSITY PRESS
New Brunswick, Camden, and Newark, New Jersey, and London

Library of Congress Cataloging-in-Publication Data

Names: Zambrana, Ruth E., author.
Title: Toxic ivory towers : the consequences of work stress on underrepresented
minority faculty / Ruth Enid Zambrana.
Description: New Brunswick, New Jersey : Rutgers University Press, 2018. | Includes
bibliographical references and index.
Identifiers: LCCN 2017055144 | ISBN 9780813592985 (hardback : alk. paper) |
ISBN 9780813592978 (paperback : alk. paper) | ISBN 9780813592992 (epub)
Subjects: LCSH: Minority college teachers—United States. | Minorities in higher
education—United States. | Faculty integration—United States. | Universities and
colleges—United States—Faculty. | Discrimination in high education—United
States. | BISAC: EDUCATION / Higher. | SOCIAL SCIENCE / Discrimination
& Race Relations. | BUSINESS & ECONOMICS / Labor. | PSYCHOLOGY /
Ethnopsychology. | SOCIAL SCIENCE / Ethnic Studies / African American
Studies. | SOCIAL SCIENCE / Ethnic Studies / Hispanic American Studies. |
SOCIAL SCIENCE / Social Classes.
Classification: LCC LB1778.2 .Z35 2018 | DDC 378.1/20973—dc23
LC record available at https://lccn.loc.gov/2017055144

A British Cataloging-in-Publication record for this book is available from the British
Library.

∞ The paper used in this publication meets the requirements of the American
National Standard for Information Sciences—Permanence of Paper for Printed
Library Materials, ANSI Z39.48-1992.

www.rutgersuniversitypress.org

Manufactured in the United States of America

This book is dedicated to all URM research faculty, who persevere and contribute creative and innovative knowledge and pay it forward through mentoring and institutional and community work so that others can follow in their footsteps. I dedicate this work in recognition of all these professionals who in the face of inequitable economic, social, and interpersonal treatment, often without rewards or institutional recognition, persist in the hope of opening new doors of change, justice, equity, and opportunity.

# CONTENTS

# TOXIC IVORY TOWERS

# 1 · WHERE IS THE DIVERSITY?

## The Importance of the Domestic Talent Pool in Elite Higher Education Institutions

> So it was very frustrating and people would say, "Well, we don't have problems here." Because I would say, "We need representation because we don't have diversity and people aren't learning," and they all—my faculty—would say, "It's not a problem. We don't have any problems here." But we do have problems here; we don't have any diversity here.
>
> —African American female

The discourse on diversity has become prolific in the last three decades.[1] It has generated a whole new lexicon of words and constructs that generate multiple definitions and interpretations in the United States due to their ambiguity. Yet the versatility of diversity and its attractiveness to the majority group in America is precisely its inability to address issues of racial and ethnic inequality. Zanoni, Janssens, Benschop, and Nkomo (2010) provide an incisive critique of the term *diversity* and the critical diversity literature. They proffer important questions regarding the evidence that diversity management increases equal opportunity and interrogate the limited empirical study on diversity and the experiences of historically disadvantaged groups (p. 6). The language of diversity eschews any thoughtful discussion of structural and racial and ethnic inequality. Most importantly, the diversity discourse overlooks the rationale and impetus of the 1960s civil rights movement and its focus on inequality, racism, and elitism. That moment in history drew attention to four racial/ethnic groups who were native born and *not* immigrant groups: Blacks of African origin, Puerto Ricans, Mexican Americans, and American Indian / Alaska Natives, the original inhabitants of the U.S. territories. The underrepresented minority (URM) faculty studied in this book are composed of those four groups.

Definitions of race/ethnicity are at the heart of the diversity discourse. Set aside but not forgotten are the definitions from fifty years ago that contributed to the unveiling of the "Other America" (Harrington, 1962) and the unequal treatment of those groups who had been silenced but not overcome. The past fifty years have widened the landscape of opportunity by a sliver and increased at best token representation in elite colleges and universities of URM undergraduate students, graduate students, and faculty. In the United States, we have narrowed opportunity by perpetuating a *testocracy*, as coined by Guinier (2015, p. ix), that undermines our democracy and continues to ensure that the avenues of opportunity are most available to the majority of economically and affluent classes both native and foreign born. In 2010, African Americans (7.4 percent) and Hispanic groups (5.8 percent) compared to non-Hispanic Whites (74.3 percent) were much less likely to hold doctoral degrees (U.S. Department of Education, 2012). Additionally, racial/ethnic faculty are much less likely to have wealth and economic resources compared to their White counterparts. The median wealth of White households is twenty times that of Black households and eighteen times that of Latino households (Taylor et al., 2011). A set of characteristics distinguish traditionally historically underrepresented groups from majority-culture and other racial and ethnic groups. These groups (African American, Mexican American, American Indian / Alaska Native) are defined as underrepresented due to their historical and contemporary underrepresentation in higher education institutions relative to their proportion in the general U.S. population. These groups share a history of involuntary incorporation into the United States (via slavery, colonization, or land acquisition) that shaped avenues of economic and social opportunity throughout the life course and across generations and has contributed to repeated hardships and a legacy of exclusionary experiences in higher education. The riveting question that haunts our education system is how these groups are being included in diversity initiatives.

Overall, URM faculty have achieved minimal progress compared to majority-culture women, other racial/ethnic groups, and foreign-born faculty in all major disciplines and professions and in the professoriate.[2] Despite trends toward greater representation of URM students in colleges and universities and university-based discourses on diversity, URM faculty are still disproportionately underrepresented across all degree-granting institutions. Concern regarding promotion, tenure, and retention of diverse and underrepresented faculty is a national phenomenon and one that is palpably felt on university campuses. The promise of the meritocracy continues to be elusive for many URMs.

In attempting to understand why URM faculty are grossly underrepresented in higher education, this work examines the social and economic inequalities and work-life experiences URM faculty face in predominantly White research institutions. In addition to making a much-needed contribution to the literature on work-family balance among URM professionals who have been understudied in the field of marriage and family, the study identifies the unique workplace stress that exists in elite academic employment settings and the impact it has on the health and mental well-being of URM faculty. Importantly, this research can be translated into practices that higher education institutions can employ to recruit, retain, and promote URM professionals.

## TARGETS OF OPPORTUNITY OR TARGETS OF OMISSION?

*Diversity*, a word that appeared in the 1980s as a backlash to any notion of affirmative action, has taken on many meanings in society, but also in higher education among faculty, administrators, and students. The epistemology of the word has contributed to a large corpus of scholarship that seeks to find not only its meaning but its utility to inform social concerns or advancement of URM faculty and students in higher education. Every discipline wants to partake of its aura without interrogation of its potential harm. For example, the academic work environment framework merges prior research on diversity climate (Hurtado, Milem, Clayton-Pedersen, & Allen, 1999; Price et al., 2009) and perceptions of campus climate (Jayakumar, Howard, Allen, & Han, 2009). Heckman, Johnson, Foo, and Yang (2017) surveyed 350 executives on several diversity-valuing behaviors, including whether they respected cultural, religious, gender, and racial differences; valued working with a diverse group of people; and felt comfortable managing people from different racial or cultural backgrounds. They defined diversity-valuing behavior as that which promotes demographic balance within organizations. Although much of the noninstitutional research on URM and "faculty of color" has focused on issues of diversity and retention, few studies have critiqued the limited impact of the implementation of traditional diversity initiatives in light of the limited presence and success of URM faculty in predominantly White institutions (Alex-Assensoh, 2003). However, does merely inserting diversity into every discourse and every discipline significantly change the social fabric of institutional policies and practices? Is there a shared meaning among faculty and/or administrators that can guide institutional policies and practices? A central question arises: Who is benefiting from the diversity mandate?

According to a 2009 National Science Foundation (NSF) report, the most impressive outcomes in fueling the pipeline have been for majority-culture White and international women as reflected in the growth of science and engineering (26.5 percent) and social sciences (59.7 percent) doctorates awarded (American Council on Education, 2016; Fiegener, 2009). At this juncture it behooves us, as Bowleg (2012) argues and common sense dictates, that the ampersand of "women & minorities" must be unlinked. The progress made by majority-culture women far outweighs the limited progress made by all under-represented men and women. Achieving the doctorate is an important educational marker that provides entry into the professoriate. Although scholars and social justice activists easily invoke the Women's Movement, the Health Consumer Movement, and the Anti-war Movement as rationales for supporting progress for women, patients, and demilitarization, the invocation of the civil rights movement and mention of limited progress for historically underrepresented groups inject citizens with a defensive alertness. In fact, one can certainly make an argument that the promise of civil rights for all historically incorporated Americans has slowly been abandoned (Valdez, 2015). What is the evidence for this statement?

In institutions of higher education, URMs constitute less than 11 percent of all faculty, compared to 34 percent of the U.S. population (Kena et al., 2015).[3] These groups represent a segment of the diversity compendium of the domestic talent pool, an important resource in institutions of higher learning. Yet, despite trends toward greater representation of URM students in colleges and universities and university-based discourses on diversity, URM faculty are still disproportionately underrepresented across all degree-granting institutions. Imperative to clarify is for whom the equality of citizenship rights was intended. Who stood to benefit from the promise is an equally critical question. Extant data on hiring practices and retention suggest that the URM domestic talent pool is not viewed by those in power as integral to the fabric of higher education institutions but is deployed only as part of a symbolic diversity discourse.

Although universities employ the language of "diversity" and "inclusion," this type of "race" talk does not disrupt the reproduction of Whiteness and leaves institutional structures of inequality unchanged (Ahmed, 2012; Brayboy, 2003). Evidently not only "fears" about violating the laws of race-conscious hiring policies (which of course do not apply in legacy admissions) but equally important fears about tipping the balance of White hegemonic power (Hoover, 2015) drive this diversity discourse. Hegemonic power is maintained and reinforced by ensuring the inclusion of groups who share a similar value orientation of competition and individualism and a belief in the meritocracy of the elite. Significant questions must be asked about how students, teachers, and administrators who share similar beliefs and values, such as racial equality and social justice, can alter the contours of higher education. As Collins observed of the gatekeepers who lived in the house of the master and wanted to change the rules, "The master's tools will never dismantle the master's house" (Audre Lorde, quoted in Collins, 2015, p. 9).

Reflecting on the role of hegemonic power begs a question: Is diversity both a target of opportunity and a target of exclusion or omission? Moreover, a review of the diversity literature reveals its multiple meanings and misuses in its efforts to accommodate a role for progress. Strong critiques have been leveled at the ambiguity of and license for unmonitored interpretations of diversity with reference to limited progress of URM in higher education. Contemporary critiques suggest that we pause and ask questions: How do we conceptualize and pursue diversity in higher education institutions? How do we engage critically with our curricula to fulfill our educational missions to provide multiple perspectives? Are we providing equal access, opportunities, and support to students from all backgrounds, considering students from URM backgrounds are relatively absent from doctoral programs? Who will teach the next generation of college-bound students, and does it matter what perspectives they present? Do we need multiple perspectives in higher education to create and respond to a more global and diverse world? How will the internalization of faculty and students in institutions of higher learning increase/decrease or replace our goals of equity? And, a remnant of an age-old question, can education be the great equalizer for URM faculty and students?

These questions are emerging as colleges and universities are under fire and states are disinvesting in higher education. They also come at a time when the United States is on the cusp of an inevitable demographic shift that will result in a majority-minority nation, making the need for URM faculty in higher education even more pressing. Research supports the premise that racial, ethnic, and gender diversity in faculty is an asset not only to institutional diversity goals but also to knowledge production, the transfer of knowledge, the attraction of URM students, and partnerships with underserved communities. Thus significant underrepresentation of URM in faculty ranks demands a more complete analysis of the institutional and social barriers that prevent a more robust presence.

Despite the attention that has been focused on the importance of diversifying the professoriate in racial/ethnic dimensions, significant inequities remain (American Federation of Teachers, 2010; American Psychological Association [APA], 2004; Moore, Acosta, Perry, & Edwards, 2010). While greater numbers of URM students are increasingly filling college and university classrooms, URM faculty representation lags far behind. Table 1.1 shows that among racial/ethnic faculty in 2013, approximately 6.0 percent were African American, 5.0 percent were Hispanic, .04 percent were American Indian / Alaska Native, and 10.0 percent were Asian (U.S. Department of Education, 2015). Many of these URM faculty are concentrated in minority-serving institutions, constitute only a small proportion of faculty at major research universities, leave the academy at greater rates than White faculty, and are more dissatisfied with their workplace environment and perceived professional rewards (APA, 2004; Moore et al., 2010; Trower, 2009). Often when there are surges in numbers of URM faculty, they reflect URM representation in contingent, non-tenure-track positions, and mask their higher attrition rates. Drawing on data from 2007, of the 10.5 percent of faculty positions held by URMs, 7.6 percent were in contingent positions. This means that 73 percent of URM faculty were in contingent positions, likely indicating inadequate wages/benefits and lack of job security and academic freedom (American Federation of Teachers, 2010).

## MOVING THE NEEDLE OF HIGHER EDUCATION POLICY TO PRACTICE TRANSFORMATION: DOES THE LAW MATTER?

David Riesman (1956) offered the classic characterization of the importance of hierarchy and stratification in American higher education when he described the system of higher education as a "snakelike" procession in which the tail (composed of institutions lower in the hierarchy) and the body (representing

TABLE 1.1    Percentage of full-time instructional faculty at degree-granting institutions by race/ethnicity and gender (1985–2013)

| Year | Gender | Asian | Black | American Indian / Alaska Native | Hispanic | White |
|------|--------|-------|-------|---------------------------------|----------|-------|
| 1985 | Total | 4.0 | 4.1 | 0.4 | 1.7 | 89.9 |
| | Male | 3.2 | 2.3 | 0.3 | 1.2 | 65.5 |
| | Female | 0.8 | 1.9 | 0.1 | 0.5 | 24.4 |
| 1991 | Total | 5.1 | 4.7 | 0.3 | 2.2 | 87.7 |
| | Male | 3.9 | 2.5 | 0.2 | 1.4 | 60.2 |
| | Female | 3.9 | 2.2 | 0.1 | 0.8 | 27.5 |
| 1995 | Total | 5.0 | 4.9 | 0.4 | 2.3 | 85.1 |
| | Male | 3.7 | 2.5 | 0.2 | 1.4 | 55.8 |
| | Female | 1.3 | 2.4 | 0.2 | 0.9 | 29.2 |
| 2001 | Total | 6.2 | 5.1 | 0.4 | 3.0 | 80.9 |
| | Male | 4.2 | 2.6 | 0.3 | 1.7 | 49.8 |
| | Female | 1.9 | 2.6 | 0.2 | 1.3 | 31.0 |
| 2003 | Total | 6.5 | 5.3 | 0.5 | 3.2 | 80.2 |
| | Male | 4.4 | 2.6 | 0.3 | 1.8 | 48.6 |
| | Female | 2.1 | 2.7 | 0.2 | 1.4 | 31.6 |
| 2005 | Total | 7.2 | 5.2 | 0.5 | 3.4 | 78.1 |
| | Male | 4.7 | 2.5 | 0.3 | 1.8 | 46.4 |
| | Female | 2.5 | 2.7 | 0.2 | 1.5 | 31.7 |
| 2011 | Total | 8.8 | 5.5 | 0.5 | 4.1 | 74.0 |
| | Male | 5.4 | 2.4 | 0.2 | 2.1 | 41.5 |
| | Female | 3.4 | 3.0 | 0.2 | 2.0 | 32.6 |
| 2013 | Total | 10.0 | 6.0 | 0.4 | 5.0 | 79.0 |
| | Male | 6.5 | 2.4 | 0.2 | 2.8 | 43.0 |
| | Female | 3.5 | 3.6 | 0.2 | 2.2 | 35.0 |

SOURCES: U.S. Department of Education, National Center for Education Statistics, 1985, 1991, 1995, 2001, 2003, 2005, 2011, and 2013 Integrated Postsecondary Education Data System.

institutions in the middle of the hierarchy) of the snake continually try to move up and catch the head (those institutions at the top of the hierarchy that serve as a model for other institutions to follow). While it is a democratic ideal of education to level social inequity and equalize opportunity, history shows otherwise, as is discussed in chapter 2.

The intensification of the civil rights movement and President Lyndon B. Johnson's War on Poverty in the mid-1960s prompted the nation to respond to the reality that historically underrepresented minorities did not have equal access to education, jobs, housing, or other valued resources (American Council on Education [ACE] & American Association of University Professors [AAUP], 2000).[4] The failure to extend equal educational opportunities in higher education institutions, especially research universities, led to many judicial decisions. The landmark 1954 *Brown v. Board of Education* Supreme Court decision was the most influential and led to integrated public schools. By the early 1960s, except for students attending historically Black colleges and universities (HBCUs), only a very small number of URM attended college. Today, minorities of any race, ethnicity, or nativity constitute upward of one in five undergraduates at four-year colleges (ACE & AAUP, 2000).

Race-inclusive admissions were recognized by the Supreme Court in its 1978 decision in *Regents of the University of California v. Bakke*.[5] Race-sensitive practices, initially introduced to redress past wrongs, have evolved into policies that support university efforts to recruit URM faculty. Taking race and ethnic origin into account in admissions decisions is one of the most controversial of these practices. Despite an attempt by institutions of higher education to create a sense of belonging for URM students and faculty through race-conscious affirmative action programs since the court's *Bakke* decision, subsequent decisions by lower federal courts (such as the initial Fifth Circuit decision in *Hopwood v. Texas*), popular referenda (such as Proposition 209 in California and Initiative 200 in Washington), and institutional policies responding to these two mandates (such as the University of Florida Board of Higher Education's decision to end affirmative action in admissions) have called into question the diversity rationale as articulated in *Bakke*, resulting in cutbacks to race-conscious affirmative action across the United States (ACE & AAUP, 2000).

As national higher education needs to evolve, so does federal policy. The past several years have brought a multitude of updates to the Higher Education Act.[6] With the convening of the 114th Congress on January 6, 2015, the Obama administration's FY 2016 budget submission to Congress proposed to increase spending on many higher education programs and achieve savings by changing some student loan and repayment options. Included in the submission were proposals to provide free community college to some students through a matching grant mechanism, to streamline higher education tax breaks, and to create a bonus grant program to reward colleges that graduate large numbers of low-income students.[7] These policies would increase equity of access to higher education and decrease the student loan debt burden on a significant number of historically underrepresented students and undocumented Latino students who aspire to college. These policies would also begin to channel financial resources to those who confront the most significant barriers to educational opportunity. But under a new administration, the long- and short-range goals of moving toward more equitable educational opportunities have diminished.

Purposively, this book focuses on the experiences of the historically underrepresented professoriate in research-extensive institutions to understand why they are relatively absent in higher education. As Trower and Chait (2002) reported more than fifteen years ago, "After decades of scholarly research, hundreds of campus committee reports and scores of disciplinary and professional commissions on faculty diversity, the needle has scarcely moved and the numbers have hardly changed. The history of the academy on the matter of faculty diversity strongly suggests that self-reform has not worked—and will probably not work" (p. 37)—goodwill on the part of many notwithstanding.

Most of the extant work exploring the lives of URM faculty is captured in anthologies of small case studies or in scholarly narratives, and much of it does not distinguish between URM and non-URM populations (Bilimoria & Buch, 2010; Gutiérrez y Muhs, Niemann, González, & Harris, 2012; National Research Council, 2010; Robinson & Clardy, 2010). However, anecdotal and autoethnographic narratives provide an essential albeit limited view of the challenges faced by and successes of this group. These narratives convey most sharply a highly stressful work environment and significant sociopolitical implications. Large-scale studies have failed to include URM faculty, mainly due to the use of random sampling and small sample sizes, or researchers have aggregated all non-White faculty into a "faculty of color" category including international faculty, masking the unique challenges and contributions of the domestic talent pool.[8]

There is an emerging plethora of scholarship in sociology, public health, higher education, and psychology on workplace stress, perceived discrimination, coping strategies, and adverse physical and mental health effects (Hart & Cress, 2008; Wang et al., 2007; Webb & Gonzalez, 2006) that has much to contribute in this area. New insights can be garnered about the experiences of professional URMs regarding workplace stress, work–family life balance, and mentoring practices and their impact on career pathways. Moreover, relationships between workplace stress including perceived discrimination, coping strategies, and health and mental well-being capture lived experiences in their elite institutional settings. This study addresses the gaps in the literature with rich data to uncover how URM faculty navigate the complex higher education system in their quest to secure economic security and a meaningful and successful career path. Additionally, these data lend support to other findings that signal the urgent need to change the ways in which higher education institutions pursue and achieve diversity.

These data focus on a segment of the U.S. workforce who will play a vital role, through their place in higher education institutions, in shrinking the social and economic inequalities in poor and racial/ethnic communities and educating future cohorts of URM and diverse students as citizens of a global society. Diverse college faculty are essential in spreading new knowledge and fostering pluralistic perspectives among young change agents who will advance equity in a diverse and global society. URM faculty who focus on community-engaged or social-problem-oriented research agendas are committed to poor and racial/ethnic students, contribute to solving community concerns, serve as good stewards of the academy, and can make significant contributions to research, service engagement, and mentoring the next generation. If we are to be a truly innovative, inclusive, and diverse society, one that moves beyond the rhetoric of racial/ethnic talk to more action, our society and its institutional gatekeepers must recognize the unique talents and resources of URM faculty, while increasing their numbers and ensuring their retention in higher education institutions.

## IMPETUS FOR THE BOOK: RESEARCH QUESTIONS AND THEORIZING LENS

Rapidly increasing evidence suggests that workplace stress related to highly demanding work roles and expectations and the brain's biological response to repeated acts of perceived discrimination and racism play important roles in the development of several types of chronic physical and mental health conditions. While we know that higher socioeconomic status (SES) equates to improved physical and mental health outcomes for majority-White populations, data demonstrate that this is not necessarily the case for URMs. Thus the educational advantages of health that are accruing to White populations are not accruing to URMs.

The purpose of this study is to examine the associations between workplace stress, academic organizational factors, coping strategies, and physical and mental health among URM faculty. The questions that guide the analyses are the following: (1) What are their perceptions of diversity and workplace climate? (2) What kind of mentoring have they experienced? (3) How have they experienced perceived discrimination? (4) How do they balance work and their family and personal life? (5) Has their physical and mental health been affected by their work environments and experiences? (6) What strategies (e.g., self-care practices, recreational activities, social support, and rational/cognitive responses) help them cope with workplace stress? A secondary, yet important, question examines whether there are sharp differences by gender, race, and Hispanic subgroup.

To accomplish meaningful interpretation of the data, several interdisciplinary scholarly traditions were drawn upon, integrated, and applied. All studies have an implicit lens or set of assumptions that guide how they are conducted, how a sample is defined, and what theory is used to understand and interpret data. One of the major theorizing arguments is that study participants are marked by coconstitutive and mutually reinforcing social status identities that shape life chances, opportunities, and, in turn, experiences in higher education institutions (see Zambrana & MacDonald, 2009). Another important theorizing challenge is to move beyond simplistic feminist discourses that focus solely on gender as a key determinant of exclusion, instead examining gender identity that is informed by multiple feminisms and multiple dimensions of inequality (Collins, 2015; Collins & Bilge, 2016; Segura, 1992, 2003).[9]

An intersectional lens incorporates a set of explicit assumptions that inform inequality of historically underrepresented groups in relationship to stress-inducing work roles. Many URM faculty share a set of historical and life experiences that include educational disadvantage and intergenerational, structurally embedded discriminatory practices that shape their perceived competence and their ability to navigate academic environments. Three basic analytic premises guide this study:

1. Sociohistoric experiences of URM incorporation into the United States (due to slavery, land takeover, or colonization) contribute to social status identity inequality throughout the life course, such as prior experiences in segregated or underserved neighborhoods and schools.
2. Historic institutional stereotypic perceptions of racial/ethnic and social status identity inequality reduce access to social and institutional capital throughout the educational pathway.
3. Patterns of interaction and the potential success of URM scholars in the professional sphere including academia are hindered by limited access to prior and current economic resources (wealth and assets) and social capital (networks of established and senior colleagues).

Intersectional analysis illuminates how the multiple dimensions of social status identity, history, and inequality uniquely shape URMs' professional experiences in higher education institutions.[10] Thus each chapter seeks to further understand how social status identity inequality (race, gender, ethnicity, and class background) influences mentoring, discrimination, work-family balance, and coping strategies and in combination potentially adversely impacts physical and mental well-being. Special attention is given to the understudied area of comparing African American, Latino, and American Indian / Alaska Native faculty by gender. I seek to engage in critical analyses and critical praxis to discern institutional processes in higher education that are operating in exclusionary fashion in spite of what appears to be, and is promoted as, impersonal and fair standard operating procedures or embedded social and organizational norms (Collins & Bilge, 2016; McDonald & Wingfield, 2008).

This book provides a rare opportunity to examine the lived experiences of an understudied and crucial segment of the domestic professional workforce in higher education. Most importantly, while research informs us about the workplace stress that is prevalent among minority and women faculty, none has to my knowledge empirically examined the multiple dimensions of workplace stress faced by URM faculty within elite academic settings. The data examined here address the long-standing issue of severe underrepresentation of URM faculty and are critical to discovering ways to increase the retention and promotion of URM faculty in elite higher education institutions. These results can inform higher education administrators and policy organizations on how to translate, develop, and promote solution-driven transformative practices and policies that can be employed in higher education institutions to recruit, retain, and promote URM faculty in a more equitable manner. However, these outcomes can be realized only if the analyses and interpretation of the data are informed by a critical understanding of structural inequality, combined with an intersectional perspective. In other words, historic social status identity has created pernicious stereotypes and implicit biases that are embedded in institutional practices and policies that in turn have shaped the life course experiences of URM faculty, including their professional experiences, and contribute to underrepresentation. The analyses included here represent a shift from an individual or person-centered determinant paradigm of understanding health to a social determinant and intersectional paradigm that can account for the experiences of URM faculty in academia. Moving beyond individual narrative experiences to systematic racial/ethnic group analyses allows for interrogating how institutional power embodied in a White racial frame maintains URM social status identity inequality (Feagin, 2010; McDonald & Wingfield, 2008).

## DATA AND SAMPLE

Data were derived from empirical research that employed a mixed-methods design. Data were collected using web-based surveys ($n = 616$), six group interviews divided by race and gender ($n = 21$), and in-depth interviews ($n = 39$) for a total sample of 676 respondents. For inclusion herein, I use data for 568 respondents from historically underrepresented groups.[11]

Data were collected on workplace stress, academic organizational factors, coping strategies, and physical and mental well-being among URM faculty. A mixed-methods approach allowed for a more coherent narrative. The mixed methods were also reciprocally validating, which is of particular importance when capturing the lives of underrepresented and understudied populations. Each method offers explanatory power for the findings of the other and allows the research design to honor both the shared patterns in the experiences of URM faculty and the struggles of individuals.[12] The web-based survey items and sample individual and group interview study questions are included in appendices A and B.

Eligibility criteria for study participants included U.S.-born women and men of African American, Mexican American / Chicano/a, American Indian / Alaska Native, and Puerto Rican descent who were early- to midcareer faculty defined as tenure-track assistant or tenured associate professors at a Carnegie-defined research university. The four groups were selected because they share involuntary historical incorporation into the United States (via slavery, colonization, or land takeover) that has shaped avenues of economic and social opportunity; and this mode of incorporation created a legacy of exclusion, marginalization, and adverse social interactions and experiences in higher education that are associated with social status identity inequality and stereotypic attributions of inferior intellect. We selected early- to midcareer faculty since the focus of the study is on URM career paths. Focusing on early-career faculty is important in uncovering potential reasons for underrepresentation and low retention and promotion in higher education institutions. Study participants were identified through network sampling techniques using existing academic personal contacts, peer networks, Faculty Advisory Board (FAB) referrals, word of mouth, and respondent recommendations. Adjuncts, lecturers, and full professors were excluded. Participants ($n = 60$) in the qualitative portion of the study provided written consent and were compensated for their time via small gift remunerations. The study was approved according to institutional review board procedures at the University of Maryland for research involving human subjects.

Table 1.2 displays demographic data for study participants. Among the sample, 333 participants (58.6 percent) self-identified as African American, 134 (23.6 percent) as Mexican American or Chicana/o, 76 (13.4 percent) as Puerto Rican, and 25 (4.4 percent) as American Indian / Alaska Native. The sample included 347 (61.1 percent) women and 221 (38.9 percent) men.[13] The mean age was 44.45, with a range of 30 to 64. A slight majority were assistant professors ($n = 276$; 52.2 percent), and the others were associate professors ($n = 253$; 47.8 percent). Of the participants, 85 percent were born in the United States or

Puerto Rico. Mexican-born / U.S.-raised participants constituted 6.5 percent of the sample. Disciplines reported were recoded into broad disciplinary areas to protect respondent anonymity: arts and humanities (21.6 percent), education (9.3 percent), ethnic studies (5.9 percent), STEM/health/medicine (41.6 percent), and the social sciences (21.6 percent).

About one-third of the total sample had fathers and/or mothers with college and graduate degrees completed. African Americans and Puerto Ricans were most likely to have high parental educational status and American Indian / Alaska Natives the least likely to have parents with a college degree or more (24.0 percent had a father and 28.0 percent a mother with a college degree or more). However, 54.0 percent of African Americans had parents with graduate degrees or more. In terms of marriage, 66.7 percent of the sample was married, 14.9 percent was divorced/separated/widowed, and the remainder reported having never been married. Approximately 37.1 percent of the sample reported no children. Although these four groups share a similar historical legacy, there are differences based on phenotype, colorism, geographic location, and indigenousness. Mexican Americans and American Indian / Alaska Natives were most likely to live in the Southwest/West (55.3 percent and 63.2 percent, respectively). Puerto Ricans were most likely to live in the Northeast (38.0 percent).

## CONTRIBUTIONS OF THE BOOK

Presenting results from the largest web-based survey of URM faculty in the United States to date, this book documents the experiences of URM faculty in elite U.S. higher education institutions while also addressing the realities of social and economic inequalities in their work-life experiences. The major goals of this book are to (1) describe and chronicle the lived experiences of historically underrepresented faculty in research-extensive institutions, (2) contribute to the literature on work-family balance among URM professionals who have been understudied in the field of marriage and family, (3) identify factors associated with the unique workplace stress in elite academic employment settings and their impact on health and mental well-being, and (4) translate this research into transformative practices that can be employed in higher education institutions to recruit, retain, and promote URM faculty.

Three major innovative contributions characterize this book:

1. The unmatched national faculty data source and rich qualitative data highlight the voices of URM faculty to interpret and enhance the meaning of their experiences.
2. The book documents URM social assets—URMs are committed to their research and teaching, are excellent citizens, and engage in institutional

TABLE 1.2   Descriptive characteristics of total respondents by race/ethnicity

| | Total sample (N = 568) | African American (n = 333; 58.6%) | Mexican American (n = 134; 23.6%) | Puerto Rican (n = 76; 13.4%) | American Indian / Alaska Native (n = 25; 4.4%) |
|---|---|---|---|---|---|
| **Age** | | | | | |
| Mean | 44.45 | 45.00 | 43.22 | 42.95 | 48.83 |
| SD | 9.42 | 9.87 | 8.73 | 7.53 | 11.06 |
| **Gender** | | | | | |
| Male | 221 | 126 | 51 | 36 | 8 |
| | (38.9) | (37.8) | (38.3) | (46.8) | (32.0) |
| Female | 347 | 207 | 83 | 40 | 17 |
| | (61.1) | (62.2) | (61.7) | (53.2) | (68.0) |
| **Rank** | | | | | |
| Assistant professor | 276 | 148 | 79 | 39 | 10 |
| | (52.2) | (47.9) | (62.2) | (55.7) | (43.5) |
| Associate professor | 253 | 161 | 48 | 31 | 13 |
| | (47.8) | (52.1) | (37.8) | (44.3) | (56.5) |
| **Primary academic discipline** | | | | | |
| Arts and humanities | 116 | 63 | 32 | 15 | 6 |
| | (21.6) | (20.3) | (24.8) | (19.7) | (27.3) |
| Education | 50 | 27 | 17 | 6 | — |
| | (9.3) | (8.7) | (13.2) | (7.9) | |

| | | | | | |
|---|---|---|---|---|---|
| Ethnic studies | 32 | 14 | 9 | 4 | 5 |
| | (5.9) | (4.5) | (7.0) | (5.3) | (22.7) |
| STEM/health/medicine | 224 | 141 | 46 | 29 | 8 |
| | (41.6) | (45.3) | (35.7) | (38.2) | (36.4) |
| Social sciences | 116 | 66 | 25 | 22 | 3 |
| | (21.6) | (21.2) | (19.4) | (28.9) | (13.6) |
| **Parental education level** | | | | | |
| *Father[a]* | | | | | |
| Less than high school | 128 | 59 | 52 | 9 | 8 |
| | (22.9) | (18.1) | (39.4) | (11.7) | (32.0) |
| High school / some college | 190 | 119 | 28 | 32 | 11 |
| | (33.9) | (36.5) | (21.2) | (41.6) | (44.0) |
| Bachelor's degree | 77 | 41 | 21 | 13 | 2 |
| | (13.8) | (12.6) | (15.9) | (16.9) | (8.0) |
| Graduate degree | 151 | 98 | 27 | 22 | 4 |
| | (27.0) | (30.1) | (20.5) | (28.6) | (16.0) |
| *Mother[a]* | | | | | |
| Less than high school | 118 | 51 | 51 | 9 | 7 |
| | (21.2) | (15.7) | (38.9) | (11.8) | (28.0) |
| High school / some college | 227 | 137 | 43 | 36 | 11 |
| | (40.8) | (42.2) | (32.8) | (47.4) | (44.0) |
| Bachelor's degree | 95 | 56 | 20 | 15 | 4 |
| | (17.1) | (17.2) | (15.3) | (19.7) | (16.0) |
| Graduate degree | 112 | 77 | 16 | 16 | 3 |
| | (20.1) | (23.7) | (12.2) | (21.1) | (12.0) |

(continued)

TABLE 1.2  Descriptive characteristics of total respondents by race/ethnicity (*continued*)

| | Total sample (N = 568) | African American (n = 333; 58.6%) | Mexican American (n = 134; 23.6%) | Puerto Rican (n = 76; 13.4%) | American Indian / Alaska Native (n = 25; 4.4%) |
|---|---|---|---|---|---|
| **Nativity** | | | | | |
| United States / Puerto Rico | 481 | 286 | 102 | 76 | 25 |
| | (85.0) | (86.4) | (76.7) | (100) | (100) |
| Mexico | 37 | — | 28 | — | — |
| | (6.5) | | (21.1) | | |
| Other | 48 | 45 | 3 | — | — |
| | (8.5) | (13.6) | (2.2) | | |
| **Geographic region** | | | | | |
| Northeast | 74 | 48 | 5 | 19 | 2 |
| | (19.2) | (20.7) | (5.9) | (38.0) | (10.5) |
| Mid-Atlantic | 68 | 47 | 11 | 10 | — |
| | (17.6) | (20.3) | (12.9) | (20.0) | |
| Southeast | 67 | 50 | 9 | 7 | 1 |
| | (17.4) | (21.6) | (10.6) | (14.0) | (5.3) |
| Midwest | 77 | 54 | 13 | 6 | 4 |
| | (19.9) | (23.3) | (15.3) | (12.0) | (21.1) |
| Southwest/West | 100 | 33 | 47 | 8 | 12 |
| | (25.9) | (14.2) | (55.3) | (16.0) | (63.2) |

| Individual annual income | | | | | |
|---|---|---|---|---|---|
| $0–$50,000 | 20 | 7 | 7 | 5 | 1 |
| | (3.7) | (2.2) | (5.4) | (6.8) | (4.2) |
| $50,001–$70,000 | 173 | 97 | 47 | 21 | 8 |
| | (31.7) | (36.2) | (36.2) | (28.4) | (33.3) |
| $70,001–$90,000 | 142 | 79 | 38 | 20 | 5 |
| | (26.1) | (24.9) | (29.2) | (27.0) | (20.8) |
| $90,001–$115,000 | 118 | 76 | 25 | 13 | 4 |
| | (21.7) | (24.0) | (19.2) | (17.6) | (16.7) |
| $115,001 or more | 92 | 58 | 13 | 15 | 6 |
| | (16.9) | (18.3) | (10.0) | (20.3) | (25.0) |
| **Home ownership** | | | | | |
| Yes | 399 | 238 | 88 | 52 | 21 |
| | (70.9) | (72.3) | (66.2) | (67.5) | (87.5) |
| No | 164 | 91 | 45 | 25 | 3 |
| | (29.1) | (27.7) | (33.8) | (32.5) | (12.5) |
| **Current household net worth** | | | | | |
| $0–$90,000 | 159 | 97 | 30 | 25 | 7 |
| | (32.3) | (34.2) | (26.1) | (35.2) | (29.2) |
| $90,001–$200,000 | 164 | 82 | 47 | 25 | 10 |
| | (33.2) | (28.9) | (40.9) | (35.2) | (41.7) |
| $200,001 or more | 171 | 105 | 38 | 21 | 7 |
| | (34.6) | (37.0) | (33.0) | (29.6) | (29.2) |

NOTE: Values in parentheses are percentages.

a. Total does not sum to 100 percent because 2.5 percent of the sample selected "not applicable."

service, while their civic-minded work and practice engage young URM students and communities in need.
3. The books offers new insights on URM coping strategies that respond to
   subtle forms of discrimination and the experience of daily microaggressions.

This book provides crucial information that can be used by higher education
institutions to broaden the discourse on diversity and inclusive excellence. It
expands the parameters of inclusion so as to reverse the trend of low representation in all prestigious occupational groups. It is also important to affirm what
this book is not about. It is concerned not with exclusion but with intentional
inclusion and embracing all the talent pools in the United States. Twentieth-
century Blacks and Hispanics who immigrated as professionals or due to civil
unrest in their countries of origin represent talent pools who have different experiences and aspirations. The intent is to encourage measures of transparence
and institutional accountability in assessing our national goal of equity. In other
words, the inclusion of multiple professional talent pools is important in and of
itself but should not serve as a substitute for the erasure of the URM domestic
talent pool. Acknowledging that academic life is a difficult terrain for all faculty
and racism and discrimination are integral to the social fabric of U.S. society as
witnessed in the recent presidential election, my intent is to feature URM academic professionals who are not and never were immigrants. Non-URM faculty
(foreign-born, Asian, African, and other Hispanic) often experience different life
course events and varied forms of welcoming receptivity in the United States.[14]
The subjects of study significantly differ in general from White, Asian, and many
foreign-born groups with respect to SES of family of origin, prior experiences of
exclusion and discrimination, and formal schooling.[15]

## ORGANIZATION AND DESCRIPTION OF CHAPTERS

Presenting data on the areas of URM professional life that hinder or facilitate academic career paths and upward social and economic mobility, the following eight
chapters explore how multiple workplace stress domains impact social interactions, family life, career milestones, and physical and mental health outcomes.
Each chapter presents relevant literature and study data to illustrate the intersections of institutional patterns of the academic workplace and their relationship to
domains of professional life including professional socialization, discrimination,
family life, career milestones, and physical and mental health outcomes.

Chapter 2 explores the history of the professoriate. It describes the foundations and development of higher education research institutions as a site of historical color and class privilege evolving as an elitist bastion and an exclusionary
space. The founders of higher education developed an invisible culture and set of

expectations that are often unfamiliar to URM faculty and thus more difficult to navigate. Second, the entrance of URM faculty into the academy in the 1960s is discussed and trends by gender, race, and ethnicity from the 1970s forward are presented for both faculty and doctoral students.

Chapter 3 draws from multiple disciplinary traditions and theories including organizational theory, social capital theory, life course perspectives, and an intersectional analytic lens that integrates multiple domains of knowledge to contextualize the factors associated with the experiences of URM faculty. Using multiple traditions allows for an expanded understanding of the complex role that social status identity (race/ethnicity, SES, and gender) has in the life experiences and career paths of study participants. An examination of structural, historical, and social forces is central in interrogating and describing the institutional forces that are associated with the challenges URM faculty face with retention, promotion, and tenure.

An important and novel set of theoretical contributions deals with the social determinants of physical and mental well-being in the workplace. Conceptualizations of organizational climate are proposed as having two components: a physical, material reality and an individual, perceptual reality. A lack of diversity or attention to diversity plays a significant role in setting the tone or climate of an organization, be it a department, school, or university. Thus chapter 3 interrogates normative definitions and assumptions about higher education. For example, perceptions of aloneness and tokenism in interpersonal relationships have a strong influence on how URM faculty experience colleagueship and organizational climate at the departmental or institutional level. Unwelcoming climates are a major concern of higher education institutions and may contribute to the academic disengagement of URM faculty as well as lower productivity. The roles of academic work environments as stressors or buffers have been largely left unexamined yet may provide insights into solving the problem of URM retention. Each chapter in the book draws on these theorizing conceptualizations.

Chapter 4 describes the mentoring experiences of URM faculty. Mentoring plays an important role in faculty development, especially in enhancing social networks that oftentimes promote career progression and retention in the academy. This chapter explores how participants encounter mentoring, the importance of mentoring across the life course, ideal attributes of and challenges to mentoring relationships, and the role of political guidance. Collectively, this chapter provides a road map for shifting how we engage with URM faculty and provides knowledge and strategies for promoting a more successful pipeline. Moreover, it discusses how to assess the effectiveness of mentoring to increase the retention of URM faculty.

Chapter 5 describes how URM faculty experience racism, discrimination, devaluing, and tokenism through consistent microaggressions at both institutional and personal levels. It discusses the difficulty of identifying and naming racism in the academy and how this process leads URM faculty to internalize metanarratives of incompetency and inferiority. The effects of perceived discrimination and hypervigilance in their work settings require protective psychological responses to avoid adverse physical and mental effects.

Chapter 6 describes the social, economic, and familial factors associated with work-family balance for URM faculty. Historical and contemporary research on families has directed attention primarily to educated, non-Hispanic White families and often failed to include URM families. As a result, little information is available on how URM, particularly those in high-prestige occupations, balance family and work obligations. This chapter focuses on family/work and life experiences of URM faculty, revealing more about negotiating family-of-origin responsibilities, and strategies for how family-work balance is maintained within a context of multiple stressors.

Chapter 7 explores the pathways to securing an academic position and the challenges confronted by URM faculty as they strive to achieve tenure and promotion. Data show that a number of social determinants including economics, lack of community belonging, hostile environment, and lack of both external and institutional social supports in confluence produce social conditions that are not conducive to productivity but rather engender fear and perceived interloper status. This chapter discusses the participants' dreams and aspirations, the challenges encountered when developing a place of belonging, the processes required to seek tenure or promotion, and reasons for staying or leaving the academy.

Chapter 8 reveals the potential consequences of unwelcoming workplaces on the physical and mental health outcomes of study participants. Racial/ethnic underrepresented groups with increased educational advantage and occupational prestige are at increased risk of adverse physical and mental health outcomes. A conceptual framework is displayed that shows the associations of workplace stressors on the physical and mental well-being of study participants.

The analyses reveal the costs of academic life and the complex and dynamic ways in which URM faculty negotiate their work lives and professional challenges. Coping mechanisms include religion and spirituality; social support; intentional ignoring; staying below the radar; and, least desirable of all, confrontation. These approaches to buffering stress proffer unique and novel contributions to understanding how a socially mobile and prestigious occupational group of racial/ethnic faculty navigates their role in higher education institutions.

Chapter 9 illustrates gender differences by race/ethnicity and class. Compelling findings are revealed for each of the four subgroups and highlight how different dimensions of disadvantage shape life chances, opportunities, stress, and sources of support and, in turn, experiences in elite higher education institutions.

The ways in which gender matters is a central question in contemporary feminist discourse. Comparisons are made using all major study variables. Data show the ways in which intersecting gender identities create compelling differences between men and women and proffer some insights into why URM men are less likely to be retained in academic professions.

Chapter 10 summarizes the unique challenges that URM faculty confront in higher education and highlights three major themes associated with institutional inequity. It capitalizes on the narratives and voices of these groups to forge new directions and create more transparent, transformative, and equitable approaches in diversity initiatives. The articulated challenges of these participants are reengineered to inform the institutional practices on the racial/ethnic problem of "leveling the playing field." This chapter also calls to task the institutional power brokers in higher education who have settled for symbolic diversity in lieu of equity.

In conclusion, this book represents the culmination of many years of thinking about the struggles and strengths of racial and ethnic minority professional communities when coping with workplace stress and the impact on their physical and mental health. During my more than thirty-five years as a faculty member at research universities, I have keenly observed that the workplace stress on URM faculty colleagues is uniquely and adversely impacting their lives. This book, a combination of personal experience and scholarly engagement, is a product of my own journey and observations as a sociologist and an underrepresented faculty member. This work builds on national quantitative and qualitative data collected on URM faculty, providing generalizable findings and giving voice to their unique experiences.

All too often, these talented racial/ethnic groups are missed or excluded from studies, but their work lives are seriously affected by the phenomenon of exclusion. They represent a segment of the U.S. workforce that is vital to strengthening higher education in important ways. As noted earlier, four major impacts have been identified: (1) historically, URM faculty entering the academy seek solutions to social problems of low-income racial/ethnic communities; (2) increasing numbers of URM faculty can yield important institutional impacts that address the needs of these groups; (3) the production of knowledge by invested and committed faculty on racial/ethnic communities can contribute to increasing understanding to promote social equality; and (4) their presence can increase the service mission of the university to help surrounding disadvantaged communities. Understanding these issues, putting them out into the open, and facing them together as scholars, university leaders, and policy makers can help us answer urgent questions that impact our nation, higher education faculty, administrators, and the student bodies that universities serve. By preparing universities to be more inclusive of URM faculty and by breaking the silence surrounding URM perceptions of exclusion, higher learning institutions can create more welcoming environments for their undergraduate and graduate students and faculty communities. The diversity of a university's faculty, staff, and students influences its strength of perspectives and innovation, productivity and intellectual sharpness. Diversity as a value capitalizes on the inclusion of U.S. talent and provides equitable opportunities. As Hurtado (2007) has posited, "It is time to renew the promise of American higher education in advancing social progress, end America's discomfort with race and social difference, and deal directly with the issues of inequality present in everyday life" (p. 186).

# 2 · THE HISTORY AND IMPORTANCE OF THE INCLUSION OF HISTORICALLY UNDERREPRESENTED FACULTY IN THE ACADEMY

Cloistered beyond the turmoil of mainstream society, the American upper classes maintain a circuit of exclusive private preparatory schools designed to calibrate youth from privileged families for participation in the top levels of power at the institutions that shape and direct the nation's foreign and domestic policy, as well as its commercial and artistic endeavors. The preparation of these schools involves not only attaining academic skill but also cultivating acumen in styles of domination required as managers and boards in commercial corporations, cultural institutions, and government bureaus and cultivating a basis for cooperation with and co-optation of new middle-class aspirants.
—Churchill and Levy (2012, p. 73)

Why do many historically underrepresented minority faculty feel like interlopers and perceive an unsettling sense of not belonging in research universities?[1] Embedded in this question is the need for further scrutiny of the foundations of higher education institutions as sites of historical and contemporary privilege. As such, these institutions were often exclusionary in regard to the lecturers and professors, as well as the students, who were permitted into these sanctuaries of higher learning. When discussing the university's climb and status as a respected and elite institution in American society, it is necessary to acknowledge the historically fractured pathways to college for women and historically underrepresented minority groups (URMs). A key barrier was high school completion. African Americans, Mexican Americans, and Native American / American Indians were denied universal access to public secondary education until the mid-twentieth century, and community-controlled secondary institutions for Native Americans did not proliferate in earnest until the Indian Self-Determination and Education Assistance Act of 1975 (Guillory & Ward, 2007; MacDonald, 2013; Manuelito, 2005; Rury & Hill, 2011). A select, resource-rich sector of these groups enrolled their youth in private, either independent or religious (Catholic and Protestant) secondary institutions as boarders or with families in urban centers with more extensive educational options than the vast rural areas where the majority of these groups lived prior to the U.S. Civil War (Anderson, 1988; MacDonald, 2004; Mihesuah, 1993). Indeed, many historically Black colleges and universities (HBCUs) and Catholic colleges' first two years of education were de facto the last two years of high school up through the Great Depression of the 1930s and beyond, until there was greater public access for high schooling and less poverty, which alleviated the need for youth to contribute to the family income (Anderson, 1988; Gleason, 1995; Goldin & Katz, 2008).

Although access for White women was more limited, access to high school completion and higher education increased for majority-culture groups including young women in the early twentieth century. Native-born White women had some access to higher education, beginning with the founding of small women's colleges in the antebellum South as early as 1836.[2] In the Northeast, young women's academies developed into tertiary institutions in the post–Civil War decades. More rigorous liberal-arts-oriented women's colleges, such as Mount Holyoke and Smith, opened to combat closed doors at the male-only Ivy League. Both men and women were granted admission to Midwestern and western state public universities founded as a result of the Morrill Act of 1862 (Beadie & Tolley, 2002; Nash, 2005; Solomon, 1985). For all of these groups, the nineteenth century represented a liminal era, when the lines between secondary and collegiate education in terms of curriculum, faculty, student preparation, and other functions were blurred and overlapping.

This chapter concisely contextualizes and historicizes the development of higher education institutions with a focus on research universities, the institutions of interest in this study. These universities were and remain the training ground for future knowledge producers and thought leaders who design policies and practices that are associated with the health and wealth of the nation. Past and current evidence paints a distressing landscape of deep-rooted institutionalized racism, with the elite professoriate remaining overwhelmingly male and more recently female, White, and upper middle class.

The following pages examine the historical forces that have shaped and curtailed the pathway to the professoriate for underrepresented minorities. The development of colleges and universities for non-White students and faculty is also described, as are the disruption of exclusionary practices during the civil rights movement of the 1960s and 1970s and the role of self-determination among URMs, which expanded access to previously narrow or closed doorways. Changes in access to the higher education pipeline are presented here from the 1980s forward and parsed by gender, race, and ethnicity, for both doctoral students and faculty. This opening of the higher education opportunity structure as a result of the civil rights movement and affirmative action legislation increased the number of historically URM in high-prestige occupations (Higginbotham, 2009). However, a deeper understanding of how URMs fare in these predominantly White spaces and how the workplace environment and institutional processes support URMs in fulfilling their work responsibilities and their contributions can be garnered only by applying a critical analytic lens to institutional mission as embedded in historical imperative.

## INSTITUTIONS OF HIGHER LEARNING: SEVENTEENTH AND EIGHTEENTH CENTURIES

The history of institutions of higher learning reveals four broad and overlapping developmental stages: elite private colleges, public state-funded colleges, racial/ethnic minority colleges, and public and private research universities. The first elite private college in the initial stage was Harvard (1636), followed by eight universities including many of the modern Ivy League institutions. These colonial colleges were modeled on Cambridge and Oxford, the most elite British institutions, and designed to train young men for a career in ministry to serve both civil and spiritual authorities. Their mission expanded somewhat in the eighteenth century to also train young men for other occupations in civic life and public service. Students of this era rarely stayed in college more than a year or two and represented a miniscule proportion of the population, less than 1 percent. College was reserved primarily for the sons of elite and prosperous families, with a small number of scholarships offered to poor, but talented, young men, including Native American students, identified by church missionaries and community leaders as potential future ministers (Thelin, 2011).

The number of colleges and universities grew in the nineteenth century, with a notable expansion of small denominational colleges and public colleges and universities. The expansion of private colleges was facilitated through the U.S. Supreme Court's verdict in *Dartmouth College v. Woodward* (17 U.S. 518, 1819), giving early colleges the authority to maintain private governance structures, although chartered by the state (Geiger, 2000). Increased student demand during the early nineteenth century and a disdain from rural Midwestern legislators toward northeastern private college elitism resulted in calls for a more practical and applied college curriculum. In response to this increased interest in higher learning, the Morrill Act of 1862 provided federal land and funding to establish land-grant colleges, intended to (1) serve the workforce goals of the state and (2) offer an applied curriculum with an emphasis on agriculture and the mechanical arts (Lucas, 2006). Many of these colleges would transition into research universities in the twentieth century. The act aided in the upgrading and extension of smaller institutions into permanent state "flagship" institutions or brand-new campuses.

Despite their creation as public institutions to serve the economic needs of the states, several groups were excluded either de jure or de facto. African Americans, Mexican Americans, and Native Americans were virtually absent until either formal desegregation occurred or more robust high school pipelines developed after World War II (Anderson, 1988; MacDonald & Garcia, 2003; Wallenstein, 2008). For instance, in the academic year of 1938–1939 at the University of Texas (Austin), undergraduate students with Spanish surnames represented only 1.5 percent of the student population and only 0.3 percent of the total graduate student enrollment (MacDonald & Garcia, 2003, p. 21).

The U.S. Congress had passed the Morrill Act of 1890, providing funding and land to build racially segregated but equitably funded institutions for Blacks excluded from the southern and border state flagships created under Morrill Act I. However, the funding intended for Black institutions was diverted inequitably to the White schools. Furthermore, southern states excluded White women from the state flagship schools and with one or two exceptions (e.g., Texas State University for Women) did not build separate institutions for White women until the twentieth century (Anderson, 1988; McCandless, 1999; Wallenstein, 2008).

## MINORITY-SERVING INSTITUTIONS (MSIS)

Minority-serving institutions (MSIs) emerged in response to a history of inequity, limited access to research-extensive institutions for minorities, and significant demographic changes in the United States.[3] MSIs—specifically historically Black colleges and universities (HBCUs), Hispanic-serving institutions (HSIs), and tribal colleges and universities (TCUs)—have carved out a unique niche in our nation, serving the needs of low-income, underrepresented minority students (Gasman, Nguyen, & Conrad, 2015). MSIs play an important role for the nation's economy, especially with respect to elevating the workforce prospects of disadvantaged populations and reducing the underrepresentation of minorities and disadvantaged people in graduate and professional schools, as well as in careers that require postbaccalaureate education and training (Gasman & Conrad, 2011).

In the antebellum period, Antioch and Oberlin colleges began admitting some free Blacks (Thelin, 2011), but higher education opportunities were rare for this group. However, by the early nineteenth century new colleges and small religious institutions, notably Lincoln University, the first degree-granting historically Black college in the nation, established in 1854, were founded to educate free Blacks in the North. Early HBCUs founded after the Civil War varied in their missions. The U.S. Bureau of Refugees, Freedmen, and Abandoned Lands (Freedmen's Bureau) founded Howard University in 1867. Howard had the first law school for Blacks in the nation, graduating many of the famous civil rights lawyers of the twentieth century. Freed slaves and missionary organizations such as the American Missionary Association founded colleges with a liberatory curriculum, emphasizing a traditional liberal arts education. With Morrill Act II land-grant funds, state-controlled institutions emphasized an applied curriculum of home economics for women and industrial arts for men rather than the more diverse curricular offerings at White colleges (Anderson, 1988; Thelin, 2011). The impetus to expand postsecondary access to African Americans derived from an effort to develop community leadership in the postslavery era, yet questions of who would define African American education loomed large.

Under a proposal by White philanthropist Samuel Armstrong, African American higher education, and consequently leadership development, was dictated by White philanthropists and businessmen (Anderson, 1988), whereby African Americans were conscribed to industrial and agricultural employment. W. E. B. Du Bois rebuked the industrial model of education and emphasized that the social mobility of all African Americans was firmly rooted in educating an elite leadership class he referred to as the Talented Tenth. Du Bois believed that providing the most talented and elite African Americans access to a quality liberal arts curriculum was the key to social mobility for the community at large (Du Bois, 1903).

Small numbers of promising African Americans were admitted into prestigious White-serving institutions; however, they were denied the opportunity to socially interact with their White peers and faculty due to segregated campus policies, resulting in their limited access to social and cultural capital, which is a central benefit of attending elite institutions (Lucas, 2006). Furthermore, these primarily White-serving institutions limited African American student campus involvement and restricted student leadership development during the early to mid-twentieth century.

Mexican Americans' admittance to higher education institutions increased in the pre–World War II era, aided by philanthropic organizations and their own determination. As in the elementary and secondary public school system, Mexican Americans were not legally excluded from public colleges or universities, but de facto their presence was discouraged (MacDonald & Rivera, 2015). While segregation and linguistic and cultural discriminatory policies and practices were being tackled at the elementary and secondary levels, significant reforms occurred in higher education for Mexican Americans.[4] One tangible result of Chicano student protests during the 1960s was the creation of Chicano studies and research centers. San Francisco State University's Ethnic Studies Department (encompassing African, Native American, Asian, and Raza studies), established in 1969, is generally considered the first such academic department and center in U.S. higher education. Newly minted Mexican American doctorate degree holders produced research, created professional organizations, and established scholarly journals to revolutionize a traditionally Anglo-centric academic culture. The Ford Foundation, considered radical among many conservative politicians, particularly President Richard Nixon, played a central role in funding both Black and Mexican research centers and individual scholars (MacDonald & Hoffman, 2012).

Although there are differences between these MSIs, all share limited resources, a reputation for minimal selectivity in student admissions, and therefore less highly skilled graduate students to assist faculty with research and grant submissions combined with less research productivity due to high faculty teaching loads and lower salaries. These factors are associated with less prestigious reputations and rankings.[5] In the next sections, brief overviews are provided of those institutions of higher education that were designated to educate historically excluded native-born U.S. citizens.

### Historically Black Colleges and Universities (HBCUs)

HBCUs were established to serve the educational needs of Black Americans. Prior to the time of their establishment, and for many years afterward, Blacks were generally denied admission to traditionally White institutions. As a result, HBCUs became the principal means for providing postsecondary education to African Americans. The HBCU designation was created by Congress in 1965 to refer to any accredited school established prior to 1964 whose principal mission was, and is, the education of Black Americans. Following the Civil War, public support for Black higher education was reflected in the enactment of the Second Morrill Act in 1890. The act required states with racially segregated public higher education systems to provide a land-grant institution for Black students whenever a land-grant institution was established and restricted for White students. After the passage of the act, public land-grant institutions specifically for Blacks were established in each of the southern and border states. As a result, some new public Black institutions were founded and a number of formerly private Black schools came under public control; eventually sixteen Black institutions were designated as land-grant colleges, offering courses in agricultural, mechanical, and industrial subjects, but few provided college-level courses or degrees (U.S. Department of Education, 1991). Today there are 105 HBCUs.

Since public HBCUs tend to enroll a greater number of low-income and underprepared students who are less likely to graduate from college, their funding has taken a hit in many states across the country because it is now tied to outcome factors such as graduation rate, a policy that is especially hard on HBCUs. A report released by the Association of Public and Land-grant Universities found disparities in states' matching funds for land-grant HBCUs versus predominantly White colleges and universities: HBCUs received more than $244 million from the USDA, while states matched just over $188 million. Several states have withheld nearly $57 million in funding that was designated for the institutions. Under congressional mandate, states are not penalized if they cannot or refuse to fund the schools, leaving HBCUs with the responsibility to match the funds up to 50 percent to keep the federal allocation. However since 2008, more than 50 percent of HBCU land-grant schools have applied to waive this requirement (Gasman, Lundy-Wagner, Ransom, & Bowman, 2010). African Americans, through many barriers and closed doors, were able to develop as intellectually prominent advocates from the mid-nineteenth century onward, in contrast to the other historically underrepresented groups. For underrepresented Hispanics and Native Americans / American Indians, access to educational opportunity for a significant number was not available until the late 1960s.

## Hispanic-Serving Institutions (HSIs)

During the civil rights era, Chicano, Native American, and Puerto Rican activists created more than a dozen colleges (sometimes together) that truly reflected grassroots needs and demands for ethnically and linguistically congruent institutions. Unfortunately, only two, Boricua College and Hostos Community College in New York, persisted. HSIs are a subset of MSIs, which differ from HBCUs and tribal colleges because they were not created to serve a specific population but evolved due to their geographic proximity to Latino populations (O'Brien & Zudak, 1998). HSIs are defined in Title V, the Developing-Hispanic Serving Institutions Program of the Higher Education Act of 1965, as amended in 1993, as nonprofit institutions of higher learning with a full-time equivalent (FTE) undergraduate student enrollment that is at least 25 percent Hispanic. Title V also requires HSIs, by definition, to ensure that at least 50 percent of their

Latino students are low-income individuals and to maintain nonprofit status (Dayton, Gonzalez-Vasquez, Martinez, & Plum, 2004; Núñez, Hurtado, & Galdeano, 2015).

As MacDonald, Botti, and Clark (2007) demonstrate, the pathway to HSIs began in the 1960s as Latinos from Mexican and Puerto Rican backgrounds in particular demanded recognition from the federal government as a distinct racial/ethnic underrepresented population, also meriting targeted aid to enhance higher education access and opportunities. HSIs became officially recognized through the efforts of Latino educators and business leaders dedicated to the advancement of Latinos in higher education. In 1986, these leaders formed the Hispanic Association of Colleges and Universities (HACU).[6] In 1992, HACU led the effort to convince Congress to formally recognize campuses with high Hispanic enrollment as federally designated HSIs and to begin targeting federal appropriations to those campuses.

Unfamiliar with the needs of the Hispanic population, the federal government and philanthropists such as the Ford Foundation tried to emulate programs and policies for Blacks, with little initial success. Although lobbying and negotiations in Congress were at times contentious due to concern from HBCU advocacy groups that their needs might be overlooked during a period of rapid growth in the Latino population, the imperiled higher education status of both groups maintained inclusion and support across both communities (MacDonald et al., 2007). However as Núñez and colleagues (2015) point out, HSIs are "more likely than other institutions to educate a significant proportion of students from populations that have historically had less access to higher education, including low-income, first-generation, and underrepresented racial/ethnic minority students, as well as students who are less academically prepared for college" (p. 4).

### Tribal Colleges and Universities (TCUs)

The TCU movement was founded in the late 1960s to counterbalance the near eradication of all things American Indian within the educational system of the United States. TCUs have developed a philosophy that protects and enhances tribal cultures while embracing much of modern education. Leaders of TCUs understood that to enhance American Indian communities, students must be knowledgeable about their own cultures and prepared to survive in the non-Indian world (Stein, 1992). Navajo Community College (Diné College), founded in 1968, was the first institution to develop the tribal college philosophy. Other communities have followed this blueprint when founding their own institutions.

Each TCU has been chartered by its respective tribal government and is governed by a local board of regents. TCUs adhere closely to their mission statements as they develop curriculum and work closely with regional accreditation agencies. Within the United States, TCUs serve approximately twenty-five thousand students; individual school enrollments range from fifty to forty-five hundred students. Although TCU students represent many racial and social backgrounds, the majority at each college come from local tribes. Students' average age is twenty-seven, and a majority are female and live below the poverty line; most are first-generation college students (St. Pierre & Stein, 1997).

Given the creation of separate institutions dependent on federal and state funding and majority-culture faculty, and the enrollment of low-income students who attended predominantly underresourced elementary and secondary segregated schools, these MSIs continue to be a potent reminder of separate and unequal (MacDonald, 2013; Núñez et al., 2015). This history of MSIs, endowed with limited financial institutional support and few research resources, informs the current lack of progress and suggests the national abdication of responsibility for these groups and the closing off of opportunities for attendance at elite research universities.

## THE TRANSITION OF PREDOMINANTLY WHITE INSTITUTIONS TO RESEARCH UNIVERSITIES

In the twentieth century, higher education initiated a shift away from the Oxford-Cambridge liberal arts model toward the German Humboldtian research university model (Lucas, 2006). Germanic research universities were characterized by a curriculum rooted in research, discovery, and experimentation; seminars and laboratory work instead of lectures and recitation; and faculty who held advanced degrees and often specialized in only one field (Veysey, 1965).[7] Harvard, Yale, and the University of Michigan are among the many colleges of higher learning that recast their mission to that of a research university (Lucas, 2006). Moreover, many traditional liberal arts and land-grant colleges embraced the research philosophy and transformed their mission and curriculum. Building on the German Humboldtian foundation, Johns Hopkins University (JHU) was established in 1876; Daniel Coit Gilman (JHU's first president) described the purpose of the research university as to provide "the acquisition, conservation, refinement and distribution of knowledge" (1885, pp. 15–16).

Although faculty members did not have influence or social prestige in early 1800s, the pedagogical technique of recitations and lecture first implemented in the colonial colleges was maintained well into the founding of research universities. Religious-affiliated boards of trustees and their chosen presidents administered colleges in a hierarchical fashion with limited input from students or faculty (Thelin, 2011). American graduate education was primarily a by-product of the research university's demand to produce domestically credentialed faculty and researchers. One of the hallmarks of research universities was faculty who conducted original research and graduate education (Geiger, 1986). Faculty professional duties at research universities expanded beyond teaching to include a required component of independent research and scholarship. Professors of this period increasingly held specialized, subject-specific doctoral degrees. This resulted in the creation of disciplinary academic departments. The faculty increased significantly and research flourished because of the expansion of an elective curriculum. The number of college professors in American higher education tripled from 1883 to 1913 (Stricker, 1988).

Institutional goals and pedagogy diverged greatly from the historical American college model (Lucas, 2006). New U.S. research universities began recruiting European-trained faculty to be both teachers and researchers focusing on graduate education (Goldin & Katz, 1999). These credentialed faculty were awarded their doctorates by the Germanic universities (Veysey, 1965) and were recruited first by elite Ivy League institutions, and later others (Schuster & Finkelstein, 2006). Faculty members' educational training placed them in the same social and economic spheres as other lettered professional men, such as doctors and lawyers; Veysey (1965) noted in a study of the family background of the nineteenth-century professoriate that the majority were the sons of businessmen from New England.

An instructor hierarchy was observed in the 1870s and 1880s, with the less credentialed faculty serving in junior or assistant professor capacities (Schuster & Finkelstein, 2006). By the late nineteenth century credentialed faculty outnumbered the others. With the increase of credentialed faculty arose the demand for professional protections that allowed for an independent research agenda with minimal interference from the university (Berdahl, Altbach, & Gumport, 2005). The tenure system of faculty self-regulation, the American Association of University Professors, and the concept of academic freedom were unknown to American higher education prior to the advent of research universities (Schuster & Finkelstein, 2006; Thelin, 2011).

In sum, American colleges and universities experienced vast institutional changes from the mid-nineteenth century to the early twentieth. The emergence of the research university, the proliferation of academic disciplines, and growing student enrollments resulted in extensive modifications to the traditional structure and management of higher education. Both colleges and universities adapted more business-like organizational practices to accommodate this expansion as well as to counter growing ambiguity in their mission and purpose (Goldin & Katz, 1999).[8] Universities nurtured and drew on strong research and funding relationships with the federal government initiated during the wars, which ushered in a transition from faculty conducting basic scientific research (or research for the sake of inquiry) to applied or military research. External funding for faculty research became a central strategy in faculty life and university financial support, and consequently increased the role of federal oversight in multiple spheres of university life (Thelin, 2011). In turn, research universities distinguished themselves from liberal arts schools and instituted faculty incentives to promote successful external funding for innovative developments as well as creative faculty contributions to their disciplines. These developments established a normative set of institutional expectations that required social capital (an external professional network, knowledge on accessing funding) and cultural capital (ideas that fit and were valued within the majority culture). Vague evaluative criteria such as "creative contributions" represented slippery benchmarks that were oftentimes subjective and varied by discipline, individual faculty, and departmental group culture. It is precisely these prestigious institutions of higher learning and leaders of the agenda for knowledge production and policy that are the focus of this study. These institutions are embedded in the national cultural and political agenda that portrays social issues and social problems as individual or racial/ethnic group dilemmas that resist solution-driven policy.

## THE ACADEMY AS A SITE OF PRIVILEGE AND EXCLUSIONARY PRACTICES: SELECTIVITY AND RANKINGS

The earliest accreditation system of colleges and universities emerged in the late 1800s as the lines between secondary academies, high schools, and postsecondary institutions remained blurred and resulted in uneven educational quality. As a result, a system was created, still in place today, that comprises five regional accrediting agencies covering the United States and its territories. The first was the New England Association of Schools and Colleges, organized in 1885; and the last was created in 1923. The Council for Higher Education Accreditation is the main body overseeing these regional affiliates, commonly known as the Southern Associations of Colleges and Schools, and other accrediting bodies for postsecondary institutions. Because states, the federal government, and most wealthy philanthropic organizations will not fund schools that fail to meet accreditation standards, the accreditation bodies are critical in protecting quality and also represent institutional gatekeepers, such as the Carnegie Foundation, that can exert power over innovative or diverse schools, including Chicano and Native American nationalist schools that closed in the 1970s due to lack of funds (Olivas, 1989).

The Carnegie Foundation has been intimately associated with the assessment and ranking of higher education institutions since the early 1900s. In 1910, the Carnegie Foundation released the highly acclaimed Flexner Report, which condemned many poor-quality medical schools in the country and recommended the consolidation and closure of several (Lagemann, 1983, 1989). Schools allowing entrance to women and Blacks and financially struggling institutions were particularly negatively impacted. In 1917, the Bureau of Education issued a study of HBCUs, criticizing schools and calling on many to consolidate or close (U.S. Department of the Interior, Bureau of Education, 1917). In the early twentieth century, the norms of higher education quality were thus partially created through influential corporate philanthropies such as the General Education Board of the Rockefeller Foundation and the Carnegie Foundation. Regional accreditation entities linked standards to the federal government's quality benchmarks when the U.S. Department of Education passed the Veterans Readjustment Assistance Act of 1952, requiring new standards for institutions receiving funds. The bill was a consequence of the high number of unscrupulous fly-by-night schools created in the 1940s to benefit from the 1944 "GI Bill of Rights" for veterans of World War II (corollary to today's online universities such as the now defunct Trump University). The 1965 Higher Education Act further raised standards for the regional accreditation councils, also tying them to the Civil Rights Act of 1964 and desegregation orders that impacted higher education, including the still largely ignored (particularly in southern states) *Brown v. Board of Education* (1954). Later, through Title IX (1974), women were provided protection in equality, first in access to athletic facilities and participation in intercollegiate sports and later in other forms of gender discrimination.

Elite doctoral programs at research universities emerged as early as 1900 when the American Association of Universities (AAU) was founded. Presidents from elite universities such as the University of California, Berkeley, Johns Hopkins, and Harvard converged on the University of Chicago to form an association that would differentiate themselves from perceived lesser quality institutions and engender respect from the German institutions they had been modeled after. The original fourteen schools (eleven private and three public) expanded to a more balanced composition of half public and half private by World War I. An important component of the AAU's mystique and elitism is that it is an "invitation only" organization and thus a key signifier of high-quality research and aspiration for other doctoral-granting universities. As of 2016, sixty-two schools, including two in Canada, belong to AAU (AAU, 2016).

Philanthropic institutions continued their strong presence in university rankings into the late twentieth century. In 1967, Clark Kerr, former president of the University of California system, was asked by the Carnegie Foundation for the Advancement of Teaching to head a new Commission on Higher Education, charged with "investigating and providing recommendations on the most vital issues facing American higher education" (Douglass, 2005, p. 3). The nineteen commission members included presidents from elite universities

(Harvard, North Carolina, Bryn Mawr) and higher education scholars such as David Riesman and Carl Kaysen (Douglass, 2005). In 1973, the commission recommended a method for classifying the wide array of American colleges and universities. Prior to the Carnegie Classification, colleges and universities designated themselves as public or private two- or four-year institutions or according to the highest degree they conferred (Douglass, 2005). The commission created six categories and thirteen subcategories. Data about each institution's degrees awarded, research funding, and curricular specialization were used to assign schools to particular levels of classification, similar to the 1960 California Master Plan for Higher Education that Kerr devised to differentiate various levels within the California system (McCormick & Zhao, 2005). Critics charged that the classification system became a guideline for how state funding was allocated (Douglass, 2005). The highest level of the classification system is assigned to doctoral-granting institutions that receive the greatest funding.

The Carnegie Classification system has been updated four times since 1973 to account for institutional changes and mergers. In 2000, the classifications were revised from Research I and II to doctoral/research university-extensive and doctoral/research university-intensive. Extensive classification was reserved for institutions awarding the most doctorates, intensive for those awarding fewer doctorates (McCormick & Zhao, 2005). An important question is, What is the premise of the Carnegie classification?[9] Clearly these classifications protect the presumptive standards of quality, prestige, and excellence that maintain the reputations predominantly White institutions, with considerable populations of legacy students and more recently the international elite. Admission standards including test scores, prior research and international experiences, and letters from a well-positioned social network are perceived as fair indicators of meritocratic and democratic institutional practices that reproduce powerful race- and class-conscious exclusionary practices (Guinier, 2015). The classification system maintains a firm boundary of selective diversity with the inclusion of, for example, predominantly majority-culture women (Johnson, 2016).

## WHITE WOMEN: EARLIER ACCESS
## AND REMARKABLE PROGRESS

In contrast to that for racially and ethnically marginalized historically underrepresented minority female students, access to higher education for White women was expanded with the founding of more rigorous liberal-arts-oriented women's colleges, such as Mount Holyoke (1837) and Smith (1871; Solomon, 1985). The elite women's colleges, commonly known as the Seven Sisters and including Wellesley, Radcliffe, and Bryn Mawr, separated themselves from the teacher-training normal schools of the nineteenth century, offering instead a classic liberal arts curriculum competitive with the male-only Ivy League schools, which shut their doors to women until about the 1970s. Women were prepared for limited careers outside the home, including teaching. As the rapidly expanding normal schools became two-year colleges and then part of state higher education systems, women sought to expand their educational and occupational options. At the elite northeastern women's colleges, strong emphasis was placed on enhancing women's leadership roles by offering a leadership model within the female faculty (Horowitz, 1993; Palmieri, 1995). Further, as women increasingly gained enrollment at universities alongside male students, they had the opportunity to develop and use their own social capital, based oftentimes on family lineage and relationships with other established and powerful male networks. As observed by Hurtado (1996), the availability of access to the social and economic opportunity structure by White women was facilitated by their material and psychological relationship with White male power (p. vii).

Moreover, a limited number of White women had gained admission to research universities beginning in the late nineteenth century. Although the "new" research universities, such as Chicago and Johns Hopkins, admitted White women to undergraduate and graduate programs, White female doctorate graduates had difficulty securing faculty positions at research universities despite having earned their credentials at prestigious universities (Thelin, 2011). Instead, White female faculty were primarily employed at women's colleges and smaller, progressive coeducational institutions, most often in the Midwest (Pollard, 1977). Wellesley College hired exclusively female faculty, and Bryn Mawr maintained a strong tradition of female leadership under Carey Thomas (Horowitz, 1993). At the turn of the twentieth century, the trend of female "coeds" was most common at public universities in the West and Midwest (Lucas, 2006), and women quickly demonstrated that they were capable students who did not impede the order of the college, as feared by campus administrators. While only 2.5 percent of women were enrolled in higher education in 1890 (Lucas, 2006), increased political activism and civic engagement of students and faculty at women's colleges on issues of suffrage, labor activism, and pacifism were manifesting. Professional avenues and economic opportunities opened very quickly to White women over the course of the twentieth century because of increased access to postsecondary education.

As tens of thousands of women poured into higher education in the post–World War II era, their numbers did not yet parallel their workforce participation (Eisenmann, 2006). However, role modeling in the form of women faculty provided the opportunity for students to perceive women as both academics and professionals separate from hearth and home (Horowitz, 1993). The number of women who were awarded undergraduate and graduate degrees in all professional fields steadily rose and was accompanied by a rise in female faculty numbers at research universities. Their ascendancy in faculty ranks and administrative leadership has contributed to tremendous gains for White women in leadership and responsive policies and practices (ACE, 2016; Rossiter, 1982, 1995). As a result, White middle-class women are the largest group of unintended beneficiaries of later twentieth-century affirmative action initiatives (Hamilton, 2011; Harwarth, Maline, & DeBra, 1997). For example, in fall 2013, of all full-time faculty at degree-granting postsecondary institutions, 79 percent were White (43 percent males, 35 percent females), 6 percent were Black (3.6 percent female), 5 percent were Hispanic (2.8 percent female), 10 percent were Asian (3.5 percent female), and less than 1 percent were American Indian / Alaska Native.

Though White women still lag slightly behind White men, middle-class White women as a group have made considerably more progress than URM women and men and members of low-income SES groups. Middle- and upper-class White women have historically been better positioned to contribute to and take advantage of new systemic opportunities because they have had fewer structural impediments to success in secondary education than their URM peers. In contrast, the social status identity of URM scholars coupled with implicit bias has resulted in less institutional support and recognition. For these groups, claims about equity in the post–civil rights era have been justified but unheard. Hegemonic class-driven claims of cultural fairness have protected structural mandates. For example, institutional resistance to integration of racial/ethnic underrepresented groups into the decision-making processes of the institution has led to practices of tokenization by majority-culture administrators. Yet majority-culture women faculty and administrators continue to exercise authority and demands for more benefits without in-depth analyses of which groups of women have gained privilege and rank in higher education institutions. Evidence demonstrates that majority-culture professional women have made significant inroads yet often fail to advocate for their domestic historically underrepresented colleagues (Evans, 2007). New directions have to be forged. One strategy that can move institutions past symbolic and selective diversity is to unlink majority-culture women, other elite international women groups, and racial/ethnic historically underrepresented women, acknowledging that majority-culture women possess a privileged position by virtue of their Whiteness and ideological viewpoints. Their partnerships with those in power and their family assets may contribute to collaborations and advocacy for expanding the opportunity structure for all nonprivileged and less-privileged women.

## HISTORICAL AND CONTEMPORARY TRENDS
## IN FACULTY PIPELINE AND REPRESENTATION

In the mid-twentieth century, American higher education was reshaped from an elite to a more universal college system by both government action and formal advocacy. The GI Bill, the civil rights movement, and the Women's Rights Movement significantly expanded the number and type of students entering American higher education. The 1944 GI Bill allowed veterans and current military personnel to obtain financial compensation for tuition and room and board in compensation for their service. The legislation is regarded as one of the most transformative policies in American higher education as it made a college degree affordable for a wave of returning veterans of modest means who had historically been excluded from higher education. Colleges and universities expanded rapidly in this period to provide increased access for these new students, including the development of the large-scale community college system (Beach, 2010; Brint & Karabel, 1991). However, Black veterans found that they had limited access to the bill's resources because of the systemic segregation of American higher education and the limited number of universities where they could be admitted (Thelin, 2011). The GI Bill served as a tremendous social class leveler for working- and middle-class White Americans while simultaneously reproducing racial inequality.

The gains of the civil rights movement significantly altered African Americans' access to higher education. By the mid-1960s, many predominately White institutions (PWIs) began aggressively recruiting highly talented racial/ethnic minority students as part of affirmative action programs (Bowen, Kurzweil, & Tobin, 2005). Affirmative action allowed a small number of URM students access to a wider array of higher education opportunities. The increase in URM undergraduate students was reflected by a very modest increase in doctoral enrollment. However, from 1988 to 2013, the number of doctorates received by African Americans, Mexican Americans, and Puerto Ricans has been relatively stagnant and the number of advanced degrees received by Native Americans has actually decreased (Fiegener, 2015; see table 2.1).

Until the 1960s, the intentional recruitment and retention of African American, Mexican American, and Puerto Rican faculty was not a priority in higher education (Weems, 2003). The pathway to graduate education and the professoriate continued to primarily be the province of White males. Prior to World War II, Mexican American and Puerto Rican (now subsumed under the general category of Latino) tenured faculty were virtually nonexistent at U.S. colleges and universities (Wilson, 1995). Most telling was the Julius Rosenwald Fund nationwide survey of PWIs in 1941 that included a question regarding the demographic composition of faculty (Wilson, 1995). This survey highlighted

TABLE 2.1 Percentage of U.S. doctorates received by race/ethnicity (1988–2013)

| | 1988 | 1992 | 1998 | 2000 | 2004 | 2010 | 2013 |
|---|---|---|---|---|---|---|---|
| Asian | 14.3 | 21.3 | 20.1 | 19.5 | 21.8 | 24.6 | 25.5 |
| African American | 3.8 | 3.7 | 4.5 | 5.1 | 5.7 | 5.2 | 5.0 |
| American Indian / Alaska Native | 0.3 | 0.4 | 0.4 | 0.4 | 0.3 | 0.3 | 0.2 |
| Hispanic | 3.1 | 3.6 | 4.4 | 4.7 | 4.8 | 5.7 | 5.8 |
| White | 69.2 | 66.6 | 62.8 | 63.8 | 58.6 | 55.1 | 52.8 |

NOTE: Percentages include U.S. citizens / permanent residents, temporary visa holders, and recipients whose citizenship is unknown.
SOURCE: National Science Foundation Survey of Earned Doctorate (1988, 1992, 1998, 2000, 2004, 2010, 2013).

that only two African American faculty members were employed in tenured positions among the hundreds of universities that responded, and both held laboratory positions that did not include teaching (Wilson, 1995). According to the historical record, URMs in the first half of the twentieth century were employed primarily at HBCUs and taught an applied industrial curriculum, which did not require advanced degrees (Weems, 2003).

It was not until the 1973 *Adams v. Richardson* case, which mandated an increase in minority faculty at public institutions, that noticeable numbers of racial/ethnic minority faculty were hired at PWIs. By the end of the 1970s, African Americans made up only 2 percent and Latinos 1.5 percent of all faculty in U.S. higher education, including at MSIs (Wilson, 1995). And even when URM faculty overcame racial obstacles to enter the professoriate, they were often confined to non-tenure-track positions. In addition, when URM faculty sought to use the legal system to address discriminatory practices they were often discouraged from filing a complaint. Reviews of fifty-three lawsuits in which faculty members challenged their denial of tenure based on racial discrimination found only six were successful, and four of the six represented White faculty members at HBCUs (Baez, 2002). Due to the structural barriers created by historic racism and segregation in the United States, URM academics continue to experience decreased opportunities to compete for tenure-track faculty positions at the most elite research universities. Historicity has engendered a narrative of exclusion and devaluing of conquered population groups that seeps into institutional practices and policies and has been politically redefined as implicit bias and stereotype threat.

## EXPANDING THE OPPORTUNITY STRUCTURE: INCREASING NUMBERS OF URMS IN THE ACADEMY

Many benefits can accrue to higher education systems by expanding the educational opportunity structure for URMs, yet current data suggest that the reverse is occurring. The limited pathways available to URM students pursuing graduate study is unlikely to reverse the trend of continued underrepresentation of URM faculty. In 1988, African Americans were awarded less than 4 percent and Latinos 3.1 percent of doctoral degrees (Fiegener, 2015). In 2013, minimal increases in doctoral degrees awarded to African Americans (5 percent) and Latinos (5.8 percent) were observed, yet the statistics in Table 2.1 indicated a growing inequity between national demographic trends and the racial/ethnic composition of doctoral programs (Cook & Cordova, 2007).[10] Increasingly, the number of URM doctoral students in the academic "pipeline" is closely linked with diversifying the applicant pools for early career tenure-track faculty positions (Turner & Myers, 2000).

Systemic and institutionalized racism continues to perpetuate inequalities within institutions, faculty ranks, and disciplines. URM faculty continue to be largely at underresourced institutions that are less prestigious. Delgado Bernal and Villalpando (2002) highlight that in 1995, 32 percent of all African American and 37 percent of all Chicano/a faculty had positions in the humanities and social sciences, while only 2 percent of each group had appointments in the physical sciences. Scholars argue that these and other inequities among URM faculty are not necessarily based on their personal choices to pursue certain fields but are more likely due to decreased access to opportunity structures and inadequate educational preparation and mentorship to pursue STEM fields. Thus, even with the affirmative action programs of the 1980s and 1990s, which attempted to increase the number of URM faculty, parity has not been achieved.

Underrepresentation of URM faculty across disciplines affects the pedagogical and innovative domains of higher education at multiple levels. These include the ability to recruit, educate, and train the best and brightest URM undergraduate and graduate students; recruit and retain the highest quality URM research faculty; and generate and nurture new paradigm shifts in thinking and innovation. Intractable challenges continue to deter the inclusion of URM (Villalpando & Delgado Bernal, 2002). Most notable is the tendency toward hiring others who share values, attitudes, and research interests with majority-culture male and female faculty. The self-fulfilling prophecy is then catapulted into action. The bodies of knowledge that are taught and valued represent the viewpoints of the majority faculty; funds for research and scholarships are designated by and support the interests of the majority; and racially and ethnically diverse student bodies are not reflected in faculty and administrator ranks, affecting the enrollment and retention of URM students (Patitu & Hinton, 2003) and inevitably maintaining a "leaky pipeline." The impact of the absence of URM faculty is best articulated by Patitu and Hinton (2003): "Their presence is crucial for the personal and academic success of minority students for whom they act as mentors, role models, and advisers and for White students, who need the opportunity to interact with URM faculty to overcome misconceptions about the intellectual capabilities of minorities. Their presence is also crucial for White faculty, who need to interact with African American faculty and other URM faculty to gain a better understanding of minority cultures" (p. 89). Additionally, the quality of the faculty, and therefore the academic environment, is compromised when URM are not included in faculty recruitment pools. Finally, innovation, creativity, and universities' ability to secure and maintain a competitive ranking are curtailed when faculty do not have a range of experiences, perspectives, and knowledge bases from which to draw, undermining innovation and socially driven problem solving. Beyond benefits to students (and other faculty), critical diversity enhances a university's reputation "because growth and innovation depend on people from various backgrounds working together and capitalizing on differences" (Henderson & Herring, 2013, p. 309). For example, in a study using the 2011 National Academy of Sciences Rankings of U.S. Research Universities, Henderson and Herring (2013) found a positive and significant relationship between racial and gender diversity among students and faculty and the program rankings of research universities.

## RACIAL FORMATIONS IN THE INSTITUTIONAL HIERARCHY: WHEN SYMBOLIC REPRESENTATION MASKS RACISM

Although the term *faculty of color* is used, data and experience show that there are indeed major differences between URM and non-URM faculty including Asian Americans, Asians, and other foreign-born faculty. *Faculty of color* is a vague, broad, and inconsistently used term describing members of academe who are not considered White in the racial American hierarchy.[11] The term, which places a focus on diversity of skin color and political status globally as opposed to histories of oppression, results in the conflation of many underrepresented groups under one umbrella based on racial and cultural differences from Whites. In some scholarship, the terms *faculty of color* and *underrepresented minorities* are synonymous, referring solely to African Americans, Native Americans, and Latinos whose specific cultural histories are rooted in centuries of colonial and racialized violence. For other researchers, however, *faculty of color* paints a broader picture inclusive of non-White faces to include foreign-born groups, Asians, and Asian Americans.

In 2013, the U.S. Census Bureau identified Latinos (all Spanish-speaking groups) and Asians as the fastest-growing racial and ethnic groups in the United States. The majority of growth in the Asian American population is attributed to international immigration (61 percent between 2012 and 2013, compared to 22 percent of Latino population growth; Brown, 2014). For Latinos, on the other hand, 78 percent of population growth between 2012 and 2013 was due to natural births, compared to 39 percent of population growth for Asians (Brown, 2014). This disparity is reflected in differences between Asian Americans' and other minorities' median ages and levels of educational attainment—higher for Asian Americans than native-born historically underrepresented groups. Social factors such as median income, age, and education level are higher among Asian Americans than among Whites, Blacks, and Hispanics (Pew Research Center, 2013). These advantages in social factors vary by Asian subgroup; for example, Indian Americans have significantly higher levels of income and education compared to other Asian subgroups; additionally, Americans with Korean, Vietnamese, Chinese, and "other U.S." origins compose a higher share of those in poverty than individuals of Indian, Japanese, and Filipino descent (Pew Research Center, 2013).

URM scholars may bristle at the use of *faculty of color* in qualifying the diversity, or lack thereof, in academe. Distinctions between the historical experiences of oppression of minority groups can shape the discourse surrounding identifiers such as *underrepresented minority* and *faculty of color*. It is indisputable that historically underrepresented minorities are "forced minorities" while non-URM minorities are "voluntary minorities," distinctions grounded in differing histories of forced incorporation into the United States (Mexican American, Puerto Ricans, African Americans, and Native Americans) and voluntary immigration (Asians; Ogbu & Simons, 1998). These different histories are reflected in (under)representation in institutions of higher education. Equally important in the claim that America is a country of immigrants is that the history of forced incorporation is ignored.

Despite these differences in history, many international or foreign-born faculty including Asian faculty may face barriers in the academy. Asian faculty report racial barriers pertaining to the model minority, stereotypes that Asians are always foreign, and persistent perception as an "invisible minority" excluded from diversity-oriented research and recruitment. Although Asian Americans and Asians have made significant gains in faculty representation, they report experiencing a "glass ceiling," suggesting that few administrators are Asian (American Council on Education, 2013; Lee, 2002). Understanding the heterogeneity and nuance of racial and ethnic struggles in the academy is necessary for moving forward—data regarding differences in nativity, ethnic subgroups (e.g., Korean, Chinese, Japanese for Asians; Mexican, Cuban, Puerto

Rican for Latinos), and SES are crucial for advancing a conceptualization of how a "diverse" academy can build knowledge and innovation to improve our society and solve social problems.

In summary, the history of American research universities and PWIs shows a long-standing pattern of exclusionary practices toward URM groups and a more inviting climate for European and other elite international groups. The perpetuation of these practices was facilitated by the simultaneous passage of the Civil Rights Act of 1964 and the Immigration and Naturalization Act of 1965, which abolished national origin quotas and established family reunification and employment qualifications as major reasons to request entry. The growing percentages of international faculty at major universities do not augur well for URM. Data show that these faculty are fully engaged in the research mission rather than the pedagogical and service mission of the university and are less likely to teach and mentor students or engage in community projects (Kim, Wolf-Wendel, & Twombly, 2011; Webber, 2012). An important question emerges in examining this new trend: is this new diverse higher education system reproducing diversity through institutional global elitism?

The diversity of a university's faculty, staff, and students influences its strength of teaching and service perspectives and innovation, productivity, and intellectual sharpness. Diversity as a value capitalizes on the inclusion of U.S. talent and provides equal opportunity for success. Undoubtedly the presence of URM faculty at universities changes the culture of the institution; it communicates to students the value of a range of life experiences and often translates to further community engagement and a rich variety of research topics. Yet history and present trends show separation and devaluing of differences. As Minow (1990) states, "Neither separation nor integration can eradicate the meaning of differences as long as the majority locates difference in a minority group that does not fit the world designed for the majority" (p. 25).

To change historic trends and seize the opportunity to capitalize on the strengths that URMs bring into institutions of higher education, an understanding of the organizational structure of these institutions is needed. In the next chapter an examination of the sociology of institutions including normative expectations and institutional processes is presented so as to contextualize the lived experiences of URM faculty in these institutions and illuminate the processes that contribute to their persistent underrepresentation in all universities, particularly research-extensive ones.

# 3 · THE ACADEMY AS A SITE OF INTELLECTUAL DETERMINISM

> And I think the catch is not how much of the institutional barriers do you want to not just overcome, yourself, but how many do you want to break down while you're here? I think that's a challenge, because you see it, and I feel like, as a woman of color, that I can't afford to be here and not tear down some of those walls.
>
> —Mexican American female

Academic spaces are prestigious and privileged institutional environments that promote intellectual and scientific activity in the interest of buttressing the social structure. The quote above is a clarion call to an academy that has largely remained unchanged and unchallenged since its inception. Arguably institutions of higher education have changed in minimal ways, but the elite class- and race-based values upon which they were built have not been disrupted. Although new terminology and goals, such as diversity, inclusion, and excellence, have become part of the university discourse of distress, their meanings have gone undefined and unevaluated yet implemented under the same value system that has used and continues to use the metrics of exclusion (Guinier, 2015). History and trend data strongly demonstrate a "separate but unequal" and an "integrated but unequal" higher education system that has begrudgingly accommodated the post–civil rights unrelenting demands from underrepresented and low-income students and faculty for inclusion, distributive justice, and fairness. The purposes of this chapter are (1) to provide an interdisciplinary overview of the sociology of inequality in work and organizational practices and norms including what is known about academic work environments and URM experiences; (2) discuss supports and stress-inducing work roles; (3) examine the mental and physical health consequences of workplace stress; and (4) present an intersectional social determinants model to analyze factors associated with the career path of URM professionals.

Employing multiple interdisciplinary scholarly traditions in critical sociology and higher education including theories of organizations, social capital, critical race, life course perspectives, and intersectionality, multiple domains of knowledge are applied to contextualize the factors associated with the experiences of URM faculty in institutions of higher learning. An intersectional lens deepens the understanding of the complex role that social status defined by historicity, race/ethnicity, and SES assumes as it interacts with power structures to produce inequality in the career opportunity structure. Structural, historical, and social forces are consequential in explaining the experiences and challenges of retention, promotion, and tenure that underrepresented professionals confront. This nesting of forces drives a novel set of theoretical considerations in the exploration of how lived experiences throughout the life course set the groundwork for adverse social interactions and institutional demands that create injurious determinants of health and mental well-being in the workplace. Workplace environments can be perceived as stress inducing when one's presence is considered anomalous or as supportive or buffering when one fits in. As observed in chapter 1, significant anecdotal narratives have been produced that illuminate the stress of being a token in academic work environments. In analyzing available qualitative data, a conclusion can be drawn that low rates of URM retention and career success may be explained by an institutional culture that promotes the phenomenon of a "push out" effect (Fine, 1991).

In order to accomplish robustness and depth in the analyses of the fit between higher education as an institutional context and URM faculty, and the powerful role that normative values and expectations assume in these organizational settings, a critical race analysis is employed to examine the perceived and experienced "misfit" between predominantly White institutions and underrepresented minority faculty. In exploring meaning in the interpretation of data, looking deeper into how organizational normative policies and practices in higher education enhance career paths is worthy of attention. Institutional climate, normative expectations, institutional support mechanisms such as mentoring, and processes for determining merit are pathways to achieving success and are seen as equal across the board so everyone has a fair chance. However, anecdotal, empirical, and statistical evidence tells a different story.

## ACADEMIC WORK ENVIRONMENT

Higher education institutions are powerfully shaped by implicit assumptions of dedication to intellectual and creative activity, long hours of individual engagement, and cordial interpersonal relations. The body of scholarship on the academic work environment reveals myriad ways that this setting is influenced by and constructed from professional relationships and social interactions. The academic work environment refers to and is composed of multiple historic and contemporary organizational domains and units that have a voice in the governance of its systems, policies, and procedures, including (1) student, faculty, and administrative bodies; (2) interpersonal dynamics at the departmental and/or institutional level, which include racial/ethnic/gendered dynamics such as marginalization, tokenism, racism, and discrimination; (3) demands and perceptions of faculty scholarly, teaching, research, and service activities; (4) departmental and institutional policies and procedures, including those related to recruitment, hiring, salary, evaluation, and tenure and promotion that influence the working environment in which faculty find themselves; (5) faculty support including mentoring and professional development; and (6) the engagement of leadership and administration in creating a work environment supportive of diversity.

Institutional cultures can be characterized by a performative and symbolic set of norms and expectations that govern both implicitly and explicitly the behavior of the major actors. These norms and expectations create an institutional culture that is enacted by the major power brokers in these institutions and must be learned. The behaviors are enacted in the work environment, professional relationships, social interactions, and mentoring relationships. For example, mentoring opportunities are important institutional support resources in helping faculty develop their political and professional understanding of the path to tenure and the process for sharing accomplishments to gain access to additional opportunities for advancement and promotion (Diggs, Garrison-Wade, Estrada, & Galindo, 2009; Turner, González, & Wood, 2008). However, access to mentoring relationships and professional networks designed to support and enhance faculty success is more limited for URMs than for non-URM faculty (Aguirre, Martinez, & Hernandez, 1993; Price et al., 2005).

Importantly, the interpersonal dimensions of the academic work environment are influenced not only by intercollegial relationships and dynamics but also by relationships and interactions with students (Bower, 2002; Diggs et al., 2009). URM faculty report concerns about how race/ethnicity influences students' perceptions of them and experience race- and ethnicity-based negative evaluations, challenges to authority and expertise, negative behaviors and attitudes, and complaints from students made to senior faculty and administrators about their teaching (Bower, 2002; Cook & Gibbs, 2009). When URM faculty are teaching on race-related topics, student reactions and resistance manifest passively (e.g., in instructor evaluations) and/or actively (e.g., through overt resistance and even harassment; Sampaio, 2006). Tuitt, Hanna, Martinez,

Salazar, and Griffin (2009) describe a growing body of literature that high-lights the costs involved in seeking a career in higher education. They cite specifically that an "unwelcoming and potentially hostile classroom environment awaits for those who choose to teach in a PWI" (p. 65). For underrepresented faculty, the questioning of their authority and legitimacy in the classroom has reached intolerable heights.

In many ways, the academic work environment is the lived expression and result of departmental and institutional policies and procedures that establish the norms and rewards for faculty engagement, participation, and retention. Though the practices that accompany the policies and procedures may not affect a given faculty member on a daily basis in the way that professional relationships and interpersonal dynamics do, the departmental and institutional structures that undergird the presence and participation of faculty have a pervasive and profound effect on the working environment (McDonald & Wingfield, 2009).

These organizational domains promote a climate that contributes to faculty satisfaction or dissatisfaction, decisions to stay or leave academic positions, and attrition from the professoriate. Climate is conceptualized as having two components: a physical and material reality and an individual perceptual reality. For example, perceptions of marginalization and tokenism in interpersonal relation-ships have a strong influence on how URM faculty experience colleagueship and organizational climate at the departmental or institutional level. An unwelcoming climate is a major concern of higher education institutions and may contribute to the academic disengagement of URM faculty. The idea of a "chilly climate" was coined with the significant increase of women in institutions of higher learning in the 1970s. In contrast, constructs of marginalization and solo status have become linked with inclusion and exclusion of URM professionals and are strongly tied with the institutional rhetoric around institutional diversity.

While the academic work of faculty involves appealing features such as autonomy, work-time flexibility, creativity, and prestige, past research has demonstrated mixed results regarding the ways in which this occupation affects one's health (Burgard & Lin, 2013; Mirowsky & Ross, 2007; Moen, Kelly, Tranby, & Huang, 2011). Time pressures and role overload associated with faculty work-load show that, on average, across institutions and departments, faculty commit over fifty hours per week to teaching, research, service, and other responsi-bilities (Jacobs & Winslow, 2004) and today are spending more time engaged in research, teaching, and classroom preparation than they have in the past (Hart & Cress, 2008; O'Meara & Braskamp, 2005). While a heavy workload may stress all faculty, it seems uniquely stressful for URM faculty who are more likely to be assigned higher teaching loads and more new course preparations (Allen et al., 2002; Martínez Alemán & Renn, 2002). Although service activities are less valued and normally count minimally toward tenure requirements and may even hinder promotion (Cook & Gibbs, 2009; Gregory, 2001; Martínez Alemán & Renn, 2002; O'Meara & Braskamp, 2005), URM faculty may feel pressure from senior colleagues to assume these roles, while simultaneously feeling an obligation to mentor minority and low-income students.

URM faculty, compared to their White colleagues, report their institutional environments as unwelcoming and a contributing factor to lower work satisfaction (Cook & Gibbs, 2009; Laden & Hagedorn, 2000). For early career faculty, campus environments can represent impersonal spaces. The Collaborative on Academic Careers in Higher Education (COACHE) survey, which assessed 8,513 college and university faculty, demonstrated significant gaps between the satisfaction of racial/ethnic minority groups and that of Whites on the interpersonal aspects of the academic work environment.[1] In particular, all racial/ ethnic minority groups except Hispanics were less likely than Whites to feel that they had satisfactory personal interactions with tenured colleagues and were a good fit in their departments. American Indian / Alaska Native and African American faculty reported fewer opportunities to collaborate with tenured faculty and were less likely to agree that junior faculty were treated fairly and equitably. American Indian / Alaska Native faculty were also less likely than other groups to believe that their tenured colleagues took an interest in their professional development and were more skeptical about the intellectual vitality of senior faculty (COACHE, 2007). Within academic medicine, URM faculty reported fewer networking opportunities and diminished access to professional and social relationships (Price et al., 2005). Prior studies such as the 1993 Study of Postsecondary Faculty found that faculty of color reported greater barriers to job satisfaction relative to their White colleagues as a result of having limited opportunities to develop working relationships with White faculty, experiencing little warmth or understanding among colleagues, and feeling socially isolated from White colleagues. In addition, racial/ethnic minority faculty satisfaction was also influenced by perceptions that their scholarly credentials were ignored or devalued by their colleagues (Laden & Hagedorn, 2000).

Without a sense of community, faculty are more likely to report feeling stressed, isolated, and intellectually understimulated (Boice, 1999; Sorcinelli, 2000). While this is reported among new faculty regardless of race/ethnicity or gender, evidence indicates the particular importance of professional, collegial relationships in the success and satisfaction of URM faculty, especially those at predominantly White institutions (Vasquez et al., 2006). For all faculty, the social climate and support, guidance, and role modeling of more experienced faculty are essential to professional success and satisfaction (Menges & Associates, 1999; Rice, Sorcinelli, & Austin, 2000). However, institutional investments in mentoring and public acclamation of diversity remain unexamined.

## INSTITUTIONAL SUPPORTS:
## MENTORING AS A NAVIGATIONAL TOOL

Professional work environments produce unique cultures that partly reflect the larger social culture and partly reflect that of the founders and their legacy peers, who are viewed as coproducers of the extant "secretive, powerful, and peculiar world" in academia (Lamont, 2009). In selecting new employees, fit in values and vision is taken into account, as is physical presence. Oftentimes a new hire is formally or informally assigned a "buddy," an advisor or formal or informal more seasoned colleague with whom the new employee can consult, ask a question, or obtain guidance on the organizational mores including dress policy. The apprenticeship model of mentoring has been a long-standing institutional practice in academic settings and is understood to be a major building block in the academic career path. This model predominates among White males and their White male protégés. This practice includes molding and strengthening scholarly contributions; transmitting social and political capital in understanding the normative expectations and hidden curriculum in institutional cultures; helping protégés access an intellectual social network; and oftentimes serving as gatekeepers, advocates, and protectors in conflicts and adverse collegial relationships. With the advent of women and historically underrepresented minorities in the 1970 and 1980s, new mentoring approaches were devised and a new set of cultural metaphors were embraced such as advisors, coaches, informal peer mentoring, and formal institutionally designed mentoring programs. A formulaic dance was devised to mentor women, URM, and in some instances first-generation faculty, and new advice was proffered on the importance of having many mentors to fulfill different needs. Not surprisingly, study after study has reported the same findings regarding mentors. For example, Blake-Beard (2011) reports that the most successful pairings are those based on a shared commonality between mentor and mentee. Matching on race and gender has been shown to be an effective strategy for helping female students and those of color to remain in STEM fields. Among URM faculty, mounting evidence unequivocally reveals the limited number of mentors who share a common value system of race consciousness, a socially driven research agenda, and commitments to community service and students (Boyd, Cintrón, & Alexander-Snow, 2010; Dancy & Brown, 2011; Zambrana, Ray, et al., 2015). URMs perceive a hostile workplace environment where they experience high levels of bias and daily microaggressions (Wingfield, 2010; Zambrana, Wingfield, Lapeyrouse, Hoagland, & Burciaga Valdez, 2016). The outcome for many early career faculty is a lack of professional socialization that is very closely tied to career path advancement. As described in chapter 5, an untenable lived experience is encountered whereby URM faculty have limited guidance on the normative and cultural expectations on how to enact their role in the university, the college, their department, and the larger disciplinary field. Without these cultural maps and access to professional socialization processes, URM faculty are often overengaged in activities that do not count toward advancement and experience high levels of duress.

## UNEQUAL INSTITUTIONAL CULTURES: WORKPLACE STRESS IN ACADEMIC ENVIRONMENTS

The major training ground for integration in academic life begins in graduate school with the assistance of mentors and peers (Segura, Brooks, Shin, & Romo, 2012; Turner, 2015). This is less likely to occur for URM students, who have limited access to social networks that can improve their ability to navigate and benefit from graduate school experiences. Moreover, many confront unique challenges such as serious life events and family kin obligations that exacerbate institutional stressors (Vallejo, 2012).

Marginalization, tokenism, and discrimination due to racial/ethnic and gender statuses are central features of workplace stress that impact job satisfaction, thus creating a sense of invisibility, isolation, perceived tokenism, and devaluation of one's work in the academy (Cook & Gibbs, 2009; Diggs et al., 2009; Laden & Hagedorn, 2000). These experiences threaten personal and collective identities, create pressures to assimilate in intolerable ways (Diggs et al., 2009), and contribute to negative academic work environments (Turner et al., 2008). A major theorizing anchor in understanding integration and adaptation of URM faculty in academic institutional cultures is the construct of vocational strain. To more fully understand vocational strain within higher education organizations, the following chapters reveal how institutional (e.g., mentoring experiences in chapter 4, perceived bias and discrimination in chapter 5) and individual factors (such as family concerns, life events, self-care practices) interact in academic work environments to exacerbate stress-inducing work roles and demands.

Recurring themes in the corpus of work on institutional cultures reveal four distinct yet consistent perceptions in the workplace: tokenism / solo status; perceived bias, discrimination, and microaggressions; devaluing and questioning of credentials; and impact of excessive work demands on physical and mental health. Regardless of race/ethnicity or gender, URM faculty are more likely to report feeling stressed, isolated, and intellectually understimulated, without a sense of community (Vasquez et al., 2006). At the departmental and institutional levels, especially at PWIs, URM faculty are more likely to report experiencing a sense of isolation, a lack of acceptance, and exclusion from formal and informal networks in the academy (Patton, 2004). Additionally, URM faculty are oftentimes the "only one" in their departments. This sense of "tenuring alone" enhances hypervisibility and expectations to be the representative of one's racial group (and at times all URMs). This solo status also leads to being stereotyped, being encapsulated and highly contrasted with other members of the department, and experiencing more vulnerability to stereotype threat and less psychological safety. The next sections of this chapter describe the studies that examine important institutional practices and experiences that continue to hamper progress in diversifying institutions by not equally drawing on the URM domestic talent pool.

Kanter (1977a) illustrated tokenism for women, and the results can also be applied to URM groups. Tokenism describes the concurrent negative processes of how being small in number leads racial/ethnic and gender minority faculty to feel highly visible; to be expected to be representative of one's own and sometimes all minority groups; to be stereotyped and encapsulated in one's respective group; to be highly contrasted with the other members of one's work environment; to be more vulnerable to stereotype threat; to bear a greater burden in the form of institutional and individual racism; and to experience diminished psychological safety (Niemann & Dovidio, 1998). In many disciplines, URMs not only have token status but also are solo members of their racial/ethnic group. The powerful role of solo status goes beyond even token status. In a survey of racial/ethnic minority and majority faculty, solo minorities were more dissatisfied with their jobs than were nonsolo minorities. Within groups, the solo-nonsolo disparity in job satisfaction was revealed for African Americans in particular by their high visibility, which exposed them to daily experiences that demonstrated the powerful impact of structural diversity on URM faculty satisfaction, success, and survival within the academy (Niemann & Dovidio, 1998). Comparing URM and non-URM perceptions of institutional diversity confirms that faculty overall were dissatisfied with diversity efforts, but in one study URM faculty were nearly four times less likely to report satisfaction with racial/ethnic diversity than were their majority colleagues (Price et al., 2009).

In a survey of Black faculty (Thompson & Louque, 2005), 84 percent of respondents reported experiencing racism. Further, of the respondents who reported experiences of racism, 70 percent experienced racism from one or more colleagues, 74 percent from students, 51 percent from immediate supervisors, and 57 percent from other administrators. Nearly 70 percent of respondents reported that the racial work climate affected their job satisfaction, and nearly 70 percent reported that it had caused stress on them. URM faculty report isolation, alienation, negative evaluation, questioning of their credentials, and overt discrimination from colleagues (Bower, 2002; Cook & Gibbs, 2009; Diggs et al., 2009). URM faculty in academic medicine report on the manifestations of bias within many aspects of the academic work environment, including interpersonal dynamics, questioning of professional competence by colleagues, and having to justify credentials to others (Price et al., 2005).

Excessive work overload combined with racial bias is exceptionally stressful. Departmental chairs often assign courses on marginalized topics (Diggs et al., 2009), assign higher teaching loads, and require service tasks related to their racial/ethnic identities. Higher teaching loads and additional university service expectations related to diversity, normally a topic assigned in terms of race/ethnicity (Agathangelou & Ling, 2002; Aguirre, 2000; Brayboy, 2003; Medina & Luna, 2000; Moses, 1989; Turner et al., 2008; Turner & Myers, 2000), are associated with higher levels of stress (Thomas & Hollenshead, 2001). African Americans and Mexican Americans perceive racial bias by faculty members in higher positions, colleagues, and students via daily microaggressions (Peterson, Friedman, Ash, Franco, & Carr, 2004). Extant data show that about 24.7 percent of White faculty report subtle discrimination, compared to 63.6 percent of African American faculty and 42.6 percent of Latinos. URMs have higher reports of discrimination than do other groups (Hurtado, Eagan, Pryor, Whang, & Tran, 2012, p. 6). Furthermore, URM faculty are frequently viewed by students and colleagues through a narrow racial/cultural lens (Salazar, 2009). Perceptions of being seen by peers as unqualified affirmative action hires and illegitimate scholars are another common form of bias (Agathangelou & Ling, 2002; Medina & Luna, 2000; Smith & Calasanti, 2005) for both URM men and women. When facing such biases, devaluing, and discrimination, faculty struggle to determine whether and when to confront bias and stereotypes in the workplace without negatively impacting their career development (Price et al., 2005).

The intersecting identities of historically underrepresented groups as defined in this book entail a set of historical and social experiences that shape their life experiences, opportunities, and interactions with majority-culture individuals (or power relations). The authors of many studies, particularly in Black feminist thought (Collins, 2000, 2015) and Chicana feminism (Hurtado, 1996; Moraga & Anzaldúa, 2015; Segura, 1989), argue that gendered experiences cannot be isolated from race, ethnicity, and class performance. The experiences of URM women have been shown to be different from those of non-Hispanic White women, and these precise differences have yielded a rich body of work on multiple feminisms. Interestingly, the data confirm that the intersection of race, ethnicity, and gender performance is prevalent for both URM men and women fighting for legitimacy and a place in the academy regardless of discipline.

Gender as a dimension of inequality has received the most attention in empirical works as well as in policy, practice, and programs such as the National Science Foundation–funded program ADVANCE and the recent report "Pipelines, Pathways, and Institutional Leadership: An Update on the Status of Women in Higher Education" by the American Council on Education (Johnson, 2016).[2]

Intersectional identities of gender/race/ethnicity and class have been largely omitted from mainstream studies due to small sample sizes. This omission perpetuates the minimal progress of professional URM women during the past four decades because their status is not part of the national discourse. Moreover, when we speak of all women, we actually reference majority-culture women, whose struggle is within the very system that privileges them by virtue of their color and most often their class. Acknowledging the discrimination against all women in United States, we nonetheless need to move beyond gender as the sole category of analysis and inquire about the privileges of being, for example, a racialized Mexican American male versus an African American woman. This section interrupts the social constructs of race, ethnicity, and gender and interrogates the homogeneity among "singular identity" groups in ways that elucidate the role of intersectional identities and institutional power. A growing literature addresses the voices of African American and Mexican American women on the nature and level of disrespect experienced in their classrooms and departments (Allison, 2008; Harley, 2008; Harlow, 2003; Pittman, 2010). See chapter 9 for a fuller discussion on gender.

Underrepresented women have not made gains as substantial as White women have in securing representation in academia (American Council on Education, 2015). Wong and colleagues (2001) analyzed descriptive data from the Association of American Medical Colleges (AAMC) and found that whereas all women faculty had risen from 15.2 to 26.6 percent in the past two decades, the proportion of URM women had grown only from 4 to 6 percent. Of the total female faculty, 4.2 percent were African American, 0.2 percent American Indian / Alaska Native, 0.5 percent Mexican American, and 1.1 percent Puerto Rican (Johnson, 2016). A recent report by Lautenberger, Moses, and Castillo-Page (2016) in conjunction with the American Association of Medical Colleges shows that in 2015, women made up 39 percent of the total full-time faculty at medical schools. In analyses by race, ethnicity, and gender, data show that White women made up 59 percent (36,609), and faculty with "unknown race" made up 13 percent (8,264). Asian women constituted 11.6 percent (6,408) of all female medical school faculty while comprising roughly 5.1 percent of the total U.S. population in 2012. African American females constituted 3.6 percent ($n = 2,002$), and Hispanic women faculty made up 3.7 percent ($n = 2,076$), of whom 61 percent ($n = 1,249$) were other Hispanic and American Indian / Alaska Native faculty ($n = 85$). Among women, the African American and other women categories occur at higher rates than their male counterparts in faculty positions. Trend data from the 1980s to the early 2000s show differences in rates of promotion and retention between men and women. Using a nationally representative sample, Perna (2001b) investigated whether the probability of holding tenure or being promoted to full professor differed by race/ethnicity and gender. At four-year institutions, although women were marginally less likely to hold tenure than men after controlling for race/ethnicity, citizenship, research productivity, and structural factors, tenured women were still 10 percent less likely than men to hold the position of full professor (2001). Interestingly, gender differences were not evident in quantitative data analyses or in qualitative sample short surveys, but narrative data revealed gender discrimination in terms of service and classroom experiences.

The common tendency to compartmentalize race/ethnicity, gender, and class prevents a deeper analyses of the inequality and inequity that lies at the multiple and layered social identity of URM faculty and that plays itself out unquestioned in the academy. The frequent masking of racism, sexism, or classism behind what appear to be and are promoted as impersonal, fair standard operating procedures or embedded social and organizational norms (McDonald & Wingfield, 2009) also contributes to the difficulty in naming and addressing these interlocking -isms within the academy and the acknowledgment of unequal institutional cultures. These inequalities can best be understood as the benefits and rewards of institutional cultures for some faculty while often having a subtractive effect on the productivity, rewards, and advancement of URM faculty. This vocational strain, which is integral to professional advancement, becomes more burdensome when additional demands are placed on early career faculty.

## SOCIAL STATUS, STRESS-INDUCING WORK ROLES, AND PHYSICAL AND MENTAL WELL-BEING

Occupational stress is a growing concern that manifests in adverse physical and mental well-being, poor work performance, reduced productivity, and lower retention of qualified employees in the workforce. A significant body of work on the effects of occupational stress has been conducted on women and early career faculty—comparing rigorous academic environments and requirements among women and men, and more recently non-tenure-track faculty (Duquette, Kérouac, Sandhu, Ducharme, & Saulnier, 1995; Eddy & Gaston-Gayles, 2008; Elliot, 2008; Hart & Cress, 2008; Lease, 1999; Reevy & Deason, 2014). Few studies, however, have addressed the intersections of race, ethnicity (Latino subgroup), and occupational status (high prestigious professionals). Most studies that have addressed coping with stress among URMs in the workplace have focused on less educated workers (Hogan, Carlson, & Dua, 2002). An important empirical finding is that the educational advantages in health status reported for upper-middle-class Whites are not as evident for higher SES Blacks and Latinos.

New lines of inquiry during the past decade have contributed to empirical evidence on the interrelationships between stress, perceived discrimination, and coping strategies and their roles in racial and ethnic health disparities, particularly among low-income groups (Gee & Walsemann, 2009; James, Lovato, & Khoo, 1994; Pearlin, 1989; Pearlin, Schieman, Fazio, & Meersman, 2005). Furthermore, associations between occupational stress specifically and racism and discrimination, coping, and adverse physical and mental well-being have been reported (Araujo & Borrell, 2006; Mays, Cochran, & Barnes, 2007; Okazaki, 2009; Williams & Williams-Morris, 2000). These results confirm a theorizing shift highlighting the relationships among race, ethnicity, work, and discrimination.

Stress-inducing work experiences oftentimes contribute to high levels of anxiety and intellectual devaluation. This devaluation is a primary source of occupational stress that impacts job satisfaction by creating a sense of invisibility, isolation, tokenism, and disregard of one's work in the academy (Cook & Gibbs, 2009), threatens personal and collective identities, and creates pressures to assimilate in difficult ways (Diggs et al., 2009). These negative interactions of bias with colleagues and students create unwelcoming spaces and increase vocational strain and anticipatory stress. High levels of stress-inducing work roles and few institutional supports can powerfully affect a person's health and mental well-being (Moen, Lam, Ammons, & Kelly, 2013; Thoits, 2011). Although an argument can be made that higher education faculty all experience difficulties, for URM groups, who are the most underrepresented in these settings, their social status as historically incorporated and subordinate groups is embedded in institutional power relations (Ridgeway, 2014), making them even more prone to workplace stress and vocational strain. The career trajectories of early career faculty combined with undesirable prior experiences in college and graduate school contribute to a difficult set of processes in preparation for tenure and promotion. A modest body of scholarship reveals the pervasive challenges to retention and promotion at research universities for URM faculty, which are linked with perceived occupational stressors that oftentimes have detrimental effects on faculty's physical and mental well-being (Gutiérrez y Muhs, Niemann, González, & Harris, 2012; Turner et al., 2008). Stressors include (1) the lack of diversity and unwelcoming work environments (Stanley, 2006; Turner et al., 2008); (2) experiences of marginalization, devaluation, benign neglect, racism, and discrimination (Boyd et al., 2010; Essien, 2003; Flores, 2011; Niemann, 1999); (3) challenges in balancing work and family lives (Castañeda et al., 2015; Childers & Sage, 2003; Elliot, 2003; Jacobs, 2004; Mason, Wolfinger, & Goulden, 2013); and (4) the lack of institutional support, such as mentoring (Boykin et al., 2003; Cross & Slater, 2002; Dixon-Reeves, 2003; Shollen, Bland, Taylor, Weber-Main, & Mulcahy, 2008). Successful retention and promotion depend on a number of unmeasurable factors such as personality, likeability, powerful departmental allies, and perceived value of research, among others. Thus, the career success milestones depend significantly on what is referred to as the accumulation of social capital over the lifetime. Bourdieu (1986) splendidly captured the construct of social networks such as family friends or friends from summer camp or school who could assist one in identifying and accessing resources with which to catapult one's ambitions and aspirations forward. In many ways, this class- and race-based social capital accumulates over the life course and facilitates the successful completion of career milestones along the way. Although exceptions exist, the patterns of success for those individuals with social capital are consistent.

Historically, higher education has excluded URM faculty through various practices (Margolis & Romero, 1998; Zambrana & MacDonald, 2009) rooted in dominant ideologies that "sustain a biased class structure; facilitating only the psychosocial and career benefits of mentoring for some groups by some groups" (Fletcher & Mullen, 2012, p. 15). These advantages are present at the earliest stages of faculty development (i.e., doctoral education), whereby students are (un)willingly socialized to fit rigid conceptualizations of the "ideal" scholar (Noy & Ray, 2011): one who displays "detachment and distance, the use of abstract concepts, assertive self-confidence, competition, independent work habits, and loyalty to colleagues—even at the expense of allegiance to one's community of origin" (Margolis & Romero, 1998, p. 9). As a result, URM faculty find it difficult and stressful to navigate the labyrinth of organizational structures that were not intended to serve historically underrepresented groups (Aguirre, 2000; Gonzáles, Murakami, & Núñez, 2013; Johnsrud & Sadao, 1998; Martínez Alemán, 1995; Turner, 2002).

Exploring inequality and inequity consists of multiple, complex, overlapping, and intertwined dimensions that converge with existing structural power arrangements. By applying an intersectional lens to explore, for example, the joint effects of social status (coconstituted identities) and life course experiences of discrimination, scholars from multiple disciplines contribute to developing and placing new knowledge into action by deconstructing the old. In a recent essay on intersectionality, Collins (2015) proffers some keen observations on the deployment of intersectionality as an overarching analytic tool to inform and guide knowledge production whose roots are embedded in and respond to social formations of social inequalities (p. 5). I argue that contextualizing the academic organization and its historically underrepresented faculty within an intersectional lens allows for a deeper interpretation of the structures of inequality within higher education, inclusive of a set of theorizing assumptions (historic, social status, life course trajectory). To repeat, social status is an identity that for my purposes encompasses the lives of subordinate groups whose historical treatment—namely, the denial of all civil rights into the mid-twentieth century—has dramatically shaped their life circumstances, the ways in which they are viewed within the larger social structures, and, in turn, the access they have to social and economic opportunities. Pursuing the importance of history in defining circumstances, a second theorizing construct claims that one dimension of identity does not fully describe another's perception of one's social status in the existing social order and its power relations. Race, ethnicity, SES, and gender are coconstitutive and mutually reinforcing dimensions that shape one's life chances, opportunities, and, in turn, life course experiences in the educational pipeline (Collins, 2000, 2015). Identities are multilayered and fluid, but color and phenotype are not readily changeable. One of the distinguishing factors of URMs is the identity markers of race, ethnicity, and gender, embedded in institutional structures (Ridgeway, 2014), that permeate the implicit biases of institutional agents such as faculty peers, department chairs, and deans. Historic and contemporary stereotypic representations of these groups as inferior and "affirmative action babies" are prevalent in the attitudes of university officials and in environments throughout the educational pipeline. These attitudes constitute structurally embedded implicit bias and contribute to a view of URM faculty as undeserving and not desiring or able to succeed academically (Baez, 2002; Gutiérrez y Muhs et al., 2012; Montero-Sieburth, 1996).

A life course perspective is central in the discussion of any professional career path, as it takes into account one's opportunities and available resources throughout one's life, including the transmission of family social capital, such as access to private schools, vacations abroad, and role models and the ability to participate in volunteer activities and research internships. Being a child of parents who graduated from an Ivy League school (legacy) and participation in extracurricular activities including summer camps open up avenues of social and economic opportunity. Life course experiences are powerfully shaped by SES, race/ethnicity, neighborhoods, and schools attended. Evidence shows that many underrepresented faculty have throughout their life course experienced educational and economic disadvantage and multiple forms of discrimination and microaggressions (Allison, 2008; Bhopal & Jackson, 2013; Griffin, Pifer, Humphrey, & Hazelwood, 2011; Joseph & Hirshfield, 2011). Particularly for those URM who are from low SES families, access to social capital in the form of well-resourced schools, extracurricular activities, and high-level professionals who serve as role models, mentors, and bridges to social and economic opportunity is oftentimes limited. At the culmination of a professional degree and/or doctorate, initial entry into an early career professional position is highly associated with family SES and quality of schooling, including access to extracurricular activities, and prior mentoring experiences. Notwithstanding strong aspirational capital, working in higher education with few professional development opportunities or mentoring resources, as well as persistent discrimination and the witnessing of unearned privilege among dominant culture groups, can greatly curtail social networks and cultural capital, which in turn negatively affects career paths (Carr, Palepu, Szalacha, Caswell, & Inui, 2007). Early career faculty consistently confront unwelcoming climates and invisible institutional barriers. For example, institutional policies and practices, such as assigned mentoring, are often informed by historical representations and racialized attitudes and practices (albeit unconscious) that may contribute to the academic disengagement of URM faculty, dampening educational expectations and aspirations (Boykin et al., 2003).

The distinguishing features of the experiences of URM faculty have been clearly articulated by Trower (2003): (1) overt and/or covert racism including being stereotyped and pigeonholed; (2) heavier teaching and service loads than those assigned to White males; (3) isolation and exclusion and the resultant lack of colleagueship, networks, and mentors, leaving them less attuned to the rules that affect academic work life, including promotion and tenure; (4) marginalization and finding that their research is discredited, especially if it concerns minority issues; (5) tremendous burden of tokenism, including feeling like they must be an exemplar of their entire race and feeling they have to work twice as hard to get half as far; (6) feeling "culturally taxed," or more obligated to show good citizenship by representing their race or ethnicity on multiple committees that help the institution but not necessarily the individuals and to mentor and advise many same-race students—a huge hidden work load that goes unrewarded in the promotion and tenure system; (7) the need to place greater emphasis than Whites do on the affective, moral, and civic development of students, the result of having been more likely to enter the academy having drawn a connection between the professoriate and the ability to effect social change; and (8) a tendency to suffer from the negative, unintended consequences of being perceived as an affirmative action or target-of-opportunity hire.

Throughout the forthcoming chapters, data are presented on the multiple domains of the lived experiences of URM academic professionals. Mentoring and institutional support, the experiences of implicit bias and discriminatory practices, work-family balance, and procedures for appointment, tenure, and promotion are embedded in the racialized institutional hierarchies that produce injurious physical and mental health outcomes for many of these promising scholars. These data initiate a new conversation that is meant to inform concerns regarding the low levels of URM representation in elite institutions in spite of a forty-year diversity discourse.

Several studies have clearly demonstrated what can be substantially changed to make diversity into a principle of change, not simply accommodation. Greater student/faculty diversity is reported to create positive departmental and institutional work environments for racial/ethnic minority faculty and, when lacking, contributes to a negative academic work environment experience (Turner et al., 2008). In 1997, Knowles and Harleston observed that "achieving diversity" in the academy requires moving beyond thinking of diversity in terms of adding more URMs to departments and toward creating an environment that will nurture faculty and students of all types. Although their work is well intentioned, they reinforced the resistance to any form of "leveling the playing field" for those who had been denied equal access to higher education for so long. Efforts to increase the number of diverse doctoral graduates through recruitment have not been effective as academic work environments continue to be perceived as unaccommodating to URM faculty.

Leadership plays an important role in establishing the conditions that support developing, maintaining, and promoting policies that create a supportive academic environment for all faculty, particularly women and URM faculty. Faculty perception of administrative and leadership commitment to helping URM faculty be successful leads to greater job satisfaction (Laden & Hagedorn, 2000; Piercy et al., 2005; Price et al., 2005; Turner et al., 2008). Activities that support the development of an institutional culture that encourages faculty to openly express opinions and differing views on social issues, makes faculty feel valued, builds social connections and professional partnership to bridge diversity lines, and incorporates faculty perspectives into the main mission and culture of the institution are important steps toward building an interpersonal culture that embraces diversity (Cook & Gibbs, 2009; Piercy et al., 2005; Ross, 2011). Moreover, ample evidence suggests that faculty mentorship is a valuable resource for imparting career guidance, transmitting social and cultural capital, and helping with the process of tenure and promotion. The next chapter focuses on mentoring, provides narratives of URM faculty who have had experiences with mentoring, and examines the consequences that occur in its absence.

# 4 · MENTORING

## Institutions Applying a Solution
## without Acknowledging the Problem

My mentors were amazing about explaining to me how things get done in departments, where money comes from, who has authority over what, how to approach in a given situation so that you're not just concerned about your own needs, but you understand the needs of the department, or the committee, or whoever's looking at reviewing your work. And I think a lot of mentoring relations don't do enough to all of those invisible things that make success possible particularly for people of color, who you know, in my family, no one had gone to graduate school before me. So it—there was nobody there who understood all of that, and could tell me things on a personal level, and I think that's true for a lot of people of color in the academy, that you don't come from a place of prior knowledge.

—Mexican American female

Universities are becoming progressively concerned about increasing the number of faculty and students of diverse backgrounds in their institutions and retaining those populations once they arrive. Faculty diversity and retention are associated with a welcoming climate and institutional resources that ensure higher quality environments. The last two decades have witnessed an institutional frenzy to institute faculty mentoring programs to predominantly redress the low representation of historically underrepresented minority (URM) groups (African American, Mexican American, Puerto Rican, and American Indian / Alaska Native) and majority-culture women in the STEM and STEAM fields.[1] In order for faculty to be retained, multiple forms and layers of mentoring have been designed to help all hires in their professional socialization. These include peer mentoring, one-on-one formal and informal mentoring, sponsorship mentors, advisors, academic coaching, and group mentorship such as launching committees.[2] Over the past two decades, early career scholars have been encouraged to rely on mentoring as a mechanism to ensure success in academia. Yet scholarly narratives and data on retention, tenure, and promotion suggest that social capital via mentoring is not being consistently transmitted or received by URM groups at the same rate as it is by majority-culture Whites. In effect, mentoring has become a symbolic form of institutional support that has served to mask authentic social change at the institutional level.

Mentoring plays an important role in professional development and navigational support, especially in enhancing social networks for all professionals. These networks are crucial for new and midcareer faculty who are navigating critically important terrains in processes and procedures associated with securing tenure and promotion. This chapter presents findings on the role of mentoring as a potential institutional support and explores how participants experience mentoring, engage in interpersonal relationships, and describe ideal attributes of and challenges to mentoring relationships and the role of political guidance in the process. Questions about the meanings of effective mentorship for URMs, why it is different for URMs versus non-URMs, and the best strategies for increasing retention of URMs in elite research institutions are best answered when those who are most affected provide us with insights on how to best help them. This chapter also employs a review of the literature to uncover the importance of mentoring across the life course, describes participants' lived experiences with multiple forms of mentoring, provides a road map for shifting how we engage with URM faculty, and presents insightful knowledge and novel and tailored strategies for promoting a more successful URM career pathway.

Significant debates exist on the most effective approaches to mentoring. A broad range of models such as peer mentoring, coaching, sponsorship, and formal and informal mentoring programs have garnered strong interest and been touted as promising solutions to career path success. Yet their effectiveness has been understudied, available results on effectiveness are mixed, and other studies have obfuscated the issue rather than shed light on its importance for specific populations such as URM men and women.

## DEFINITIONS OF MENTORSHIP: WHY IS IT PROBLEMATIC?

Mentoring has multiple dimensions and definitions that affirm the value of an early career scholar's work, uplift the confidence of that individual through constructive feedback, and inform the mentee on next steps in both direct and indirect ways throughout the life course. URM students participating in mentoring programs in college and/or high school have demonstrated higher grade point averages, lower attrition, increased self-efficacy, and better defined academic goals (Tsui, 2007; Zambrana, Dejesus, & Davila, 2015). A caring mentor relationship between a high school teacher and a student or a faculty member and an undergraduate student is pivotal in fostering future professional goals (Crawford, Suarez-Balcazar, Reich, Figert, & Nyde, 1996; Tsui, 2007). Mentorship at the graduate level serves two important functions: teaching doctoral students how to work in tandem with colleagues, which is essential to building a professional reputation and network in the academy (Felder, 2010), and providing graduate URM students with essential supports, particularly at PWIs. Brown, Davis, and McClendon (1999) note that "mentors have the ability to assist graduate underrepresented students of color with adjustment to both the academic and nonacademic aspects of graduate education" (p. 110).

Effective mentorship is not merely advising or supervising (Bozeman & Feeney, 2007; Crisp & Cruz, 2009); it emphasizes the informal transfer of knowledge, social capital, and psychosocial support between an individual with perceived knowledge and experience and one without over a sustained period (Bozeman & Feeney, 2007). Social learning theory regards "mentoring as a developmental process of modeling and vicarious reinforcement . . . where a protégé acquires important skills by observing and modeling the mentor's behaviors" (Kay, Hagan, & Parker, 2009, pp. 72–73). Yet the importance of the accumulation of advantage via mentoring or prior research experiences, which is often reported absent by study participants, is not adequately accounted for in the career path of the URM professoriate.

Almost three decades ago, Jacobi (1991) conducted a comprehensive review of the role of mentorship in student academic success. She examined not only the competing definitions of mentoring and the role of the mentor in the relationship but also the role of mentorship wherein shared ethnicity, race, and/or gender were present (p. 511). She explicated several important findings: a distinction between formal and informal mentor relationships, the importance of early mentorship initiatives for undergraduates, and the need for rigorous mentorship of graduate students. She states, "Describing the theoretical link between mentoring and academic outcomes is more than an intellectual exercise. Different theoretical approaches shift the focus of investigations and emphasize different aspects of the mentoring relationship" (p. 522).

In 2009, the authors of an updated comprehensive literature review (1990–2007) on college student mentorship reported that mentorship was a policy priority with national, state, and institutional programs (Crisp & Cruz, 2009, pp. 525–526). Yet the authors poignantly stated that the field had not kept pace with the program development, nor had it maintained a "consistent definition and conceptualization of mentorship" (p. 540). Confirming other critiques, the definition of what constitutes mentorship varied between and within disciplines. The findings reveal primarily positive effects for mentored students, which are the focus of the empirical work. The authors conclude that an emergent trend in the literature is investigating the benefits of mentoring for underserved and underrepresented student populations. Divergent mentoring theories suggest that mentoring can enhance learning engagement, facilitate integration of the academic and social spheres, provide social support, and/or enhance professional and personal development.

An overall consensus exists in the literature of a nebulous and broad construct of the practice of mentorship. This is illustrated by mentorship situations that are often poorly defined and rarely theoretically constructed with little or no expectations for mentors or mentees (Boykin et al., 2003; Daley, Wingard, & Reznik, 2006). This is so common that underrepresented minority faculty in general tend to identify mentorship as poor or nonexistent and as a hindrance to advancement (Boyd, Cintrón, & Alexander-Snow, 2010; Robinson & Clardy, 2010; Thomas & Hollenshead, 2001; Turner, 2002).

Two major mentoring modalities are frequently discussed: informal and formal. The findings on informal mentorship have identified it as superior to structured firm-wide mentorship programs (Bozeman & Feeney, 2007; Kay et al., 2009) and capable of supporting better career outcomes including overall career satisfaction as well as a greater sense of workplace fairness, superior job placement, and higher earnings (Kay et al., 2009). Yet early career faculty may experience barriers in accessing and developing informal mentoring relationships and professional networks in highly selective educational contexts (Daley et al., 2006; Diggs, Garrison-Wade, Estrada, & Galindo, 2009). Informal mentorship relationships and networks are often developed in graduate school or through active participation in professional organizations but are less useful in current work environments. A strong body of evidence in multiple fields such as law, sociology, and medicine, among others, demonstrates that informal supports are not readily available nor frequently carried over from graduate school to the professional work setting (Higginbotham, 2009; Segura, Brooks, Shin, & Romo, 2012). As a result, URM faculty more often than not enter PWIs with little knowledge of what to expect, of how to obtain support, or of the challenges they will confront in teaching and collegial relationships (Tuitt, Hanna, Martinez, Salazar, & Griffin, 2009).

In contrast, institutionalized university-wide support via formal mentoring programs focuses on "socializing new faculty into the culture, mission, goals, and characteristics of the university and the communities it serves" (Otieno, Lutz, & Schoolmaster, 2010, p. 77). Although formal mentoring may provide a valuable format for transmitting navigational guidelines, career guidance, and psychosocial support, oftentimes the match in terms of intellectual interests, relationship building, and empathy presents serious barriers to effective mentoring. Bozeman and Feeney (2007) regard "formal mentoring as an oxymoron" (p. 732) and suggest that formal mandated mentorship programs become another responsibility of supervision. In response to the mixed results these approaches have yielded, alternative mentorship paradigms have blazed forward in an attempt to improve individual mentoring. These include group and peer mentorship interactions (Boykin et al., 2003; Thomas & Hollenshead, 2001). However, a positive interpersonal relationship between the mentor and the mentees is pivotal to a successful mentor relationship. All faculty, but particularly URM faculty who are visible as the "only one" in the department or college, are looking to construct mentorship relationships where they feel valued and supported in their careers (Boykin et al., 2003; Cerecer, Elk, Alanis, & Murakami-Ramalho, 2011; Espino and Zambrana, forthcoming 2019).

Because of the small number of URM faculty and senior administrators, racial/ethnic matching between mentor and mentee is often not possible. Cross-racial/ethnic mentorship processes require careful consideration to ensure effectiveness. These cross-race/ethnicity/gender matchings should involve an understanding of how race/ethnicity influences personal interaction, collegiality, social systems, and organizational structures (Cowin, Cohen, Ciechanowski, & Orozco, 2011; Stanley, 2006). Ideally, developing an effective and meaningful cross-racial/ethnic match in formal mentoring opportunities requires a sense of trust, acknowledgment of covert and overt forms of racism, strategies for helping faculty manage potential risks pertaining to their research agendas, and acknowledgment of the extent to which URM faculty are "othered" in their departments and universities (Diggs et al., 2009). Cross-gender mentoring can sometimes present challenges because the members of these relationships may not acknowledge power dynamics, implicit bias, paternalism, racism, and unwritten dominant culture norms within departments and university policies (Brown et al., 1999; Cowin et al., 2011; Thomas & Hollenshead, 2001). In these mentorships, gender stereotyping can create a paternalistic dynamic. Notably, male mentors can be uncomfortable providing advice on balancing career and family responsibilities, the development of romantic interests can undermine the relationship, and relationships may be subject to romantic rumors or innuendos (Zellers, Howard, & Barcic, 2008). While racial/ethnic matching is not necessary for successful mentoring, cross-racial/ethnic mentoring can present obstacles. The disengagement of White mentors and often elite foreign-born faculty undermines the dynamics of power, race, and embedded systemic racism in the lived experiences of URM faculty. Available mentors are often not informed or interested in performing the roles of effective mentors to historically underrepresented faculty (Essien, 2003; Feagin, 2006, 2013; Moore, 2008).

In summary, mentorship is a critical tool for success in the lives of all individuals and is an "invisible" resource for privileged, upper-income majority-culture male and female students yet a scarce resource for URM students and in turn faculty. Positive mentorship can be a key leveler in the academic careers of URM undergraduates, graduate students, and faculty members to assist them in moving through the educational pipeline. The often cited leaky pipeline is as strongly associated with lack of access to financial resources as with mentoring. For example, in a study of doctorate students of color in public affairs, insufficient mentorship was the second most significant problem for retention, following only funding deficiencies (Farmbry, 2007). Although universities emphasize the value of diverse student populations and faculty, these values are overwhelmingly symbolic (Brown et al., 1999). The absence of mentorship has contributed to a high degree of mistrust in university commitments to diversifying their ranks (Farmbry, 2007) when URM faculty continue to be underrepresented. Further compounding this mistrust are poorly executed institutionalized mentorship programs, which URM faculty often perceive as inferior to the mentorship interactions of their colleagues. Although a significant body of evidence has accrued to show that mentorship can be a hindrance to advancement, due to its poor or nonexistent quality (Boyd et al., 2010; Carr, Palepu, Szalacha, Caswell, & Inui, 2007; Price et al., 2009; Robinson & Clardy, 2010; Thomas & Hollenshead, 2001; Turner, 2002; Ward, 2010; Wong et al., 2001), a growing body of scholarship informs the disciplines of insightful and responsive mentoring practices. In the study undergone here, participants were well positioned to articulate the contours of effective mentoring experiences to showcase ways to improve mentoring practices and to draw lessons from these experiences of innovative workplace approaches to mentoring.

## STUDY FINDINGS: THE ROLE OF MENTORING IN CAREER SUCCESS

A description of workplace characteristics is provided to capture the climate in which mentoring is provided to enhance understanding of the lived experiences of mentoring as reported by participants. Frequency data and scale means are presented on the following self-reported items: (1) number of full-time faculty in the department, (2) number of full-time URM faculty in the department, (3) participation in a formal mentoring program, (4) whether the participant had a mentor in the past three years, (5) whether the participant currently had a mentor, (6) number of mentors, (7) gender of mentor, (8) race/ethnicity of mentor, (9) activities facilitated by mentor, and (10) perception of impact of inadequate mentoring.

As displayed in table 4.1, more than 50 percent of respondents were in relatively large departments of twenty-one or more faculty, while only 21.6 percent of faculty were in departments with six or more URM faculty, with African Americans being the least likely to be in departments with six or more URM

TABLE 4.1  Departmental and mentoring characteristics of respondents by race/ethnicity

| | Total sample (N = 568) | African American (n = 333; 58.6%) | Mexican American (n = 134; 23.6%) | Puerto Rican (n = 76; 13.4%) | American Indian / Alaska Native (n = 25; 4.4%) |
|---|---|---|---|---|---|
| **Number of full-time faculty in department** | | | | | |
| 0–10 | 101 | 52 | 30 | 13 | 6 |
| | (20.5) | (17.3) | (27.0) | (22.0) | (26.1) |
| 11–20 | 144 | 95 | 33 | 10 | 6 |
| | (29.2) | (31.7) | (29.7) | (16.9) | (26.1) |
| >21+ | 248 | 153 | 48 | 36 | 11 |
| | (50.3) | (51.0) | (43.2) | (61.0) | (47.8) |
| **Number of full-time URM faculty in department** | | | | | |
| 1 | 104 | 67 | 19 | 14 | 4 |
| | (21.8) | (23.3) | (17.8) | (24.1) | (17.4) |
| 2 | 101 | 64 | 24 | 9 | 4 |
| | (21.2) | (22.2) | (22.4) | (15.5) | (17.4) |
| 3–5 | 168 | 106 | 34 | 21 | 7 |
| | (35.3) | (36.8) | (31.8) | (36.2) | (30.4) |
| 6+ | 103 | 51 | 30 | 14 | 8 |
| | (21.6) | (17.7) | (28.0) | (24.1) | (34.8) |

| Participated in formal mentoring | | | | | |
|---|---|---|---|---|---|
| Yes | 151 | 87 | 38 | 21 | 5 |
| | (27.4) | (27.3) | (28.8) | (27.6) | (20.8) |
| No | 400 | 232 | 94 | 55 | 19 |
| | (72.6) | (72.7) | (71.2) | (72.4) | (79.2) |
| **Mentor in last three years** | | | | | |
| Yes | 335 | 201 | 77 | 44 | 13 |
| | (59.5) | (61.1) | (57.9) | (57.9) | (52.0) |
| No | 228 | 128 | 56 | 32 | 12 |
| | (40.5) | (38.9) | (42.1) | (42.1) | (48.0) |
| **Currently have mentor** | | | | | |
| Yes | 301 | 171 | 75 | 42 | 13 |
| | (53.6) | (52.0) | (56.8) | (55.3) | (52.0) |
| No | 261 | 158 | 57 | 34 | 12 |
| | (46.4) | (48.0) | (43.2) | (44.7) | (48.0) |
| **Number of mentors** | | | | | |
| 0–1 | 74 | 35 | 19 | 15 | 5 |
| | (24.4) | (20.5) | (25.3) | (34.1) | (38.5) |
| 2 | 96 | 55 | 26 | 13 | 3 |
| | (31.7) | (32.25) | (33.3) | (29.5) | (23.1) |

(continued)

TABLE 4.1  Departmental and mentoring characteristics of respondents by race/ethnicity (*continued*)

| | Total sample (N = 568) | African American (n = 333; 58.6%) | Mexican American (n = 134; 23.6%) | Puerto Rican (n = 76; 13.4%) | American Indian / Alaska Native (n = 25; 4.4%) |
|---|---|---|---|---|---|
| 3–5 | 113 (37.3) | 65 (38.0) | 28 (37.3) | 16 (36.4) | 4 (30.8) |
| 6> | 20 (6.6) | 16 (9.4) | 3 (4.0) | — | 1 (7.7) |
| **Race/ethnicity of mentor** | | | | | |
| White, non-Hispanic | 153 (51.3) | 94 (55.0) | 36 (49.3) | 19 (46.3) | 4 (30.8) |
| Black, non-Hispanic | 74 (24.8) | 63 (36.8) | 2 (2.7) | 8 (19.5) | 1 (7.7) |
| Hispanic/Latino | 46 (15.4) | 7 (4.1) | 26 (35.6) | 12 (29.3) | 1 (7.7) |
| Native American / Alaska Native | 6 (2.0) | — | 1 (1.4) | — | 5 (38.5) |
| Asian or Pacific Islander | 12 (4.0) | 6 (3.5) | 4 (5.5) | — | 2 (15.4) |
| Other | 7 (2.3) | 1 (0.6) | 4 (5.5) | 2 (4.9) | — |
| **Gender of mentor** | | | | | |
| Male | 149 (50.2) | 83 (48.8) | 32 (43.8) | 29 (70.7) | 5 (38.5) |

| | | | | | | | | | |
|---|---|---|---|---|---|---|---|---|---|
| Female | 148 | (49.8) | 87 | (51.2) | 41 | (56.2) | 12 | (29.3) | 8 | (61.5) |

| **Mentor-facilitated activities** | | | | | | | | | | |
|---|---|---|---|---|---|---|---|---|---|---|
| Journal editorial boards | 45 | (7.9) | 27 | (8.1) | 8 | (6.0) | 9 | (11.8) | 1 | (4.0) |
| Invitation to conferences | 138 | (24.3) | 81 | (24.3) | 31 | (23.1) | 21 | (27.6) | 5 | (20.0) |
| Chairing of conferences | 42 | (7.4) | 24 | (7.2) | 7 | (5.2) | 8 | (10.5) | 3 | (12.0) |
| Opportunities for research collaboration | 181 | (31.9) | 97 | (29.1) | 49 | (36.6) | 30 | (39.5) | 5 | (20.0) |
| Coauthoring | 143 | (25.2) | 81 | (24.3) | 38 | (28.4) | 21 | (27.6) | 3 | (12.0) |
| Reviews career annually (yes) | 224 | (39.4) | 125 | (37.5) | 59 | (44.0) | 32 | (42.1) | 8 | (32.0) |

| **Impact of inadequate mentoring** | | | | | | | | | | |
|---|---|---|---|---|---|---|---|---|---|---|
| Very significantly / a great deal | 138 | (24.9) | 89 | (27.2) | 25 | (19.5) | 17 | (22.7) | 7 | (28.0) |
| Somewhat | 182 | (32.8) | 94 | (28.7) | 56 | (43.0) | 23 | (32.0) | 9 | (36.0) |

(continued)

**TABLE 4.1** Departmental and mentoring characteristics of respondents by race/ethnicity (*continued*)

| | Total sample (N = 568) | African American (n = 333; 58.6%) | Mexican American (n = 134; 23.6%) | Puerto Rican (n = 76; 13.4%) | American Indian / Alaska Native (n = 25; 4.4%) |
|---|---|---|---|---|---|
| Hardly / not at all | 235 | 144 | 48 | 34 | 9 |
| | (42.3) | (44.0) | (37.5) | (45.3) | (36.0) |
| Impact of inadequate mentoring mean[a] | | | | | |
| M | 3.23 | 3.24 | 3.22 | 3.30 | 3.00 |
| SD | 1.32 | 1.40 | 1.16 | 1.21 | 1.38 |

NOTE: These data include both web-based and qualitative data of total study participants. Values in parentheses are percentages.

a. Five-point Likert-type scale, 1 = *very significantly* to 5 = *not at all*. No significant differences between means (based on ANOVA analysis).

faculty. Only about one-quarter of respondents reported participation in a formal mentoring program, with American Indian / Alaska Native faculty least likely to have done so. Eight additional questions were asked about characteristics of the mentor and types of activities performed. A cognitive appraisal of perceived impact of mentoring on the participants' academic career was also measured. Approximately 59.5 percent of the respondents could identify someone as a mentor in the past three years, as well as a current mentor (53.6 percent). Almost 43.9 percent reported three or more mentors.

More than 50 percent of respondents reported their mentor was White, non-Hispanic. African American respondents reported the highest rates of racial/ethnic matching in their mentoring relationships, at 36.8 percent, and more than one-third (35.6 percent) of Mexican Americans reported having a Hispanic/Latino mentor. These higher rates of racial/ethnic matching are associated with geographic location, as many Mexican Americans held positions at PWIs in the West and Southwest, while African Americans were most likely to hold positions in the South or large urban areas of the Northeast.

Respondents equally reported male/female mentors, with Puerto Ricans least likely to have a female mentor (29.3 percent), while American Indian / Alaska Natives were most likely to have a female mentor (61.5 percent). The most frequent mentor-facilitated activities reported were collaboration (31.9 percent), coauthoring papers and books (25.2 percent), invitations to attend conferences (24.3 percent), and an annual career review (39.4 percent). Puerto Ricans were the most likely to report mentor-facilitated activities, American Indian / Alaska Natives the least likely. One notable finding was that about half the participants reported that inadequate mentoring had impeded their career growth, with about 24.9 percent of them feeling inadequate mentoring had impeded their career growth a great deal or very significantly. No differences in reported mean of mentoring experiences were found by race, ethnicity, gender, or discipline, although close to 30 percent of African Americans and American Indian / Alaska Natives reported that inadequate mentoring very significantly impacted their career. No differences across disciplines or STEM versus non-STEM fields were observed. This is not surprising given that across all academic areas URM faculty are severely underrepresented.

The qualitative data provide rich insights into three areas that emerged from the participants' experiences and observations: (1) the role of mentoring experiences across the academic life course, (2) barriers in mentorship relationships, and (3) ideal mentorship characteristics, particularly political guidance that transmits knowledge about institutional norms and the role of race/ethnicity and power in higher education.

## MENTORS ACROSS THE LIFE COURSE: GETTING THE INSIDE SCOOP

One central finding was that the undergraduate and graduate school experiences were tremendously influential in terms of both inspiration or discouragement and "getting the scoop" or not. Many reported excellent guidance across the life course, while others experienced racism and/or were poorly advised. Another crucial component of effective or helpful mentoring is recognition of the mentee's personhood and overall personal development, as captured in this response: "I really had an extraordinary graduate school experience. I didn't realize as much, while I was a graduate student, as I did when I became a postdoc, that I had had much better mentoring than most people I knew, that I had been intellectually supported, but also loved and cared for as a human being, in ways that most of my colleagues around the country, I don't think, had that level of experience. So, I—that's a big reason why I'm so concerned about issues concerning people of color in the academy. Both of my advisors are very political, have done a lot of activist work in their careers, and they modeled that for me" (Mexican American female).

Although respondents noted positive, influential experiences with mentors, respondents also vocalized the consequences of poor mentoring throughout their academic life course. One African American male described his undergraduate experience with a mentor:

And he pulled me aside and he said, "This is outstanding work. I really enjoy it. I encourage you to continue to pursue it for your thesis. And where are you thinking? What are your plans?" And I said, "Well, the plan is to go to a top 25 or so doctoral program and I want to study race and class and equality and probably urban sociology, something like that." And he said, "Well, one, you're not *going* get into a top tier program. Your best thing is to try to get to your mid second tier. That's reasonable and that's what's likely. So you should change your expectations there. And secondly, just studying race is trite. You don't want to do that. That's what everybody does. It's so stereotypical. You want to study organizations or something else and that's the way I would go." And I remember hearing it and just being insulted and upset about it.

All too often, the uninformed, demeaning, even racist comments by predominantly majority-culture White males not only were demoralizing but also provided limited guidance along the way. Many first-generation respondents (those with parents with less than high school educations), particularly Puerto Ricans and Mexican Americans, had limited cultural institutional capital—knowledge of how institutional culture works, where the resources are, and how one can access them. A Puerto Rican male stated, "I think, in retrospect, I didn't have a lot of people to give me guidance throughout the entire way and what I mean by guidance is kind of inside scoop, what should you be doing to really maximize your opportunity to get into medical school? What should you be doing to maximize your opportunity to get into residency? Now certainly there was general information you get but I'm talking about inside scoop. I didn't have a lot of that."

A Mexican American female echoed these sentiments, stating, "And another one is maybe just—maybe not knowing, not always having access to information, like the informational resource is not always there. And so sometimes I think I personally get a little bit left behind just not knowing things that I should know or that other people seem to somehow know and I don't." A Puerto Rican female respondent discussed her lack of savvy about what she needed to succeed: "I would say there is just—coming into a doctoral program without a whole lot of savvy around doctoral study and how oftentimes people have the opportunity for graduate research assistance support and that kind of thing. I was, you know, admitted to a program with no support. And others were admitted to the program with support. And I'm not sure to this day on what basis incoming students were offered or not offered the support. So what you don't know, you can't complain about or you can't identify it."

One participant identified how graduate school itself can be a barrier to certain types of knowledge and career trajectories. He described how his career path was influenced by his graduate medical school experience:

We didn't learn disparities. We didn't learn about health equity issues. We didn't learn about language issues. We never learned how to use an interpreter in a clinical encounter. We didn't learn issues about gender and sexual minorities. All of this stuff was not there. . . . So I can't say that medical school got me to think about the issues that are now the focus of my career. That happened much later in my training through the experience of master's in public health and a minority health policy fellowship. Had I not done that, I would have been in practice and a clinician somewhere, doing heart catheterizations and making sure that the BMWs were all lined up and ready to go. (Mexican American male)

Other respondents noted how integral mentors across the life course had been to their career trajectory. A Mexican American female stated,

Well, I would say that she, who was my mentor . . . she continues to be my mentor. She made it clear at—I don't know. I think at some point she just said you can't get rid of me. She said, "I am going to be your mentor forever." And that was really nice when she said that. I was very touched. She said just because you're finished with your graduate degree, you know that you still have a lot of things ahead of you, a lot of challenges. She's, like, so now I'm going to help you get tenure . . . and to continue on in your career. So that mentoring relationship has just transitioned out of me being a graduate student to her helping me, as a new faculty member, do what I need to do to be successful.

Repeatedly the participants discussed not knowing or not having a lot of savvy about how to negotiate their academic environment in terms of accessing scholarships, identifying a well-positioned mentor, or obtaining a research assistantship in a funded research project. None of the participants mentioned a faculty member approaching them to be part of their large projects. Feeling unprepared to integrate themselves into the doctoral program environment put them at a disadvantage in developing fruitful mentoring relationships for the next milestone along the trajectory to a faculty position. Participants perceived limited valorization of their intellectual and socially driven agenda among their instructors and mentors (Essien, 2003; Segura et al., 2012); thus all too frequently URM "graduate students were left behind." While some respondents indicated the potential benefits of mentoring throughout their academic careers, for many others there was an absence of or inadequate mentoring. In general, graduate school was a deciding force and served as an anchor during their next stage of professional development. An African American female respondent succinctly underlined this point: "There were moments in grad school that really help shaped the type of faculty person I was going to be."

## BARRIERS IN MENTORSHIP RELATIONSHIPS: BURNOUT AND DISINTEREST

Professional socialization into faculty life takes many forms. It involves transmitting normative expectations, "teaching" skills to engage in faculty development, and supporting and valuing the individual and his or her research, as the quotations above demonstrate. Yet a common theme was an explicit acknowledgment that there were many unknowns in the new environment, few guideposts, and few mentors. Participants characterized their mentoring experiences with senior faculty as benign neglect, uninformed, and a patchwork-like. Overall participants perceived that mentors were not available and uninterested and that URM mentors were burned out. Many participants reported both surprise and disappointment at the lack of institutional interest in their career success and their own intuitive sense that they did not know what questions to ask. A primary aspect of a mentoring relationship is to validate the research direction of the mentee and promote the research agenda within a scholarly network. Study participants had been well informed about the importance of mentors, and the majority were disappointed and/or stunned by mentorship's absence and inadequacy, with only about half reporting a current mentor.

The following quotes are representative of participants' mentoring experiences and their perceptions of professional socialization interactions. An African American female stated, "I kept thinking that there would be sort of this magic mentoring and that it never has really materialized, and maybe that's just what that is and you have to kind of—there is a level at which you do have to figure this stuff out on your own. That's part of academia. The ideal is that you wouldn't, but a lot of it, you do." A Mexican American male shared a similar perspective: "But it's still pretty hands-off. I think just my whole career has been sort of based on doing it on my own."

Respondents identified a lack of mentoring resources, so individuals found their own. A Puerto Rican female described her experience in the following way: "We don't have senior faculty. The senior faculty that we have, especially the seniors of color, have been so—they're burnt out and they are not entities. They separate themselves. And, of course, who would want to be—they have gone through too much pain now. It is time for them, we should be somebody else's responsibility, too. But nobody steps in. So we get—so we get together and this is what we do. We talk about grants. We share job position announcements." Many respondents who did have mentors characterized their experience as uninformative or unhelpful. An African American female stated, "Everyone is so busy and so the few people that I consider mentors, they're just so busy. And I'm asking, 'Am I asking the right questions?' They're like, 'Well, yeah. I guess.' And I'm thinking okay, I need some criticism. I need someone to tell me, 'You're being narrow' or 'You haven't considered—' or 'What about—' and I don't get that." Similarly, a Mexican American man stated, "So I'm at an institution now where my mentor is a URM, and I think it's great. It's actually been a really great relationship. But again, it has to do with knowing the bureaucracy of this institution and how it works and trying to get me through that process. I'm not entirely sure that this person would be the person who is the strongest in that process."

The few participants who had a URM mentor observed that their mentor was often burdened with multiple responsibilities and was not part of the insider power-broker network. In some cases, respondents experienced direct negative consequences as a result of poor mentoring. An African American female shared this experience: "She told me, 'Get your thing in. Get it in at least two weeks before and I'll read it.' She never did. She's like, 'Oh, you'll have another chance afterwards.'"

Experiences of benign neglect and being uninformed led respondents to identify and create their own mentoring networks. While this required more time and energy, respondents were forced to do so to get what they needed. An African American male stated, "I had to build a larger network and not solely rely on one single person or a couple of people at my institution because they could be gone." A Mexican American male went into detail stating: "I'm like I'm mentoring myself with the intelligence to realize [the university is] a big place. I have found people I can work with, you know, who are willing to—I'm not at their particular institute or their particular department, but we collaborate. But I did those things. I went over there. I emailed them. I said, look, I think this, that and the other, kind of what we do here."

For many, it was quickly learned that self-initiative was the only viable option, and they were expected to simply find their way. Oftentimes this meant seeking advice and direction from a multitude of peers and senior faculty. While some participants felt burdened by the idea of juggling a patchwork of mentors in terms of time and energy, others commented on the strengths of this approach. Multiple mentors do not always fill all of the needs, however. A Mexican American male described the gaps in his mentoring network stating, "I do feel I have one mentor outside of [the university] and one within. The one outside is . . . good at reading my papers and giving me the honest feedback. But as an outsider, he doesn't have much to say about the politics. My other mentor here is also very good at the research stuff . . . but politically, relatively new. So on the politics side, I do feel I have been lacking."

Another participant (African American female) benefited from multiple mentors: "And those relationships have varied. Some have just—one person was very instrumental and helped me when I had the job offer, which I hadn't gone through before. And she's a senior person and she was able to tell me what kinds of things I should ask, how to ask for them. And then the person who's my formal mentor here in the department that I was pretenure, he was good mostly about reading my work. And his area was close to mine, so he would give me insights on actual work. And then another person was the one who originally brought me to [the university] on the predoc. . . . I go to him for—call him up you know—I don't know, you're offering me this much money, is that enough."

Effective mentoring relationships proved useful in overstepping barriers for some participants. One Puerto Rican female participant described in detail how her mentor taught her the ropes:

First of all, in the second or third year, she got a grant and she chose me as her teaching assistant. Well, no. Before that, I had taken a course with her, and she was merciless in teaching me how to write, merciless, but she did it in a way that you knew she wasn't being mean. She was really wanting you to learn, and so I learned how to write in that course with her, and then she hired me as her research assistant for this special grant that she had. . . . And she was very active in the division of women in the American Psychological Association, and she belonged to a committee in New York City of that organization, and she invited some of us every time to go with her to see the proceedings of the committees. I mean she was a mentor [in] every way, right?

These lived experiences provide insights into the difficulty of identifying mentors. Three major barriers emerge from these data: time constraints on all faculty, lack of interest by majority-culture faculty, and severe underrepresentation coupled with excessive work demands of URM senior faculty. The central point emphasized by participants is their perception of not entering these "sacred groves" (Cooper & Stevens, 2002) with the same social capital as majority-culture faculty—that is, not possessing the necessary tools to navigate the institutional processes and demands to be successful. Others described the requisites of a helpful mentor.

## IDEAL MENTORSHIP CHARACTERISTICS: FINDING YOUR WAY

The process of socialization was essential, especially as it related to navigating tenure expectations and departmental and institutional culture. Study participants made explicit their need for guidance, especially about informal rules, in order to make informed decisions about their time and priorities, as well as professional socialization and mentors' honest perspectives on normative expectations for promotion criteria and access to social networks. One first-generation Mexican American male assistant professor described the role of a mentor with a strong reference to the importance of decision-making guidance: "I think it's someone who provides guidance and help and steers someone in the right direction and stops them when they're making a mistake, intervenes." Another first-generation Mexican American male longed for someone to provide career pathway options so that he would be better equipped to make career-related decisions: "The process of promotion should be made transparent by your mentor. There's no way to advance the career if you don't know what the hoops really are, not what's on the website at [the university]. And . . . they really should make the connections for you for collaborative work, so that not only do you have an increased paper count, but that you have the ability to learn how to collaborate with someone who is not your mentor."

An African American male respondent eloquently explained how a mentor can best help an early career faculty member and what the mentor can say: "Here are the dynamics of the academy. Here are the people that you watch out for. Here are the kind of relationships . . . he provided tremendous exposure, the different kind of conferences that he held, he would always bring us in. He would introduce us to people that he knew. So scholars that you read, he would make the introduction. And he always has been the kind of person, again, just like a parent who—not only does he introduce, but he praises you in front of them so that he leaves them with a strong impression and does what he can." One compelling insight was the recognition that access to skills and knowledge in conjunction with access to social networks can significantly increase collaborations, publications, and overall productivity. It cannot be understated that mentors who direct faculty to collaborative opportunities prove beneficial for early career scholars, as evidenced by a Mexican American male who did not have those opportunities: "I wish I had a mentor there that would have told me right when I got there, you can't do this all on your own and build your own empire. You have to build yourself into existing projects and collaborations."

In addition, professional academic socialization included mentors who provided participants with the technical knowledge, content expertise, and feedback on research and grant development and writing for publication to successfully navigate their careers. Participants expressed a desire for someone to "discuss [my] work with me on a consistent and continuous basis and get feedback" and "someone who is very willing to deliver potentially painful feedback, someone who is brutally honest." A Mexican American male discussed the challenge of finding such mentors: "At the end of the day, when I'm imagining what an ideal mentor would look like, I think there is the mentor who would help you and at least have the real conversation with you in terms of 'These are the numbers you ought to be targeting for publications. These are the type of journals. This is kind of what you are working on. Target these journals.' . . . But then I think there is the mentor that can also have you navigate the process. And those don't always go hand in hand. At least the mentor doesn't usually have both of those things."

Beyond technical knowledge, scholarly opportunities, and content expertise, respondents characterized the ideal mentoring relationship as one of mutual respect. A Mexican American female narrated the importance of feeling valued and perceived as a colleague with something to contribute. She described the collegial and welcoming interaction with her mentor: "And she really, again, was one of those people who, for whatever reason she did it, you know, believed that I had something to contribute and so she fostered that. You know, she actually invited me to work as an equal with her, not as this little Chicana from New Mexico, saying, 'You were at Berkeley. You know, we have some commonalities and I'd like you to come and help me think about this and write about this and work with us on this.'"

In sum, the most notable finding is that life course mentoring is crucial to the academic path of many URM faculty. Many of the respondents described mentors within and outside of educational systems from early on in their journey. These mentors' belief in respondents' intellectual abilities and encouragement in their pursuit of education were critical in promoting their aspirational capital (Yosso, 2005). Social capital in the form of material, social, and emotional investments to direct, guide, and teach skills as well as language to access the opportunity structure and navigate the dominant culture networks shapes the academic life course of URM faculty. Closely related to these experiences are participants' commitments to mentor others or "pay it forward," engage in a research agenda that aims to solve community issues, and participate in community engagement. These commitments are not necessarily valued in higher education yet are the professional drivers of many URM scholars. Moreover, participants reported that they welcomed mentoring and sought continued guidance in how to negotiate institutional norms. However, prior experiences, particularly in graduate school, influenced their ability to connect with mentors in the academic workplace. For example, minority graduate students, and minority women in particular, reported significantly less respect for their research ideas and received significantly less instrumental support from their faculty advisors compared to their White peers.

## MENTORING AS CARING INVESTMENTS

Unequivocally intensive efforts have been invested in the design of mentoring programs *for all* during the past two decades. However, this solution precisely misses the point that not *all* require mentoring at the same level of intensity or at all for that matter and that some groups are at a greater disadvantage than others. Deeper investments such as quality mentoring, research release time, and research support funds do not challenge equality but affirm equity. Indeed, what is needed to position URM professionals for success is valuing their research agenda and understanding the consequences of aloneness and tokenism and its potential impact on work productivity.

Four conclusions are drawn from this study: (1) life course mentoring is crucial in the career success of many URM faculty, (2) a lack of institutional fit exists between the research interests and sociopolitical commitments of underrepresented minority and non-URM faculty, (3) a mentoring glass ceiling that limits quality and type of mentoring is apparent, and (4) senior faculty are perceived as disengaged and ambivalent toward the professional development of early career URM faculty.

Table 4.2 presents a schema of the life course milestones of how study participants acquired social capital via key "bridge persons" who guided and informed them regarding mainstream cultural and institutional norms. Zambrana, Ray, et al. (2015) depict the unique mentoring practices throughout the stages of the life course that were most helpful to study participants. In all stages of their career, the valuing of their aspirations and intellectual interests was paramount in the mentoring relationship. A disconcerting experience in higher educational institutional settings is the unexpected devaluation of the person and his or her intellectual interests and commitments. An unspoken divide is the lack of value placed on the research areas of many URM faculty. In other words, the conundrum seems to lie in the lack of shared intellectual interests and socially driven commitments between URM faculty and the faculty who can serve as mentors, rather than the number of faculty mentors available. Many URM participants report limited opportunities to engage in positive mentoring relationships, while others have had negative experiences with well-intentioned mentors. Institutions have moved forward in a frenzy to develop mentoring programs at all levels of the institutions with little or no attention to the internal barriers to effectively mentoring and retaining URM faculty. The unchanging

TABLE 4.2    Life course mentoring pathways for URM populations

| K–12 schooling | College | Graduate school | Early career faculty |
|---|---|---|---|
| **Valuing the intellect and potential of the URM** | | | |
| Opportunities to access intellectual debates specific to URM communities | Providing opportunities for critical engagement and access to both dominant culture knowledge and marginalized knowledge | Reciprocity in intellectual exchange<br><br>Supporting research focus on marginalized populations | Supporting research focus on marginalized populations<br><br>Understanding the connection between service/commitment to community and scholarly work |
| **Affective support** | | | |
| Serving as URM role models and sources of inspiration in the community<br><br>Understanding the historical experiences of URM populations and sites of resistance and strength | Acknowledging the struggle for URM populations<br><br>Language/skills to be able to name/identify oppression<br><br>Encouraging URM students to apply to graduate school | Supporting commitment to issues of justice and community<br><br>Building connections with other URM scholars across campus and the discipline<br><br>Language/skills to be able to name/identify oppression and strategies for dealing with microaggressions | Encouraging further development of research pertaining to issues of justice and community<br><br>Developing a campus-specific URM faculty community that includes senior URM faculty and/or administrators<br><br>Strategies for dealing with microaggressions |

| K–12 schooling | College | Graduate school | Early career faculty |
|---|---|---|---|
| Political guidance: learning the norms, skills, and strategies of the academy | | | |
| Providing instrumental support in accessing opportunity structures such as college readiness courses and college entrance exam preparation | Support in developing a competitive application for graduate school | Advocating for external and departmental funding for URM graduate students | Including early career URM faculty in major grant proposals |
| Teaching to harness assets found in the home and community while navigating dominant culture etiquette and protocols without demanding assimilation | Research opportunities that shepherd URM students through the elements of research design, implementation, and analysis | Support in accessing opportunity structures | Support in accessing opportunity structures |
| | Dominant culture etiquette and protocols without demanding assimilation | Dominant culture etiquette and protocols without demanding assimilation | Offering strategies for framing commitment to issues of justice and community in tenure and promotion portfolios and evaluations |
| | | | Dominant culture etiquette and protocols without demanding assimilation |

SOURCE: Zambrana, Ray, et al. (2015).

barriers such as implicit bias of faculty peers and senior faculty and a perceived hostile climate remain untouched. Rather than explore peer devalorization of the intellectual research interests of URM scholars, institutions have rushed to provide solutions without understanding the problem and in turn redefining the problem to suit the solution.

Thus important questions arise regarding how academic work environments and structural mechanisms intended to address the needs of all faculty, including URM faculty, may facilitate as well as potentially hinder career advancement. For example, in response to laments regarding the absence of mentors among URM faculty, universities mandated formal mentoring programs to be implemented at the department level and then expected an increase in promotion and tenure without any intentional or structured formats to foster this process or any changes to values, attitudes, or resources. Furthermore, clear evidence has been available for decades that URM faculty were not being mentored voluntarily by precisely those individuals who now were mandated to mentor them. Did universities really expect a successful match? Pifer and Baker (2013) assert that the current format of formal mentoring programs allows the university administration to absolve itself of responsibility for inadequate mentoring and promotion failures and place blame on the department. These data yield two provocative questions particularly with respect to formal mentoring programs: Can mentoring for URM faculty by any faculty member work without monetary incentives and release time? Can mentoring for URM faculty by any faculty member work without training for empathy and knowledge of particular background experiences and needs?

Institutional policies and practices such as assigned or formal mentoring are often informed by historical representations and racialized attitudes and practices (albeit unconscious) that often contribute to the academic disengagement of URM faculty, dampening educational expectations and aspirations (Espino & Zambrana, forthcoming 2019). The academy requires a critical examination of the values and philosophy of the institution and an incorporation of diverse U.S. faculty to capitalize on the talents, perspectives, and values they have to offer. Mentoring of URM faculty and students needs to be a shared responsibility in higher education institutions, not just the purview of a few. Acknowledging that racial/ethnic concordance in mentoring relationships is neither necessary nor required for a successful career path compels us to seek other answers to the lack of fit or the absence of quality mentoring at PWIs. Mentoring is important to all early career professionals. However, they do arrive at higher education institutions with a varied armamentarium of skills, and many non-URM faculty are more welcomed and more easily engage with their like-minded peers.

Data suggest that institutions cannot enact a one-size-fits-all solution such as assigning senior mentors of any race or ethnicity who may not have an interest in similar research areas, who harbor implicit bias, or who do not wish to invest their personal time in the success of early career URM faculty. Senior mentors, both majority-culture and senior URM faculty, require financial incentives. Unquestionably, the work of career development can no longer be the sole responsibility of senior URM faculty. Institutions must create a policy to redirect their resources to ensure equity. For example, they must invest in programs that change the climate and incorporate URM-specific advancement practices that comprehensively address implicit biases that exist among faculty and administrators. They must invest time in designing mentor training for majority-culture and elite foreign-born faculty. Dominican novelist Junot Díaz captures this theme when he states, "Colleagues are a wonderful thing—but mentors, that's where the real work gets done" (Conway, 2016).

# 5 · UNWELCOMING CLIMATES
## The Costs of Balancing Belonging and Inequality

> Race matters, because of the long history of racial minorities being denied access to the political process ... because of persistent racial inequality in the society. ... Race matters to a young man's view of society when he spends his teenage years watching others tense up as he passes. ... Race matters to a young woman's sense of self when she states her hometown and then is pressed, no, where are you really from. ... Race matters because of the slights, the snickers, the silent judgments that reinforce the most crippling thoughts: "I do not belong here."
>
> —Supreme Court Justice Sonia Sotomayor

Many studies have documented the challenges that underrepresented minority faculty experience in predominately White institutions of higher education (Griffin, Pifer, Humphrey, & Hazelwood, 2011; Hurtado, 1992; Joseph & Hirshfield, 2011; Stanley, 2006). Some of these challenges include racism, discrimination, devaluation of research, and tokenism through microaggressions. Double troubling is that for URM faculty, these challenges are experienced throughout their time in the educational pipeline and across their life course. As undergraduate and graduate students, URM also battle institutional racism and are forced to engage in unwelcoming climates that condone microaggressions and stereotyping. Indeed, in December 2015, during the opening arguments for the latest Supreme Court case about the University of Texas's affirmative action program, Justice Antonin Scalia made headlines after he cited a theory suggesting that Black students might be better off attending "a slower-track school where they do well" rather than elite schools (Green, 2016, p. 4).

The widespread claims that higher education is objective, meritocratic, and color blind, providing equity for all (Astin, 1982; Carnevale, 1999; Delgado

Bernal & Villalpando, 2002; Guinier, 2015), do not hold up despite an official end to de jure segregation. As universities pursue diversity-based hiring initiatives in an attempt to mitigate the hegemonic structures of academia, scholars have investigated the extent to which institutions have gone beyond mere "talk" and approach critical diversity.[1] Although racism, discrimination, microaggressions, tokenism, and stereotypical threats to URMs have been part of the conversations at PWIs, there is still no effective language for the ways universities police their boundaries or help identify the allusive forms of racism that haunt the academy (Back, 2004; Harley, 2008).

## DEFINITIONS AND CONCEPTUALIZATIONS

Many definitions of racism in the literature (Bonilla-Silva, 2015; Harper, 2012; Harrell, 2000) have centered on the question of power. Harper (2012) defines racism as "individual actions (both intentional and unconscious) that engender marginalization and inflict varying degrees of harm on minoritized persons; structures that determine and cyclically remanufacture racial inequality; and institutional norms that sustain White privilege and permit the ongoing subordination of minoritized persons" (p. 10). According to Back (2004), "Most White academics consider it unreasonable that an accusation of racism should be leveled at them" because they believe "that the face of racism is that of the moral degenerate, the hateful bigot" (p. 4). Oftentimes, White individuals pretend not to notice differences and attempt to explain that "color" was not involved in their actions (Sue et al., 2007). This color blindness can be explained by the "ethnocentric monoculturalism" construct, which argues that a self-defined worldview keeps Whites from noticing ethnocentric beliefs, values, and assumptions (Sue, 2004, p. 761). This is the reason why it is practically impossible to have a serious discussion of racism in the academy; Bonilla-Silva and Baiocchi (2001) eloquently describe it as "call it anything but racism" (p. 117).

Racism can be overt or covert, blatant or unintentional. Discrimination (unfair treatment), prejudice (negative judgments and attitudes), stereotypes (distorted and overgeneralized cognitive labels), and devaluing (underestimating worth or importance) can be based on a wide range of human characteristics (Harrell, 2000). Tokenism (the policy or practice of making only a symbolic effort), as to desegregate, has long been held as a common occurrence in professions (the professoriate) dominated by White people. Alexander-Snow and Johnson (1999) suggest that "many new and junior White faculty experience loneliness, intellectual isolation, lack of collegial support, heavy workloads, and time constraints. Unlike their White colleagues, however, faculty of color enter the predominantly White institutions with the legacy of tokenism" (p. 92). Last, scholarship on microaggressions illustrates the everyday verbal, nonverbal, and environmental slights, snubs, and insults—whether intentional or unintentional—that have a powerful impact upon the psychological well-being of racial/ethnic groups (Solórzano, Ceja, & Yosso, 2000; Sue et al., 2007). Research suggests that Whites often dismiss racially problematic statements or actions as simple jokes or unimportant asides to which minorities—and some Whites—overreact (Picca & Feagin, 2007). The repeated occurrence of these incidents reinforces unwelcoming climates and shows how institutional racism can survive and renew itself in more resilient forms in response to changing circumstances. For example, the term *postracial* referred to the idea that U.S. society had moved beyond the complications, problems, and violence around race and that racism and prejudice no longer or minimally existed (see Bonilla-Silva, 2015). In denial of the contemporary political climate, the myth of postraciality continues to permeate academic circles within the institutional diversity discourse.

This chapter describes how study participants perceive discrimination and illustrates the ways in which discriminatory institutional practices become manifest in their daily lives and contribute to workplace stress. It discusses the difficulty of spotting and naming racism in the academy and how this leads to internalizing metanarratives of incompetency and inferiority. The effects of perceived discrimination and hypervigilance in the workplace require protective psychological responses to avoid injurious personal effects. Perceived class, race, ethnic, and gender discrimination and the self-reported coping strategies used by respondents as recipients and witnesses of discriminatory practices and encounters are the focus of this chapter.

## RACISM IN THE ACADEMY: BURDENS AND RESPONSIBILITIES

The last fifteen years have witnessed a plethora of scholarship on racism in public health, medicine, higher education, and the professional world at large. A substantial body of knowledge has also emerged from the field of higher education describing the experiences of URM graduate students and their aspirations for entry into the professoriate. Although they have slowly gained entry into the faculty and administration, evidence confirms that URMs have been consistently denied full inclusion within academic institutions and experience a variety of discriminatory encounters (Allison, 2008; Griffin, Pifer, et al., 2011; Hassouneh, Lutz, Beckett, Junkins, & Horton, 2014; Robinson, 2014). Moreover, URMs often have difficulty naming these experiences as racist acts as they are often covert (Bhopal & Jackson, 2013). URMs are judged by their social group membership rather than as individuals, their scholarship is devalued and differentially assessed, and they are tokenized and experience both structural and personal racism. Examples of structural racism include the additional diversity-based responsibilities in the name of university service that URMs assume without remuneration due to pressure from other faculty and staff (Dunbar, 2014; Laymon, 2014) and the all too frequent questions from students regarding their qualifications, credibility, and capability (Allison, 2008; Bhopal & Jackson, 2013; Robinson, 2014; Tuitt & Carter, 2008).

URM faculty often hear White colleagues make comments that imply they are only affirmative action hires and are unqualified for their position (Griffin, Pifer, et al., 2011; Harley, 2008), which create stress, stereotype threat, and hypervigilance. For example, Garza (1993) contends, "Chicano/Latino faculty believe that they are viewed as second-class academics because they and their teaching, research, and publications are undervalued" (p. 37). Though most new and early career faculty have time constraints because of their work commitments, many URM faculty feel they are overburdened compared to their White colleagues.

When discussing the experiences of URM faculty, Fong (2000) states, "We get lonely for familiar foods, the familiar lilt of a tongue, the familiar face that hearkens to our own, the sense of not always having to explain ourselves, justify ourselves, in order to be understood and accepted" (p. 57). Moreover, faculty scholarship that has a racial/ethnic focus is oftentimes dismissed and undervalued, which contributes to URM feeling unwelcomed (Johnsrud & Sadao, 1998; Stanley, 2006; Turner & Myers, 2000). What is most astonishing is that the reports of isolation, overwhelming responsibility to racial/ethnic minority students, hostile work environments, and lack of institutional support have been ubiquitous in the literature since the early 1980s (Garza, 1993; Gutiérrez y Muhs, Niemann, González, & Harris, 2012; Jarmon, 2001; Johnsrud, 1993).

Institutional racism can take many forms such as implicit bias, blatant racism, devaluing of accomplishments, and excessive role burdens, including advising and serving as role models to URM and other students. These demands are unique to URM and often lead these faculty to become overburdened and over-committed, which can yield differential rates of workplace stress when compared to White colleagues (Joseph & Hirshfield, 2011; Segura, 2003) and inevitably a reduction in research productivity and adverse mental well-being. According to DeJesus and Rice (2002), "While the literal twine of the noose of racism that chocked our throats is relatively obsolete, the figurative rope continues to cut the breath of our psychological well-being" (p. 52). The intersectional identities of historically underrepresented groups contribute to excessive burdens and expectations from students and non-URM faculty. These expectations, combined with racist encounters throughout their life course, may deter URM scholars from entering academia or may lead to an early departure from an institution or, more significantly, the professoriate (Griffin, Pifer, et al., 2011; Ponjuan, 2005;

Trower & Chait, 2002). Importantly, the nature and force of discriminatory practice vary by institution and racial/ethnic color privilege, phenotype, and ideology (traditional vs. nontraditional).

Multiple institutional practices serve to underscore the ways in which racism, stigmatization, tokenization, and stereotype threat—the threat of being perceived as intellectually inferior by teachers and peers based on negative racial/ethnic stereotype—are maintained. For example, the unconscious negative framing of URM hiring associated with affirmative action policy sets the stage for tokenization and stigmatization (Niemann, 1999). Other forms of microaggressions may be experienced in recruitment, on campus visits, in protocol, and when negotiating contracts, such as offering to URM lower salaries than were recently given to comparable faculty.

If they overcome the barriers and are hired, URM faculty identify microaggressions with respect to teaching, academic segregation, devalued research, heavier service requirements / diversity taxation, and nebulous standards and guidelines for tenure (Guzman, Trevino, Lubuguin, & Aryan, 2010). In response, some faculty may feel as though they are being set up to fail (Griffin, Bennett, & Harris, 2011). Using excessive emotional labor to manage conflicting expectations may result in less time for research and collaboration and less likelihood of receiving research grants on the first or second attempt. In fact, this may be a contributing factor to lower rates of prestigious grant awards among URM faculty. Blacks and Hispanics are less likely than White counterparts to resubmit a revised application. Black investigators who do resubmit have to do so more often than White faculty to receive an award (Ginther et al., 2011). These findings are alarming and again raise the specter of the role of racialized hierarchies in promoting what appear to be exclusionary processes.

In effect, career milestones, including grant awards and important collaborations, may be sidetracked due to the racialized hierarchies that deter the intellectual efforts of URM faculty and instead compel them to engage in self-protective efforts. Additionally, URM faculty rarely can muster all the coping mechanisms necessary to manage discrimination stress. The overwhelming majority of empirical works on work stress focus on women and majority-culture early career faculty (Eddy & Gaston-Gayles, 2008; Elliot, 2008; Hart & Cress, 2008; Hendel & Horn, 2008; Lindholm & Szelenyi, 2008)—comparing rigorous academic environments and requirements among women and men. Studies identify higher stress levels among female and early career faculty and link stress levels to perceptions and events, which include isolation, familial responsibilities, and substantial workloads (e.g., research production). Identified stressors in the academic workplace (see chapter 8) include dissatisfaction, impetuses to leave or change fields due to stressors, decreased productivity, burn-out, stress-related health problems, and notions of perceived stress (Rosser, 2004). Patterns of productivity, retention, and promotion among URM have not been well understood, nor have their history of incorporation, racism, and intersectional coconstituted identities. These factors assume an important role in extending the conversation on the low rates of representation and retention in higher education institutions (see chapter 7).

## INTERSECTIONAL IDENTITY AND INEQUALITY

Theorizing traditions support the view that U.S. institutions of higher education have embedded ideologies that work to preserve inequalities (Giroux, 1983; Hurtado, 1992). An intersectional lens allows for an expanded understanding of the complex role that discrimination and other institutional factors play in how URM faculty are faring in research universities. Additionally, an examination of structural, historical, and social forces is essential to analyzing and understanding their experiences and challenges navigating the academy. Using an intersectional perspective (see chapter 3) allows for analyses of the social location of historically underrepresented racial/ethnic groups within the larger social, economic, and political context and the exclusionary racial hierarchy (Bonilla-Silva, 2006; Dill & Zambrana, 2009; Wingfield & Alston, 2014). Findings on perceived discrimination not only illustrate how intersectional processes of power relations affect individuals in their everyday lives but also provide further evidence, in a nationally representative sample, of one of the central claims of intersectionality: that race/ethnicity and class are gendered and that gender and class are racialized (Penner & Saperstein, 2013).

Bonilla-Silva (2009) illustrates a range of ways by which people make sense of the salience of race, racial stratification, and experiential differences between racial/ethnic minority groups and Whites' claim that they are unable to see "color." According to Bonilla-Silva, the *minimization of racism* suggests that discrimination is no longer a central factor affecting minorities' life chances (p. 28) and compels Whites to view discrimination through the narrow lens of overt, outrageously racist acts. Anything less is often misperceived as URMs playing the "race card" (Harper, 2012). This position is consistent with critical race theory (CRT), which critiques claims of neutrality, objectivity, and color blindness in U.S. institutions (Delgado Bernal & Stefancic, 2001; Dixson & Rousseau, 2005). CRT suggests that URM faculty bring perspectives and "voices" that can move us toward the elimination of all forms of subordination and teach us how to create a more equalitarian institution of higher education (Delgado Bernal & Villalpando, 2002). One of the most important functions of voices and narratives in CRT scholarship is to counteract the stories of the dominant group (Delgado, 1989; Dixson & Rousseau, 2005). The dominant group tells stories that are designed to "remind it of its identity in relation to outgroups and provide a form of shared reality in which its own superior position is seen as natural" (Delgado, 1989, p. 240). Drawing from intersectional and critical race theorists (Cobas, Duany, & Feagin, 2009; Feagin, 2010, 2013), I outline a perspective called White racial framing that captures major tenants of institutional racism. The perspective is defined as a set of beliefs, stereotypes, sincere fictions, and emotionally driven actions that collectively reinforce a racial hierarchy of White dominance and superiority over non-Whites. This body of beliefs can characterize institutional practices or individual beliefs (conscious or unconscious). In the former case, aspects of organizational culture, routinized interactions, and discrimination can maintain racial/ethnic inequities (Feagin, 2006). Underlying beliefs, attitudes, and stereotypes promote the practices of institutional racism that permeate the functioning of an institution; "allow whites to collude in or rationalize the systemic processes that facilitate and maintain ongoing racial privilege and inequality; . . . [and] obscure attention to the existence and consequences of these deep structural inequalities" (Wingfield & Feagin, 2012, p. 144). Building on this strong evidence that supports the intersectional social status identity groups as being at greatest risk of discrimination, the participants' voices illuminate their lived experiences of systemic institutional racism in PWIs and identify coping strategies used to buffer the impact of discrimination.

## MEASURES AND QUESTIONS ASKED

Three questions are addressed in this chapter: (1) Is there a relationship between respondents' demographic characteristics and perceived discrimination? (2) What types of discrimination (based on race/ethnicity, gender, or class) are most likely to be encountered? and (3) What coping strategies are most likely to be used in response to work-related perceived discrimination?

Measures include perceptions of discrimination and bias scales in both web-based and pencil-and-paper individual and group interview surveys. A perceived gender, race/ethnicity, and class bias scale measured perceptions of discrimination in professional advancement. Respondents were asked six items to assess whether in their professional career they have ever encountered gender, racial/ethnic, and/or class discrimination by a superior or colleague. Additionally, respondents were asked whether in their professional career they have ever been left out of opportunities for professional advancement based on gender, race/ethnicity, and/or class. Responses were coded on a 3-point scale (1 = *never* to 3 = *often/always*). A cognitive appraisal scale asked respondents to rate how upsetting these experiences were on a 3-point scale (1 = *extremely/very upsetting* to 3 = *not upsetting at all*). Cronbach's alpha reliability tests were conducted for the entire sample ($\alpha$ = .900) and as stratified by race and ethnicity ($\alpha$ = .907 for African Americans, $\alpha$ = .887 for Mexican Americans and Puerto Ricans).

Qualitative data were employed to interpret the meaning of the discrimination scale data. Participants were asked, "What types of incidents have you observed in the workplace that you consider racial or gender discrimination?" and "Have you ever had experiences of racism and/or gender discrimination in the work environment?" They were also asked to describe three institutional challenges that most hindered and three that most helped their career path and advancement. These last two items provided a rich understanding of instances of discrimination and racism, their meaning, and respondents' perceptions of the impact on their lives and careers.

## WORKPLACE ENCOUNTERS, EMOTIONAL WORK, AND OPPORTUNITY

Table 5.1 displays the descriptive statistics by race and ethnicity for the six-item perceived racial/ethnic, gender, and class discrimination scale and perceived level of distress with discriminatory encounters. Data show that 46.3 percent of the total sample report racial/ethnic discrimination "often/always" by a superior or colleague, 31.8 percent report gender discrimination, and 25.9 percent report class discrimination.

Across racial/ethnic groups, differences are evident. American Indian / Alaska Natives are the most likely to report all forms of discrimination by superiors or colleagues and being left out of opportunities based on all three of the social statutes. For class and gender, American Indian / Alaska Natives are almost twice as likely to report these forms of discrimination, while for race and ethnicity, 68 percent report racial/ethnic discrimination often or always versus 46.3 percent for African Americans. Puerto Ricans, in comparison to African Americans and Mexican Americans, are most likely to report gender and class discrimination by superiors and colleagues, although Mexican Americans and Puerto Ricans are equally likely (about 20 percent) to report being left out of opportunities based on gender and class. Overall, respondents are most likely to report experiencing racial/ethnic discrimination compared to gender or class discrimination and are more likely to report being left out of opportunities based on race/ethnicity rather than on gender or class. Higher reports of discrimination based on class are associated with URM Latinos most likely being the first in their families to graduate from high school, college, and beyond. In this study, slightly more than 40 percent of African American participants had mothers (40.9 percent) and fathers (42.7 percent) who had completed college and graduate degrees, compared to mothers (27.5 percent) and fathers (36.4 percent) of

TABLE 5.1 Perceived race, ethnic, gender, and class discrimination by race/ethnicity

| Variable | Total sample (N = 568) | African American (n = 333; 58.6%) | Mexican American (n = 134; 23.6%) | Puerto Rican (n = 76; 13.4%) | American Indian / Alaska Native (n = 25; 4.4%) |
|---|---|---|---|---|---|
| **Racial/ethnic bias by superior or colleague** | | | | | |
| Never | 79 | 46 | 16 | 11 | 6 |
| | (14.3) | (14.3) | (12.3) | (14.7) | (24.0) |
| Rarely | 217 | 126 | 62 | 27 | 2 |
| | (39.4) | (39.3) | (47.7) | (36.0) | (8.0) |
| Often/always | 255 | 149 | 52 | 37 | 17 |
| | (46.3) | (46.4) | (40.0) | (49.3) | (68.0) |
| **Gender bias by superior or colleague** | | | | | |
| Never | 176 | 113 | 34 | 25 | 4 |
| | (35.3) | (35.3) | (26.2) | (33.3) | (16.0) |
| Rarely | 199 | 115 | 53 | 24 | 7 |
| | (34.0) | (35.9) | (40.8) | (32.0) | (28.0) |
| Often/always | 175 | 92 | 43 | 26 | 14 |
| | (31.8) | (28.8) | (33.1) | (34.7) | (56.0) |
| **Class bias by superior or colleague** | | | | | |
| Never | 188 | 112 | 42 | 26 | 8 |
| | (34.5) | (35.1) | (33.1) | (35.1) | (32.0) |
| Rarely | 216 | 135 | 53 | 24 | 4 |
| | (39.6) | (42.3) | (41.7) | (32.4) | (16.0) |
| Often/always | 141 | 72 | 32 | 24 | 13 |
| | (25.9) | (22.6) | (25.2) | (32.4) | (52.0) |

TABLE 5.1  Perceived race, ethnic, gender, and class discrimination by race/ethnicity (*continued*)

| Variable | Total sample (N = 568) | African American (n = 333; 58.6%) | Mexican American (n = 134; 23.6%) | Puerto Rican (n = 76; 13.4%) | American Indian / Alaska Native (n = 25; 4.4%) |
|---|---|---|---|---|---|
| **Left out of opportunities based on gender** | | | | | |
| Never | 241 | 136 | 62 | 36 | 7 |
|  | (44.6) | (43.2) | (48.1) | (49.3) | (30.4) |
| Rarely | 171 | 103 | 40 | 22 | 6 |
|  | (31.7) | (32.7) | (31.0) | (30.1) | (26.1) |
| Often/always | 128 | 76 | 27 | 15 | 10 |
|  | (23.7) | (24.1) | (20.9) | (20.5) | (43.5) |
| **Left out of opportunities based on race/ethnicity** | | | | | |
| Never | 146 | 77 | 42 | 21 | 6 |
|  | (27.1) | (24.7) | (32.3) | (28.8) | (25.0) |
| Rarely | 200 | 109 | 55 | 28 | 8 |
|  | (37.1) | (34.9) | (42.3) | (38.4) | (33.3) |
| Often/always | 193 | 126 | 33 | 24 | 10 |
|  | (35.8) | (40.4) | (25.4) | (32.9) | (41.7) |
| **Left out of opportunities based on class** | | | | | |
| Never | 261 | 157 | 60 | 35 | 9 |
|  | (48.6) | (50.3) | (46.9) | (47.9) | (37.5) |
| Rarely | 187 | 113 | 43 | 24 | 7 |
|  | (34.8) | (36.2) | (33.6) | (32.9) | (29.2) |

| | | | | | |
|---|---|---|---|---|---|
| Often/always | 89 | 42 | 25 | 14 | 8 |
| | (16.6) | (13.5) | (19.5) | (19.2) | (33.3) |
| Discrimination scale[a] | | | | | |
| M | 14.38 | 14.34 | 14.14 | 14.25 | 16.35 |
| SD | 4.91 | 5.00 | 4.56 | 4.87 | 5.24 |
| Impact of discrimination | | | | | |
| Extremely/very upsetting | 274 | 155 | 67 | 34 | 18 |
| | (52.2) | (50.7) | (54.5) | (46.6) | (78.3) |
| Somewhat/mildly upsetting | 218 | 131 | 49 | 34 | 4 |
| | (41.5) | (42.8) | (39.8) | (46.6) | (17.4) |
| Not upsetting at all | 33 | 20 | 7 | 5 | 1 |
| | (6.3) | (6.5) | (5.7) | (6.8) | (4.3) |

NOTE: These data include both web-based and qualitative data of total study participants. Values in parentheses are percentages.
a. No statistically signifcant differences.

Mexican Americans (see table 1.1). Thus it may be that class privileges conferred greater social capital and cultural resources to African American faculty than to their Latino counterparts, enabling them to navigate professional workplace settings more effectively (Bourdieu, 1986; Lareau, 2002). The gender differences are furthered interrogated in chapter 9.

Out of a total score of 18, the mean sample discrimination scale score was 14.38, with American Indian / Alaska Natives reporting the highest mean. Just over half (52.2 percent) of this sample reported discrimination incidents to be extremely/very upsetting, with American Indian / Alaska Natives and Mexican Americans reporting the highest levels of distress. These data suggest that URM faculty experience racism or microaggressions on a regular basis and most likely expend a high level of emotional energy coping with these incidents.

Data on the frequency of experiences and cognitive appraisal of participants' levels of distress, however, do not provide insight into the context and types of incidents that can be categorized as discriminatory practices. Qualitative data informed the understanding of the numeric data and yielded rich narratives on how participants interpreted discriminatory practices so as to protect their well-being and career security.

## INTERPRETATIVE CONTEXT: THE LIVED EXPERIENCES OF DISCRIMINATORY PRACTICES

The respondents provided a description of a range of discriminatory incidents around three themes: outright, subtle, and nuanced racism; the devaluation of URM faculty's scholarship and credentials; and the racial/ethnic tax that comes with the burden of representing diversity in university, college, and departmental committees. In addition, these data expand the body of scholarship on specific role tasks and interpersonal relationships that increase workplace stress, inform on strategies employed to buffer those racialized assaults, and extend our understanding of institutional climate and its role in URM retention, promotion, and career trajectory.

## THE STRUGGLE TO NAME IT (OUTRIGHT, SUBTLE, AND NUANCED RACISM)

When asked about their experiences of racism and discrimination, many of the participants struggled to name and identify experiences as racism or discrimination. Especially for female faculty, sometimes because of intersections of race, gender, and age, respondents were unable to identify in which dimension they were being discriminated. Consider the words of this Mexican American female respondent: "But there are subtle ways, and I think you never know what it is people are discriminating on. Is it because you're a woman? Is it because you're an out gay woman? Is it because you're a Chicana that doesn't talk academically theoretical lingo."

In other cases, the experiences were more subtle, nuanced, and insidious. In some cases, faculty hesitated to name these exchanges clearly as racism: "I can't say definitively that I've experienced it. I think I should be clear with that. But there are subtleties that could border on that. And I guess the example is I've been a faculty member in my department for going on six years, and I have gone to enough faculty meetings to know who my colleagues are. And I've run into them in the hallway, the very hallway of my building, and said hello to them. And I feel that they simply didn't know who I was. . . . And then there is the other piece about, again, I don't know if it's discrimination or it's just the way the academic climate is. I have a harder time distinguishing between those two" (Mexican American male).

However, other URM faculty were able to identify subtle acts as racism. A Mexican American female respondent named it and considered it the worst kind: "I mean, it's that kind of very nuanced sense of what I would call racism, you know. So it's kind of having such a low opinion of what people of color are able to do, that when you can do a little bit more or when you're actually on par with other people, it creates surprise. And that's, I think, the worst kind to deal with."

However, there were still numerous blatant and overt examples of racism that indicated a strong lack of knowledge, awareness, and sensitivity among some members of the respondents' institutions and an overall degree of tolerance for blatant racism at the departmental and institutional levels, as this African American female noted: "Well, I certainly felt racially discriminated against the whole time I was at the [research center]. I felt like a complete token. It was clear to me that they wanted me there because I was Black and during the time I was there, they had an external review and this was around the time that I quit and they would not—they didn't tell the reviewers that I had quit. And so that was clearly discrimination."

Notably, for another respondent, a blatantly racist interaction caused her to quit her position: "So the day I quit we were having a meeting and the other guy, the guy who thinks he's my best friend, said to me, 'You know, I just really think that once we get this achievement gap thing under wraps or whatever, America can move forward. Once we get those Black kids achieving, America can really meet its potential.' I was like, 'Wow.' And so I just got up and I left and I never came back."

Other respondents noted similar blatant racist interpersonal experiences: "I had one White male, senior professor, ask me, 'So what do you call yourself now?' I said, 'Excuse me?' He said, 'First when we were growing up, it was Negro, and then it turned to Black, now it is African American, so what do you call your-self?' I just looked at him, just so perplexed, like I can't believe that's coming out of an intellectual's mouth" (African American female).

One African American male respondent echoed eloquently the difficulty in naming racism, yet he identified systemic racism within his institution: "I can't think of instances where I felt like someone was directly discriminating me in some way, based on race. I think—I think if you look at the pattern of the institu-tion, in general, there are obviously things there that speak to your inability to progress within it" (African American male).

For many respondents discriminatory practices in the forms of actual exclu-sion, inappropriate questions or comments about race/ethnicity and/or gender, and perceived expectations due to racial/ethnic background (e.g., not being "as smart or competent" as others) represented an integral part of their academic workplace encounters. Being involved in these situations, whether as the recipi-ent or as a witness, was unsettling to participants and engendered feelings of not belonging or being unwelcomed. These encounters and their aftermath have been aptly labeled by Wingfield (2010) as emotional labor that occurs in racial-ized hierarchies. These incidents were tangible and visible, unlike the subtle comments, innuendos, and silences URM experienced regarding their research agendas and methodologies.

## DEVALUING URM FACULTY'S SCHOLARSHIP AND CREDENTIALS

Respondents observed that one of the ways discrimination and racism are expressed is through the devaluing of the accomplishments, credentials, and successes of URM faculty. The suggestion that faculty who have been recruited as target-of-opportunity hires are in a different category, will need extra help, and should be treated differently is an example of how the credentials of URM faculty are devalued and alternative explanations for their success are generated. Multiple and subtle forms of implicit racism were identified by the respondents, confirming the existing research. One Mexican American female discussed areas of study and their centrality in the selection for academic positions: "It's a subtle beast. To me, it seems to play out more in the topics that you want to study and how those topics are judged. When you get to the job market, it plays out in the extent to which topics that you study will be valued and departments will want you." Implicit bias was a major theme in the narratives of participants. A URM scientist collected the material in the text box. The five points capture succinctly the lived experiences of the messages embedded in the institutional work envi-ronment of many URM faculty.

Five Examples of Implicit Bias (a.k.a. Academic Bigotry) against
Underrepresented Minorities (URMs)

1. Presumes incompetence: Belief that URMs do not have knowledge, skill, or experience equal to non-URM colleagues even if there is evidence to the contrary. In some instances, this perception never changes.
2. Assumes the worst: URM faculty are never given the benefit of the doubt (i.e., a grant not renewed, a temporary decline in productivity is seen as a stalled career by non-URM faculty).
3. Demands a higher level of performance: URM faculty are expected to publish more, teach more, and serve more to progress at the same pace as non-URM faculty.
4. Minimizes achievements and accomplishments: No discovery or publication of URM faculty is seen as impactful enough to warrant the same degree of recognition as that of non-URM faculty.
5. Persistent marginalization: URM faculty are isolated to keep them from creating a critical mass.

SOURCE: URM scientist

A Mexican American male explained the challenges of embracing a social agenda and its consequences: "Well, scholars of color have to have better, more succinct, more accurately written proposals. They have to justify if they have a social agenda. . . . So scholars of color who have magnificent skill sets and great talents, who are less interested in pursuing sort of the entrepreneurial disciplinary goals of the moment but really want to build social justice agendas. There's fewer sources of funding, so they're competing for less money, with a lot more people." Other respondents noted the systemic racism throughout their department, beginning with the structure of the graduate program and continuing through the hiring and promotion and tenure process: "My mentor, who means well, actually circulated this note to all of the doctoral students and faculty about her concern about the students of color taking a lot longer and needing a lot more resources to graduate. She just assumed it was a characteristic of them rather than how the program was organized. It's just the most blatant stuff. There's a lot. It happens all the time" (Native American female).

## REPRESENTING DIVERSITY BURDEN
## AND RACIAL/ETHNIC TAX

A growing body of scholarship suggests that the excessive burdens placed on URM faculty to "represent" and to engage in service and committee activities require significant sacrifices of their time in addition to teaching and mentoring URM students (Harley, 2008) because they are often the one person on campus who can "check the box" (Wingfield, 2013). These expectations and demands are not shared by non-URM faculty and thus represent an inequitable burden and a form of discriminatory practice. As the sole URM representative on committees or in meetings, URM faculty face the pressure to represent the voice of diversity and/or the indignity of being expected to speak for all URM students or faculty. Faculty recognize that there is an inequitable division of service and that while they are expected to carry the greater load, these activities are not rewarded or accorded value during promotion and tenure review. The institutional procedures in hiring, tenure and promotion, and salary emerged strongly as indicators of the racism that is embedded in institutional policies and procedures that are touted as fair, impersonal, and standard, contributing to the difficulty in naming and addressing the inequity. One Mexican American female, describing an interaction with a search committee member, explained how institutional cultural norms often disregard the values and norms of the candidate: "I reminded her, I said, we need to be careful with these applications because some people come from societies where saying this is my strength would count as boasting and that's not what they're going to do on these applications. We need to be culturally aware that somebody might say, 'Well, I'm not very good at such and such' and that doesn't mean they're not. We need to look a little deeper. Majority culture member responded: 'Well, if that's what people do, if they're self-deprecating, we don't need any of those here.' She said it in the presence of other people and nobody said a thing."

An African American male discussed how search committee criteria change depending on a particular "color or ethnicity" of the candidate. "And I just watched, particularly the last two years, how we've had very highly qualified people who have applied to our department and then at first it was, like, well, they don't have NIH grants. That was in 2006. So they didn't bring in somebody, who ended up going to a more prestigious institution, because they didn't have NIH grants. Then the next year, somebody came in that had 3 million in NIH funding and then it was, like, they're not a psychologist. They don't work in a department of psychology, right, because they're located in public health but they are trained in psychology and so that worked against them. So they made an offer to a person who had just graduated from grad school over someone who already had demonstrated what you want them to do as a faculty member. And these were all people of color? The person out of grad school that they brought in was not. So that was a White female."

Another African American male participant discussed the normative criteria for tenure that float in an aura of neutrality: "So even when tenure cases come up, you'll hear the way that—they want to talk about citation index and so on. Again, things that are heavily flawed, right, and discriminatory in terms of how they actually are—the outcomes, what we see. But they use these variables again as though they're color blind." In addition to the observed departmentally embedded discriminatory practices within the structure of the program and hiring policies, respondents also noted the unwelcoming departmental climate. A Mexican American female described a polarized racialized climate: "When I first entered the department, I think people were even less conscious than they are now, that I'm a person of color. And people would say things in front of me that were appallingly racist. And they would joke about the angry Black man down the hall, and things like that. So, I was made to understand that I was in a place of polarized racial politics, from the moment I arrived."

An African American female drew the connection between the structure of the university and the interpersonal attacks experienced by URM faculty: "The way in which people behave is a response to structure. I mean, those types of microaggressions that you experience in your department, the off-the-wall things that the dean and provost say about race, it is tolerated on this campus. And so, I don't necessarily think that people will say those racial insults if it wasn't necessarily favored, because I think that the structure dictates the way in which people respond to racism and the ways in which people talk about racism and sexism."

## MECHANISMS FOR COPING WITH DISCRIMINATION AND RACISM

One of the most serious challenges facing URMs is the need to acquire a broad repertoire of racism-related coping strategies. These protective mechanisms fortify them and ensure appropriate responsiveness to different types of situations. Depending on the severity of the situation, coping responses are calibrated to decrease provocation and increase protection (Brondolo, Brady ver Halen, Pencille, Beatty, & Contrada, 2009). Lease (1999) observed stress coping mechanisms among academic faculty and their experiences of isolation and psychological, physical, and interpersonal strain: "In order to adapt, particularly early career female faculty must become assertive and must attempt to find supportive mentorship" (p. 287). Attempting to be more assertive as a coping mechanism, an African American female respondent stated, "Because I'm an assistant professor, I don't want to make too many waves right now. I kinda just wanna kinda go with the flow as much as I can. . . . Now associate or full, I'll unleash on 'em [laughs]."

One female African American was told by her mentor, "Pick your battles and swallow some stuff because you just need to get [tenure]. Then you can deal with stuff when you get tenure." URM faculty frequently participate in university and faculty meetings in which they are the token URM or one of a few minority faculty. URM faculty may find themselves in positions such as these in which they must either confront discrimination or become resigned to the fact that White faculty use color-blind frames to absolve themselves. One African American female expressed,

> I've sat in on faculty meetings where people have said things that I've found offensive about other faculty of color. Suggestions that faculty who are here as I am through target of opportunity hires are a different category should be treated differently, are gonna need extra help citing that we're not as qualified as others. So I've sat in on meetings like that and when I've said something—course you know they haven't said it about me, but they've been saying it about others. So of course I know they've said it about me when I'm not there. Or I can suspect that they have because I don't know for sure. And when I've raised it, it hasn't gone over well. So it has meant to me no longer raising it.

Opportunities to form support systems or find like-minded colleagues within PWIs are limited. Networks of support to cope with discrimination are most often cultivated formally and informally and often are external to the work setting (Harley, 2008; Shorter-Gooden, 2004). URM faculty who connect and network with other professionals with similar experiences of discrimination can strategize with them about nonthreatening ways to respond and how to examine the pros and cons of various situations. Whether formed through affiliations with ethnic studies departments or professional organizations, opportunities to discuss workplace challenges with other URMs provide participants with the support they need to persist within challenging climates. One Mexican American male respondent clearly articulated the importance of these relationships: "If it were not for my relationships with colleagues in other national professional associations, I probably would not have survived the tenure review process. The criteria for getting tenure at my institution were vague and some senior colleagues in my department did their best to prevent me from getting tenure because they discriminate against Chicanos and queer people. I also survived at my institution by developing relationships with faculty in other departments who deal with racism, homophobia, and patriarchy—all very much alive at my institution" (online survey comments).

Spirituality was an important coping mechanism for African Americans and American Indian / Alaska Natives more so than for URM Latinos/Hispanics. Spiritual rituals (such as prayer, meditation, and dance) all served an important role in alleviating the demands and stress of professional roles and institutional experiences. Spiritual practices were personal as well as group based. Connecting with others who share their spiritual beliefs, confiding in their spiritual leaders, and participating in spirituality provided a safe, healing, and nurturing environment. As one female African American pointed out, "Prayer, meditation, exercise, keeping connected. I have an amazing partnership. So keeping connected with people."

An African American male reported that his family and friends and God were all important supports in his life: "I would say friends and family and then also my relationship with God, my spiritual journey, my spiritual path. All those things are very important to me." Family and friends were important outlets of relief from the demands of work for all professionals. They lauded their accomplishments rather than erased them. However, as will be discussed in the following chapter, social and economic caretaking of their family of origin was at times draining. Other ways of coping included practical approaches such as working only forty to fifty hours per week and not taking work home on weekends and disconnecting from work email in the evenings and on weekends. Those who employed these strategies were predominantly married or partnered and/or had children. Yet none of the respondents mentioned vacations, nannies, or second homes as sources of relaxation for "getting away from the stress." The reported high levels of stress and the few mechanisms used to buffer it are cause for concern. Evidence clearly pinpoints the effects of stress on the physiological functioning of the body, its role in both physical and mental health conditions, and the effects of racism on well-being (see chapter 8). Other coping strategies mentioned, such as assertiveness and confrontation, cannot possibly be effective for any faculty member and may incur severe consequences for URM faculty. Ideally, one approach is to transform the institutional culture to minimize racism and discriminatory practices, "increasing hope, and buffering the impact of racism on health" (Brondolo et al., 2009).

## GAZING AT THE VISIBLE COLOR LINE

Contrary to suggestions that America has become a postracial society or that society is color blind, these findings suggest that encounters with racism are common in the everyday experiences of URM faculty in research universities. Although research identifies discriminatory and racist experiences of URM faculty and institutional ways to respond and diminish the effects of these experiences, the recommendations have two main limitations. First, the research relies primarily on accounts by African Americans, excluding other URMs. Second, the associated studies were primarily conducted with small sample sizes (Allison, 2008; Griffin, Bennett, et al., 2011; Robinson, 2014). Additionally, although URM experiences have been examined within scholarly journals and the popular media (Dunbar, 2014; Laymon, 2014), little is known regarding how universities have addressed these concerns. Understanding the historical and contemporary nature of racism is critical for higher education scholars, policy makers, and practitioners to comprehend the complexity of the ways in which racism permeates postsecondary institutions as well as how they might engage in efforts to address them (Museus, Ledesma, & Parker, 2015).

Institutional racism and microaggressions present a heavy burden for URM faculty that results in daily vigilance, which in turn leads to physical and mental fatigue or excessive emotional labor (Wingfield, 2013). Microaggressions are defined as everyday slights, insults, and indignities directed toward one group by another group (usually but not always White) or by structural institutional Whiteness. Microaggressions are an example of broader institutional discriminatory practices. By inscribing race and ethnicity as identity markers signaling social status in institutional settings, everyday social interactions and experiences in predominantly White spaces are filtered through a lens of implicit bias that increases discriminatory practices such as microaggressions. An understanding of workplace perceived discrimination (actual or imagined) may provide some insight into the revolving door phenomenon of URM faculty in higher education (Moreno, Smith, Clayton-Pedersen, Parker, & Teraguchi, 2006).

Respondents expressed that they experienced a sense of solitude and did not know whom to ask for help or support. Due to the low numbers of URMs in departments, colleges, and entire universities, all respondents reported some degree of isolation, though this was particularly the case among assistant professors. These experiences may account for low rates of retention of URM faculty. A plethora of extant evidence demonstrates that racism and all its manifestations are an integral part of occupational settings, especially higher education institutions (Moore, 2008; Wingfield & Alston, 2014). Campuses would be well served to cultivate awareness that racism is endemic to higher education beyond overt discrimination.

Our findings provide insights into strategic actions universities can take to improve retention and nurture a more welcoming climate for URM faculty. Drawing from extensive scholarship (Bonilla-Silva, 2009; Collins, 2015; Delgado & Stefancic, 2001; Dill & Zambrana, 2009; Feagin, 2006, 2013; Griffin, Bennett, et al., 2011; Griffin, Pifer, et al., 2011; Museus et al., 2015; Wingfield, 2010), research universities can address discriminatory practices by engaging in the following actions:

- White faculty and administrators must engage in critical self-reflection regarding personal bias and prejudice (Robinson, 2014).
- White faculty must understand how bias influences tenure and the promotion process. Additionally, other forms of scholarship and service must be valued (Griffin, Pifer, et al., 2011).
- URMs should have access to mentoring, support systems, and assistance with establishing contacts within the URM community (Patitu & Hinton, 2003).
- Institutional leaders should implement focused and specific initiatives to improve interactions between URM and White faculty (Griffin, Pifer, et al., 2011).

To that end, it is useful to consider whether and how diversity discourses can potentially ameliorate the challenges facing URM faculty (Bhopal & Jackson, 2013; Whittaker, Montgomery, & Acosta, 2015). Many universities express a commitment to building a diverse faculty and often mention in recruitment ads that they enthusiastically welcome applications from underrepresented minorities (Zanoni, Janssens, Benschop, & Nkomo, 2010). However, the findings shed light on the challenges associated with both recruitment and retention. Inasmuch as racial/ethnic minorities cite increased stress associated with the discriminatory behavior of their White colleagues, it might be beneficial to universities to devote greater attention to intentional ways that they can become more hospitable work environments.

Given the pervasive implicit bias and racial stereotyping that suggest that Whites are more intelligent and, by extension, more deserving of academic positions, URM faculty repeatedly find themselves in situations where they confront perceptions that they did not earn and therefore do not deserve their occupational standing. As respondents noted, this persists in the face of exemplary research records, hard work, and proficiency. This is important given that URM faculty are often the ones who are expected to "carry the entire" burden of ensuring knowledge of and sensitivity to issues of diversity. Despite the minimal numerical gains for URMs in research universities in recent decades, universities' inability to better comprehend their own discriminatory practices and the consequences of these practices on URM faculty significantly undermine future progress in diversifying the professoriate.

# 6 · WORK-FAMILY BALANCE
## The Quandary of URM Professionals

I just want to say as an African American with a family, I feel, like, an extra responsibility to make the family work, just because of the dynamics and the statistics. I came from a divorced household. My wife did too. So there's a whole psychological piece of wanting to be extra daddy.

—African American male

Current and past research on work-family balance among professional occupational groups has focused primarily on White nuclear families (Sayer, England, Bittman, & Bianchi, 2009), often failing to include URM professional families—namely, those of African American, Mexican American, and Puerto Rican descent.[1] A limited body of research provides some insights on professional URM dual-career families and how they negotiate daily activities at home and work (Lacy, 2007; Pattillo-McCoy, 1999; Vallejo, 2012). Recently, a small body of empirical literature has emerged on work-family balance in the academy (Evans & Grant, 2008; Marotte, Reynolds, & Savarese, 2011) and on work-family issues for URM faculty (Nzinga-Johnson, 2013). As Wight, Bianchi, and Hunt (2013) observe, "There are enough differences across race/ethnic groups to raise questions about whether the dominant perspectives in the literature on housework 'fit' other groups as well as Whites" (p. 401). Indeed, the work-family issues affecting URM faculty are shaped by an economic and social context that differs from those affecting non-URM faculty (Landry & Marsh, 2011; Rockquemore & Laszloffy, 2008). These differences may include unique work strains such as encounters with discrimination and racism and extensive demands for diversity-related university service, economic strains, and significant obligations to the family of origin. Collectively, these factors may increase family strains and imbalance the work-family nexus.

Key to understanding work-family balance is the role of the intersections of education level, economic resources, and the racialized systems that shape family opportunity structures and life chances. In light of the focus on upward social mobility, work-family balance, and professional socialization, academia as a site of work-family strain is important yet has largely been unexamined in relation to URM families. Whereas Gerson (2010) argues that family functioning is one of the "new moral dilemmas of work and care" for the twenty-first century, the limited research that does address URM families finds that the processes are not the same across racial/ethnic groups. The study of how professional URMs balance work and family obligations remains largely absent in the work-family national and higher education discourse. Work-family balance can be broadly conceptualized as integrating individual priorities with family (marital, partner, children, and family-of-origin relationships), work (career and ambition), institutional resources, and self-care practices (spiritualism, recreation, and strategies to relieve stress).

In this chapter, I present study data that illustrate how participants were able to balance their multiple roles and responsibilities, particularly obligations to family caretaking. Questions were asked about social, economic, and familial factors and how these roles impacted work demands or how work demands disrupted the work-family balance. In interviews, I asked participants how they manage work and family responsibilities; what major barriers they face to managing work and family demands; and what personal, family, social, and institutional supports increase their capacity to cope with multiple demands. The findings fill a major gap in the family science and sociology of marriage and family scholarship.

## THE ONGOING SCHOLARLY CONVERSATION: ABSENT OF THE URM PROFESSORIATE

A significant corpus of work on dual-career families and family dynamics evolved in the 1970s when majority-culture women began to enter the labor force in significant numbers. Noteworthy is the fact that historically underrepresented women (African American, Mexican American), who had been laboring in the fields and as both laborers and handmaidens to majority-culture women and their families, were ignored in this plethora of research on work and women (Harley & the Black Women and Work Collective, 2002; Higginbotham, 2009; Zambrana & Hurtado, 2015). Initial foci of the research associated with family dynamics included job characteristics and the type of work (Clark, 2002; Hammer, Kossek, Anger, Bodner, & Zimmerman, 2011; Judge & Colquitt, 2004; Keene & Quadagno, 2004; Kelly, Moen, & Tranby, 2011; Moen, Kelly, Tranby, &

Huang, 2011; Moen, Lam, Ammons, & Kelly, 2013; Weigt & Solomon, 2008), family structure and the ages of children (Higgins, Duxbury, & Lee, 1994; Martinengo, Jacob, & Hill, 2010), and the frequency of time pressures and multitasking (Offer & Schneider, 2011).

In the late twentieth century, a shift was observed and a significant body of research emerged around three additional themes: time use in the work and family spheres (Milkie, Raley, & Bianchi, 2009), a "second shift" for working women in dual-earner families who continued to shoulder household duties with limited household and caregiving contributions from their husbands (Sayer et al., 2009; Spain & Bianchi, 1996), and factors that contribute to men's participation in the home (Orbuch & Custer, 1995). For example, among married men, Black and Mexican American men were more likely to participate in household labor than White men (Wight et al., 2013). In another study, Mexican American men contributed more than White men when their wives made significant economic contributions to the household (Pinto & Coltrane, 2009). Factors likely to influence how households balance responsibilities included economic assets and income, flexible work hours, autonomy, and access to social capital (e.g., social support networks; Amato, 1998; Golden, 2001), areas that differed between URM and non-Hispanic White families. In a study of predominately White professional women, those with the highest incomes and the highest educational achievements reported fewer problems with employment interfering in personal and family lives because they were able to control the events of their lives outside of employment and have more flexibility (Damiano-Teixeira, 2006). These options, due to lower economic resources and higher workplace stress, may not yield the same benefits for URM men and women. Another line of inquiry has examined gender differences with professional non-Hispanic White women as the focal point. Keene and Quadagno (2004) explored predictors of perceived work-family balance using 1996 General Social Survey and 1992 National Study of the Changing Workforce data and found that greater work demands (as measured by number of hours) led to less balance in women than in men and that when men reported having little personal time due to work, their feelings of balance were affected to a greater degree than were women's (see also Mattingly & Sayer, 2006). Another predictor of balance was control over one's own schedule, which reduced work-family conflict for both women and men (Clark, 2002; Kelly et al., 2011).

The fit between academic life and home life is not a comfortable one. Jacobs and Winslow (2004) found that those who worked the longest—more than sixty hours per week—were by far the most productive in terms of books and articles. Parents of both genders were less likely to be in that group but were also more satisfied in general with their workload. The level of commitment necessary to obtain tenure took a particular toll on women with children. They confronted greater obstacles that resulted in fewer publications, slower self-perceived career progress, and lower career satisfaction. Although men and women were equally productive, men spent more time on research while women spent time on household responsibilities and less free time on themselves (Sax, Hagedorn, Arredondo, & Dicrisi, 2002). Xie and Shauman (1998) explained a decrease in the difference in productivity over time between female and male faculty in scientific fields: "A major reason for this trend is that the distribution of resources and structural positions, albeit still unfavorable to women, has become more equitable over . . . time" (p. 863). Differences in productivity have often been explained by the presence of a partner and children.

Childbearing decisions and fertility patterns vary by gender, race/ethnicity, and rank. Women with tenure are less likely to have children, and if they do, in general they have fewer children than they would want (Ecklund & Lincoln, 2011; Mason & Goulden, 2002; Perna, 2001a). Another study found that women with doctorates who had decided on early childbearing decreased their chances of getting tenure and experienced more career barriers (Damiano-Teixeira, 2006), including opting out of tenure-track positions because they believed it was not possible to reconcile their career with having children (Williams & Ceci, 2012). Less is known about racial/ethnic faculty and their decisions and the impact of childbearing. The overwhelmingly majority of literature has included samples of predominantly White women but has not included information on family-of-origin background, spousal occupation, or wealth and assets. Economic resources and family of origin and spouse/partner SES (as defined by education and income) are central to the ability to manage balance and employ options such as outsourcing family and domestic tasks including full-time day care, household help, and live-in child care, among others. Yet the use of these resources has generally been ignored. One study confirmed that class significantly alleviated many of the challenges faced by highly educated mothers through options such as outsourcing domestic labor, while working-class mothers engaged in a great deal of gendered interpersonal work and had less control over their choices (Weigt & Solomon, 2008). Although these data broaden our understanding of the multiple processes involved in decisions about family, work, child care, and housework among all professionals (single, married/partnered), the intersecting roles of economic resources and race/ethnicity are imminent concerns among URM faculty (Hurtado, Eagan, Pryor, Whang, & Tran, 2012) and have lasting effects across the life course. Yet these critical determinants of how to manage work-family balance have been overlooked in prior studies.

Powerful tensions exist in the discourse regarding how to manage, balance, and/or integrate work demands, family life, and personal self-care. Although much has been learned regarding how White middle-class families' choices are influenced by their work lives and how their work lives influence many family decisions (e.g., Hammer et al., 2011; O'Neil & Greenberger, 1994), economic, structural, and demographic shifts in the past few decades have complicated the portrait of family life and work life and the multiple components that shape individual choice (see Bianchi & Milkie, 2010, for a review of the past decade of work). Much more work is needed to investigate and understand these choices and how they intersect with wealth and social inequities in our society to affect racial/ethnic families, particularly high-prestige professional URMs (Childers & Sage, 2003; Clark, 2002; Roehling, Jarvis, & Swope, 2005).

Understanding work-family balance among URM professionals is important because it has implications for work-family conflict (Nomaguchi, 2009), role strain (Grzywacz, Almeida, & McDonald, 2002), marital distress (Simon, 1995), relationship disintegration (Thornton & Young-DeMarco, 2001), parent/child relationships, and intensive parenting (Lareau, 2002, 2011). As Burton, Bonilla-Silva, Ray, Buckelew, and Freeman (2010) discuss, family research necessitates the incorporation of the basic tenets of what we know about race and that "acknowledges race as a social construction that create[s] racial realities with real effects." This study provides rich insights into the pathways in which race/ethnicity intersects with class, gender, and other social statuses to shape in multiple ways the work-family dynamic.

## OCCUPATIONAL WHITE SPACES: PRIVILEGE, ECONOMICS, AND ROLE STRAIN

Generally, professional status is strongly marked by higher social capital resources, perceived middle-class status, economic resources, access to safe and well-resourced public spaces, economic and social support from family of origin, and a supportive personal and professional social network. However, the benefits of professional status vary by race/ethnicity due to salary disparities, family-of-origin SES, occupational demands and expectations, and additional workplace stress such as discrimination. A modest emerging body of research provides some insights on professional URM dual-career families and how they negotiate daily activities at home and work (Lacy, 2007; Pattillo-McCoy, 1999; Vallejo, 2012), work-family balance in the academy (Evans & Grant, 2008; Marotte et al., 2011), and faculty work-family issues (Nzinga-Johnson, 2013). Although a satisfying balance between family and work lives has been reported to be a myth (Hall & MacDermid, 2009), prior investigations have suggested that the work-family issues affecting URM faculty are shaped by an employment, economic, and familial context that differs from that affecting non-URM faculty (Gutiérrez y Muhs, Niemann, González, & Harris, 2012; Landry & Marsh, 2011; Rockquemore & Laszloffy, 2008). For example, a study of professional

Mexican American women examined how life role status (i.e., having a partner and no children, having a partner and children, being single with no children, being single with children) is associated with personal and professional role satisfaction. Personal satisfaction was highest for women with partners but no children and lowest for those with children but no partners. Thus personal satisfaction, but not professional satisfaction, appears to be influenced by role status (Zambrana & Frith, 1988, p. 356). Contextualizing both women's perception of employment attributes and their satisfaction with childbearing status informs our interpretation of workplace strain.

Workplace strain is associated with discriminatory treatment and diversity work demands as well as lower salaries and less access to family support benefits. As Bonilla-Silva (1997) observed, Whites receive greater "economic remuneration, are granted higher social estimation, often have the license to draw physical as well as social boundaries, and receive a 'psychological wage'" (pp. 469–470). Beyond these challenges, socioeconomic disparities linked to institutional discrimination in labor, education, and housing markets exacerbate wealth gaps over the life course between highly educated URMs and Whites (Lacy, 2012; Lareau, 2011); impact individual and family strains and family functioning (Rothwell & Han, 2010); decrease the outflow of resources from families of origin to their offspring (Heflin & Pattillo, 2006); and dampen upward mobility (Burton et al., 2010; Vallejo, 2012). URM families are more likely to experience cycles of upward and downward mobility that prevent them from taking advantage of the educational attainment of previous generations (Shapiro, 2004; Telles & Ortiz, 2009) and are more likely to incur responsibilities to parents and siblings that affect their ability to accumulate assets during their work life.

A significant corpus of work reveals that URM professionals face significantly more stress than their White counterparts from workplace discrimination, unsafe neighborhood spaces, and caregiving responsibilities to family of origin. Few studies have examined the strategies that URM professionals use to cope with race/ethnicity-specific workplace role strains and their impact on family life (Roehling et al., 2005). Individuals within similar social structures tend to employ similar coping strategies (Pearlin, 1989). Professionals may cope with role strain and stress in race/ethnicity-specific ways such as institutionalized religion and spiritual practices (Adams, Aranda, Kemp, & Takagi, 2002; Clark, 2002); seeking community support (Shorter-Gooden, 2004); refocusing energy away from workplace stress; relying on social support from other URM professionals within and outside of the institution; engaging in problem-focused strategies (Thomas & Hollenshead, 2001; Wingfield, 2010); and utilizing available family-friendly support services that help with work-family balance (Siemieńska & Zimmer, 2007; Ward & Wolf-Wendel, 2012). Other strategies, which are potentially harmful, include passive coping, such as ignoring, remaining silent, or doing nothing (Ek, Cerecer, Alanis, & Rodriguez, 2010) and emotion-focused coping that often does not address the stressor directly (Plummer & Slane, 1996). As observed by Wingfield (2010), URM professionals engage in significant emotional labor in their work environments that may deplete the emotional and social resources necessary to fully engage in social and family relationships.

Data on work-family balance among the professoriate illustrate in multiple ways the lingering inequalities in career pathways. The nature, intensity, quantity, and timing of career demands are important considerations for faculty who are making family-related decisions (Jacobs, 2004; Mason & Goulden, 2002; O'Laughlin & Bischoff, 2005). Given the autonomous and flexible nature of faculty work life, many faculty sit at the nexus of experiencing great privilege in the workplace while also facing persistent discrimination, increased competition for fewer tenured positions, and a workload that is unending and continuously flows over into home life. The work lives and successes of URM faculty, because of their relatively tenuous history within the academy, are consistently put at risk by the demands and sacrifices required to achieve the golden ticket of tenure.

Three primary conclusions are drawn from this body of knowledge that distinguishes URM faculty from their majority counterparts: workplace experiences place a heavy role strain on URM professionals due to their racial/ethnic social status (Wingfield & Alston, 2014); professional class standing does not provide equivalent economic benefits to URMs compared to non-URMs due to gaps in wealth (Oliver & Shapiro, 1995); and caregiving supports in the form of material resources and emotional labor are more likely to flow from URM professionals to their family of origin than the reverse. Together, these factors may exacerbate family and work role strain that is specific to the URM professional experience.

## FAMILY CHARACTERISTICS OF THE SAMPLE AND QUESTIONS ASKED

Family is conceptualized as extending beyond members of the nuclear family (parents and children) to include family of origin, extended kin, fictive kin, and even community members (Vallejo, 2012). In interviews, four prompts and questions were used to explore work-family responsibilities, life events, and coping strategies: (1) "Describe how your family (partner and/or children) and personal obligations and responsibilities have an effect on your career path"; (2) "Have there been any major family events in the last five years that affected work, or work events that affected family life?"; (3) "What types of supports are available to you to balance the competing demands of work and family/personal life, e.g., financial resources, level of satisfaction with child care arrangements?";

and (4) "What are the ways (strategies) you balance the competing demands of work and family/personal life, e.g., how do you care for yourself?" An important limitation of this study is that data were not collected on respondents' partner's education, employment, or income.[2]

The following sections provide a profile of demographic, family structure, and caregiving responsibilities to family and friends and responses to the following self-reported survey items: (1) level of satisfaction with family, work, and personal balance; (2) department chair's level of respect for balance; and (3) perceived level of support for balance through institutional policies. Following the descriptive survey data, qualitative thematic findings are presented to provide a deeper understanding of the context of work-family experiences.

## DECISION-MAKING: DIFFICULT
## CAREER CHOICES AND PRIORITIES

As displayed in table 6.1, 18.4 percent of the sample had never been married, 66.7 percent were married or living with a partner, 14.9 percent were divorced/ separated/widowed, and more than half (62.9 percent) had children. Puerto Ricans, American Indian / Alaska Natives, and Mexican Americans were most likely to be married, while African Americans and Mexican Americans were most likely to report no children. Among faculty with children, 46.1 percent had children younger than 10. More than a third, 38.4 percent, stated they planned to have children in the future, with African Americans and Puerto Ricans more likely to report future plans for family formation.

Table 6.2 provides descriptive data on caregiving responsibilities and social resources including institutional support and satisfaction with balance. Since family includes not only nuclear but also extended family, caretaking questions were asked. In addition to work-related obligations, 21.7 percent of respondents reported caretaking responsibilities for family or friends. Among those with caretaking responsibilities, 24.3 percent reported caretaking less than once a week, 37.4 percent one to two times per week, and 27.1 percent five or more times per week. American Indian / Alaska Natives were most likely to report caretaking responsibilities (30 percent), but about 20 percent of each of the other groups also reported "helping at least one sick, disabled, or frail family member or friend on a regular basis." In the item regarding "how often in the last month have you helped a friend or family member," about one-quarter of racial/ ethnic groups except for Puerto Ricans indicated five or more times per week.

Almost one-third (31.8 percent) of respondents found their department chair to be respectful of their work-life balance most of the time, 39.2 percent stated that this was usually or often true, and 28.5 percent reported occasionally, rarely, or never true. Of respondents, 19.5 percent reported institutional policies

TABLE 6.1  Demographic and family profile of respondents by race/ethnicity

| Variable | Total sample (N = 568) | African American (n = 333; 58.6%) | Mexican American (n = 134; 23.6%) | Puerto Rican (n = 76; 13.4%) | American Indian / Alaska Native (n = 24; 4.4%) |
|---|---|---|---|---|---|
| **Marital status** | | | | | |
| Never married | 104 | 75 | 19 | 7 | 3 |
| | (18.4) | (22.8) | (14.3) | (9.1) | (12.0) |
| Married, living with spouse / not living with spouse / living with partner | 376 | 205 | 97 | 57 | 17 |
| | (66.7) | (62.3) | (72.9) | (74.0) | (68.0) |
| Separated/widowed/divorced | 84 | 49 | 17 | 13 | 5 |
| | (14.9) | (14.9) | (12.8) | (16.9) | (20.0) |
| **Household size** | | | | | |
| 1 | 138 | 93 | 29 | 12 | 4 |
| | (24.5) | (28.4) | (21.8) | (15.6) | (16.0) |
| 2 | 283 | 158 | 75 | 38 | 12 |
| | (50.3) | (48.2) | (56.4) | (49.4) | (48.0) |
| 3+ | 142 | 77 | 29 | 27 | 9 |
| | (25.2) | (23.5) | (21.8) | (35.1) | (36.0) |
| **Number of children** | | | | | |
| 0 | 210 | 128 | 50 | 25 | 7 |
| | (37.1) | (38.7) | (37.6) | (32.5) | (28.0) |
| 1 | 138 | 79 | 38 | 18 | 3 |
| | (24.4) | (23.9) | (28.6) | (23.4) | (12.0) |

| | | | | | | | | | |
|---|---|---|---|---|---|---|---|---|---|
| 2 | 142 | (25.1) | 77 | (23.3) | 38 | (28.6) | 21 | (27.3) | 6 | (24.0) |
| 3+ | 78 | (13.4) | 47 | (14.2) | 7 | (5.3) | 13 | (16.9) | 9 | (36.0) |

**Ages of children[a]**

| | | | | | | | | | |
|---|---|---|---|---|---|---|---|---|---|
| 0–4 years | 153 | (26.9) | 74 | (22.2) | 46 | (34.6) | 28 | (36.4) | 5 | (20.0) |
| 5–10 years | 109 | (19.2) | 62 | (18.6) | 21 | (15.8) | 19 | (24.7) | 7 | (28.0) |
| 11–14 years | 55 | (9.7) | 34 | (10.2) | 9 | (6.8) | 6 | (7.8) | 6 | (24.0) |
| 15–18 years | 46 | (8.1) | 22 | (6.6) | 14 | (10.5) | 8 | (10.4) | 2 | (8) |
| 19+ years | 96 | (16.9) | 66 | (19.8) | 16 | (12.0) | 7 | (9.1) | 7 | (28.0) |

**Interest in future children (having or adopting)**

| | | | | | | | | | |
|---|---|---|---|---|---|---|---|---|---|
| Yes | 89 | (38.4) | 57 | (42.2) | 17 | (28.8) | 14 | (46.7) | 1 | (12.5) |
| No | 88 | (37.9) | 46 | (34.1) | 32 | (54.2) | 7 | (23.3) | 3 | (37.5) |
| Unsure | 55 | (23.7) | 32 | (23.7) | 10 | (16.9) | 9 | (30.0) | 4 | (50.0) |

NOTE: These data include both web-based and qualitative data of total study participants. Values in parentheses are percentages.

a. Percentages do not sum to 100 percent, as individuals may have children in more than one category; the value indicates the percentage of faculty who have one or more children in that age range.

**TABLE 6.2** Descriptive percentage responses of caregiving responsibilities and perceived institutional support by race/ethnicity

| Variable | Total sample (N = 508) | African American (n = 310; 61.0%) | Mexican American (n = 113; 22.2%) | Puerto Rican (n = 62; 12.2%) | American Indian / Alaska Native (n = 23; 4.5%) |
|---|---|---|---|---|---|
| **Caregiving** | | | | | |
| *Helping at least one sick, disabled, or frail family member or friend on a regular basis* | | | | | |
| Yes | 107 | 63 | 24 | 13 | 7 |
| | (21.7) | (21.0) | (21.6) | (21.7) | (30.4) |
| No | 387 | 237 | 87 | 47 | 16 |
| | (78.3) | (79.0) | (78.4) | (78.3) | (69.6) |
| *In the last four weeks, how often have you helped this friend or family member?* | | | | | |
| Less than 1 time a week | 26 | 15 | 5 | 4 | 2 |
| | (24.3) | (23.8) | (20.8) | (30.8) | (28.6) |
| 1–2 times a week | 40 | 21 | 11 | 6 | 2 |
| | (37.4) | (33.3) | (45.8) | (46.2) | (28.6) |
| 3–4 times a week | 12 | 8 | 2 | 1 | 1 |
| | (11.2) | (12.7) | (8.3) | (7.7) | (14.3) |
| 5+ times a week | 29 | 19 | 6 | 2 | 2 |
| | (27.1) | (30.2) | (25.0) | (15.4) | (28.6) |
| *How satisfied are you with the balance between professional and personal or family time?* | | | | | |
| Very dissatisfied | 83 | 53 | 16 | 11 | 3 |
| | (16.9) | (18.0) | (14.4) | (18.0) | (13.0) |

| | | | | | |
|---|---|---|---|---|---|
| Somewhat dissatisfied | 167 (34.1) | 102 (34.6) | 39 (35.1) | 17 (27.9) | 9 (39.1) |
| Neutral | 79 (16.1) | 48 (16.3) | 21 (18.9) | 8 (13.1) | 2 (8.7) |
| Somewhat satisfied | 127 (25.9) | 70 (23.7) | 26 (23.4) | 22 (36.1) | 9 (39.1) |
| Very satisfied | 34 (6.9) | 22 (7.5) | 9 (8.1) | 3 (4.9) | — |

*Department chair is respectful of my efforts to balance work, family, and/or personal responsibilities*

| | | | | | |
|---|---|---|---|---|---|
| Rarely or never true | 60 (12.4) | 35 (12.0) | 9 (8.2) | 10 (16.7) | 6 (26.1) |
| Occasionally true | 80 (16.5) | 47 (16.2) | 23 (20.9) | 5 (8.3) | 5 (21.7) |
| Often true | 80 (16.5) | 45 (15.5) | 25 (22.7) | 8 (13.3) | 2 (8.7) |
| Usually true | 110 (22.7) | 62 (21.3) | 24 (21.8) | 20 (33.3) | 4 (17.4) |
| True most of the time | 154 (31.8) | 102 (35.1) | 29 (26.4) | 17 (28.3) | 6 (26.1) |

*Institutional policies are supportive of faculty efforts to balance work and family responsibilities*

| | | | | | |
|---|---|---|---|---|---|
| Rarely or never true | 67 (14.0) | 36 (12.5) | 19 (17.4) | 6 (10.0) | 6 (27.3) |

(continued)

TABLE 6.2   Descriptive percentage responses of caregiving responsibilities and perceived institutional support by race/ethnicity (*continued*)

| Variable | Total sample (*N* = 508) | African American (*n* = 310; 61.0%) | Mexican American (*n* = 113; 22.2%) | Puerto Rican (*n* = 62; 12.2%) | American Indian / Alaska Native (*n* = 23; 4.5%) |
|---|---|---|---|---|---|
| Occasionally true | 99 | 60 | 21 | 14 | 4 |
| | (20.7) | (20.9) | (19.3) | (23.3) | (18.2) |
| Often true | 101 | 58 | 27 | 13 | 4 |
| | (21.1) | (19.9) | (24.8) | (21.7) | (18.2) |
| Usually true | 118 | 66 | 29 | 18 | 5 |
| | (24.7) | (23.0) | (26.6) | (30.0) | (22.7) |
| True most of the time | 93 | 68 | 13 | 9 | 3 |
| | (19.5) | (23.7) | (11.9) | (15.0) | (13.6) |

NOTE: These data include only web-based study respondents. Values in parentheses are percentages.

to be supportive of work-life balance most of the time, 45.8 percent stated usually or often, while 34.7 percent reported occasionally, rarely, or never. About one-half (51.0 percent) of the respondents stated that they were somewhat or very dissatisfied with their level of work-family balance.

## BEYOND BALANCE: NARRATIVES OF JUGGLING AND STRUGGLING

Four major themes are notable with regard to work-family balance: (1) balance as an oxymoron that contributed to sacrifice of either work or family responsibilities, (2) postponement of marriage and children due to work demands, (3) response to stressful role demands by focusing on a positive perspective, and (4) desire for institutional resources to assist with work-family life. These themes were salient for the majority of respondents and were consistent across gender, race, and ethnicity. Quotes that are representative of the experiences of the majority of respondents are presented in the following sections.

## BALANCE AS AN OXYMORON: SACRIFICE AND ROLE STRAINS

Participants viewed work-family balance as an oxymoron, with the majority reporting work-family balance as a sacrifice and role strain that required a difficult juggling act. A Mexican American woman explained it as follows: "But I think work-family balance is an oxymoron. I don't know that I've ever spoken to anybody who has been able to tell me how to balance it at my institution. Everybody that I speak to is like, well, you know, I put my kids to bed, and then I work until twelve o'clock. And, you know, that's kind of what—that's kind of like what I've been doing, you know." Interestingly, none of the respondents mentioned having a nanny or other household help. Outsourcing domestic labor and child care is often recommended as a strategy to decrease parental strain but requires economic resources that are often not available to URM professionals. Oftentimes the women reported feeling disappointed and even angry at not having time with their children when they were young. An underlying dilemma that emerged in discussing work-family balance was the choice to focus on either work or family. Respondents discussed the notion of sacrifice required in multiple arenas: the balance of multiple roles with work demands and decisions to forgo childbearing or partnership due to work demands or to focus on family versus work due to personal reasons or caregiving responsibilities at the expense of a lifelong investment in a career. These choices were difficult because not working was impossible. Although there is a consensus in the extant literature that family-work balance is a myth, the empirical literature of mainly

White dual-career families and professional women do not frame the notion of balance as sacrifice of work or family and/or sacrifice of personal self. An African American female respondent commented on the "myth" of work-family balance and addressed the sacrifice of self that is often required to ensure that work and family responsibilities are accomplished: "I don't know. I've actually come to think that the balance idea is something of a myth. I don't know that you can really truly balance it. I can juggle it. But I don't know how I'm balancing it where everything is sort of working out where there's equal time to everything and everything's getting its due. Right now, I don't feel that I'm achieving that balance and I don't feel that the attention to myself is very strong." As her observation illustrates, although juggling may keep work and family life in motion, all too often personal life gets left behind. In other cases, work and family life begin to blend with no clear demarcation of roles or time. A married African American male respondent with two children spoke to this point: "It's something that I still probably don't manage quite well, the balance between family life and work because in academia, even when you're at home you're at work."

Some respondents relied on their partners to balance work and family life, but even with a support system balance remained elusive: "I started graduate school with a one-year-old and was juggling. So it was juggling things all along and I had a supportive husband at the time and all. So it has always been a juggle" (Puerto Rican female). Because of the myth of work-family balance, the majority of respondents perceived they were making a choice between prioritizing either work or family. Some argued that balance is difficult for all couples and parents. However, for URM balancing is more difficult due to simultaneous life stressors, persistent stereotype threat, and more limited economic resources, particularly when considering family choices.

## Work Demands and Family Choices: Postponement of Marriage and Children

An extensive body of literature, particularly dating to the late twentieth century, has provided evidence of the extensive demands and requirements of professionals in terms of investment of hours and productivity. Despite academia's high level of autonomy, there are immense pressures and expectations that acutely impact URM faculty. URM faculty learn that there are no clear-cut strategies for balancing work and family life and frequently perceive that if they are to succeed they must favor one dimension over the other. An African American woman reflected, "My whole personal life has been organized around making my professional life as efficient and effective and productive as possible. So there are all kinds of things that I gave up, hobbies that I gave up, friends that I gave . . . the only thing that made that possible for me is not having people who needed me."

These decisions can be particularly difficult in terms of postponing marriage/ partnership and childbearing. One Puerto Rican man, married without children, shared his decision to postpone children: "I have been resistant to having a child until I have tenure or have the security of the possibility of tenure." An African American woman with one child acknowledged the consequences of prioritizing work: "I regret not having had a second one. There is regret on either end."

Other early career scholars studied their environment and the lives of other academics and were unable to find viable lifestyles. "Well, for example, I was looking at the lifestyles of all the other Latino women in my field who are prominent scholars and none of them are married and none of them have kids. Not one. And I was like, 'Oh, crap.' Is this really—and I was, like, well would it be different for me, or would I follow the same path? I don't know. But this seems like the likelihood of that" (Mexican American woman). A Native American woman echoed these sentiments: "I would love to have a partner, but I don't. That allows me to work harder. I think that contributes to my success. I won't say I don't feel like I've given up something for both my spiritual practices and my career, but I feel like in some people's lives, they have wonderful relationships, wonderful kids, or a great career. You don't often get all of it."

In addition to delaying childbearing, other participants indicated prioritizing work to the extent of forgoing partners and even dating. One participant stated, "I am single and living alone. Don't have any children. Don't have a mate. Don't have a partner. Up until this point, I've been—from postdoc to the first couple years as an assistant professor, I was one-dimensional. Monday through Saturday I was at my office or working" (African American female). Similarly, a Mexican American male discussed sacrificing his relationship with his partner but could not imagine having children: "I don't have a family. I don't have children. I have a partner, but that's very different. If I had children, I don't know how I would have done the 100-hour effort that I did for the last two and a half years. . . . Well, in retrospect, I basically decided to sacrifice my personal relationship with my partner for my job."

This strong undertone of sacrifice also reflects fear of not being able to successfully manage too many additional roles alongside work obligations and a profound understanding that success depends on galvanizing all their intellectual and, by implication, physical and emotional energy.

## Family versus Career as a Priority: The Dilemma of Successful Careers

Many of the respondents found work and family life incompatible. For those who chose family over work, it was a taxing relationship. When discussing prioritizing their family life, respondents often indicated that those decisions come at a cost. "And I'm—you know, like, right now, we're planning, hopefully, to have another child. So I'm like, okay, this year, I'm working on four to five articles so that, when I have the baby, all these articles hit. So I kind of plan it that way. But it takes quite the commitment. So it affects how I plan out my career" (Mexican

American female). Beyond the potential disruption of their career planning, two respondents noted the potential uncertainty of their career trajectory when making family the priority:

> I have a kid, so I cannot be working at all hours of the day. When she comes home, its homework time, and I'm not going to be responding to emails at seven o'clock at night because we're eating dinner and we are going to be doing homework. And I take Sundays off. I'm sorry, but I'm not doing work all weekend long because I have to spend time with my family. And if that makes me less productive, oh, well. I only get her young for a certain amount of years, and that's just the way it is. (Mexican American female)

> There are people who keep the candlelight burning. I make the decision not to do that, and I may pay for it, so we'll see, but the family thing, I have to keep that intact. (African American female)

Another Mexican American male participant shared how he came to change his values regarding work to engage in more family time: "And now I say no. But I needed to get to the point where I finally had my self-esteem sorted out. It cannot be attached to my mentors. It can't be attached to my institution. It can't be attached to any of this. And it's been liberating for me to be able to realize, okay, this is not anything I want to replicate for the rest of my career. I do not want to be working a hundred-plus hours a week just to show people that I can do this."

Family is an important and central social system in the lives of all individuals. These narratives reveal that having a career, due to its extraordinary demands, coupled with the emotional work required to confront and cope with race/ethnicity/gender discrimination, comes at the high of negative consequences on family relationships, the personal life course, and asset building and wealth accrual.

URMs do not benefit from intergenerational mobility in the same manner as Whites do, and status advantages gained by one generation do not necessarily transfer to the next (Shapiro, 2004; Telles & Ortiz, 2009). For example, the median wealth of White households is twenty times that of Black households and eighteen times that of Latino households (Taylor, Kochhar, Fry, Velasco, & Motel, 2011). Discrimination in the labor and housing markets has resulted in a large racial/ethnic wealth gap for URMs (Lacy, 2012; Oliver & Shapiro, 1995; Shapiro, 2017; Sternthal, Slopen, & Williams, 2011). Beyond these challenges, access to economic resources impacts work-life balance, individual and family stress, and family functioning (Rothwell & Han, 2010). Many participants did not benefit from family-of-origin economic support. Instead, they often contributed economic resources to their family of origin, which impacted quality of life and upward mobility (Burton et al., 2010).

### Caretaking Responsibilities for Family Members

Participants who prioritized family did so for two major reasons: a strong commitment to being good parents and family caretaking responsibilities. Some noted family responsibilities or a change in family circumstances (e.g., financial, health) that required their primary attention. One Mexican American female shared, "Then my mother became very sick. My mother has diabetes and has had it for fifty years but then she got very sick and I called [tenure review chair] and said take my hat out of the ring. I can't do it. I'm under too much pressure for family situations. Pull my name out." Likewise, other respondents noted caretaking responsibilities as a determinant of their career decisions:

> So initially I wanted to go into clinical medicine, and I pretty-much decided that I could not go into clinical medicine because of my family responsibilities. So I had a little baby, and my mother is mentally ill, and I'm her full-time caretaker. So I didn't think that that would be feasible. (Mexican American female)

> I waver back and forth because the reality is I need to make more money than what I do right now because I am supporting two people on my income. I have responsibilities to my parents that maybe other people don't have. And so that unfortunately, that does play a big factor where I'm going to go with the next step with my career. (Mexican American female)

> Well I worked in our medical school as a graduate student and because I had a family I could not afford to have a graduate assistantship that was over here [in one place] and my work as my doctoral dissertation work was over there. Everything had to mesh. My brain could not go in two different directions. (African American female)

In addition to perceived career costs, respondents also indicated the physical and mental tension from work-life decisions. "I think that my—all my health problems are related to the fact that I am trying to be the kind of mother my mom is, at the same time that I have a job that is incredibly demanding and my mom didn't have that job. So I have an idea of what it is to be a mom, and I kill myself in order to be able to do that" (Puerto Rican female).

Participants reiterated their multiple responsibilities at work, at home, and with their parents but also with siblings and other extended family members. All too frequently, self-care practices to cope with these multiple responsibilities were not considered, which contributed to compromised physical and mental well-being. Preventive self-care strategies are important to ameliorate the consequences of stressful life demands and daily and chronic stressors. In the next section, strategies to manage and balance self-care and work and family demands are described.

## COPING BY SHIFTING THE PERSPECTIVE

The major coping strategies included shifting the perspective, having faith and spirituality, and using mental health services, coupled with resignation and passive coping (complaints and fear). A major set of coping strategies involved reframing perspectives and shifting values of the definitions of success. Not only is work-life balance more of a juggling act and one that often requires a prioritizing of one domain of life over another, it can inevitably contribute to adverse physical and mental effects. In order to adjust to the reality of academic work life, some participants reframed their expectations. Across racial/ethnic groups, a persistent concern around meeting the demands of the workplace was omnipresent. An African American female respondent described her shift in perspective as follows:

> Yeah, it's very interesting because I, in the past, I was more so in the mind-set of I want to be this top academic—it's like superstar academic, just does all this, and as I've continued through the pathway, I realized that I changed my values. There's just sort of things that were more important than that, and that was like family and things like that and just having a more balanced life.

Other respondents mirrored her comments:

> You can't be superman or superwoman forever and continuously. And I'm not willing—I'm interested in having a family. I'm not willing to sacrifice those things. I'm now there. I can say that. I couldn't say that a year ago or two years ago or three years ago. I'm not willing to sacrifice those things for the glory of saying I'm an associate professor, full professor at [a university], and I'm okay with that now. (Mexican American male)

> I do things like I put a lot of time into my child's school. I volunteer for everything. I'm the PTA president. . . . It's a lot of work, and if anything, I give up sleep, but I like it. It's rewarding. I think those things take my time, but they give back in terms of having some balance, having a sense that my job is not everything and that if I don't get a grant or if I don't get a paper published, it's not the end of the world. (Mexican American female)

Participants also described resolving pressure to prove their worth to others. An African American female respondent described the added expectation of being a URM faculty member and also a woman within the historically White male professoriate: "That's one of the attitude changes, too, that I think—from earlier, where I was like, 'Okay, I gotta prove to whoever this because I'm a woman or because I'm African American,' and those different things. Now I feel like, I mean, I actually believe in God. I believe that there's something higher than me that is in control, so if I don't make it, I don't make it. Like there's some other path for me, so I don't put as much—beating myself up about it, you know?" This respondent clearly drew on her faith to overcome the external pressures and adjust her expectations within academia. Similarly, participants indicated how shifting their perspectives to define new views about success changed their career trajectory. One Puerto Rican female respondent described, "It also happened because I gave up being director of the research center, and two people came to me and said, 'How can you give up your power?' and I said to them, 'My power is my power, it doesn't reside in my job,' and I realized that I had a point of view that was different from theirs in that I didn't feel that I was giving up my power. I was giving up this position, but I wasn't giving up my power. And so that awareness, and the idea that I didn't need to be a full professor, that wasn't part of my definition of success."

As respondents indicated, their shift in values stemmed from the unattainable work-life balance embedded in the academic work environment. As a Mexican American female summed up, "I've become more aware of the things that are important to me which is family and taking care of myself. And, again, that's something that came out of these not-so-happy experiences in academia. I put my heart and soul into it, and it wasn't giving me the things I needed, so I felt like I had to go somewhere else to feel fulfilled."

The effects of role strain were most injurious because many participants reported that they had to abandon self-care practices to fulfill other role demands. Mental health services were reported as critical resources to assist respondents in achieving work-family balance. These strategies ranged from positive to negative, such as soliciting the help of advocates who could listen to their concerns, to not exercising or going to yoga classes. The boundaries between work and family presented a serious conundrum. An African American female respondent spoke to the need for mental health care to initiate a balance in her work-family life: "To be honest, I've kind of said to myself, 'Maybe I need to do some type of therapy to kind of help myself find how to eke out these lines of demarcation with the family, the job, the social life and get some balance.'" An African American male echoed these concerns and partly in jest suggested year-round access to mental health services: "Well, beyond good mental health care, and good insurance that covers that [laughs], which I have, but most university programs that I'm aware of cover about—I can't remember if it's twenty sessions a year, but I mean, something like—kind of nuts. Like, you know, how about fifty-two? Give me one each week through the year, you know."

The majority of participants reported that role strains were taking a toll on their personal selves and family and social relations. Their inability to cope effectively was deeply embedded in a stressful workplace environment where participants expressed that the general environment was unwelcoming and lacked family supportive services, collegiality, and a general sense of support for their presence. Respondents' desire for a supportive work environment was not without reason. A Mexican American male described his experience as follows: "I think child care and those things are pathetic here at [the university]. Coming in, I was told these were things I could benefit from, but nothing is guaranteed here. . . . We have quality child care, but no one is guaranteed a slot."

In addition to participants not feeling as though they had the necessary access to supportive institutional policies, they also noted the negative perceptions of using the institutional policies they did have. The latter often expressed fear of even using institutional benefits. Similarly, an African American female described having to hide her family's health challenges: "Well it was difficult that when I first went on tenure track, which was 2004, and my significant other who's now my husband, had a stroke. I did not tell the people. I told one person who was down the hall from me, but I did not tell those that I worked with" (Castañeda et al., 2015; Castañeda & Isgro, 2013). These fears are associated with high visibility within research universities, perceptions of being "affirmation action" hires, and oftentimes less availability of economic assets such as family assistance or savings to supplement their salary to enhance family quality of life (Castañeda & Isgro, 2013; Turner & Myers, 2000). Even though they sometimes felt uncomfortable about using these policies, the overwhelming majority of respondents sought resolution in their institutional environments with supports.

## DESIRED INSTITUTIONAL RESOURCES: MONEY, TIME, AND CREDIT FOR ADDITIONAL SERVICE WORK

Participants identified four key areas related to institutional resources that would contribute to their ability to manage work and family obligations: resources for child care, equitable salary, faculty research grants and information and skills on how to successfully compete, and departmental support such as teaching assistants for large classes that would reduce their workload and aid in achieving work-family balance. Though respondents noted the importance of additional personal financial resources such as the ability to pay for the university day care center, their desired resources reflected the importance of having a departmental and institutional environment that was welcoming and generally supportive of their presence. As observed in prior chapters, respondents perceived their environment as unwelcoming and were self-vigilant about their behaviors and requests so as to not become more visible. However, participants also were cognizant of what was most needed for them to succeed in the workplace environment financially and in terms of professional development, as described in the next two quotes.

An African American female respondent stated, "Well, listen, if I had more money, then I could afford to hire help that would help me take care of [my son]. . . . And if I had course reduction or more assistance with teaching assistants in [my] department, those sorts of things. That can lighten the load as well." Similarly, another African American female respondent noted the required adjustments to time constraints: "I would love if there was some like publication grant, some kind of faculty development money. We could take a course or just to do something else, some type of additional incentive to help with the work. I mean I literally write so many proposals. I have so many irons that I'm just trying to figure out like, how do I do this? I feel like I'm in a trap. And it's a catch-22 that the teaching—I can't apply for opportunities unless I'm an assistant professor at an institution, but being assistant professor at this particular institution I can't get anything done." A Puerto Rican female noted the importance of the departmental work environment for allowing faculty to utilize their benefits. "Well I think I'll tell you one thing that definitely makes a difference is feeling like you have vacation time and you can take vacation. That's not always the case. So I think there certainly are places where you get the chance that yes, these are your benefits, and yes, you have personal time and vacation time, but you never feel comfortable taking time off." Similarly, an African American male commented on the importance of departmental support: "At work I would probably want the environment that I had at [prior university]. A supportive environment. An environment that enables me to succeed, like it does with others—like with my colleagues. So supportive work environment via my chair, program director, and dean I think would be quite helpful, what I don't have."

The inability to fully utilize available workplace resources increases workplace and family strains. Despite available work-family resources, many URM faculty report the fear of negative consequences on tenure and career progression when taking advantage of work-family policies related to child care, the birth of a child, or a family emergency (Reybold, 2014). Some barriers to using these policies included lack of a strong social network of peers in the department or college who can assume their classes, lack of connection and trust with the chair to negotiate a plan that would permit a full semester leave with pay, and fear to reinforce stereotypes of "less than competent" (Castañeda et al., 2015). These fears compounded workplace strain.

## SACRIFICED ON THREE PLATFORMS: RACE/ETHNICITY, CLASS, AND INTERGENERATIONAL LEGACIES

In conclusion, this study presents new information on the struggles of participants in maintaining a healthy work-family balance. The unique challenges faced by study participants—particularly related to unwelcoming workplace environments, covert racism, and legacies of family economic disadvantage—compound work-family balance. Moreover, participants described a lack of information on how to access work-family policies, their fears of being regarded as a challenging faculty member, and a lack of belonging within their collegial network. Respondents reported excessive work demands, particularly a racial/ethnic tax due to burdens of university, college, and departmental service on diversity committees. These findings extend prior work on family role strain and illustrate the additional stressors experienced by URM faculty as they navigate a difficult work environment and juggle multiple family roles including limited economic resources and caregiving obligations. Struggling to achieve balance and sacrifice as parents, caregivers, and employees were persistent sources of role strain. For the majority of participants, obligations to their family of origin were a source of both support and strain. Overall, the participants' narratives show the conflicts and tensions that permeate the management of work and family demands yet reveal a determination to achieve work success despite forms of excessive labor and the sacrificing of their personal well-being. Many participants were able to come to terms with their stressful lives and find peace in the midst of chaos. Other participants demonstrated acceptance of work-family tensions in the context of academia. Yet many respondents expressed fears of raising a "red flag," which demonstrates a perceived culture of fear rather than one of care (Castañeda et al., 2015; Thompson & Louque, 2005).

Throughout the life course, URM individuals, compared to their non-Hispanic White counterparts, are more likely to experience stressful life events, specific family and kin obligations, limited economic resources, and multiple forms of discrimination and microaggressions that exacerbate vocational strain in unwelcoming institutional environments (Sue, 2010). Safe spaces for Whites, such as workplaces and neighborhoods, may be additional sites of racial discrimination for URMs, including racial profiling for high SES minorities via their increased social interactions with Whites (Chávez, 2011; Feagin, 2010; Feagin & McKinney, 2003; Landry & Marsh, 2011). Black and Latino neighborhoods are largely less affluent and have fewer resources, such as public recreational spaces, than White neighborhoods (Charles, 2003; Pattillo-McCoy, 1999). These conditions may increase family and work role strain as URM professionals often need to engage in additional emotional labor (compared to their White colleagues) to navigate neighborhood settings to ensure the safety of their family members and assist in caregiving. All these factors contribute to a high-pressure environment that often squeezes out those who are unable or unwilling to reduce their time spent on family life (Mason & Goulden, 2002). These data show a set of important determinants and consequences of what it means to be a URM academic. What is described in the literature as role strain was dramatically described by respondents as sacrifice of family responsibilities and self or of work obligations. The data show that work overload was persistent in terms of excessive time demands, high diversity service demands, and immense pressure to publish. In addition, family-of-origin responsibilities and nuclear family demands commandeered additional time. Yet the coping resources were not readily available to overcome the emotional drain and workplace racial battle fatigue (Fasching-Varner & Albert, 2015). Work-family balance was further jeopardized by the lack of economic resources available to assist in caretaking and support of the family of origin, to outsource domestic labor, or to engage in extensive leisure time activities. In effect, work-family balance seemed like a fantasy due to exceptional demands and unwelcoming workplace environments.

An extraordinary institutional and national investment on work-family support has been observed over the past fifteen years. Work-family policies for faculty, regardless of race/ethnicity, often highlight that they provide resources and benefits for all, yet few address the barriers in accessing the available resources. The data suggest that an active pursuit of strategies to manage work, family, and personal selves is not enough if the cultural climate of the academic institution is discouraging. Two institutional investments to decrease workplace strain include transparent family-friendly support policies that are equitable and fair to minimize the power of academic gatekeepers who may not otherwise apply policies evenhandedly (Castañeda et al., 2015); and chairs serving as institutional agents to assist faculty with access to and use of work-family policies and additional resources related to vacation and accrued leave time. Investments in responsive policies, such as mentoring department chairs on how to implement family-responsive policies and managing with flexibility (UC Hastings College of the Law, n.d.), would contribute to improving institutional climate. Recruitment and retention are associated with an overall welcoming climate that includes attention to other important policies such as addressing domestic partnership, supporting the career of the faculty member's partner/spouse, eliminating salary inequity, and providing regular salary increases that are commensurate with market trends (Piercy et al., 2005). Contemporary family-work policies are moving in the right direction, but more specific attention to the needs of URM professionals is imperative. The ability to navigate multiple spheres of family life presents myriad challenges and, combined with relatively rigid professional career markers in unwelcoming environments, creates additional stressors. In the next chapter, institutional processes related to appointment, tenure, and promotion are presented to examine how study participants perceived and surmounted the obstacles.

# 7 · THE INTERSECTION OF HIRING, APPOINTMENT, TENURE, AND PROMOTION

## Is It Possible to Survive and Thrive?

> Every day, I walk a lonely walk down the long corridor that leads to my office, passing office after office inhabited by White colleagues who I may never really know, who cannot understand, and who would likely negate my lived experience with numerous examples of how they cannot possibly be racist. In the solace of my office, I often close my door and turn on some soul-nourishing music as I reflect on my experiences in this place. When I began my tenure as a professor of color in a predominately White university, I anxiously anticipated the reality that I would constantly be faced with attempts to devalue my expertise, to question my authority, and to put me in my place.
>
> —Tuitt, Hanna, Martinez, Salazar, and Griffin (2009, p. 67)

Professional observations and personal interactions with URM early career scholars jointly with study data show that many of them do not have knowledge of the institutional culture and norms of their academic workplace and/or their rights and responsibilities, beginning with hiring expectations and protocols. Ambiguity about formal and informal institutional rules is a source of stress for most, especially new faculty. The primary way faculty learn about their institutional culture is through interactions with colleagues and peers (Menges & Associates, 1999; Rice, Sorcinelli, & Austin, 2000). Yet feelings of discomfort, of being on the edges of their department, and of not belonging permeate the lives of many URM faculty. Although formal institutional culture is embedded in human resource policies and handbooks, the unwritten and informal rules are most important for faculty. For example, informal culture may prescribe how often faculty should be seen in their office working to be viewed as a "serious academic." Discretionary funds (and how to access them) and the number of publications required for tenure may also be a part of informal institutional culture. Deep questions that require serious consideration and institutional acknowledgment include the following: What are the rules URM faculty need to know to survive and thrive in an academic environment? How should they translate vague instructions such as "just work hard" and/or interpret the imprecise construct "intellectual contributions"? How is all that defined and interpreted and by whom?

The processes entailed in achieving tenure are complex and entrenched in life course meanings and experiences throughout the educational pathway. A robust body of scholarship clearly demonstrates that the social capital networks developed in college and graduate school are associated with success in recruitment, appointment, and tenure and promotion milestones. Drawing from prior studies, a survey, and narratives, the previous chapters provided an in-depth assessment of obstacles to academic career paths. Unequivocally, mentoring relationships, experiences of discriminatory and exclusionary practices, and managing work-family balance all weigh heavily on the achievement of successful career milestones. The ability to navigate institutional and departmental cultures, whether based on past experiences or institutional political advisors such as chairs, deans, senior mentors, and/or peers, plays a determinant role in securing tenure and/or promotion. This chapter probes the unique challenges that study participants reported in navigating the tenure and promotion processes successfully. In addition, the participants' dreams and aspirations, the obstacles they encountered in developing a place of belonging, the processes detailed in seeking tenure or promotion, and their reasons for staying or leaving the academy are explored.

Scholars attempting to explain reasons for low rates of hiring, retention, and promotion and to find solutions to the underrepresentation of URMs in institutions of higher learning have focused on several domains of interest: existing pathways of doctoral graduates seeking entry into the academy, departmental and university policies and procedures addressing recruitment, hiring and retention processes, and employment in industry or other private and public sectors that may explain the lower rates of URM faculty in colleges and universities (Hurtado, Eagan, Pryor, Whang, & Tran, 2012; Moreno, Smith, Clayton-Pedersen, Parker, & Teraguchi, 2006; Xie & Shauman, 1998). While each of these points of examination brings us closer to understanding underrepresentation and push for full inclusion, it is equally important to contextualize the factors associated with the processes of hiring, tenure, and promotion and the reported experiences of URM faculty. Significant challenges in seeking academic positions include the devaluing of research topics and methods; limited or no access to mentors and even less so to mentors who understand and value their work; and racial/ethnic or cultural taxation in engaging in diversity teaching and institutional service jointly with their own commitments often to "pay forward" and help the next generation of URM and other students. Yet institutions perhaps are not aware of the commitments, enthusiasm, and energy that many URM faculty bring to their departments or the sources of inspiration that propelled them forward and that they seek in their institution. These antecedents are important fountains of knowledge for institutions to build upon and nurture among URM faculty and others. Central questions for institutions to ask are these: Why did you want to enter the professoriate? What mattered to you?

The majority of respondents identified early sources of inspiration, a strong need to achieve, and role models of hard work, including parents, parents' friends, community members, and teachers and counselors during their elementary and secondary schooling years. Although they confronted financial, racial, and ethnic obstacles during those first twelve years, they endured to college, where many of the participants encountered professors who encouraged them to pursue graduate degrees. It was then that they discovered pathways to the professoriate and entry into the sacred halls of predominantly White institutions where many experienced a sense of alienation. Yet they were fiercely committed to the professoriate to help others and ensure the success of the next generation. They reported a strong commitment to engage in research that informs social change and produces knowledge to find solutions to social problems including poverty, prison reform, health inequity, and educational inequity, among others. Those who received fellowships often had no mentors or invitations to participate in faculty research; others were not funded and needed to work as graduate research assistants or elsewhere to pay for their tuition and expenses. Few received the social capital or political guidance to prepare them for faculty positions. In graduate school, they used multiple survival strategies such as staying below the radar, working excessively, treating those around them with deference, and resigning themselves to their difficult situation. A few opted to confront the blatant discrimination and racism they faced. The majority of study participants were not well prepared to engage the difficult process of being recruited, hired, and engaged as a faculty member. In fact, few understood the strategies to navigate the "hidden curriculum" of norms and expectation in their university setting. The following section presents a brief overview of the corpus of institutional dynamics, such as normative expectations and practices in recruitment, hiring, and tenure and promotion processes, as a context to interpret the narratives of participants.

## RECRUITMENT AND HIRING PREFERENCES

While higher education institutions have been striving to improve the hiring of diverse faculty, progress has been steady but relatively slow (Flaherty, 2015). Multiple challenges have been identified that hinder the successful hiring of URM faculty. Several barriers to hiring have been proffered by institutions such as the inability to identify qualified applicants. Informal systems of preference rather than qualifications and merit often dominate hiring decisions, and both attitudinal and structural barriers influence hiring (Smith, Turner, Osefi-Kofi, & Richards, 2004). For example, hiring barriers include some or all of the following: faculty candidates are eliminated based on which graduate school they attended (Gasman, Kim, & Nguyen, 2011), and positions are listed in traditional venues as opposed to racial/ethnic sections of professional organizations or journals (Adams & Bargerhuff, 2005; Price et al., 2005). Furthermore, *dysconscious racism* is invoked in explaining why search committees often prefer candidates with similar backgrounds, values, behaviors, and research interests.[1] Faculty perceptions of the bias and lack of departmental/institutional effort to recruit and hire URM faculty contribute negatively to faculty professional experiences in their institutions (Turner, 2002; Turner, González, & Wood, 2008). For example, while fewer than a third of all faculty (majority and URM) reported experiences of bias in most of the areas assessed, only half of all faculty felt recruitment and promotion were unbiased. However, URMs were significantly less likely than majority faculty to agree that faculty were recruited to their department in an unbiased manner (Price et al., 2009).

A common rationale for unsuccessful searches is the pipeline defense, which claims that the absence of URM faculty is due to a paucity of students obtaining doctoral degrees (Acosta-Belen & Bosen, 2012; Cross, 1994; Kayes, 2006). Although the numbers of URM graduate students have increased in the past decade, faculty hiring has not experienced parallel growth. In fact, the number of Latinos/as among full-time faculty has actually decreased (Acosta-Belen & Bosen, 2012). To explain this pipeline stagnation, scholars have offered varying arguments: underrepresented minority graduate students may not be encouraged to seek faculty careers and may not have the networks to get to these positions (Spalter-Roth, Mayorova, Shin, & White, 2011), universities may recruit faculty from other institutions including European universities, and elite institutions use the pipeline defense to limit recruitment of Black faculty to recent college graduates with less experience.[2] These hires may not be able to compete successfully with more experienced faculty due to absence of mentoring and undervalued research areas. Both these latter strategies dismiss problems of search committee cultures overtly and covertly undermining goals of faculty and staff diversity (Kayes, 2006).

Frequently URM faculty hires occur for positions related to the study of race or ethnicity through the use of special hiring interventions such as exceptional hires, search waivers, spousal hiring, targeted hiring for specific fields, modification of usual search requirements to meet program needs, shortened search process, cluster hiring, out-of-cycle hiring, and incentive funds of some sort. An overreliance on diversity indicators is associated with hiring interventions most likely to involve the study of race topics (Evans, 2007; Smith et al., 2004). Although these interventions can lead to increasing representation of URM faculty, overuse of these approaches can contribute to three detrimental outcomes: their ghettoization in racial/ethnic departments, low representation in traditional disciplines, and exclusion of faculty who engage in non-racial/ ethnic research. Moreover, the use of diversity interventions requires support and endorsement by department leadership and colleagues. Otherwise, the faculty member will be part of an unwelcoming department that can compromise his or her career (Smith et al., 2004). Unsurprisingly, diversity interventions are fraught with resistance by faculty and administrators who are deeply influenced by myths of inferior intelligence, unearned privileged, or the abandonment of perceived quality. These efforts often create unwelcoming climates and hostile departmental environments.

A common myth that hinders diversification efforts is the perception that search committees need to sacrifice quality to achieve diverse hires. Gasman et al. (2011) illustrate this point in a quote from a White female associate professor: "Diversity is like apple pie; most people would find it hard to say no to. However, there are some people who might say it's a bigger priority to have eminent [read White] scholars on our faculty" (p. 216).

This statement reflects majoritarian culture sentiments regarding the competence and potential of URM qualifications versus distinguished scholars, emphasizing the perception that URM faculty may lower the quality of the department due to having attended nonelite schools (Gasman et al., 2011). Although differences in race/ethnicity and institution of origin (Smith et al., 2004) have not been shown, definitions of quality tend to exclude nontraditional scholars' use of particular perspectives such as CRT and community-engaged and applied research methods, thereby denying academic career opportunities to many URM faculty (Light, 1994; Turner, 2002; Williams, Phillips, & Hall, 2014). In effect, the narrow definition of quality needs to be broadened to include multiple and diverse perspectives in research and teaching. Undoubtedly, broadening definitions of quality will encounter powerful resistance among faculty who want to hire candidates similar to them with traditional training and career trajectories (*Chronicle of Higher Education*, 2015). Distressingly, the Thomas Meyer study found that people will judge applicants differently based on their race, even if they have the same qualifications (Godsil, Tropp, Atiba Goff, & Powell,

2014). Majority-culture strategic resistance can and often does undermine the best-intentioned efforts. Institutional, departmental, and search committee cultures can overtly and covertly undermine the goal of faculty and staff diversity via implicit bias—that is, by simply including token minority scholars in the hiring pool, which does not result in hiring from underrepresented groups (Acosta-Belen & Bose, 2012; Kayes, 2006). If campuses don't have a positive climate for URM, it is equally difficult to recruit candidates (Flaherty, 2015). Candidates may become aware of high turnover rates and/or challenges URM faculty face, which may lead them to decline job offers. Even if a faculty member accepts the position, he or she may choose to leave, resulting in a "revolving door" for URM faculty due to the hostile institutional climate (Kayes, 2006). In effect, attitudes and perceptions represent central forces in climate creation and influence the hiring of faculty as well as their ability to thrive in the academic workplace.

Once a faculty member accepts an academic position, he or she often faces a tension between becoming incorporated into the institution and maintaining his or her unique personal identity (Turner, 2003). While integration into the institutional culture is key to improving access to resources, social networks, and research opportunities to accomplish the career goal of tenure and promotion, there are also personal and emotional costs. While remaining on the edge can allow for space for resistance to find and maintain one's voice, moving toward the center might put that voice at risk (Rockquemore & Laszloffy, 2008). In effect, tensions between professional marginalization and intersectional identity go beyond race/ethnicity (Stanley, 2006). Receiving and accepting an offer of employment is the beginning of a journey through unchartered terrain to tenure and promotion.

## THE MYSTERY OF TENURE AND PROMOTION PROTOCOLS

Tenure and promotion protocols are embedded in institutional practices, departmental culture, and demographic and political attitudes and perceptions of faculty peers. The academic work environment is the lived expression and result of departmental and institutional procedures that establish the norms and rewards for faculty engagement, participation, and retention. Though the practices that accompany the policies and procedures may not affect a given faculty member on a daily basis in the way that professional relationships and interpersonal dynamics do, departmental and institutional structures have a pervasive, embedded, and profound effect on the working environment (McDonald & Wingfield, 2009). Departmental and institutional policies and procedures that determine assessment procedures and tenure and promotion protocols are powerful mechanisms for shaping and reflecting the values of a department and/or institution with respect to diversity. Departmental norms inform what is considered legitimate scholarship (as judged by journal ranking and impact factor). Scholarly efforts on social problems such as low-income Mexican American female gangs or community violence are not perceived as highly innovative or creative work, and the results are less likely to be published in high-impact journals, generating what is oftentimes referred to as a crisis of legitimacy. The devalorization of their scholarly activity, negative student evaluations often arising from racial/ethnic dynamics, disproportionate time spent in the pedagogical activities of advising/mentoring URM and other students of color, diversity committee work, and community service hinder the achievement of tenure for URM faculty.

The criteria for tenure and promotion evaluation are all too often embedded in what majority-culture peers value as worthy. The unspoken criteria represent the unwritten rules and policies or the hidden curriculum of the tenure process (Laden & Hagedorn, 2000; Stanley, 2006; Turner & Meyers, 2000). Invisible criteria are complex and multilayered roadblocks and are best described by Ridgeway (2014) in her discussions of how the intersecting identities of race, class, ethnicity, and gender are inscribed in institutional power arrangements, influence the perceptions of peers, and inevitably exercise power over the outcomes of nontraditional academic subjects.

Three significant counterforces are at work in URM career advancement: unwritten and unspoken institutional expectations and norms, absence of consistent socialization in majority culture via mentoring, and a socially focused, nontraditional research agenda coupled with a strong commitment to service. URM faculty often experience challenges adjusting to the departmental and institutional culture, as cultural norms may differ or be unfamiliar from their own experiences. For example, one study explored the experiences of African American women faculty. The authors reported that participants found the institutional environment jarring and uncomfortable because they needed to promote their individual accomplishments and engage in competitive rather than collaborative strategies. Study participants employed different resistance strategies, including silence and disengagement, such as self-imposing isolation, in an attempt to cover up discomfort with this individualistic orientation (Patitu & Hinton, 2003). URM faculty may also perceive significantly more pressure than White early career faculty to conform to departmental colleagues in their political views (Trower & Bleak, 2004). Collegiality can be another source of discomfort; URM faculty have to prove and "overprove" their presence and worth in the academy, are aware of being held to a higher standard, and are not acknowledged when they make an effort to respond to all requirements (Stanley, 2006). Central to potential differences in perspectives is the importance of a bridging agent or mentor to guide URM faculty in the adjustment to institutional or departmental culture.

Preparation for tenure and promotion processes requires steady and clear guidance once a faculty member is hired. URM faculty oftentimes need additional guidance due to prior life course experiences of limited or absent academic career path mentoring. Though many studies have revealed the importance of mentorship to faculty professional success, access to mentoring relationships and professional networks designed to support and enhance faculty success is more limited for URMs (Aguirre, Martinez, & Hernandez, 1993; Diggs, Garrison-Wade, Estrada, & Galindo, 2009; Price et al., 2005). Faculty professional development programs as well as mentoring opportunities have been cited as important in helping faculty develop their political and professional understanding of the path to tenure and the process for sharing accomplishments to gain access to additional opportunities for advancement (Diggs et al., 2009; Turner et al., 2008). However, as Price and colleagues (2009) found, only one-third of all (majority and URM) faculty believed networking was inclusive of ethnic minorities, women, and foreign-born faculty. URM faculty were three times less likely to believe that networking opportunities and mechanism included minorities (see chapter 4 for mentoring discussion). The rules and power relations involved in the tenure and promotion process operate in masked ways that rationalize racism, sexism, and classism in order to screen out persons who do not fit the academy's designation of who and what the faculty should be. A central guideline in the process of tenure is creative, intellectual achievement combined with a nebulous notion of institutional fit into the "departmental culture." Notwithstanding this ambiguous term, the quality and quantity of the dossiers vary dramatically depending on what individual is being judged and the nature of the work. Frequently, as Agathangelou and Ling (2002) conclude, the bureaucratic guidelines often serve as a pretext for spurious reasoning that allows tenure and promotion committees to defend their positions citing adherence to guidelines often not applied to majority faculty. Beyond the judgment evoked by quality and quantity of the scholarship, other important considerations are often omitted yet counted on for departmental administrative service. For example, majority peers generally have a more privileged position whereby they do not usually have the same responsibilities or commitments such as community-engaged research or advising and mentoring URM students, nor do they confront the discriminatory practices in teaching and colleagueship that URM faculty face. A consistent burden that URM confront is being the face of diversity in all areas of the university and their legitimacy being interrogated in all spheres of their academic life. In other words, university and departmental service in conjunction with pedagogical activities (advising and mentoring) are viewed as integral to faculty obligations and as good citizenship. However, since diversity service, informal and/or formal advising, and mentoring students are not heavily weighted in the tenure and promotion process, majority-culture faculty can select their set of obligations, while URM faculty often perceive pressure to not only serve a "diversity role" in the department and on behalf of the department but also to assist with racial/ethnic students who are often ignored or are lost in large departments or the university. The push and pull to serve the interests of the university and the department often takes a heavy toll on URMs' time for scholarship.

## DEMANDS AND PERCEPTIONS OF FACULTY SCHOLARSHIP, TEACHING, AND SERVICE

Challenges to the legitimization and valuing of their work in research, teaching, and service as well as additional demands and responsibilities related to their role as representatives of their racial/ethnic group are ever present. Participants also reported that their love of teaching and their contributions to service often explain their persistence in the academy, providing inspiration and passion and fueling many URM scholars in the face of challenging work environments. However, their aspirations are often deflated by the devaluation of scholarly research interests, approaches, and theoretical frameworks (Diggs et al., 2009; Laden & Hagedorn, 2000; Turner et al., 2008) as well as unrealistic expectations that they uphold all of their academic responsibilities while also responding to often excessive service and committee responsibilities as representatives of their racial/ethnic group (Brayboy, 2003; Thompson & Louque, 2005). Pressure to "implement diversity" through specific forms of service, not usually performed by White faculty or foreign-born faculty, can be detrimental to professional advancement as these service activities are not given serious weight in evaluation, tenure, and promotion, take time, and detract from their ability to meet other scholarly responsibilities (Cook & Gibbs, 2009; Turner et al., 2008). In addition, those who teach diversity courses report that their work is seen as less valuable and less rigorous by their peers, and their authority and credibility are challenged by students in the classroom (Moore, Acosta, Perry, & Edwards, 2010). Teaching and research in diversity can result in being typecast as an "ethnic specialist" rather than a qualified expert in one's discipline, leading to greater dissatisfaction among URM faculty due to expectations to handle minority affairs and speak as a minority expert and to represent the university in service activities.

Service activities include advising and mentoring URM and other students of color from other departments in addition to their departmental advisees, serving on strategic planning committees and McNair and Mellon scholarship selection committees, engaging in multicultural community events and activities, and serving on multicultural or diversity committees (Eddy & Gaston-Gayles, 2008; Evans, 2007; Harley, 2008; Harlow, 2003; Hendrix, 2007; Johnson &

Harvey, 2002; Tippeconnic Fox, 2005; Turner, 2002; Williams, 2015; Williams et al., 2014). This phenomenon is commonly referred to as cultural taxation or the racial/ethnic tax. URM female faculty may be especially vulnerable to this cultural taxation, as they tend to mentor students more than do their male colleagues (Blackwell, Snyder, & Mavriplis, 2009; Boyd, Cintrón, & Alexander-Snow, 2010). Although service activities may help alleviate isolation and enhance a sense of community on campus (Stanley, 2006), they decrease time spent on research, place extra stress on URM faculty, and extract personal costs (Griffin & Reddick, 2011). Although the university and department oftentimes benefit from the service-related activities of URM faculty, including increasing diversity visibility while decreasing the service workload of majority faculty, diversity service is not valued in promotion and tenure processes.

A significant career disadvantage of overparticipation in diversity activities is having little opportunity to participate in nonminority affairs at the departmental level. Engagement in departmental and college committees provides inclusion and learning in mainstream decision-making sectors rather than being pigeonholed as institutional buffers with the minority community both on and off campus. Importantly, the lack of opportunity to participate in nonminority affairs decreases access to the high-level network alliances and power structures that are responsible for the decision-making that shapes department policies and procedures and determines resource allocation. By decreasing opportunities for faculty involvement across contexts, the institution succeeds in making faculty both visible and invisible and strips faculty of any real voice or power (Aguirre et al., 1993). The research reviewed has begun to unravel the mystery of hiring, tenure, and promotion procedures and how outcomes are powerfully impacted by workplace climate, especially social networks and collegial relationships, unspoken expectations and attributions of expertise (Boyd et al., 2010; Eddy & Gaston-Gayles, 2008; Johnson & Harvey, 2002; Patitu & Hinton, 2003), and the assignment of diversity teaching and service responsibilities that may undermine the intellectual responsibilities required for career advancement.

The combined impact of these practices in the academic work environment exerts a powerful effect on faculty satisfaction, retention, and tenure and promotion. URM faculty are significantly less likely than majority faculty (42.6 percent vs. 70.5 percent) to report intentions to be at their current institution in five years. A combination of individual characteristics, work-life issues, and satisfaction predicts faculty intentions to leave their institution or career (Rosser, 2004). Individual characteristics such as gender and racial/ethnic minority status and rank are strong predictors of faculty satisfaction and intentions to leave. Female faculty are significantly less satisfied than male faculty, and ethnic minority faculty status is positively related to intentions to leave. The negative experience of distinctiveness and its manifestation in the workplace mediate the relationship between racial/ethnic/gender status and satisfaction (Niemann & Dovidio, 1998), with stigmatization and tokenization contributing to faculty leaving (Thompson & Louque, 2005). In addition, an inability to connect with mentors to help navigate the institutional, departmental, and discipline demands, limited networking opportunities, and inadequate retention efforts also contribute to URM faculty attrition, through hindering faculty success (Cook & Gibbs, 2009). Tensions between becoming integrated into the institutional culture of their department while maintaining their identities permeate their lived experiences. At both the departmental and institutional levels, participants report and support prior evidence on the importance of colleagues, allies, networks, and the social climate in general (Turner et al., 2008; Vasquez et al., 2006). In summary, upon entering academic positions, one of the most significant aspects affecting professional success and satisfaction is the kind of climate, culture, and collegiality that they encounter. These three factors most determine their satisfaction with work and capacity to succeed and their achievement of career milestones as teachers, scholars, and members of the academic community (Trower, 2009). The organizational determinants of career success have received limited attention, with an unwavering focus on individual characteristics. The following section describes the educational preparation of study respondents and their perceptions of how facilitative academic institutional settings are. These data provide rich insights into what has often been referred to as "institutional fit."

## WHO ARE THE PARTICIPANTS? TALENTED WITH ELITE ACADEMIC PREPARATION

Table 7.1 displays respondent educational and employment characteristics and mean scale scores by race and ethnicity on role ambiguity scale and work hours. The overwhelming majority of participants (96.7 percent) received their doctorate in public and private research universities. Puerto Ricans spent significantly more time in their doctorate program than did Mexican Americans ($M = 7.2, SD = 2.4$ vs. $M = 5.3, SD = 1.9$). More than 80 percent of all participants received postdoctoral training at a very high or high research activity institution (82.8 percent), with an average of 2.2 years ($SD = 1.29$) in postdoctoral training.

The majority of participants were new hires, with 58.0 percent at their current institution for less than six years. African American males and Mexican American females were the most likely to be assistants, while American Indian / Alaska Native and Puerto Rican females were the most likely to be associate professors. Close to 30 percent of respondents were in the social sciences, 20 percent were in the arts and humanities, and close to 10 percent were in STEM-related fields and education. On average, the completion of the doctoral program took a little

(continued)

TABLE 7.1 Education and employment characteristics by race/ethnicity

| Variable | Total sample (N = 568) | African American (n = 333; 58.6%) | Mexican American (n = 134; 23.6%) | Puerto Rican (n = 76; 13.4%) | American Indian / Alaska Native (n = 25; 4.4%) |
|---|---|---|---|---|---|
| **Doctorate: type of institution** | | | | | |
| *Public* | | | | | |
| Very high / high / doctoral research activity | 288 | 158 | 77 | 38 | 15 |
| | (64.6) | (59.8) | (76.2) | (64.6) | (68.2) |
| *Private* | | | | | |
| Very high / high / doctoral research activity | 143 | 99 | 19 | 18 | 7 |
| | (32.1) | (37.5) | (18.8) | (30.5) | (31.8) |
| Other | 15 | 7 | 5 | 3 | — |
| | (3.4) | (2.7) | (5) | (5.1) | |
| **Postdoctorate: type of institution** | | | | | |
| *Public* | | | | | |
| Very high / high / doctoral research activity | 83 | 45 | 23 | 8 | 7 |
| | (49.1) | (45.5) | (67.6) | (32) | (63.6) |
| *Private* | | | | | |
| Very high / high / doctoral research activity | 57 | 38 | 5 | 13 | 1 |
| | (33.7) | (38.4) | (14.7) | (52) | (9.1) |
| Other | 29 | 16 | 6 | 4 | 3 |
| | (17.2) | (16.2) | (17.6) | (16) | (27.3) |

TABLE 7.1   Education and employment characteristics by race/ethnicity (*continued*)

| Variable | Total sample (N = 568) | African American (n = 333; 58.6%) | Mexican American (n = 134; 23.6%) | Puerto Rican (n = 76; 13.4%) | American Indian / Alaska Native (n = 25; 4.4%) |
|---|---|---|---|---|---|
| **Years of postdoctoral training** | | | | | |
| 1 year | 55 | 34 | 8 | 8 | 5 |
| | (30.7) | (32.1) | (22.2) | (22.2) | (45.5) |
| 2 years | 74 | 41 | 18 | 13 | 2 |
| | (41.3) | (38.7) | (50) | (50) | (18.2) |
| 3–4 years | 37 | 23 | 8 | 4 | 2 |
| | (20.7) | (31.7) | (22.2) | (15.4) | (18.2) |
| 5+ years | 13 | 8 | 2 | 1 | 2 |
| | (7.3) | (7.5) | (5.6) | (3.8) | (18.2) |
| **Mean years in postdoctoral training** | | | | | |
| M | 2.2 | 2.2 | 2.4 | 1.9 | 2.4 |
| SD | 1.29 | 1.33 | 1.30 | 0.95 | 1.64 |
| **Time at current institution (web-based only)** | | | | | |
| <6 years | 279 | 158 | 77 | 33 | 11 |
| | (58.0) | (54.7) | (68.8) | (56.9) | (50.0) |
| 7–14 years | 130 | 75 | 24 | 21 | 10 |
| | (27.0) | (26.0) | (21.4) | (36.2) | (45.5) |
| 15+ years | 72 | 56 | 11 | 4 | 1 |
| | (15.0) | (19.4) | (9.8) | (6.9) | (4.5) |

| 9-month or 12-month appointment | | | | | |
|---|---|---|---|---|---|
| Years in PhD program (qualitative only) | | | | | |
| M | 6.1 | 6.0 | 5.3* | 7.2* | 6.0 |
| SD | 2.1 | 1.7 | 1.9 | 2.4 | 2.8 |
| Joint appointment (yes responses only) | 123 | 72 | 23 | 21 | 7 |
| | (24.4) | (23.5) | (20.4) | (33.9) | (30.4) |
| Serves an administrative position (yes responses only) | 386 | 237 | 85 | 46 | 18 |
| | (76) | (76.5) | (75.22) | (74.2) | (78.3) |

NOTE: These data include both web-based and qualitative data of total study participants. Values in parentheses are percentages.

*$p < .05$.

more than six years. Surprisingly, about 75 percent served in some administrative capacity, which shows that many early career scholars were engaged in non-research activity, which represents a potential barrier to career advancement. Yet only 25 percent reported a twelve-month appointment, and about 24.4 percent held a joint appointment, which similarly suggests that many work twelve months without economic remuneration, respond to two departmental requirements, and most likely have less time and resources to conduct research. These activities most likely impact research productivity and in turn achieving successful tenure and promotion benchmarks.

Table 7.2 presents data on participants' understanding of priority of role obligations (role ambiguity scale). The majority of participants understood what their responsibilities were and how they were evaluated, with a slightly lower mean for what was expected by the chair and dean. American Indian / Alaska Natives were less likely than their racial/ethnic counterparts to report developing priorities and understanding the criteria on which they were evaluated ($M = 3.2$).

A strong investment of time was observed in the data. Approximately one-third (30.2 percent) of the respondents reported an average of 11 to 20 hours per week on research, while close to 40 percent reported 21 or more hours per week on research activity. Teaching represented a significant portion of time, with 40.6 percent of respondents reporting 11 to 20 hours of teaching per week and about 24 percent reporting more than 21 hours. One-third (31.1 percent) reported 6 to 10 hours of university service, and slightly more than a quarter (29.3 percent) devoted 6 to 10 hours to other professional activities. Interestingly, teaching and university service show a pattern similar to research time allocation, which suggests less time for research. Overall, these data suggest multiple demands on academic personnel and the need for support from peers and institutional agents in order to achieve success in such a demanding environment.

Study participants were unequivocally highly qualified, well trained at elite institutions, and meritorious. This being the case, it would be expected that institutions and departments would welcome these early career scholars and facilitate their navigation through the institutional maze. (See the table in appendix A for a description of the scales.) Although study participants performed their responsibilities with devotion, their interpersonal and institutional interactions were not perceived as welcoming, nor were their peers and senior colleagues perceived as supportive.

**TABLE 7.2** Role ambiguity scale items and self-report of hours worked per week by race/ethnicity

| | Total sample (N = 568) | African American (n = 333; 58.6%) | Mexican American (n = 134; 23.6%) | Puerto Rican (n = 76; 13.4%) | American Indian / Alaska Native (n = 25; 4.4%) |
|---|---|---|---|---|---|
| **Role ambiguity scale items** | | | | | |
| The priorities of my job are clear to me | | | | | |
| M | 4.0 | 4.0 | 3.9 | 4.2 | 3.6 |
| SD | 1.03 | 1.03 | 1.01 | 0.93 | 1.33 |
| I have a clear understanding of how my department chair/dean wants me to spend my time | | | | | |
| M | 3.5 | 3.6 | 3.4 | 3.7 | 3.4 |
| SD | 1.22 | 1.22 | 1.23 | 1.27 | 1.14 |
| I know the basis on which I am evaluated | | | | | |
| M | 3.6 | 3.6 | 3.6 | 3.8 | 3.2 |
| SD | 1.25 | 1.29 | 1.15 | 1.25 | 1.34 |
| **Number of hours worked per week by area of responsibility** | | | | | |
| **Research** | | | | | |
| 0–10 | 152 | 103 | 27 | 18 | 4 |
| | (31.2) | (34.9) | (24.5) | (30.0) | (18.1) |

*(continued)*

TABLE 7.2   Role ambiguity scale items and self-report of hours worked per week by race/ethnicity (*continued*)

| | Total sample (N = 568) | African American (n = 333; 58.6%) | Mexican American (n = 134; 23.6%) | Puerto Rican (n = 76; 13.4%) | American Indian / Alaska Native (n = 25; 4.4%) |
|---|---|---|---|---|---|
| 11–20 | 147 | 82 | 39 | 17 | 9 |
| | (30.2) | (27.7) | (35.4) | (28.3) | (40.9) |
| 21–30 | 106 | 60 | 31 | 11 | 4 |
| | (21.8) | (20.3) | (28.2) | (18.3) | (18.2) |
| 31 + | 82 | 50 | 13 | 14 | 5 |
| | (16.8) | (16.9) | (11.8) | (23.3) | (22.7) |
| *Teaching* | | | | | |
| 0–10 | 173 | 107 | 35 | 26 | 5 |
| | (35.3) | (35.8) | (31.8) | (43.3) | (23.8) |
| 11–20 | 199 | 113 | 52 | 22 | 12 |
| | (40.6) | (37.8) | (47.3) | (36.7) | (57.1) |
| 21+ | 118 | 79 | 23 | 12 | 4 |
| | (24.1) | (26.4) | (20.9) | (20.0) | (19.0) |
| *University service* | | | | | |
| <5 | 221 | 133 | 52 | 25 | 11 |
| | (47.1) | (46.7) | (49.1) | (43.9) | (52.4) |
| 6–10 | 146 | 86 | 34 | 18 | 8 |
| | (31.1) | (30.2) | (32.1) | (31.6) | (38.1) |

| | Total sample (N = 568) | African American (n = 333; 58.6%) | Mexican American (n = 134; 23.6%) | Puerto Rican (n = 76; 13.4%) | American Indian / Alaska Native (n = 25; 4.4%) |
|---|---|---|---|---|---|
| 11+ | 102 | 66 | 20 | 14 | 2 |
| | (21.7) | (23.2) | (18.9) | (24.6) | (9.5) |
| *Outside professional activities* | | | | | |
| <3 | 109 | 70 | 21 | 14 | 4 |
| | (27.3) | (29.1) | (23.8) | (27.4) | (19.0) |
| 4–5 | 130 | 76 | 31 | 19 | 4 |
| | (32.5) | (31.6) | (35.2) | (37.2) | (19.0) |
| 6–10 | 117 | 69 | 29 | 12 | 7 |
| | (29.3) | (28.7) | (33.0) | (23.5) | (33.3) |
| 11+ | 44 | 25 | 7 | 6 | 6 |
| | (11.0) | (10.4) | (8.0) | (11.8) | (28.6) |

NOTE: For the role ambiguity scale, only web-based participants are included, *n* = 508. Data include participants who responded *often/usually/true most of the time.* Other data include both web-based and qualitative data of total study participants. Values in parentheses are percentages.

## NARRATIVES OF LIVED EXPERIENCES: THE PAIN OF BELONGING

To extend our knowledge of the perceptions of respondents in preparing for tenure (among assistant professors) and promotion (among associate professors), questions were asked with probes about perceptions of the process. For all respondents, questions were asked about future plans and aspirations. Questions for assistant professors included the following: "Describe your experience and/or plans for the tenure and promotion process. (Do you think it will be a difficult process? Why or why not?) What type of resources and supports do you have to help you through this process?" Those for associate professors included the following: "Describe your experience in the tenure and promotion process. (Was it a difficult process? Please explain.) What type of resources and supports did you have to help you through the process?" A second set of questions assessed future career plans: "What are your future academic dreams and aspirations? Do you aspire to become a full professor? How difficult do you think that will be? Why? In the future do you aspire to any sort of academic administrative position, such as department chair? Or somewhere outside the academy? Do you aspire to a career outside the academy?" The following sections highlight expectations and perceptions of tenure and promotion processes, resources used, workplace responsibilities and demands, and future aspirations and plans.

## TENURE PREPARATION AND ANTICIPATION: "GOING BY THE BOOK" OR "LOCKDOWN DIRTY BRAWL"

Data analyses revealed several themes: fear, anxiety, and the unknown. Overall, respondents reported that they were unsure of what to expect and how to find the right balance in terms of work, departmental, and institutional effort without "going crazy." Four major themes characterize the process: (1) expectations that the tenure process would be difficult, with associate professors expecting it to be a repeated "nightmare"; (2) lack of transparency coupled with fear and mistrust of fairness and equity in the process; (3) perceptions that the process was political and that the nature of their work and contribution would be undermined in different ways by other faculty and committee members; and (4) the importance of institutional agents (chairs and deans) as resources of support who really made the difference in their ability to successfully negotiate departmental "rules" and achieve tenure and promotion.

For many respondents, the initial years entailed excessive hours of work and building research and collaborative networks within the department and across campus. The overwhelming majority of participants expressed strong commitments to research, teaching, and university and community service. The overwhelming majority also saw their future as being within the academy. Overall, participants reported working very hard, and yet they were not clear about the expectations for periodic reviews and tenure even after they read the faculty handbook or sought clarification.

One African American female discussed how when she was coming up for a review she "was dropped in the middle" by her mentor, and when she asked what she should submit, she was told her CV. The respondent described the communication exchanges and the lack of information she received prior to submitting her dossier: "So I thought that's all I have to send. I'm thinking it was just reviewed in house. So I didn't know the process. My chair didn't know the process. The person who was supposed to be my mentor didn't tell us the process. When I came up for the tenure process, I wanted everything to go by the book, because I know that these people will then say oh I missed this and I didn't do that. I wasn't going to allow anybody—I had worked too hard to get this."

Many nontenured respondents were more cautious yet expressed more optimism. Many reported that they knew what to do—publish—but many also reported getting mixed signals and a lack of certainty about what really counted in the end. One Mexican American male stated, "You send out the signals that show people you are doing things. And then it can be read in different ways. 'Why are you doing that? You should be doing this.' And the other person says, 'Oh that's an important committee to be on. Very good.' The other person says, 'Oh you're wasting your time.' I can't please everybody, so I just kind of weigh it all out and move forward. There's no template. Everyone's done it differently—and so that's a little stressful around expectations."

Many respondents reported that the expectations for promotion and tenure were confusing and not clearly defined, which other researchers have also found (Boyd et al., 2010; Eddy & Gaston-Gayles, 2008; Johnson & Harvey, 2002). Specifically, respondents cited conflicting information, unwritten rules, and the absence of mentoring and direction from others about the promotion and tenure process (Patitu & Hinton, 2003). Additionally, URM faculty, who may be more isolated and marginalized, tend to lack the communication networks to receive this information informally (Johnson & Harvey, 2002). Overwhelmingly, lack of transparency generated strong feelings of mistrust that exacerbated the tenure and promotion processes. Participants expressed mistrust of colleagues who ignored them and then made judgments about them, while others feigned friendship and then turned on them. The process of promotion was described by several participants as a "nightmare" and a "horrible experience." An African American female participant observed, "No one prepares you for [promotion]. I mean it doesn't sound like fun on paper but it was a nightmare. It was just an awful process. The whole time these people are ignoring you, not paying attention to you and then all of a sudden they put you under this microscope . . . and you know this is going to happen but you have no idea how awful an experience it is going to be."

One Mexican American female told her story about her concern regarding fairness and equity in her departmental review after a senior faculty member pulled her aside to inform her that two faculty were arguing against her tenure: "I was blown away. I thought, Wow. I've done what I was told to do. I managed to get the publications in the top journals of our top tier. I did it and I'm going what? Why? What's there to complain about? He's telling me well, some have questions about whether your book should count for tenure. I'm going, huh? What?"

A similar narrative of surprise was relayed by an African American male respondent. He explained how the unexpected challenge during a tenure and promotion process occurred in which a published book lost its luster when the committee decided to focus on teaching evaluations. This surprise almost derailed his career path. He reflected on this incident: "But that changed the way I saw my department, that it didn't matter that in faculty meetings I didn't make a fuss. It doesn't matter that I do my work. They use my teaching and then they try to say something about my being published in such and such a press that was referred to as alternative. So they kind of just started making things up and when I saw that, I was like, 'Wow these folks are really out here to get me' kind of thing. Then they looked at my grade distribution which they had never done anywhere in the department."

Overriding themes in the data and scholarly literature are flagrant ethical violations in the devaluing of scholarship, accomplishments, and good academic citizenship during the tenure and/or promotion process, even after meeting all the university and departmental guidelines, and implicit and explicit expectations. These discriminatory practices are exercised in myriad ways such as "making up new criteria," using "coded words" (areas of focus that have not been applied equitably across the board), or simply stating that a well-known university press is an alternative press, as in the case referenced above. For these reasons, many faculty who were consciously/unconsciously aware of these strategies wanted everything to "go by the book." One Mexican American female proffered her opinion on the tenure process: "I think it is also a political process, and because it is a political process, I'm not quite sure how to play that game." This point is well illustrated by an African American male in deciphering the political process or the power of the committee: "So I can point to the metrics and say, 'This is what other folks have had, and this is what I have.' And they can always use the statement that they have, that he's yet to show sustained productivity or productivity. Who knows what that means?"

The constant fear and concern of equitable practice was countered by other participants who expressed a plea for fairness in evaluative assessments of their scholarship:

> I'm really hoping that guidelines will be more reflective of the kind of work that I do and reflect community-engaged scholarship. (Mexican American female)

> The issues with promotion and tenure, I think that it's been clearly along the lines of some racial discrimination. (African American male)

A Puerto Rican male captured the collective perceptions of the participants:

> Again there is a weird double standard, because the last person who came up for tenure, he ended up with two peer-review journal articles and one book that wasn't even published by the time he submitted his package. So the question is how you compare that work, that amount of work for somebody who had twice the amount of time that I had to complete this work with my package, which is four times larger than his.

A high sense of vigilance toward procedural protocol was observed to ensure that their hard work was rewarded and their career milestones achieved. Many of the participants shared their experiences of witnessing vastly different portfolios, and these experiences raised questions of what constitutes meritoriousness. The ever-lingering questions of defining tenure-worthy creative intellectual contributions and attaining the "good citizen label" without unbearable stress were omnipresent. As a result, many were unable to decipher the rules, but did understand that they were political and depended on key gatekeepers who could assist them. All participants acknowledged that publications were key, grants and funding were extremely helpful, teaching evaluations had to be adequate, and excessive work was required. However, many perceived that they had "to have more, be more and work more" than comparable non-URM peers to attain the same milestone.

Even acknowledging these perceived biases, they yearned for some reassurance from institutional agents or gatekeepers, whom they knew had influence in the decisions, that their dossiers were adequate or met the departmental expectations and that they were on the right track. Chairs and deans repeatedly refused to meet with early career scholars to discuss what they needed, and some chairs stated that they did not know the process involved in tenure and promotion. Two male respondents felt the anxiety of lack of support from a chair and a dean:

In terms of plans for tenure and promotion, yes it will be difficult, particularly in this department where I do not feel the support of my chair, although I have the support of the faculty. The chair is really important. (Puerto Rican male)

[The dean] wouldn't meet with me, and when he met with me in his office, with his feet upon his desk. . . . I don't think that would have happened with a colleague who was White. (African American male)

For those who reported a process that was not too difficult, a chair or a dean served as a point of support and guidance in how to navigate the process. One female mentioned, "My department has told me what my timeline is for promotion. In that way, they're supportive. They want me to be promoted. . . . Obviously they think I belong here" (Native American female). Another respondent stated, "Well, the dean is very supportive as far as him being upfront and telling you what you need to do to get tenure and what you need to do to be successful at the school. . . . I would say he has a good batting average. He tells you how it is and tells you exactly what you need to do in certain ways. So that's great" (Mexican American female).

Uneasiness in their perceived sense of (un)belonging and concerns that the themes of their research would not be well received were demoralizing. The participants expressed strong passion and commitment to their scholarship, teaching, and service. Respondents spoke to the opportunity to give forward and participate in the campus community, although many realized it did not count. Fretting about their community service counting and the long hours they invested in helping students was paramount in their minds. One participant noted, "I just think I am going to get hung up in the service area. I think that's where they will get me. . . . My outside steering committee assignments they don't think that I make a contribution" (African American female).

Another African American male discussed the conundrum of the larger importance of service, as he was aware of community and economic disadvantage and his own ability to ameliorate some of the determinants of that disadvantage. Yet it was also understood that this service had little value in the work log. He stated, "I think service means a lot, a different thing for minority faculty, if you do work in the community, it's just part and parcel of what you do, you know, and you really are penalized for that because there's just no way around it . . . you're doing it and you're going to do it. You can't not do it. . . . And there's just no reward for that within the academy."

Overall there was a strong commitment to those communities that were disadvantaged, and the overwhelming majority of respondents wanted to give back to their communities of origin. Moreover, participants wanted to promote change and make a difference in the world through their scholarship, teaching, and service. The point is best illustrated by one Puerto Rican male who, when asked why he was an academic, responded, "I want my life to make a difference."

Prior studies have illustrated that majority-culture and non-URM faculty do less diversity service work and teaching than URM scholars, which extends time for their regular faculty obligations. Invisible forms of additional workload include serving on more committees; teaching diversity courses (as URM faculty are assumed to have expertise in this area); helping local communities; mentoring URM students and faculty, or other racial/ethnic or White students who want to do a diversity project; and educating majority-culture White faculty, administrators, and students about diversity (Brayboy, 2003; Stanley, 2006). These service activities present a conundrum: they are time-consuming and do not count in the overall assessment of tenure and promotion, but they reveal the powerful commitment and dedication that respondents had for their research, students, and community. What an unrecognized gift to higher education. However, workplace strain and role overload may be major determinants of low retention and physical and mental health conditions among URM faculty. In spite of these difficulties and uncertain career paths, respondents remained entrenched in their avocation to serve others and promote socially focused, high-quality scholarship through the professoriate.

## LEAVE OR REACH THE ACADEMIC MILESTONES

The question of their aspiration to leave or reach full professor was for many a quandary. Assistant professors' plans were short range: "My professional goals are strictly focused on gaining tenure here at this institution" (Mexican American, male). An African American female shared that her plan "is to get [tenure]." A significant number of associate professors discussed the pathway to the administration so that they could change the institutional culture and open pathways for other URM students and faculty. There was hesitancy about the process to attain full professorship yet a desire to follow the steps to reach it. For example, one early career Mexican American female stated, "I think for me, becoming a full professor would be that I did it because I was good . . . not because it's going to . . . give you stature. It gives you credibility. It gives you a higher salary. But it would be the satisfaction of knowing that I could compete in an academic world that's both political and intellectual." Others specifically wanted to achieve full professorship to help others succeed and ensure fairness:

> So I can make an effort on making certain that processes are done objectively and there are more efforts to retain URM groups in academia. They come, but they leave quickly, usually less than the three-year period. (African American male)

Potentially I'd like to be a full professor just because when bad things happen, I can try and help the next group. (Mexican American female)

Others felt somewhat discouraged because early on in their careers they had engaged in extensive administrative duties and were assessing if they could "catch up" and do the type of intellectual work required to meet the criteria. This was particularly the case for associate professors who "felt stuck" because they had assumed administrative positions for additional compensation but often-times spent considerable amounts of time pleading for additional resources from superiors and/or a commitment to build an alternative structure (Dill, 2009). Undoubtedly, these participants felt committed to their research, students, and communities and repeatedly inspired themselves with the hope of having an impact on the lives of others. Institutional agents often ask early and midca-reer faculty to serve in administrative roles, such as graduate director, assistant director of a center, or administrator of a new diversity initiative, that provide no intellectual or social capital rewards but fulfill a departmental "diversity" obliga-tion or relieve a senior faculty member of administrative work. As experience dictates, URM faculty are hesitant to say no to superiors in environments where they consistently have to prove their merit and good will. Sources of discontent included a lack of administrative support, being expected to be the "minority" expert, and perceptions of inequitable salary. Concerns about salary, financial pressures ("just scraping by after sacrificing so much"), and self-questioning as to whether academia was the best place to have an impact were all considerations.

The respondents all wanted to stay or reach in spite of the obstacles. Their major reasons for staying were two: to open pathways for the next generation of URM faculty and students and to contribute to solving local community con-cerns and giving voice to those who are silent. Many participants echoed the sentiment that they wanted to serve as a voice for less privileged communi-ties. A respondent discussed his relationship to his area of research: "So I see myself having a significant impact on the communities that I study. I don't think I would have gotten into this work if I wasn't in it for that and to be able to be a voice for people who have no voice" (African American male).

Although none of the participants were planning to leave, those who dis-cussed potential reasons for leaving were enveloped with fear and ambivalence, weighing the financial and emotional toll of being in an academic envi-ronment where there were daily questions about belonging, institutional fit, respect, work overload, and the need for hypervigilance. One Mexican Ameri-can participant asked me a question: "Did you know that Latinos take a beat-ing in administration? Absolutely, absolutely." Laden and Hagedorn (2000) have shown the proportion of faculty members who predicted that they were likely to leave their present faculty position for a different institution: 20 percent of

White faculty, 31 percent of Latinos/as, 33 percent of American Indians, and 28 percent of African Americans.

Minority faculty are more likely than majority faculty to leave. In addition to the toll that persistent discriminatory practices have on this group, economic pressures around salary issues were particularly significant. Men make more than White women and White and Asian women make more than other women. Financial concerns and discriminatory practices are more likely to be reported by URM faculty than by their White or Asian counterparts and to contribute to their departure (Hurtado et al., 2012).

## UPLIFTING THE NEXT GENERATION OF URMS

These data confirm that the institutional climate in research universities is perceived as capricious, inequitable, and nontransparent. Throughout the academic trajectory from hiring through awarding of full professorship, the majority of respondents were unclear as to the informal rules and oftentimes the formal rules. Few colleagues and administrators were willing to lend a hand or provide guidance on what was needed or the unspoken requirements. Two scenarios are particularly injurious: respondents did not know what to ask and therefore were unprepared to engage successfully in the processes; and when respondents perceived the expectations of promotion and tenure as confusing and nontransparent and asked for clarification, they were denied information. Moreover, the majority of respondents reported isolation, not belonging, and tokenism in their academic departments. Academic environments were described as "chilly," and respondents experienced difficulty in connecting with colleagues and their departments. The absence of mentorship affected respondents' adjustment and impacted their overall career. Respondents expressed a strong love of their work and have engaged in a difficult climb into academic circles. They have sacrificed much to ensure their small legacy in opening doors for others, being recognized as intellectuals, and providing a better future for their families. Institutions of higher education and their gatekeepers have historically included scholars who embrace a dominant culture philosophy. These data raise questions regarding how "professors think" about scholarship that focuses on social problems and seeks to move beyond seeking knowledge only for the sake of knowledge (Lamont, 2009). For example, Turner (2015) elaborates on distinctions between pre–civil rights sociological scholarship and post–civil rights sociological scholarship: "Whether conceived as 'practice,' 'radical sociology,' or 'activist sociology,' many sociologists in the 1960s were hell-bent on changing the social world (mostly capitalism and all of its evils, such as the military-industrial state, or the clear oppression of various subpopulations)." He continues his argument on the perils to research of activist sociologists by suggesting that most of the sociologists at the time were not (and still are not) interested in: first, the value of neutrality or objectivity in research; second, following the protocols of the rigors of science (Turner, 2015, p. 356). These views provide insight into the devaluation that permeates the research of those investigators who aim for social change and problem-driven solutions to national social problems.

Incongruence exists in expectations and the actual criteria by which all faculty are evaluated during the promotion and tenure process. Confusion regarding written policies and unwritten expectations generally occurs because of historical shifts in the mission or aspirations of the university or because the unviable or hidden curriculum remains only within the purview of the dominant group. Thus quality and merit are both subjective and objective. One possible explanation for the unchanging nature of promotion and tenure processes is that senior faculty may maintain more stringent and traditional standards for tenure. Unmitigated concerns about "quality" often exclude scholars who draw from critical theories and innovative methodologies, as well as scholars engaged in research related to social inequities on underserved racial/ethnic populations. Broadening definitions of what constitutes quality research can create tensions among faculty who prefer to hire candidates who share similar traits, thinking (political preference) training, and research interests. Faculty will evaluate applicants differently based on their race, even if they have the same qualifications.

Study data confirm prior knowledge that barriers to navigating the institutional processes successfully included conflicting information, unwritten rules, and the absence of mentoring and formal direction from others about the promotion and tenure process. Assessment protocols for both tenure and promotion were unclear with respect to what counts as science, what methods are most acceptable, what weight teaching evaluations carry, and what service counts as important. All too often and inexplicably their research topics, their community-engaged methods and service, and their teaching evaluations were under scrutiny (Garza, 1993; Sampaio, 2006; Stanley, 2006; Turner, González, & Wood, 2008). A provocative question emerges: why is it that when majority-culture scholars such as Alice Goffman, a non-URM sociologist, conduct ethnographic work, community observations, and active participation it is praised, or when non-URM faculty such as Raj Chetty do work on economic communities of opportunity it is rewarded, while URM faculty such as Dolores Acevedo are penalized and their scholarship ghettoized? While non-URM scholars often increase their legitimacy, authority, and intellectual capital and are likewise rewarded with promotion and tenure by elite institutions for their study of critical social issues of race/ethnicity and economic opportunity, many URM scholars' research is interrogated and undervalued by majority faculty and students. This is referred to as the crisis of legitimacy.

These data leave us with questions regarding the best strategies for change. Two guiding principles in higher education are apparent: focus on minimums and do no wrong are not feasible solutions. Furthermore, institutions "have a tendency to hide behind the cloak of affirmative action lawsuits, rather than work to create viable, creative, alternatives to achieving a diverse university" (Patitu & Hinton, 2003, p. 85). One would expect that institutions hire qualified individuals and do everything in their power to nurture and retain early career faculty. However, respondent data contradict this goal and signal the need for institutional self-reflexivity. URM respondents love the work and exhibit high enthusiasm and passion about contributing to the university, community, and nation. They are on the cutting edge of nontraditional interdisciplinary scholarship and innovative methodologies. Why are universities disinvesting in this domestic talent pool? Experiences of racism, exclusionary practices, and the devaluation of their scholarship on national social problems take a powerful toll on their bodies and minds. Institutional racism presents a heavy burden for URM faculty that results in daily vigilance and anticipatory stress and inevitably contributes to physical and mental fatigue. The next chapter discusses the injurious outcomes on physical and mental health of working in unwelcoming institutions and the daily struggle with the pain of (un)belonging.

# 8 · WORKPLACE STRESS

## Impact on Well-Being and Academic Career Path

I am close to the end of my career and wish I had chosen another career. For so long I thought mine was an individual issue, but when talking with other African American female colleagues, we have come to the conclusion that academe is killing us. I know so many African American women professors/ administrators who have died young, especially from cancer. With no other real health problems, we can only conclude that job stress is responsible. It's just not been worth it!

—African American female

Two burning questions are evoked by the quotation above: Does the professional academic workplace harm the physical and psychological well-being of URM professionals? And can these difficult workplace environments account for lower numbers of URM professionals who successfully navigate the pathway to successful academic careers? Attention given to workplace stress and coping among URM faculty is noteworthy by its absence in the empirical literature. Compared to studies investigating job stress in the general working population, research on the impact of job stress on academics is less understood (Gillespie, Walsh, Winefield, Dua, & Stough, 2001). To understand and address racial/ethnic health inequities, research has for some time explored the relationships among workplace stress, racism and discrimination, coping strategies, and physical and mental well-being (Araujo & Borrell, 2006; Mays, Cochran, & Barnes, 2007; Okazaki, 2009; Paradies et al., 2015; Williams & Williams-Morris, 2000). Most of this research has focused on low-status, historically disenfranchised groups as defined by race, class, and gender (Gee & Walsemann, 2009; Pearlin, Schieman, Fazio, & Meersman, 2005), yet a limited body of evidence has revealed that the health advantages experienced by high-status Whites are not as evident for high-status African Americans, Mexican Americans, and Puerto Ricans (Dinwiddie, Zambrana, & Garza, 2014; Schieman, Whitestone, & Van Gundy, 2006; Sellers & Neighbors, 2008). The purpose of this chapter is to provide a portrait of the everyday workplace experiences of study participants and, more specifically, to examine their perceptions of mentoring, departmental and university service, collegial relationships, and career milestones and their reported impact on participants' well-being. Interview data are used to contextualize survey data on the physical and mental health of respondents. Three principal questions guide the presentation of the descriptive data: (1) What are the stress-inducing workplace roles associated with physical and mental health symptoms of URM faculty? (2) What coping strategies (e.g., self-care practices, recreational activities, social support, and rational/cognitive responses) are used to decrease workplace stress? And (3) Do health and mental symptoms vary by race/ethnicity and gender?

## STRESS-INDUCING WORK ROLES

Stress-inducing work roles or workplace stress, as observed in prior chapters, include heavy workload demands, little control over work, role ambiguity, role overload, perceived discrimination, and difficult interpersonal relationships with coworkers and supervisors. Workplace stress has been defined as the interaction between three elements: perceived demand, perceived ability to cope, and the perception of the importance of being able to cope with the demand (McGrath, 1976). When these elements exist in the workplace, the relationship between a person and the environment is appraised as taxing or stressful and endangers his or her well-being (Lazarus & Folkman, 1984). Workplace stress oftentimes contributes to noxious physical and emotional responses that occur when the requirements of the job do not match the capabilities, resources, or needs of the worker and can lead to poor health (National Institute for Occupational Safety and Health [NIOSH], 1999). Moreover, factors such as work and family balance issues may also be stressors, especially for women (NIOSH, 2001). "Thus, when the extant literature reports that faculty experience stress (and women faculty are reported to experience greater stress than men), it is an issue of broad concern for an institution and one that must be addressed, rather than to assume that it is an isolated incident that will rectify itself" (Hart & Cress, 2008, p. 177).

Unwelcoming climates create a highly stressful environment. For example, perceived discrimination, including unfair treatment and social disadvantage as well as other workplace stress, such as inadequate levels of institutional resources and collegial support, adverse life events, and chronic vocational strain, can predispose URMs to adverse mental health outcomes (Mays et al.,

2007). Earlier studies examining the consequences of perceived discrimination have documented that simply the anticipation of being treated badly or unfairly has as powerful an impact on individuals (Clark, Anderson, Clark, & Williams, 1999; Kessler, Mickelson, & Williams, 1999; Lewis, Cogburn, & Williams, 2015). Increasing demands of stress-inducing roles coupled with perceived discrimination, based on both race/ethnicity and gender, hampers productivity and advancement as faculty need to engage in self-care practices to regain or maintain optimal health and well-being. Few studies have examined the relationship between workplace stress, unwelcoming climates, and physical and mental well-being for URM faculty (Shaw, 2014). This chapter offers rich insights into the complex and dynamic ways that discriminatory practices and implicit bias permeate the lives of participants and what coping strategies respondents employ to negotiate their work lives and protect their physical and mental health. These data contribute to filling an important gap in the scholarly body of work on workplace stress as a determinant of physical and mental health symptoms among URM professionals.

## WORKPLACE STRESS AND PHYSICAL AND MENTAL HEALTH

In the past thirty years, investigators have explored the relationship between stress-inducing work roles, mortality, and health conditions such as mood and sleep disturbances, upset stomach, headache, and disturbed relationships with family and friends (McEwen & Lasley, 2003; National Research Council, 2004; Tennant, 2001). Health outcomes of workplace stress can be physical, such as increased susceptibility to infections (Frone, Russell, & Barnes, 1996), or psychological, such as anxiety, burnout, and depression (Alamilla, Kim, & Lam, 2010; Sauter, Hurrell, Murphy, & Levi, 1997). These early signs of workplace stress are usually easy to recognize, but the effects of stress-inducing work roles on chronic conditions are more difficult to pinpoint as chronic diseases develop over the life span and are influenced by myriad factors.

Nonetheless, evidence is rapidly accumulating to suggest that stress plays an important role in several types of chronic conditions—especially hypertension and cardiovascular disease progression (Wang et al., 2007; Webb & Gonzalez, 2006), musculoskeletal disorders, and psychological disorders (Israel, Baker, Goldenhar, Heaney, & Schurman et al., 1996; Lepore et al., 2006; McEwen & Kalia, 2010; NIOSH, 1997). Race-associated stressors contribute to racial/ethnic inequities in health outcomes (Brondolo, Brady ver Halen, Pencille, Beatty, & Contrada, 2009; Mays et al., 2007; Williams & Williams-Morris, 2000). Prior scholarship has shown that the brain's biological response to repeated acts of perceived discrimination and racism—whether real or perceived—raises an individual's cortisol levels. Cortisol in low amounts helps control the body's immune system but in large amounts can increase stress and the inflammation that causes heart disease, diabetes, infection, and obesity (Dedovic, Wadiwalla, Engert, & Pruessner, 2009; Kirschbaum, Bartussek, & Strasburger, 1992).

As has been described throughout this book, discriminatory practices are an integral part of our respondents' life course experiences and are strikingly acute in their higher education, graduate school, and faculty pathway. They experience feelings of anger, frustration, doubt, guilt, or sadness when they encounter discrimination and microaggressions (Sue et al., 2008). Racism or discrimination is a major threat to mental health. Like other chronic stressors, perceptions of unfair treatment, such as insults, discourteous treatment, name-calling, and poorer service, are psychologically burdensome to African American women (Keith, Lincoln, Taylor, & Jackson, 2010; Weber & Higginbotham, 1997). Less knowledge is available on the effects of racism and discrimination and their potential harm to Latinos (Arrellano-Morales et al., 2015; Comas-Díaz, 1997; Rodriguez-Calcagno & Brewer, 2005; Sanchez & Brock, 1996) but Latinos in the workplace report more subtle forms of discrimination and darker skinned Latinos experience more racial discrimination than lighter skinned Latinos, with adverse physical health outcomes for both men and women regardless of age, education, or income (Araujo & Borrell, 2006). Various studies have confirmed a positive correlation between discrimination and distress, and those who report being discriminated against have been found to have poorer mental health outcomes than their same-race counterparts who did not report discrimination (Roberts, Swanson, & Murphy, 2004; Williams, Neighbors, & Jackson, 2003). Responses to race-related stressors can put URM professionals on guard for signs of expected discrimination. This chronic vigilance for discrimination may result in continual workplace stress exposure and be detrimental to health (Lewis et al., 2015; Sawyer, Major, Casad, Townsend, & Mendes, 2012).

In addition to stress, other psychological factors are predictive of differences in racial and ethnic health outcomes. For instance, depression, anxiety, and anger that may be associated with chronic stress have all been prospectively linked with increased cardiovascular and all-cause mortality (Rozanski, Blumenthal, & Kaplan, 1999). Anxiety disorders range from general anxiety to panic attacks and can become severe and disabling. Adverse working conditions and high workplace stress are associated with depression and anxiety and increased risk of suicide (Feskanich et al., 2002; Melchior et al., 2007). Relatively few studies have investigated the link between working conditions, work attitudes, and suicide (Schneider et al., 2011). Furthermore, stressful life events predict mortality in initially healthy populations (National Research Council, 2004; Rosengren, Orth-Gomer, Wedel, & Wilhelmsen, 1993). In particular, vocational strain, the death or serious illness of a family member or close friend, and providing care for a chronically ill relative have been predictive of all-cause mortality and heart disease (Nyberg et al., 2013; Schulz & Beach, 1999). Vocational strain has also been associated with negative coping strategies including increases in smoking, alcohol use, and physical inactivity (Dougal & Baum, 2001; Kivimäki et al., 2013). Therefore, workplace stress may be examined as a both proximal and distal potential cause of illness and mortality.

## "I WANT TO BE IN A PLACE THAT IS NOT KILLING ME" (MEXICAN AMERICAN FEMALE)

The analyses draw on multiple interdisciplinary lenses to promote a more comprehensive understanding of the relationships among workplace stress and social support nexus (Pearlin, 1989, 1991; Pearlin et al., 2005; Thoits, 2011), social status (Collins, 2000; Ridgeway, 2014), discrimination, coping strategies, and physical and mental well-being (Williams et al., 2003; Williams & Williams-Morris, 2000). Workplace stress is multilayered and is oftentimes associated with role overload, role ambiguity, and vocational strain, all of which are intensified by racial/ethnic social status and micro-level encounters with racism and discrimination. A major claim that can be made is that these relationships constitute chronic workplace stress that results in deleterious effects to physical and mental health and decreases scholarly productivity among study participants.

A modest body of scholarship has revealed that faculty who engage in non-traditional research topics and methods, such as qualitative and community-engaged approaches, may experience lower levels of productivity. These more time-intensive methods and workplace stressors contribute to decreases in retention and promotion. Well-documented workplace stresses include (1) total absence or low numbers of URM peers and unwelcoming work environments (Stanley, 2006); (2) experiences of feeling unwelcomed (Essien, 2003; Feagin, 2006); (3) devaluation of research areas and methods (Bell & Nkomo, 2003; Browne & Misra, 2003; Wingfield & Feagin, 2012); (4) benign neglect, racism, and discrimination (Boyd, Cintrón, & Alexander-Snow, 2010; Flores, 2011; Niemann, 1999); (5) challenges in balancing work and family lives (Castañeda et al., 2015; Childers & Sage, 2003; Elliot, 2003; Jacobs, 2004; Mason, Wolfinger, & Goulden, 2013); and (6) the lack of institutional support, such as mentoring (Dixon-Reeves, 2003; Shollen, Bland, Taylor, Weber-Main, & Mulcahy, 2011; Turner & González, 2014).

The ways in which higher education institutions create environments that are exclusionary and unwelcoming produce highly invisible toxins. These environments are embedded in an aura of traditional norms and values that are driven by an unquestioned belief that progress and innovation are inherent to institutional growth. Analyses of these institutions using traditional sociological theories yield boundary claims and normalize processes of individual achievement, meritocracy, and fairness. The application of these time-honored "value-neutral" paradigms to explain social phenomena fails quite miserably in uncovering the reasons for the underrepresentation in the professoriate of African American, Puerto Rican, Mexican American, and American Indian / Alaska Native peoples. Using existing theorizing paradigms leads to an inevitable conclusion that these groups are simply unable to manage normative processes in existing institutional hierarchies. These implicit theoretical assumptions support an elite cognitive map that reifies the status quo. Implicit assumptions include that historical patterns of incorporation and treatment of specific racial and ethnic groups have no effect on career paths, that meritocracy promotes a level playing field, and that life course experiences are favorably additive rather than subtractive.

Study respondents engaged in varying strategies of resistance and protective behaviors to successfully navigate the White habitus. The descriptions of the use of varying coping strategies to buffer stress represent novel contributions to the discourse on how members of a socially mobile and prestigious occupational group navigate their career role in elite institutions.

## BUFFERING RESOURCES AND COPING STRATEGIES

Coping skills and strategies are critical for attenuating the association between workplace stress and physical and mental health symptoms (Lazarus & Folkman, 1984; Pearlin, 1991; Thoits, 2011). Healthy coping strategies, such as exercise and healthy eating, as well as negative coping strategies, such as hyperdrive and hyperprofessionalism, are critical determinants of good health.[1]

Understanding how URM professionals who experience daily surveillance and engage in frequent identity accommodation (Castro, 2012; Jones & Shorter-Gooden, 2003) use coping strategies to avert adverse health consequences can proffer unique insights on factors associated with physical and mental health outcomes.

Coping strategies as moderators of workplace stress are well documented in relation to gender and campus role (Brown et al., 1986), gender and tenure (Richard & Krieshok, 1989), faculty members' productivity (Blackburn & Bentley, 1993), their intention to leave academia (Barnes, Agago, & Coombs, 1998), and rigorous academic environments and requirements among women and men (Eddy & Gaston-Gayles, 2008; Elliot, 2008; Hart & Cress, 2008; Hendel & Horn, 2008; Lease, 1999; Lindholm & Szelenyi, 2008). Other studies have focused on workplace stress among professionals and women (Amatea & Fong, 1991; Hogan, Carlson, & Dua, 2002; Segura, 1992). Although stress impacts all professional and faculty groups regardless of tenure status, few studies have focused on coping strategies such as exercise, meditation, and social support by racial/ethnic group and gender to evaluate which are the most effective in moderating workplace stress. In a national study of licensed social workers, all respondents across race (including African American, American Indian / Alaska Native, Mexican American / Chicano/a, and other Latinos/as) reported exercise as the leading strategy for coping with stress, followed by meditation and therapy. Puerto Rican social workers were more inclined to utilize meditation as a method for alleviating stress. In addition, other Hispanic/Latinos/as were more likely to attend therapy as a means for stress alleviation (Arrington, 2008). The study data suggest that respondents perceive an inhospitable environment and thus their coping tends to be external to their institutions, and few if any mentioned institutional social support from coworkers.

Work environments that facilitate mutual support among coworkers can reduce job stress and may provide a buffer against physical and mental health symptoms. High levels of social support have protective effects on mental health and are linked with reduced risk of illness-related absence (Stansfeld, Fuhrer, Shipley, & Marmot, 1999), while low levels of social support are associated with increased risk of psychiatric disorders (Williams et al., 2003). Social support as a coping strategy in response to race-related stressors and perceived discrimination can provide beneficial effects. For example, African American men participating in an African American–centered support group for confronting racism reported decreases in levels of anger and anxiety (Elligan & Utsey, 1999). Similarly, discussing racist events among peers was a constructive and useful way to cope (Swim, Hyers, Cohen, Fitzgerald, & Byslma, 2003), as were exercise, relaxation, and taking action (e.g., time management, reduction of responsibilities; Brown et al., 1986; Ek, Cerecer, Alanis, & Rodriguez, 2010). Less effective strategies were confrontation, being passive, avoidance/withdrawal, and talking to others (McDonald & Korabik, 1991). Self-care / personal activities like getting enough sleep, exercise, and relaxation techniques are related to reductions in stress and improvements in health (Burgard & Ailshire, 2009; Saint Onge & Krueger, 2011). Data by gender show mixed results. In an earlier study, women entering academia became more assertive, found supportive mentoring relationships, and put their careers first when they confronted role overload and work tasks that lack natural closure (Fouad & Carter, 1992), while Lease (1999) reported no significant differences on measures of stress or strain between male and female and new and more experienced faculty. While scholars agree that role overload and avoidant coping are significant predictors of vocational strain measures, perceptions of social interactions in the work environment, such as mentoring support and peer relationships with senior-level faculty, and at home responsibilities (parenting and caretaking) provide a critical context for understanding stress. Little is known, however, about how URM professionals negotiate workplace stress (for exceptions, see Ek et al., 2010; Higginbotham, 2009; Segura, 1992).

Recent research has placed a greater emphasis on coping strategies and social aspects of the work environment and their influence on stress (Miller, Buckholdt, & Shaw, 2008), yet strategies such as team-building activities and social events were not found to reduce workplace stress (Wood & Budden, 2006). Although these studies did not include racial/ethnic minority faculty, investigation of the social context of the work environment suggests that intangible types of support (e.g., emotional support) coupled with informal sources (e.g., colleagues, family, and friends) may provide the most effective resources (Bailey, Wolfe, & Wolfe, 1996). Collectively, individuals with social support are normally able to buffer stress and improve their physical and mental well-being (Thoits, 2011). URM faculty are less likely to seek help from their peers and supervisors due to a lack of interpersonal trust and peer perceptions of being interlopers. As a result, they experience high levels of isolation as well as psychological, physical, and interpersonal strain (Lease, 1999, p. 287). Coping strategies might be particularly important given the unique workplace stress associated with their work lives (Gutiérrez y Muhs et al., 2012; Turner & Myers, 2000). Inquiries into coping strategies have shown that URM faculty rely upon social support from other URM faculty and individuals outside of the institution (Thomas & Hollenshead, 2002); engage in problem-focused strategies such as "playing the game" to combat workplace stress (Baez, 1998); use emotional labor and rarely directly address workplace stress due to the perceived vulnerability of their status in the academy (Baez, 1998; Harlow, 2003; Plummer & Slane, 1996; Wingfield, 2010); and employ passive coping strategies such as avoidance, silence, and withdrawal (Aranda, Castaneda, Lee, & Sobel, 2001; Coker, 2003; Feagin, 1991; Krieger, 1990).

## GUIDING LENS AND MODEL

By examining the career trajectory and effects of multiple layers of workplace stress in the lives of academic URM professionals, including the availability of institutional mentoring and coping strategies, study data inform current thinking on the ways in which intersectional racial/ethnic/gender social status is associated with workplace stress and in turn impacts physical and mental symptoms. Drawing from the existing corpus of knowledge, a stress-driven conceptual model is particularly useful in bridging indicators of stress-inducing work roles, discrimination, work-family balance, life events, institutional mentoring (senior faculty engagement), and coping strategies, all factors found to influence well-being outcomes by race/ethnicity. Prior work has too often been remiss in accounting for differences in the intersectional identities of race/ethnicity/ gender and SES. To help shed light on these interrelationships and fill this void, multiple interdisciplinary theorizing approaches are applied to explain the multiplicative and cumulative impact of work stress, social status, discrimination, life events, and coping strategies on the physical and mental well-being of URM faculty (Kreiger, 2012; Marmot, 2006; Ridgeway, 2014; Pearlin et al., 2005; Thoits, 2011; Williams, 2012). The conceptual model depicted in figure 8.1 was derived from the results produced in this study.

These data show that social status identity factors (race, ethnicity) are structurally interlinked with SES of family of origin, workplace factors (stress-inducing work roles), perceived discrimination, and work-family balance. As observed in chapter 6, oftentimes the participants had an outflow of economic and emotional resources and caretaking responsibilities for their family of origin, in contrast to financial support flowing from the family of origin to participants. These factors in turn may contribute to work-family tensions rather than balance and are all responsive to adverse life events such as financial issues or difficulty with a colleague. Life events can negatively impact work performance and work-family balance with, for example, work experiences that engender emotional fatigue, leaving little energy left for family. Conversely, high levels of family responsibilities such as caretaking for a parent with mental health issues oftentimes deplete emotional resources, decreasing active engagement in work demands. It is also notable that institutional senior faculty mentoring on how to secure and navigate resources to improve work-family life balance was minimally available or absent and participants were often afraid to "raise red flags" by requesting support for family needs/concerns such as the illness of a partner or parent (Castañeda et al., 2015). Nonetheless, the data suggest that moderating coping strategies such as exercise, prayer, mediation, yoga, and family social support can decrease stressful impacts of work roles, discrimination, and life events on physical and mental well-being (Pearlin, 1989).

However, perceived discrimination permeated the life experiences of participants at all levels, particularly as reported in chapters 4, 5, and 7. The model shows that perceived discrimination was directly associated with work-family balance, mentoring, and well-being. Participants reported stress-inducing discrimination in that their work and career goals and areas of interest were devalued; they received limited institutional mentoring from senior faculty on career advancement or work-family strategies and had limited access to advice from administrators; and all too often they were perceived as institutional servants for the department, college, or university in the interest of showcasing a value of diversity. A considerable body of knowledge has found that chronic experiences with racial/ethnic discrimination contribute to Physical and mental

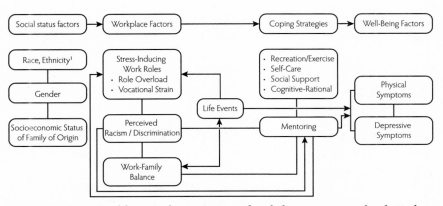

FIGURE 8.1. Conceptual framework: associations of workplace stressors on the physical and mental well-being of respondents

health conditions (e.g., high blood pressure, increased heart rate, biochemical reactions, depression, and hypervigilance) that may lead to adverse physical or mental conditions. In effect, coping strategies and resources may *not* be able to buffer the physical and mental consequences of role strain, work overload, and discrimination for racial and ethnic groups (Brondolo et al., 2009).

In sum, the data-driven model shows direct and indirect links between racial/ethnic status and well-being. I argue that racial/ethnic and economic social status factors predispose URM study participants to a range of social determinants such as chronic role strain, unfair treatment, social disadvantage, discrimination, inadequate levels of mentoring supports in career advancement, and the occurrence of adverse personal and work life events that oftentimes result in high levels of physical and mental health symptoms. The data also confirm a portrait of participants who overwhelmingly report a lack of belonging and support in what is perceived as unwelcoming toxic ivory towers. Thus the data-driven model provides some preliminary insights into the potential reasons for lower representation and retention patterns of historically underrepresented groups in elite research universities.

## METHOD AND DATA

Descriptive survey and qualitative data are presented in this section.[2] To complement the quantitative findings, qualitative narratives are drawn from two specific questions in the individual and group interviews to contextualize the meaning of participants' experience with workplace stress and physical and mental health symptoms. Respondents were asked two questions: (1) "In the last five years, have you ever been told by a doctor or other health care professional that you had/have a physical condition and/or psychological distress?" and (2) "Do you think workplace stress was a contributing factor? If so, how?" Data are reported first by combined survey responses, followed by narrative responses.

## HIGH SYMPTOMATOLOGY, LIFE EVENTS, AND PERCEIVED DISCRIMINATION: DEEPENING THE EXPLANATION OF WORKPLACE STRESS

Table 8.1 displays physical and mental health symptoms of participants by race and ethnicity. The five most frequently mentioned physical health conditions are high cholesterol (24.3 percent), high blood pressure (22.3 percent), asthma (14.0 percent), arthritis (10.2 percent), and diabetes (6.3 percent). Similar to national data, Mexican American respondents are most likely to have diabetes (Schneiderman et al., 2014) while African Americans are most likely to report high blood pressure (Akinbami, Moorman, & Liu, 2011) and Puerto Ricans most likely to have asthma (Akinbami et al., 2011). American Indian / Alaska Natives had the highest percentages for high cholesterol, high blood pressure, and diabetes. The historical and systematic oppression of American Indian / Alaska Native populations has impacted their current health (Harding, Hudson, Erickson, Taualii, & Freeman, 2015). For example, they consistently show health inequities, such as higher rates of chronic diseases, compared to the overall U.S. population (Rainie, Jorgensen, Cornell, & Arsenault, 2015).

The majority of participants (67.0 percent) self-reported their health status as being excellent or very good. However, large numbers of participants reported experiencing in the past four weeks one or more of the eighteen physical symptoms on the physical symptoms index (PSI). Almost 80 percent (78.9 percent) reported at least one symptom related to tiredness (including trouble sleeping), a majority (57.8 percent) reported at least one digestive tract symptom (upset stomach or nausea, acid indigestion/heartburn, diarrhea, stomach cramps, constipation, loss of appetite), and 43.8 percent reported backaches. Mexican Americans were the most likely to experience one or more of these symptoms in each of the categories except stress-related symptoms (shortness of breath, chest pain, heart pounding when not exercising, and dizziness). Close to one-third of all participants reported stress-related symptoms, which were most likely to be reported by American Indian / Alaska Natives (40 percent). High cholesterol and blood pressure were most frequently reported by American Indian / Alaska Natives and African Americans. Moreover, 318 of the 568 participants (47.0 percent) checked four or more symptoms on the PSI. The maximum number of symptoms any individual checked was sixteen (of eighteen). Among individuals who checked four or more symptoms, the average number of symptoms selected was 6.7 ($SD = 2.60$).

Table 8.2 displays life events over the past year. The measure included twelve life events, and a cognitive appraisal scale was used to measure the perceived

**TABLE 8.1** Self-reported health status, physical symptoms, and illness conditions by race/ethnicity

| Variable | Total sample (N = 568) | African American (n = 333; 58.6%) | Mexican American (n = 134; 23.6%) | Puerto Rican (n = 76; 13.4%) | American Indian / Alaska Native (n = 25; 4.4%) |
|---|---|---|---|---|---|
| **Health status** | | | | | |
| Excellent / very good | 370 | 220 | 85 | 51 | 14 |
| | (67.0) | (68.3) | (64.9) | (67.1) | (60.9) |
| Good | 150 | 84 | 39 | 18 | 9 |
| | (27.2) | (26.1) | (29.8) | (23.7) | (39.1) |
| Fair/poor | 342 | 18 | 7 | 7 | — |
| | (5.8) | (5.6) | (5.3) | (9.2) | |
| **Physical symptoms[a]** | | | | | |
| Tiredness-related symptoms (tiredness/fatigue, trouble sleeping, headache) | 427 | 241 | 110 | 58 | 18 |
| | (78.9) | (76.8) | (84.0) | (81.7) | (72.0) |
| Digestive tract symptoms (upset stomach or nausea, acid indigestion/heartburn, diarrhea, stomach cramps, constipation, loss of appetite) | 307 | 159 | 85 | 44 | 19 |
| | (57.8) | (52.1) | (64.9) | (62.9) | (76.0) |
| Backache | 329 | 118 | 71 | 39 | 11 |
| | (43.8) | (37.1) | (54.2) | (53.4) | (45.8) |
| Stress-related symptoms (shortness of breath, chest pain, heart pounding when not exercising, dizziness) | 169 | 101 | 35 | 23 | 10 |
| | (31.5) | (32.5) | (26.9) | (32.4) | (40.0) |

(continued)

TABLE 8.1  Self-reported health status, physical symptoms, and illness conditions by race/ethnicity (*continued*)

| Variable | Total sample (N = 568) | African American (n = 333; 58.6%) | Mexican American (n = 134; 23.6%) | Puerto Rican (n = 76; 13.4%) | American Indian / Alaska Native (n = 25; 4.4%) |
|---|---|---|---|---|---|
| Other symptoms (skin rash, fever, eye strain, infection) | 252 | 135 | 66 | 38 | 23 |
| | (47.0) | (43.3) | (51.2) | (53.5) | (52.0) |
| Chronic conditions[b] | | | | | |
| High cholesterol | 132 | 81 | 27 | 15 | 9 |
| | (24.3) | (25.6) | (20.9) | (20.5) | (36.0) |
| High blood pressure | 122 | 83 | 21 | 10 | 8 |
| | (22.3) | (26.0) | (16.2) | (13.7) | (32.0) |
| Asthma | 75 | 41 | 16 | 15 | 3 |
| | (14.0) | (13.4) | (12.3) | (20.0) | (12.0) |
| Arthritis | 55 | 37 | 11 | 5 | 2 |
| | (10.2) | (11.9) | (8.5) | (6.8) | (8.3) |
| Diabetes | 34 | 19 | 10 | 3 | 2 |
| | (6.3) | (6.0) | (7.7) | (4.1) | (8.0) |
| Ulcers | 32 | 21 | 8 | 1 | 2 |
| | (6.0) | (6.8) | (6.2) | (1.4) | (8.0) |

NOTE: These data include both web-based and qualitative data of study participants. Values in parentheses are percentages.

a. In this measure, individuals were asked to check all symptoms that they had experienced in the past four weeks. These data include individuals who selected one or more of the symptoms in a given category.

b. Numbers do not sum to 100 percent due to missing data, which ranged from 3.1 to 6.5 percent of the total sample.

TABLE 8.2  Self-reported life events, depression symptoms (CES-D), and impact of discrimination by race/ethnicity

| Variable | Total sample (N = 568) | African American (n = 333; 58.6%) | Mexican American (n = 134; 23.6%) | Puerto Rican (n = 76; 13.4%) | American Indian / Alaska Native (n = 25; 4.4%) |
|---|---|---|---|---|---|
| **Five most frequently mentioned life events over the past year** | | | | | |
| Death of close friend or family member or have serious illness | 188 (38.6) | 117 (39.8) | 39 (35.1) | 19 (32.2) | 13 (56.5) |
| Major problems with money | 184 (37.8) | 108 (36.9) | 35 (31.5) | 26 (43.3) | 15 (65.2) |
| Major conflict with colleagues | 147 (30.1) | 85 (28.9) | 32 (28.8) | 20 (33.3) | 10 (43.5) |
| Family member or close friend lost job or retire | 117 (24.0) | 68 (23.1) | 26 (23.6) | 16 (26.7) | 7 (30.4) |
| Divorce or break-up of family member or close friend | 60 (12.3) | 33 (11.3) | 12 (10.9) | 8 (13.3) | 7 (30.4) |
| **Mental health (CES-D)[a]** | | | | | |
| Sleep was restless | 0.93 (1.01) | 0.95 (1.05) | 0.90 (0.93) | 0.91 (1.05) | 0.92 (0.81) |
| Felt sad | 0.67 (0.84) | 0.66 (0.84) | 0.65 (0.83) | 0.65 (0.84) | 0.84 (0.90) |
| Felt lonely | 0.63 (0.92) | 0.64 (0.92) | 0.61 (0.92) | 0.59 (0.95) | 0.80 (0.96) |
| Felt depressed | 0.53 (0.80) | 0.50 (0.78) | 0.57 (0.81) | 0.54 (0.81) | 0.64 (0.86) |
| Felt fearful | 0.49 (0.81) | 0.49 (0.84) | 0.52 (0.75) | 0.39 (0.74) | 0.64 (0.95) |

(continued)

TABLE 8.2  Self-reported life events, depression symptoms (CES-D), and impact of discrimination by race/ethnicity (continued)

| Variable | Total sample (N = 568) | African American (n = 333; 58.6%) | Mexican American (n = 134; 23.6%) | Puerto Rican (n = 76; 13.4%) | American Indian / Alaska Native (n = 25; 4.4%) |
|---|---|---|---|---|---|
| Could not shake off the blues even with help from family or friends | 0.48 | 0.50 | 0.41 | 0.42 | 0.64 |
| | (0.80) | (0.82) | (0.72) | (0.78) | (0.95) |
| Thought my life had been a failure | 0.28 | 0.28 | 0.26 | 0.27 | 0.28 |
| | (0.64) | (0.63) | (0.65) | (0.69) | (0.68) |
| Crying spells | 0.20 | 0.18 | 0.25 | 0.16 | 0.28 |
| | (0.53) | (0.49) | (0.58) | (0.52) | (0.74) |
| Mental Health Status Scale (CES-D8)[b] | 4.16 | 4.15 | 4.16 | 3.93 | 5.04 |
| | (4.66) | (4.48) | (4.80) | (4.97) | (5.26) |
| Mental Health Status Scale (CES-D8) score[c] | 11.14 | 10.58 | 11.82 | 12.71 | 11.63 |
| | (3.70) | (3.21) | (4.34) | (4.34) | (3.81) |
| **Perceived impact of discrimination** | | | | | |
| Extremely / very upsetting | 321 | 155 | 68 | 33 | 18 |
| | (47.4) | (46.5) | (50.7) | (43.4) | (72.0) |
| Somewhat / mildly upsetting | 186 | 99 | 26 | 23 | 3 |
| | (27.5) | (29.7) | (19.4) | (30.2) | (12.0) |
| Not upsetting at all | 114 | 52 | 17 | 16 | 3 |
| | (16.8) | (15.6) | (12.6) | (21.0) | (12.0) |

NOTE: These data include both web-based and qualitative data of total study participants, except for life events (n = 508). Values in parentheses are percentages for life events and perceived impact of discrimination. Values are means, with standard deviations in parentheses, standard deviations for CES-D.

a. Values are means, with standard deviations in parentheses. Respondents were asked to indicate if during the past week they had experienced the items using a 4-point Likert-type scale (0 = *rarely or none of the time*, 3 = *most or all of the time*).

b. For this measure, scores range from 0 to 24. A score ≥7 suggests a clinically significant level of psychological distress.

c. Mean scores for those individuals with a score ≥7, which suggests a clinically significant level of psychological distress.

impact of those life events on the individual. The highest frequencies were reported for five major events that deeply affected our participants: death or serious illness of a close friend or family member (38.6 percent), money problems (37.8 percent), major conflict with colleagues (30.1), family member or close friend lost job or retired (24.0 percent), and divorce or breakup of family member or close friend (12.3 percent).[3] Scores for life events ($M$ = 2.83, $SD$ = 1.7) and their perceived impact ($M$ = 5.91, $SD$ = 4.1) were highest for American Indian / Alaska Natives.

Mental health was measured by an eight-item depression scale (CES-D) that asked participants whether they had experienced certain symptoms during the past week. Participants were asked to rate each item on a 4-point Likert-type scale (0 = *rarely or none of the time*, 3 = *most or all of the time*). Average ratings were highest for restless sleep ($M$ = 0.93, $SD$ = 1.01), followed by feeling sad ($M$ = 0.67, $SD$ = 0.84), feeling lonely ($M$ = 0.63, $SD$ = 0.92), feeling depressed ($M$ = 0.53, $SD$ = 0.80), and feeling fearful ($M$ = 0.49, $SD$ = 0.81). African Americans had higher means for their restless sleep, feeling lonely, and feeling sad, while Mexican Americans had higher means for feeling depressed and feeling fearful.

On the Mental Health Status Scale (CES-D8), which has a range of 0 to 24, a score greater than or equal to 7 suggests a clinically significant level of psychological distress. For all participants, the CES-D8 mean was 4.16 ($SD$ = 4.66); and for individuals who had a score of 7 or higher, the mean was 11.14 ($SD$ = 3.70). No statistically significant differences were observed by racial/ethnic social status on either depression or clinical depression measures. For the perceived impact of discrimination, which is strongly associated with mental health, nearly half of the participants (47.4 percent) reported being extremely or very upset by encounters with discrimination, with American Indian / Alaska Natives and Mexican Americans reporting the highest impact.

Table 8.3 displays means for vocational strain and role overload items that inform us about the domains of work that are associated with stressful events and indirectly showcase faculty commitments to the professoriate. Responding to the vocational strain scale, URM faculty reveal that few participants "dreaded going to work," found their work boring, or made errors or mistakes in their work. Participants reported a mean score of 4.1 ($SD$ = 1.06) for the item "I find my work interesting and/or exciting." These data illustrate and confirm prior evidence that participants are deeply committed to their work and careers. Role overload data provide some possible reasons for why vocational strain has such a significant impact on physical and mental outcomes. Although faculty reported confidence that they were doing a good job ($M$ = 4.3, $SD$ = 0.83), they also identified areas of perceived demands that led to work overload. Participants reported that they worked in several equally important areas at once. Perceived

TABLE 8.3   Scale item means of vocational strain and role overload of respondents by race/ethnicity

| Variable | Total sample (N = 508) | African American (n = 310; 61%) | Mexican American (n = 113; 22.2%) | Puerto Rican (n = 62; 12.2%) | American Indian / Alaska Native (n = 23; 4.5%) |
|---|---|---|---|---|---|
| **Vocational strain** | | | | | |
| Lately, I dread going to work | 1.9 | 2.0 | 2.0 | 1.8 | 2.1 |
|  | (1.21) | (1.23) | (1.19) | (1.10) | (1.25) |
| I am bored with my work | 1.5 | 1.4 | 1.5 | 1.4 | 1.4 |
|  | (0.82) | (0.82) | (0.95) | (0.67) | (0.58) |
| I find my work interesting and/ or exciting | 4.1 | 4.1 | 4.1 | 4.3 | 4.3 |
|  | (1.06) | (1.09) | (1.04) | (0.91) | (0.99) |
| I can concentrate on the things I need to at work | 3.4 | 3.3 | 3.4 | 3.6 | 3.7 |
|  | (1.16) | (1.2) | (1.07) | (1.10) | (1.02) |
| I make errors or mistakes in my work | 1.7 | 1.7 | 1.7 | 1.7 | 1.6 |
|  | (0.69) | (0.73) | (0.63) | (0.65) | (0.58) |
| Total scale mean of vocational strain | 18.68 | 18.85 | 18.89 | 17.51 | 18.32 |
|  | (0.69) | (0.73) | (5.7) | (5.1) | (4.9) |
| **Role overload** | | | | | |
| I am expected to do too many different tasks in too little time | 3.1 | 3.0* | 3.3 | 3.4* | 3.4 |
|  | (1.36) | (1.33) | (1.38) | (1.40) | (1.34) |
| I feel that my job responsibilities are increasing | 3.6 | 3.5* | 3.7 | 3.9* | 3.3 |
|  | (1.27) | (1.27) | (1.31) | (1.09) | (1.32) |

| | | | | | |
|---|---|---|---|---|---|
| I am expected to perform tasks on my job for which I have never been trained | 2.6 (1.35) | 2.4** (1.32) | 2.9** (1.45) | 2.6 (1.27) | 3.0 (1.30) |
| I have to take work home with me | 4.4 (1.00) | 4.4 (1.02) | 4.4 (0.99) | 4.6* (0.69) | 4.0* (1.26) |
| I have the resources I need to get my job done | 3.3 (1.20) | 3.3*** (1.15) | 3.3*** (1.28) | 3.3*** (1.20) | 2.4*** (1.12) |
| I'm good at my job | 4.3 (0.83) | 4.3 (0.83) | 4.1 (0.82) | 4.3 (0.81) | 4.3 (0.93) |
| I work under tight time deadlines | 3.8 (1.06) | 3.6* (1.08) | 3.9* (0.98) | 4.0 (1.02) | 4.0 (1.02) |
| I wish that I had more help to deal with the demands placed upon me at work | 3.6 (1.32) | 3.5 (1.35) | 3.7 (1.25) | 3.7 (1.29) | 3.7 (1.23) |
| My job requires me to work in several equally important areas at once | 4.1 (1.07) | 4.0 (1.09) | 4.1 (1.09) | 4.3 (0.91) | 4.0 (1.15) |
| I am expected to do more work than is reasonable | 3.0 (1.39) | 2.9 (1.36) | 3.2 (1.40) | 3.3 (1.32) | 3.3 (1.67) |
| Total scale mean of role overload | 33.10 (7.7) | 31.56 (7.6) | 33.53 (8.1) | 33.98 (6.7) | 33.35 (8.4) |

NOTE: These data include only web-based respondents. Values are means, with standard deviations in parentheses.

* $p < 0.1$; ** $p < 0.05$; *** $p < 0.01$

stressors, such as "have tight deadlines," "have to take home work," and increasing job responsibilities, were identified, with Puerto Ricans most likely to report the latter. Racial/ethnic differences are evident, with Mexican Americans reporting that they were "generally asked to perform tasks for which I have never been trained" ($M = 2.6, SD = 1.35$). About 60 percent of respondents reported that "I am expected to do more work than is reasonable" ($M = 3.0, SD = 1.39$) and "have limited resources." American Indian / Alaska Native were significantly more likely to report that they "do not have enough resources to do their work" ($M = 2.4, SD = 1.12$; total $M = 3.3, SD = 1.20$). No significant differences were observed on vocational strain or role overload, although African Americans reported slightly lower scores on role overload than the other three groups.

Table 8.4 shows coping resources related to self-care, rational/cognitive coping, and recreation. The most common strategies used for self-care were avoiding excessive use of alcohol ($M = 4.32, SD = 1.06$), getting regular physical checkups ($M = 3.60, SD = 1.39$), flossing teeth regularly ($M = 3.47, SD = 1.48$), being careful about your diet ($M = 3.28, SD = 1.24$), and exercising regularly ($M = 3.20, SD = 1.47$).

Respondents were least likely to practice deep breathing, practice relaxation techniques, and get an adequate amount of sleep. There were no statistically significant differences between racial/ethnic groups in regard to self-care. The most commonly used rational/cognitive coping skills that participants utilized were to think through the consequences of choices one might make when faced with the need to make a decision ($M = 4.16, SD = 0.98$), being able to identify important elements of problems one encounters ($M = 3.75, SD = 1.05$), using a systematic approach when faced with a problem ($M = 3.62, SD = 1.15$), establishing priorities for the use of one's time ($M = 3.55, SD = 1.12$), and, once priorities are set, being able to stick to them ($M = 3.22, SD = 1.17$). Puerto Ricans ($M = 4.33, SD = 0.77$) and African Americans ($M = 4.24, SD = 0.99$) were significantly more likely than Mexican Americans ($M = 3.90, SD = 0.97$, $p < .05$) to report that "when faced with the need to make a decision I try to think through the consequences of choices I might make." However, about 80 percent reported that they are unable to get the job out of their mind when they get home.

With respect to recreation, participants were less likely to agree with being able to do what they want in their free time ($M = 2.76, SD = 1.34$), spending their time on weekends "engaging in activities they enjoy most" ($M = 2.57, SD = 1.34$), and "setting aside time to do things they really enjoy" ($M = 2.57, SD = 1.23$). Mexican Americans were significantly more likely than African Americans to report that they "hardly ever watch television" ($M = 2.81, SD = 1.365$ vs. $M = 2.28, SD = 1.356, p < .01$). The highest mean score ($M = 3.49, SD = 1.25$) was for the item "When I am relaxing, I frequently

TABLE 8.4 Coping resources scales: means of self-care, cognitive/rational coping, recreation, and social support of respondents by race/ethnicity

| Variable | Total sample (N = 508) | African American (n = 310; 61%) | Mexican American (n = 113; 22.2%) | Puerto Rican (n = 62; 12.2%) | American Indian / Alaska Native (n = 23; 4.5%) |
|---|---|---|---|---|---|
| **Self-care[a]** | | | | | |
| Careful about my diet | 3.28 | 3.30 | 3.18 | 3.31 | 3.57 |
| | (1.24) | (1.24) | (1.31) | (1.19) | (1.12) |
| Get regular physical checkups | 3.60 | 3.63 | 3.52 | 3.59 | 3.70 |
| | (1.39) | (1.38) | (1.35) | (1.41) | (1.40) |
| Avoid excessive use of alcohol | 4.32 | 4.39 | 4.20 | 4.31 | 4.17 |
| | (1.06) | (1.38) | (1.14) | (0.92) | (1.07) |
| Exercise regularly | 3.20 | 3.22 | 3.17 | 3.15 | 3.35 |
| | (1.47) | (1.49) | (1.49) | (1.44) | (1.43) |
| Practice relaxation techniques | 2.11 | 2.12 | 1.95 | 2.31 | 2.17 |
| | (1.30) | (1.32) | (1.19) | (1.42) | (1.27) |
| Get the sleep I need | 2.68 | 2.60 | 2.69 | 2.90 | 3.04 |
| | (1.22) | (1.33) | (1.20) | (1.46) | (1.11) |
| Avoid eating or drinking things I know are unhealthy | 3.18 | 3.14 | 3.21 | 3.16 | 3.57 |
| | (1.22) | (1.23) | (1.18) | (1.31) | (1.16) |
| Engage in meditation | 1.70 | 1.77 | 1.57 | 1.62 | 1.61 |
| | (1.15) | (1.25) | (1.25) | (0.97) | (0.99) |
| Practice deep breathing exercises a few minutes several times each day | 1.52 | 1.56 | 1.50 | 1.34 | 1.57 |
| | (0.97) | (1.03) | (1.34) | (0.73) | (1.04) |

(continued)

TABLE 8.4  Coping resources scales: means of self-care, cognitive/rational coping, recreation, and social support of respondents by race/ethnicity (*continued*)

| Variable | Total sample (N = 508) | African American (n = 310; 61%) | Mexican American (n = 113; 22.2%) | Puerto Rican (n = 62; 12.2%) | American Indian / Alaska Native (n = 23; 4.5%) |
|---|---|---|---|---|---|
| Floss teeth regularly | 3.47 | 3.38 | 3.51 | 3.68 | 3.91 |
| | (1.48) | (1.50) | (1.46) | (1.46) | (1.28) |
| **Rational/cognitive coping** | | | | | |
| Able to put my job out of mind when I go home | 1.89 | 1.83 | 1.97 | 1.85 | 2.35 |
| | (1.07) | (1.06) | (1.09) | (1.01) | (1.15) |
| Feel that there are jobs I could do besides my current one | 3.08 | 3.14 | 2.95 | 2.88 | 3.39 |
| | (1.43) | (1.45) | (1.34) | (1.40) | (1.50) |
| Periodically reexamine or reorganize my work style and schedule | 2.83 | 2.79 | 2.86 | 2.97 | 2.83 |
| | (1.21) | (1.25) | (1.16) | (1.17) | (1.15) |
| Can establish priorities for the use of my time | 3.55 | 3.49 | 3.53 | 3.80 | 3.70 |
| | (1.12) | (1.15) | (1.03) | (1.12) | (1.15) |
| Once set, I am able to stick to my priorities | 3.22 | 3.16 | 3.20 | 3.48 | 3.52 |
| | (1.17) | (1.21) | (1.08) | (1.16) | (1.04) |
| Have techniques to help avoid being distracted | 2.97 | 2.94 | 2.93 | 3.23 | 2.96 |
| | (1.28) | (1.29) | (1.26) | (1.18) | (1.40) |
| Can identify important elements of problems I encounter | 3.75 | 3.73 | 3.70 | 3.97 | 3.61 |
| | (1.05) | (1.07) | (1.01) | (0.94) | (1.20) |
| When faced with a problem I use a systematic approach | 3.62 | 3.59 | 3.62 | 3.83 | 3.43 |
| | (1.15) | (1.16) | (1.13) | (1.10) | (1.31) |

| | | | | |
|---|---|---|---|---|
| When faced with the need to make a decision I try to think through the consequences of choices I might make | 4.16 | 4.24* | 3.90* | 4.33* | 3.91 |
| | (0.98) | (0.99) | (0.97) | (0.77) | (1.04) |

**Recreation[b]**

| | | | | |
|---|---|---|---|---|
| When I need a vacation I take one | 2.39 | 2.41 | 2.27 | 2.61 | 2.14 |
| | (1.37) | (1.40) | (1.30) | (1.44) | (0.96) |
| I am able to do what I want to do in my free time | 2.76 | 2.77 | 2.75 | 2.79 | 2.59 |
| | (1.34) | (1.36) | (1.29) | (1.43) | (1.18) |
| On weekends I spend time doing the things I enjoy most | 2.57 | 2.56 | 2.51 | 2.62 | 2.73 |
| | (1.19) | (1.20) | (1.13) | (1.32) | (1.12) |
| I hardly ever watch television | 2.48 | 2.28* | 2.81* | 2.72 | 2.77 |
| | (1.39) | (1.36) | (1.37) | (1.47) | (1.34) |
| A lot of my free time is spent attending performances | 1.80 | 1.81 | 1.77 | 1.79 | 1.95 |
| | (0.80) | (0.95) | (0.99) | (1.00) | (1.33) |
| I spend a lot of my free time in participant activities | 1.97 | 1.97 | 1.91 | 1.90 | 2.45 |
| | (1.20) | (1.20) | (1.17) | (1.12) | (1.47) |
| I set aside time to do things I really enjoy | 2.57 | 2.59 | 2.45 | 2.66 | 2.59 |
| | (1.23) | (1.25) | (1.18) | (1.21) | (1.26) |
| When I'm relaxing, I frequently think about work | 3.49 | 3.45 | 3.58 | 3.51 | 3.45 |
| | (1.25) | (1.24) | (1.25) | (1.35) | (1.26) |
| I spend enough time in recreational activities to satisfy my needs | 2.17 | 2.23 | 2.05 | 2.05 | 2.29 |
| | (1.20) | (1.22) | (1.12) | (1.15) | (1.42) |

(continued)

**TABLE 8.4** Coping resources scales: means of self-care, cognitive/rational coping, recreation, and social support of respondents by race/ethnicity (*continued*)

| Variable | Total sample (N = 508) | African American (n = 310; 61%) | Mexican American (n = 113; 22.2%) | Puerto Rican (n = 62; 12.2%) | American Indian / Alaska Native (n = 23; 4.5%) |
|---|---|---|---|---|---|
| I spend a lot of my free time on hobbies | 1.79 | 1.84 | 1.69 | 1.72 | 1.86 |
| | (1.01) | (1.10) | (1.02) | (1.08) | (1.13) |
| **Social support** | | | | | |
| I have help with tasks around the house | 418 | 194 | 82 | 45 | 15 |
| | (67.8) | (62.5) | (72.5) | (72.5) | (65.2) |
| There is at least one sympathetic person with whom I can discuss my work problems | 520 | 257 | 96 | 56 | 23 |
| | (84.4) | (82.9) | (84.9) | (90.3) | (100.0) |
| If I need help at work, I know who to approach | 439 | 214 | 83 | 51 | 12 |
| | (71.2) | (69.0) | (73.4) | (82.2) | (52.1) |
| OSI social support scale (no statistically significant differences) | 41.36 | 40.95 | 40.92 | 42.74 | 41.52 |
| | (7.94) | (8.60) | (7.76) | (5.68) | (7.23) |

NOTE: These data include only web-based study respondents. Values are means, with standard deviations in parentheses, except for social support, whose values are *ns*, with percentages in parentheses.

a. Missing data range from 1 to 3 percent.

b. Missing data range from 1 to 2 percent

think about work" (75 percent), while the lowest scores for participants were associated with not using free time for hobbies, performances, or personal activities. Suggested in these responses is that free time is used up with thinking about work and that nonwork activities are not an integral part of their leisure time. The social support scale reveals that slightly more than two-thirds of the respondents have help with tasks around the house (67.8 percent), with Mexican Americans and Puerto Ricans reporting the highest percentages (72 percent) compared to the other two groups (62–65 percent). Affirmative responses to the item "If I need help at work, I know whom to talk to" were lowest for African Americans (69 percent) and American Indians / Alaska Natives (52.1 percent) and highest for Puerto Ricans (82.2 percent). However, no statistically significant differences were observed by race/ethnicity.

This panoply of findings provides a glimpse of how URM faculty perceive their responsibilities, what in the actual execution of their responsibilities presents barriers, the resources available (or not available) to them, and how they take care of themselves (self-care and recreation). Yet survey data do not provide information on the quality of the work life and what findings mean in one's everyday life experiences with respect to mainstream and personal definitions of career success.

## PARTICIPANT VOICES: NARRATIVES OF HEALTH IMPACT OF UNWELCOMING WORK ENVIRONMENTS

The collected data provide insights into the contextual processes in institutional cultures that contribute to deleterious physical and mental health. They provide a deeper understanding, through narrative experiences, of how institutional cultures contribute to vocation strain and role overload and how normative practices impact life events and family-work (un)balance.

### The Impact of Stress on Work Roles and Well-Being

Participants vividly described stress-inducing work contexts and the physical and mental health consequences that accumulated as a result. In response to the question "In the last five years, have you ever been told by a doctor or other health care professional that you had/have a physical condition and/or psychological distress?," participants often spontaneously shared health conditions they were experiencing in alarming numbers and severity. Despite a mean sample age of forty-four, several participants described acute and chronic physical symptoms, seeking medical help, and eventually learning that their symptoms were stress-related or somatic. An African American male commented, "So many other people . . . whom I have seen, you know, deal with this burden of being in the academy and you know, succumbed to all kinds of different, I think, stress-related diseases that are directly tied to taking on this kind of huge burden of being in the academy."

These participants were also often told that their mental well-being was affected while the physical health conditions manifested. A Mexican American male stated, "When I first started out, like my first couple of years as a faculty member . . . and I just didn't know what I was doing. So, I was just scrambling around like crazy. I developed a pretty bad stomach issue, and my wife had me go see, like, every specialist. Man, I was at the doctor like every other week. And it turned out it was all mental, you know, stress driven."

In response to the second question, "Do you think workplace stress was a contributing factor? If so, how?," participants characterized their institutional culture as unwelcoming, showing that institutions are perceived to express insincere concerns about racial/ethnic diversity. "I am a part-time disabled faculty member which was a result of two cerebral aneurysms. I believe that the stress of my workplace significantly contributed to the raised blood pressure that preceded the aneurysms. The workplace has not changed and I will leave it!" (African American female web-based survey comments).

Respondents experienced role overload related to service, teaching, and mentoring requirements that exacerbated the normal pressures and research demands of being an early career professor. For example, a Mexican American female commented, "As much as I love teaching and research, I have often felt the academy to be a hostile environment, and it often takes a toll on my health." Moreover, the contradictory messages from colleagues and institutional agents about their worth and what is important for promotion and tenure are oftentimes confusing and stressful. One participant explained how she preserved her health during a very stressful tenure process: "[Tenure] really took a toll on my health, so I have been forced to exercise more and eat more, be more conscious about the hours that I devote to this profession, because if I were to continue to go at that pace, I'm not making tenure and I'm thirty-seven years old, and I don't want to have a heart attack by the time I'm forty" (African American female).

They also reported a sense of peers devaluing race-related scholarship and making implicit assumptions about the intelligence and work effort of URM students and job applicants. These microaggressions and race-related stressors negatively affect health. "I had a third of my faculty in my department vote against my tenure because they do not value qualitative work on racialization processes. As the first woman of color ever hired in a tenure track at my department I have been bullied, ostracized, and treated like I am an outsider in the department. It is very distressful to be constantly attacked and disregarded. I know these microaggressions have impacted my mental health and physical health as I was asked to serve as graduate advisor before I earned tenure and I was in the hospital frequently with gallstone problems and general stomach problems during the two years I served" (African American female web-based survey comment).

In addition to workplace stress, many respondents reported life stressors such as concerns about money, family of origin, or extended family. Life events were central in the additional burdens and caregiving responsibilities carried by respondents. The three primary life events reported by participants and confirmed in qualitative findings were conflict with colleagues, financial problems, and the death or serious illness of a family member or close friend. One Puerto Rican respondent noted, "My father's death was horrifying for me, I mean I didn't know how depressed I was, but I do remember taking an hour to decide which shoes to put on, so that's how depressed I was." Another respondent described how three family members died in a short period of time: "[It's] really hard because here's those first deaths in your family. No one had died before then. So my two grandparents died, and my aunt died. And so I had some of those pivotal moments where you're very close as a Latino. As a Chicana, I'm very close to my family" (Mexican American female).

Similar to the findings of other research (Heflin & Pattillo, 2006), respondents reported pressure to be responsive to family members financially and emotionally and to be caretakers while striving toward tenure and dealing with vocational strain and role overload. As one Mexican American female pointed out, "A major stress for me is helping and supporting an adult daughter with bipolar disorder." A striking finding is that respondents discussed similar stressors (such as excessive work demands and work-life balance) in graduate school that continued to manifest during their careers, which suggests a cumulative effect of life course stress for many. For a Mexican American female, the costs to her health continued to be problematic: "So now, whenever I get stressed, I don't have full-blown shingles, but I get pockets, I get patches. But I know when I have . . . to work long hours, when I have big deadlines, when I don't feel like I can find a balance between personal and academic life . . . I think I tend to react physically."

Respondents reported significant physical, emotional, and social burdens that taxed their ability to perform all their roles satisfactorily. Another respondent (Puerto Rican male) expressed the multiple domains of impact that career demands imposed on his physical well-being: "I am concerned about my health, lifestyle and weight and while I have not yet reached any risk categories, I'm concerned that I may because I feel that the demands of the tenure track directly compete with the time and resources I need to invest in improving my physical health—not to mention my interest in having children—a decision my wife and I have delayed because of the need to be more established in our academic careers and live in the same city."

Others were deeply impacted by depression, hypervigilance, and anxiety. A Black female respondent stated, "I've learned how to just shave back my involvement . . . I'm just not going to be bothered with it. . . . I try not to sweat the small stuff . . . at the end of the day I do whatever I can to protect my mental health."

Mental health is also deeply affected by lack of self-care, which includes poor eating habits and erratic sleeping patterns. The result is often physiological imbalance. A Mexican American female described the harmful process that occurs when stress is overwhelming: "And that takes a toll on how I feel about myself and then if that [the stress] disrupts my mental health then there comes the bad eating, the bad sleeping, I'm not working enough so I need to put even more of an effort in. And then I start getting sick all the time or all these other things—like I've gained a tremendous amount of weight because of the stress. The eye twitches and everything, so I think I'm very much affected—my health, by what's going on."

An African American male discussed his chronic condition and how the stress of his department impacted his physical, emotional, and mental health: "Yeah. Again, with the high blood pressure, the tenure stuff with the amount of forgetfulness that I had that year. . . . And I wasn't so concerned about getting tenure. I figured I would get that so it was really the stress of the department and having to deal with it in that regard. So yeah, definitely feel like that stress mentally, emotionally, physically."

In navigating their work environments, excessive demands, emotional labor, difficult personal interactions with colleagues and superiors, and balancing family and caretaking roles all too often resulted in adverse physical and mental health symptoms and health conditions. These oftentimes served as a wake-up call, motivating faculty to seek more active coping strategies to help manage their stress and its impact on their well-being.

## Coping Strategies: Doing the Best We Can!

Coping skills are critical in the managing of workplace stress and physical and mental health symptomatology (Lazarus & Folkman, 1984; Pearlin, 1991). Physical and emotional overload, if left uninterrupted, contributes to diminishing immune systems, inflammatory conditions, and susceptibility to chronic illnesses such as diabetes and hypertension. Coping strategies can decrease the adverse physical and mental effects. Self-care / personal activities like getting enough sleep and exercise and relaxation techniques are related to reductions in stress and improvements in health (Burgard & Ailshire, 2009; Saint Onge & Krueger, 2011). When asked what types of strategies they used to buffer the workplace stress and balance the competing demands of work and family life, participants most commonly reported using self-care, such as religious practices, spirituality, exercise, appropriate diet/nutrition, and socializing with family and friends outside the workplace.

Close to three-quarters of African Americans (71 percent) and American Indian / Alaska Natives (73.9 percent) reported a religious affiliation and regular attendance at services, compared to slightly more than half of Mexican Americans and Puerto Ricans. For example, an African American male respondent stated, "I think through prayer over the last years it's been clear through my faith that while you're at work you work, and you do the best you can. And then you can't stress about it once you leave it, and you move on to the other part of your life." Another African American male stated, "I've gone through bouts of being consistently depressed. And if it wasn't because of the prayer and working out and family, it probably would have overtaken me. . . . [I] talked to my primary care provider, and he thought that maybe I should have probably for a period of time been on some antianxiety or depressive medication. I said I don't do that. I'll increase my level of working out and prayer" (African American male). Religious/spiritual coping may involve the use of cognitive and behavioral techniques related to religion and spirituality (Tix & Frazier, 1998). Historically, spirituality has been an important coping mechanism for Black men and women living in an oppressive, racist society (Bacchus, 2008; Ellison & Taylor, 1996). In general, individuals with a strong spiritual foundation or religious beliefs tend to have fewer stress-related health problems, and spirituality significantly buffers the relationship between perceived racial stress and psychological health outcomes (Bowen-Reid & Harrell, 2002). Bacchus (2008) argues that spiritual and/or religious responses to stress are not passive but proactive, culturally specific ways of managing stress: "When a Black woman says that a stressful situation is in the hands of God, she may be engaged in behaviors she believes will bring about positive results" (p. 76).

Female participants were generally more likely to report religion being important in their lives. Female participants were also more likely than male respondents to engage in different forms of self-care. For example, one African American female respondent engaged in exercise to cope with distress and stay balanced: "I do yoga, Pilates, I run. I'm all about this kind of balance of healthy mind and spirit. I just think you have to have that because otherwise there's no relief. There's no relief and I really feel like I'm dancing as fast as I can." For some participants, social support is not easily available in their work environments. Therefore, they create social and academic support mechanisms such as writing groups, make time for friends and family, take advantage of counseling/therapy, and establish friendships with nonacademics. A Mexican American female participant mentioned, "Well, I think the way that I try to manage my stress sometimes is I don't keep an 'only academic world.' It grounds me more and makes me think that my suffering is a very privileged suffering."

A Puerto Rican female recognized the stress symptoms, engaged in proactive self-care behaviors, and sought social support: "As soon as I notice that I'm starting . . . where my mood is being affected or my stress level is affected, I do things to make myself feel healthy and good again. Like working out and eating healthy and putting things away and spending time with family and friends. So I try to be aware of . . . that it can't all be career." Another respondent acknowledged the importance of self-care if she was to successfully navigate the institutional culture: "So lately, it's been, like, I can't do anything about it, except for the way I treat people every day, and how I treat myself. That's been my coping skill, lately. It's like, I need to treat myself better, take care of my health, and I need to take care of the people I am working with. I'm not tearing any walls down [laughs]."

The participants generally reported that they were using as many strategies as they could muster and often found solace in family because family did not understand or know what it was they were going through but were simply proud of them. However, family pride and support have costs for these highly educated professionals. Closely aligned with social mobility is the fact that URM professionals are often viewed as the *talented tenth* of not only their race but also their families (Du Bois, 1903). In effect, family members are often less likely to have the economic and social resources to be self-sufficient, which may place a burden on URM faculty members' economic resources. Heflin and Pattillo (2006) found that middle-class Blacks regularly gave money to extended family members, and at times this inhibited their ability to save and build wealth. Whereas many White faculty may have parents who provide economic resources or at least do not require financial support, URM faculty oftentimes experience excessive demands on their social and economic resources from family members and extended kin. Those in high-prestige occupations are often expected to promote functioning and stability for all family members and at times even for the local community. In effect, their extended families can be both a source of support and an economic burden. Major life events in the family of origin such as an illness, loss of a job, or injury/death often have adverse effects on the ability of participants to dedicate their time and attention fully to their work responsibilities. Although prior research on low-income minorities (Stack, 1974) shows that they rely on a larger and more supportive social network than do Whites, respondents are part of a select group that *is* the social network. In other words, many URM professionals become the social and economic resource that their less affluent family and community members draw upon (Heflin & Pattillo, 2006; Vallejo, 2012). Other sources of support both within and outside of the work environment are often not readily available.

Positive mentoring support was reported by respondents as critically important to thriving in academic spaces. A Puerto Rican female described the role of mentoring as a social support resource: "She's connected me to people. She's introduced me. She's really served as that sort of liaison and contact with the outside world." Although the quality of mentorship she received was not the norm for our sample, prior evidence shows that social support in the workplace has important protective effects for physical and mental well-being (Thoits, 2011; Williams et al., 2003).

Mixed support has been reported for the view that social support moderates workplace stress (Holder & Vaux, 1998; Stroman & Seltzer, 1991). In a study of professional Black women's experiences with workplace stress, social support among peers and colleagues was not perceived as a key coping resource (Bacchus, 2008). This may indicate a social disadvantage for African Americans, compared to Whites, in terms of relationships with coworkers (Sloan, Evenson Newhouse, & Thompson, 2013). These findings suggest preliminary support for homophily in workplace social support ties (Bacchus, 2008).

Two other important thematic findings shed light on coping strategies that served to ameliorate workplace stress and keep it from spilling over into personal life—namely, rational cognitive strategy and supportive institutional family work policies. While the survey data did not show that rational/cognitive coping is a significant moderator of physical and mental well-being, many URM faculty relied on cognitive coping strategies such as learning to say "enough is enough" to limit commitments that do not count for tenure and placing events into a broader perspective about privilege and inequality. For example, rationalizing incidents displaying bias and microaggressions as having nothing to do with their actual performance allowed many to buffer the impact of these incidents. Equally important, many participants perceived that institutional support for work-family balance decreased experiences with depression and poor physical health, though some respondents felt otherwise. As one Puerto Rican female commented, "So I was supposed to go up for tenure again, but I'd been so sick as you can imagine dealing with this situation has been quite painful, that I requested a delay. And the university denied it, which makes me get even— more sick."

The cumulative effects of acute and chronic workplace stress, combined with limited coping resources, contribute to adverse physical and mental health outcomes. Strategies for coping with race and workplace stress are necessary to counteract the effects of the hostile campus ethos that accumulate over time and can take an exceedingly heavy toll on their mental and physical well-being and subsequently advancement.

## MEANING OF INSTITUTIONAL INEQUITY AND ITS INJURIOUS IMPACT ON URM PROFESSIONALS

The guiding intersectional lens sought to examine the relationships between social status identity, workplace stressors, coping strategies, and physical and mental health symptoms. A mixed-methods approach permitted us to capture reported levels of strain, overload, discrimination, mentoring, and responses to these demands and descriptions of the impact on respondents' physical and mental health. In other words the data increased our understanding of why the participants reported high vocational strain and role overload. The qualitative data provided the following thematic insights: respondents occupy a social location of tokenism that is associated with high interpersonal and intellectual isolation, excessive work demands, and high levels of interpersonal and intellectual discrimination with limited or absent mentoring support from senior colleagues. Discrimination and daily microaggressions across the life course (see chapters 4 and 7) may increase stress-driven biological vulnerability and chronic hypervigilance, which may have long-term biological consequences (Lewis et al., 2015). Chronic daily stressors are associated with physiological imbalance and dysfunction that can contribute to physical breakdown and mental stress (Brondolo et al., 2009; Brondolo et al., 2012) Exacerbating the effects of daily workplace stress was that stressful life events outside the workplace, such as restricted economic resources and adverse family events, had a significant impact. Workplace stressors are compounded by obligations that many participants reported with familial connections and responsibilities to family of origin and extended and fictive kin (Heflin & Pattillo, 2006; Higginbotham & Cannon, 1992; Vallejo, 2012). These relationships oftentimes involve additional emotional labor and economic outputs that can increase an already stressful set of work-related experiences. Furthermore, these findings lend support to prior anecdotal and narrative data (Agathangelou & Ling, 2002; Gutiérrez y Muhs, Niemann, González, & Harris, 2012; Medina & Luna, 2000; Smith & Calasanti, 2005) and recent empirical findings of an inverse relationship between health advantage and higher education level for Black and Latino URMs (Dinwiddie et al., 2014; Dinwiddie, Zambrana, Doamekpor, & Lopez, 2016; Schieman et al., 2006).

This study is one of the first to provide insight into the ways in which social status and workplace stress contribute to the inverse relationship between educational and occupational advantage and physical and mental well-being. These data proffer an interpretive lens for extending our understanding of vocational strain as encompassing multiple domains: institutional, family, economic, and social status. Social status racial/ethnic effects (devaluation, disrespect, inequitable access to opportunity and resources; Ridgeway, 2014) and a life course lens are particularly important for explaining how social status shapes economic and social opportunity. As argued by Ridgeway (2014), social status is embedded in institutional settings and evokes implicit bias. Everyday social interactions and experiences are filtered through a lens of implicit bias that increases the vocational strain in the workplace. In order to cope with workplace stress, a range of strategies are employed: strategic engagement, disengagement (Hassouneh, Lutz, Beckett, Junkins, & Horton, 2014), ignoring, suppressing, responding aggressively, responding with humor, and direct confrontation (Robinson, 2014). While some URM faculty ultimately respond with institutional departure, studies have shown that Black faculty members use a variety of responses to racism such as building external relationships, managing stereotypes through accommodating behavior, using spiritual practices (Patitu & Hinton, 2003), engaging in service, especially with students, and using the campus climate as a source of motivation (Allison, 2008).

This chapter has extended the body of knowledge on workplace stress and the meaning of the structural forces that play an important role in the institutional and family domains of URM professionals. Regardless of discipline, the intersectional social location of race/ethnicity is a powerful marker for both URM men and women, leading them to contend with paternalistic or disinvested mentoring and to fight for legitimacy and a place in the academy (Rodríguez, Campbell, Fogarty, & Williams, 2014; Zambrana, Harvey-Wingfield, Lapeyrouse, Hoagland, & Burciaga Valdez, 2017; Zambrana et al., 2017a).

Respondents' narratives suggest that workplace stress accumulates over time. These data show that inhospitable work environments (un)intentionally contribute to low productivity (publications), a push-out effect, and low retention rates. Future research can benefit from examining how different social contexts among high SES URM professionals help to explain group differences in perceived treatment and mental and physical well-being. Persistent undermining of one's competency and hypervigilance due to implicit biases and unconscious discriminatory practices take a toll on participants' physical and mental health, which may help explain the lower rates of retention, promotion, and tenure. Yet a lingering question remains: What accounts for the growing disparity between the retention of male and female URMs in institutions of higher education? In the next chapter, gender differences by race and ethnicity are explored.

# 9 · DOES GENDER MATTER?

Because I'm deeply convinced that this man [faculty colleague] treats me the way that he does because there's something about me that unsettles him, or that threatens him, that he didn't—that when I was hired, he thought I was this sweet, cute, young girl, and now... I've challenged something about the way he thinks the world works.

—Mexican American female

A central question in contemporary feminist and national discourse is, In what ways does gender matter? Gender inequality is critically important for analyzing the power and privilege dynamic among White men and women. However, the same lens and determinants are inadequate for explaining the experiences of intersecting race, class, ethnic, and gender social status identities. Intersecting identities erect visible and invisible barriers that impede successful integration of URM men and women in educational and career pathways. Important questions that have not been fully explored are centered in this chapter: Are there differences in the experiences of URM men and women? Where are these differences most likely to appear? What matters most in their perceptions of role overload, vocational strain, and discrimination? Deeper examination of their perceptions of institutional experiences can provide an alternative explanation for their continued severe underrepresentation. Notably, focus groups were constructed by both gender and race and ethnicity (e.g., one group was composed of five African American women, another contained five Mexican American women, and two additional groups were made up of African American and Mexican American men) to capture the voice of gender by race/ethnicity. The analyses reveal remarkable similarities across groups in overall experiences of discrimination, racial/ethnic battle fatigue, racial/ethnic diversity service tax burden, and concerns about family-work balance. The perceptions of isolation and devalorized research agendas did not differ significantly by gender, race/ethnicity, or discipline but were expressed as a deep concern regarding legitimacy and belongingness across the entire sample. One respondent captured the perceptions of the participants: "It's a subtle beast. To me, it seems to play out more in the topics that you want to study and how those topics are judged. When you get to the job market, it plays out in the extent to which the topics that you study will be valued and departments will want you. And for me it played in this really unexpected, subtle way that distracted the conversation from research to things that I didn't want to talk about" (Mexican American female).

This chapter illustrates gender differences by race/ethnicity and class. Compelling findings are evident for each of the four subgroups. Most revealing is how different dimensions of inequality (race/ethnicity, gender, and class) shape one's life chances, opportunities, stress, and sources of support in higher education institutions. Moving beyond academic isolation and absence of effective mentoring, three areas were the most pernicious for participants across race/ethnicity: dual identities, institutional taxation, and encounters with discrimination and racism. All these experiences deeply undermined URMs' ability to engage the passion they feel for their work and to be productive scholars, which impacted their careers. Although the White mainstream gender discourse has revolved around the privileges of males compared to females, for URMs gender cannot be easily separated from race, ethnicity, and class. Significant differences were observed by gender in discrimination scores. These data suggest the importance of exploring how institutional racism manifests itself in the lives of URM males and females and its impact on their retention.

## INTERSECTIONAL FEMINISMS: DECONSTRUCTING POWER AND PRIVILEGE

Intersectional feminist scholarship emerged predominantly from the voices of African American, American Indian / Alaska Native, and Chicana women whose social location and embodied experiences at the intersections of multiple systems of oppression did not echo the framing or assumptions of White feminist knowledge production or the privileged position of White native-born women in American society (Collins, 1991, 2000; Crenshaw, 1991; Hurtado, 1996; Romero, 1997; Sandoval, 2000; Segura, 1989, 1992, 2003). Intersectional feminist scholarship arose as a critique of mainstream scholarship and scholarly institutions and of the exclusionary practices of emerging interdisciplinary and critical movements, including women's studies and ethnic studies (e.g., see Baca Zinn & Dill, 1986; Dill & Kohlman, 2012; Dill & Zambrana, 2009). Intersectional scholarship built on and benefitted from the ways that CRT opened up new intellectual spaces that promoted innovative approaches to knowledge production. It arose primarily to understand and address the multiple and simultaneous dimensions of power and social inequality (e.g., class, race, ethnicity, and gender) that manifest at both the macro level of institutions and the micro level of the individual experiences of people who live "at the intersections" of multiple inequalities. Finally, feminist intersectional scholarship extends the category of women as a sole category to locate it in constructions of hierarchies of privilege and power across all social institutions, including the economy, family, education, law, religion, and media.

Building on the momentum of earlier women of color activism and resistance and critiquing the first and second waves of the White women's movement along with its intellectual presence in academic circles, African American, American Indian / Alaska Native, and Chicana women inserted themselves into a discourse that had overlooked how these women were historically racialized and gendered and provided the domestic and farm labor for the very group of White middle- and upper-class women who were advocating additional privileges for themselves. The role of structural inequality and the systematic exclusion of racialized women in all spheres of education, for example, were hidden disadvantages that racialized/ethnic groups interrogated. In response to a generalized women's feminism, a push for recognition of multiple feminisms took hold in the early 1980s and 1990s. Although a more public platform around women's issues was created by White feminist thought, African American intellectual forces drew from historical feminist roots to develop a Black feminist thought (Collins, 2000; Mays & Ghavami, 2017). Simultaneously, critical race theory (CRT) emerged to engage in a discourse of resistance to legal theorizing and omissions of conditions that contributed to the economic and social conditions and consequent social location of historic racial/ethnic groups in the United States (Almaguer, 1994; Delgado & Stefancic, 2013; Matsuda, Lawrence, Delgado, & Crenshaw, 1993). Building on these scholarly developments, intersectionality as a complicating approach to understanding the social location of historic racial/ethnic groups took hold (men and women) and rendered implicit assumptions of superior master narratives visible. Specifically, it offered historical and structural inequality arguments and explicit assumptions for uncovering institutional and systemic arguments rather than individual arguments to explain social location (Crenshaw, 1991; Delgado & Stefancic, 2001; Hancock, 2016; Higginbotham, 2001; Weber, 2013). However, not surprisingly, White feminist discourse has continued to serve as the master discourse on women.

The discourse on gender has revolved mainly around White women, and the narratives have been written predominantly by women. The data on women privilege White and European women who have advanced significantly and perpetuate another "myth of progress" for all women (American Council on Education, 2015). To be acknowledged is that majority-culture women are high-level aspirants to White male power and privilege in a social system where they are often the progeny and daughters, wives, and sisters of the network of power and privilege (Hurtado, 1996). Thus not all women have equal access to the social capital of networks and invisible norms and expectations of the institutional power circuit, and career advancement processes differ among URM and non-Hispanic White women (Higginbotham & Cannon, 1992; Weber, Hancock, & Higginbotham, 1997). These precise differences have yielded a rich body of work on multiple feminisms (Anzaldúa, 2007; Collins, 2000; Moraga & Anzaldúa, 2015) and have been echoing their distress from inside the ivory tower. Experiential accounts have been employed as first-person testimonies and analytic narratives to describe their challenges and difficulties within the academic environments (Balderrama, Teixeira, & Valdez, 2004; Cueva, 2014; González, 2007; Harley, 2008; Niemann, 2012; Ramirez, 2011, 2013; Robinson & Clardy, 2010).

## CORPUS OF KNOWLEDGE ON
## URM WOMEN IN THE ACADEMY

Although both URM men and women have experienced unequal treatment, women have been most vocal in expressing their distress. For example, Harley (2008) asserts that African American women at PWIs are overwhelmingly recipients of deprivileged consequences: "To be deprivileged illustrates why African American women faculty are metaphorically referred to as *maids of* academe" (p. 20). For American Indian / Alaska Natives, their past mistreatment and historical legacies have resulted in them perceiving and experiencing significant racism and harassment (Perry, 2002). American Indian / Alaska Native women in higher education report peers either supporting or denying their historical legacies (Cook-Lynn, 1996). Chicanas have also decried their mistreatment (Hurtado, 1996; Segura, 2003), while other studies have found that Chicano men have classified themselves as second-class citizens within academe (Castellanos, Gloria, & Kamimura, 2006; Castellanos & Jones, 2003; Reddick & Saenz, 2012). Four powerful and consistent themes emerge from this literature: the impact of stereotypes, the role of service demands, the lack of institutional support, and the policing of professional behaviors.

URM women and men experience the workplace and cope with stereotypes in different ways. Studies that describe URM women's experiences are presented to illustrate how gender as a coconstituted identity of race/ethnicity/class reveals powerfully complicated challenges compared to those faced by majority-culture women. At present, more studies are available on the experiences of URM women than on those of men. For men, we draw on data of what we know about male URM stereotypes and on participant data to extend our thinking about how gender role strains may differ for URM men and women.

Race/ethnic stereotypes, gender bias, and discrimination affect women's and men's experiences (Williams, Phillips, & Hall, 2014). Williams and colleagues (2014) found that women often have to provide more evidence of competence than men in order to be seen as equally competent.[1] In effect, their competence is consistently observed and questioned. These women feel as though they are under surveillance and engage in what is referred to as "Prove-It-Again" bias that is more common among Black and Mexican American women than any other group. For example, Latina and Black women faculty must combat stereotypes that behaving assertively means being perceived as angry or emotional (Williams et al., 2014). Latina faculty discussed the impact of stereotypes and reported that when they raised objections, they were perceived as being overly sensitive and emotional or relegated to the "angry/bitch" Latina stereotype. Yet in another study Latina faculty participants reported a lack of guidance at various levels of their careers and that their White male colleagues were disproportionately mentored and thus at an advantage. Oftentimes these observations resulted in internalizing these inequities as personal failures. Race/ethnicity combined with gender was specific to their experiences here, as they reported that males of color were not dismissed in the same way (Garcia, 2005). It is noteworthy that an absence of literature disallows the confirmation of the experiences of URM males.

Generally, URM women experience additional barriers in the academic workplace that include difficulties transitioning to an academic culture that is less communal and values self-promotion of individual accomplishments (Boyd, Cintrón, & Alexander-Snow, 2010); extensive participation in additional service activities and mentoring, often called cultural taxation, that is not typically counted in the promotion and tenure process (Eddy & Gaston-Gayles, 2008; Evans, 2007; Harlow, 2003; Johnson & Harvey, 2002; Laden & Hagedorn, 2000; Stanley, 2006; Turner, 2003);[2] heavier teaching and committee workloads; joint appointments (Reyes, 2005); and advising/mentoring a larger number of students compared to male colleagues (Blackwell, Snyder, & Mavriplis, 2009; Boyd et al., 2010; Griffin & Reddick, 2011; Harley, 2008). At times gender bias fuels conflict among women and decreases potential social support. Although in one study three-quarters reported that their female colleagues supported one another, 41.7 percent agreed that "some women just don't understand the level of commitment it takes to be a scientist." Black women were far less likely to agree that women support each other, while Latinas were more likely to report difficulty in receiving administrative support, a form of gender discrimination (Williams et al., 2014). In another study, African American women administrators and faculty reported that they were placed outside of the periphery of the decision-making process; had limited access to resources, minimal participation in organizations, and budget constraints; lacked support associated with sexual harassment from an immediate supervisor; were denied programming to increase diverse student enrollment; received verbal abuse from men; and were ignored, isolated, and alienated. These factors contributed to ineffectiveness in their positions.

Gender also matters in interactions with students, mentoring, and work-family balance. URM women are more susceptible to difficulties with students inside and outside of the classroom. URM women and other women are prone to challenges in the classroom, particularly from White male students who challenge their authority, fail to address them as "doctor" or "professor," question their teaching competence, engage in misidentification by assuming they are secretaries or other staff, disrespect their scholarly expertise, threaten their persons and career, and hurl accusations that course materials were biased in favor of their gender (Young, Furhman, & Chesler, 2014). Ford (2014) reported instances of being disrespected based on appearance or mannerisms by racial/ethnic background: African American women primarily described differences based on hairstyle or style of dress, whereas Asian American and Latina women often focused on speech patterns or voice. These experiences often resulted in career dissatisfaction. In another study of women of color, few race differences in workplace satisfaction were observed. The differences emerged when race/ethnicity and gender intersected. Women of color were significantly less satisfied than men of color in a number of areas, including professional interactions with colleagues, how well they fit into their department, the racial and ethnic diversity in their department, and work-family balance (Trower & Bleak, 2004).[3] Women are particularly vulnerable to being discouraged in academia because they may feel like failures at home and at work (DeCastro, Griffith, Ubel, Stewart, & Jagsi, 2014) and often lack institutional support to balance family responsibilities (Boyd et al., 2010). In fact, women may be actively discouraged from using family leave policies (Kachchaf, Ko, Hodari, & Ong, 2015) and reported (66 percent) that the most damaging form of gender bias is the stereotype that women lose their commitment to work and competence after they have children. In particular, URM female faculty who have children navigate additional tensions as they fight stereotypes about their work commitment and competence while having a family but also feel a need to spend time with their families to maintain work-family balance and meet responsibilities for quality community environments. Women without children reported being disadvantaged because of expectations to work additional hours to make up for schedules of colleagues who had children (Williams et al., 2014).

Another significant challenge in the workplace setting is access to mentoring. Due to gender discrimination and work-life challenges, URM professionals benefit from mentoring support (DeCastro et al., 2014; Patitu & Hinton, 2003). Mentoring can increase the mentee's performance and productivity, thereby promoting career success and advancement, and play a key role in the process of socializing early career faculty into the academic culture by providing guidance and emotional support (Chadiha, Aranda, Biegel, & Chang, 2014). Griffin and Reddick (2011) investigated mentoring relationships among Black men and women and found that Black male participants restricted their mentoring relationships because of concerns that their intent would be misinterpreted. The heightened gender and political sensibilities between men and women and across racial/ethnic groups has created divides that have increased the marginalization of URM faculty.

Although cross-gender and cross-racial/ethnic mentoring is absolutely necessary due to the majority of faculty being White males and females and increasingly international faculty, how these relationships are facilitated is a more difficult question. To develop effective cross-racial/ethnic mentoring relationships, mentors and mentees require mutual trust; building this trust means that in cross-racial/ethnic and -gender mentoring, the mentor acknowledges racism and sexism in the workplace and helps provide the mentee with strategies for managing sexism in academia (Diggs, Garrison-Wade, Estrada, & Galindo, 2009). Anecdotal experiences have uncovered a powerful hierarchy of protectors and gatekeepers of sexism and racism. All too often early career faculty, especially URM faculty, fear disclosing sexual harassment due to loss of position or a negative third year review. The intersection of sexism and racism operates more subversively. Wingfield and Feagin (2012) describe the invisible normative beliefs that are embedded in the individual and are part of everyday institutional interactions: "Underlying beliefs, attitudes and stereotypes promote the practices of institutional racism that can permeate the way an institution functions; allows whites to collude in or rationalize the systemic processes that facilitate and maintain ongoing racial privilege and inequality; . . . [and] obscures attention to the existence and consequences of these deep structural inequalities" (p. 144).

In turn, an inhospitable institutional climate contributes to race/ethnicity and gender marginalization, which leads to high levels of stress among all URM faculty, including sources of stress outside of the academic walls. Thompson and Dey (1998) posit that time constraints, promotion concerns, and overall stress were the most common for African American women but also varied by institutional climate. While stressors outside of the academy were not significant for African Americans by gender, Hernandez and Morales (1999) argue that racial and gender discrimination in academic institutions jointly affect the career development of all Latina faculty due to barriers and glass ceilings. For example, a Latina is often perceived as "someone who is in some manner expected to compromise her own career objectives because of her gender or ethnicity" (p. 53). American Indian / Alaska Native women are often showcased as being committed to diversity but perceive a strong disrespect and devaluing of their person and their work by institutional agents. One respondent reported her perceptions: "I was a targeted diversity hire at my university, charged with the task of expanding American Indian / Alaska Native and Indigenous Studies, but placed in a department under a chair who does not respect me or my discipline" (Native American female web-based survey comment).

## LIFE COURSE MILESTONES OPERATE IN DISEMPOWERING WAYS FOR URM PARTICIPANTS: CLASS, RACE/ETHNICITY, AND IDENTITY PERFORMANCE

Class and its attendant constructs such as income inequality, wealth gap, and intergenerational transmission of assets are unspoken and silent factors in the study of prestigious professional groups. The assumed high SES in academic circles and the concomitant advantages are not often available to URM professionals. Moreover, the historic links between racism and wealth inequality are ignored in the majoritarian mythical narrative of meritocracy and equal opportunity. The discourse on racial/ethnic prestigious professional groups is imbued with invisible assumptions that disempower and undermine lived experiences and impact outcomes for both men and women—namely, SES of family of origin or class background and links between wealth gaps, race, and ethnicity. A prominent and impactful factor that is not often discussed in the literature on academic life is the economic resources necessitated by the intellectual life. A small body of literature has been written about middle-class or professional Latina and African American women (Bowleg, Huang, Brooks, Black, & Burkholder, 2003; Rosenberg, Palmer, Adams-Campbell, & Rao, 1999; Vallejo, 2009), but little is available on the role of economic resources and the flow of family-of-origin resources. An earlier study observed the relationship between economics, professional status, and race: "Future research should address the various types of economic stressors that may adversely affect the health status of educated Black women" (Lawson, Rodgers-Rose, & Rajaram, 1999, p. 283). Among the few studies on Latinas on upward mobility, Jody Vallejo (2009) concludes that many upwardly mobile Latinas have achieved their mobility in one generation and lack the social and human capital resources that middle-class Whites take for granted. Persistent economic and caregiving responsibilities were confirmed as contributing to increased role strain and demands among study participants, which often depleted energy available to engage in research, produce grants and publications, and engage in quality family and social life. Thus the intersection of race, ethnicity, class, gender, and historical incorporation represents a legacy of economic disempowerment that is shared among many URM scholars.

Recent emerging scholarship is contesting sociological paradigms that fail to incorporate conceptualizations and measurement indicators of the role of racialized systems and the effects of class on the social location of racial/ethnic groups (Burton, Bonilla-Silva, Ray, Buckelew, and Freeman, 2010; Newman & Massengill, 2006). Newman and Massengill (2006) denote the salience of including class in sociological analyses: "The reintroduction of the language of class has been a hallmark of the past decade, drawing it closer to some of the original concerns of sociologists in the 1940s, contrasted with a nearly universal emphasis on race and ethnicity characteristic of more recent decades" (p. 423).

Class (SES), as it intersects with race/ethnicity in the context of this study, is a key indicator of access to social capital, particularly influential networks, quality schooling, high-resourced residential areas, and life course exposure to mainstream performance of roles and expectations. Well known is that SES benefits are not conferred across African American or racialized Mexican American and Puerto Rican or American Indian / Alaska Native populations due to racism, historic income inequalities, and wealth gaps, particularly for African Americans (Shapiro, 2017). A significant number of study participants were raised in ethnic enclaves, attended public segregated institutions, and experienced less exposure to the transmission of social capital that could effectively help them to navigate predominantly White institutions.

Lareau (2011, 2014) cogently describes the advantages of having parents with a college education. She claims that middle-income parents have more economic resources to provide multiple access points to the economic opportunity structure for the development and growth of their children in their specific talents, or in activities such as sports, which will serve them well in accomplishing future goals; middle-income families who are more educated tend to engage in parenting practices that stress communication, negotiation, logic and reasoning; and values of assertiveness and competitiveness are associated with high parental education level in all cultures. She concludes, "Looking at social class differences in standards of institutions provides a vocabulary for understanding inequality. It highlights the ways in which institutional standards give some people an advantage over others as well as the unequal ways that cultural practices in the home pay off settings outside the home. Such a focus helps to undercut the middle-class presumption of moral superiority over the poor and the working class" (2011, p. 257). Factoring into these class advantages are predominantly white parents who have completed several years of college at PWIs but did not graduate from those institutions as well as individuals who come from high SES families and are provided support throughout the life course as they transition into different phases including the professoriate. In this case, parents may provide a down payment for a home or resources to cover the costs of child care.

Professional socialization skills and institutional knowledge are much-needed resources for those who bring strong aspirational capital from families, communities, and formal schooling but have limited social capital to negotiate their agency in predominately affluent "white habitus" (Bonilla-Silva & Embrick, 2007). Socioeconomic inequality for these groups is linked to intergenerational institutional discrimination in labor and housing markets that exacerbates family wealth gaps between highly educated URMs and Whites (Lacy, 2012; Lareau, 2011), impacts individual and family strains (Rothwell & Han, 2010), and determines the outflow of resources from families of origin to their offspring (Heflin & Pattillo, 2006) and upward mobility (Burton et al., 2010; Shapiro, 2017; Vallejo, 2012).

Although professional status is strongly marked by higher economic resources, access to safe and well-resourced public spaces, economic and social support from family, and a supportive personal and professional social network, many URM professionals experience less access to family-of-origin resources and lack social networks to access additional resources. For example, this economic context of class has serious ramifications for both men and women and is further complicated by those groups whose parents have less than a high school education, namely Mexican Americans and American Indian / Alaska Natives (see Zambrana et al., 2017b). Women often experience the triple or quadruple jeopardy of race and/or ethnicity, class, and gender. One Mexican American female respondent discussing her intersectional identity and multiple risks stated, "But racism and gender? Yeah, I think so. . . . There's multiple interactions that I've had in the two . . . years that I've been here that you can deconstruct . . . on all those levels, definitely. It's in the relationships, you know." Although African American women have parents with higher SES, benefits accrued are not parallel to those of non-URM women. These shared experiences of racial/ethnic and class determinants that contribute to exclusion may mask the gender differences between URM women and men.

The recent body of research conducted by URM women scholars has illuminated two important constructs on identity performance and self-policing or accommodation (Castro, 2012; Jones & Shorter-Gooden, 2003; Shorter-Gooden, 2004). One Mexican American female respondent commented on the recognition of her own accommodation of gender discrimination: "I just kind of blew it off because stuff like that happens so much. I'm not going to waste my time getting all bent out of shape over it. And I just, you know, whatever. And I just try to blow it off. But when he had that reaction, I hadn't realized how much I—that it was really wrong and really inappropriate and that

I normalized it." An African American female midcareer participant spoke to policing her responses: "So I put up with a lot of crap to be really quite honest with you."

URM women's visibility due to their phenotype, physical appearance, or style of dress oftentimes contributes to a crisis of legitimacy whereby they feel compelled to engage in daily practices such as policing their looks or being hypervigilant about the presentation of sensitive materials in their classrooms to decrease the probability and minimize the assaults on their credentials and authority. Jones and Shorter-Gooden (2003) describe these policing behaviors as shifting, while Castro (2012) defines it as identity accommodation and policing of bodies. Shifting describes the lived experiences of many African American women in terms of language, dress, and affect. This shifting into a different self has also been referred to as code switching. The authors posit that these women feel pressure to compromise their true selves as they navigate America's racial and gender bigotry. Black women "shift" by altering the expectations they have for themselves or their outer appearance. They modify their speech. They shift inward, internalizing the searing pain of the negative stereotypes that they encounter daily. And sometimes they shift by fighting back. Notably for many racially and ethnically marked URM women, a repertoire of daily practices are employed to control and discipline their bodies in order to maintain and embody appropriate professional signals and comply to avoid ultravisibility within the unspoken majority cultural standards and expectations. URM women who are both ethnically and racially marked are often viewed as exotic, emotional, and flashy. In effect, URM women often manage "dual femininities" due to racialized gendered boundaries, as in the case of Chicana attorneys (García-López & Segura, 2008). Moreover, "doing" the professional role often requires one to perform both masculinity and Whiteness (Carbado & Gulati, 2013; Cheney & Ashcraft, 2007; Davies, Spencer, & Steele, 2005; Rivera, Forquer, & Rangel, 2010). Trethewey (1999) discusses what it takes to successfully perform and display professionalism to achieve credibility. She observes that women are required to continually control their bodies, whether in regard to curbing their weight or containing their emotions. Unlike their male counterparts, they must regularly tend to the details of sitting, walking, and moving professionally.

The study data show that both men and women are persistently confronted with gender-derived stereotypes that are problematized by class, race, and ethnicity. For Mexican American men and women, misidentification as blue- or pink-collar workers in professional settings is a persistent lived experience. For URM male respondents, their identities as "dangerous criminals who do not belong" on college campuses shape their interpersonal interactions (Nadal, Mazzula, Rivera, & Fujii-Doe, 2014; Smith, Allen, & Danley, 2007; Smith,

Yosso, & Solórzano, 2007). Limited narratives are available on the lived experiences of URM males in academic environments. Yet anecdotal tales speak to a strong set of experiences that are categorized as misidentification in the workplace, similar to tokenized others in professional settings (García-López & Segura, 2008; Pierce, 1995; Reddick & Saenz, 2012), and the prevalence, and respondents' avoidance, of the "angry Black man" stereotype (Evans & Moore, 2015). The absence of URM male voices is disconcerting as they are less likely than URM women to be retained in academic positions. One noteworthy observation is that more women than men are graduating from colleges, and women outnumbered men in the faculty in 2013 (African American females represented 6.8 percent of faculty vs. 4.3 percent males, and Latino women represented 4.5 percent vs. 3.9 percent males; U.S. Department of Education, 2015a). These data raise some questions regarding whether institutional racism is a deterrent to academic careers for URM men and suggest the importance of exploring how racism manifests itself in their lives and throughout the course of their education. Williams et al. (2014) noted the importance of understanding how patriarchy operates in tandem with racism, economic inequality, and heteronormativity to formulate the crisis that surrounds URM men in higher education.

Several conclusions can be drawn from this corpus of work: the body of knowledge on URM women and sexism remains limited, particularly for Puerto Rican and American Indian / Alaska Native women; URM women have high levels of perceived discrimination, with Mexican American and American Indian / Alaska Natives reporting the highest levels of discrimination based on race/ethnicity, gender, and class compared to their female and male counterparts; the challenges confronting URM males are relatively absent in the discourse on White patriarchal hegemonic academic spaces; and role strains experienced by both URM males and females are complicated and compromised by social and economic life course disadvantages such as the wealth gap, limited access to social capital, and absence of institutional support systems.

## THE VOICES OF URM: GENDER MATTERS

The sample consisted of more women (60 percent) than men. The females overall were younger than their male counterparts and more likely to be married and have children. Women were more likely than their male counterparts to have attended very high or high public and private research-extensive institutions, with about two-thirds of the sample attending public doctoral institutions. Among the 568 participants, 169 (29.8 percent) received a postdoctoral fellowship. Mexican American and Puerto Rican females were more likely than African American females to hold a two-year postdoctoral appointment. American

Indian / Alaska Native women (87.5 percent) and Mexican American males (85.7 percent) followed by African American (80.3 percent) women were the most likely to hold administrative positions compared to other URM women and men. About one-third of Puerto Rican men (34.5 percent) and women (33.3 percent) and American Indian / Alaska Native women (37.5 percent) held joint appointments, and about 25 percent of Puerto Rican and African American women held twelve-month appointments. The analyses show that early and mid-career faculty received doctorates from highly prestigious research universities, with women twice as likely as their male counterparts to have completed their doctorates at public universities, except for Puerto Ricans. African American and Mexican American females were more likely than their male counterparts to have two years of postdoctoral training, and women overall were more likely to have spent two years or more in postdoctoral training. For all racial/ethnic respondents, high levels of administrative service responsibility were evident due to either joint appointments or twelve-month appointments.

## GENDER DIFFERENCES FOR TOTAL SAMPLE

Table 9.1 presents scale means for the total sample to assess the domains of difference by gender. Of the fifteen variables, ten show significant differences by gender. In nine study areas, females were more likely than males to report higher mean scores. However, male respondents reported less impact of inadequate mentoring ($n = 3.44$) than females, lower means on mentor-facilitated activities, and lower frequency of mentoring contacts than females. Females overall reported higher scale scores on discrimination, role overload, vocational strain, role ambiguity, self-care, physical conditions, and mental symptoms.

Paradoxically, data on perceived discrimination are significantly higher for women than for men across all racial/ethnic groups. Women are more likely than men to report both gender and racial/ethnic discrimination. These data support URM women's perception of being viewed as passive and subservient academics who are doing "all the caretaking work" and are most likely to have their authority and legitimacy questioned by students. Moreover, higher visibility in administrative roles and navigating different departmental cultures due to joint appointments most likely increase demands and workplace stress. These responsibilities may account for women's higher reports of role strain, role ambiguity, and vocational strain. These measures highlight demands and time constraints as well as clarity in role functions. Not unexpectedly, women were more likely to report higher physical symptoms without seeing a doctor, significantly higher mean physical symptoms and depressive symptoms, and higher self-care scores overall compared to men. This aggregated profile by gender suggests a heavily taxed female group with a perceived overload of work and disclosure

TABLE 9.1 Mean scale scores for total sample by gender

| Variable | Total sample (N = 568) | Male (n = 221; 38.9%) | Female (n = 347; 61.1%) |
|---|---|---|---|
| Mean of mentor facilitated activities | 1.36 | 1.29 | 1.40 |
| | (1.61) | (1.67) | (1.57) |
| Mean of frequency mentoring functioning[a] | 13.20 | 12.94 | 13.36 |
| | (5.89) | (5.86) | (5.91) |
| Impact of inadequate mentoring[b] | 3.23 | 3.44*** | 3.10*** |
| | (1.32) | (1.25) | (1.35) |
| Mean discrimination scale | 14.38 | 12.76*** | 15.38*** |
| | (4.91) | (4.70) | (4.77) |
| Mean of physical symptoms index—doctor (individual went to see a doctor) | 0.63 | 0.52 | 0.69 |
| | (1.50) | (1.34) | (1.59) |
| Mean of physical symptoms index—other (individual did not go to see a doctor) | 3.68 | 3.34** | 3.89** |
| | (3.24) | (3.32) | (3.32) |
| Mean of physical symptoms index—total | 4.30 | 3.86** | 4.59** |
| | (3.36) | (3.22) | (3.42) |
| Mental health status scale (CES-D8)[c] | 4.16 | 3.61** | 4.51** |
| | (4.66) | (4.41) | (4.78) |
| **Occupational stress inventory scales[d]** | | | |
| Role overload scale | 32.39 | 32.21** | 32.50** |
| | (7.71) | (7.71) | (7.73) |
| Social support scale | 41.19 | 41.18 | 41.20 |
| | (8.04) | (8.20) | (7.96) |
| Role ambiguity scale | 22.57 | 22.10** | 22.86** |
| | (7.29) | (6.94) | (7.49) |
| Vocational strain scale | 18.67 | 17.62*** | 19.32*** |
| | (5.66) | (5.30) | (5.78) |
| OSI self-care scale | 28.95 | 27.71*** | 29.70*** |
| | (7.45) | (6.89) | (7.69) |
| OSI rational cognitive coping scale | 28.99 | 29.41 | 28.74 |
| | (6.77) | (6.18) | (7.10) |
| OSI recreation scale | 23.99 | 24.69 | 23.56 |
| | (7.84) | (7.76) | (7.87) |

NOTE: Values are means, with standard deviations in parentheses.

a. Mentoring scale that consists of five items with five response options. Scores range from 5 to 25, with higher scores indicating more activity (1 = *never*, 5 = *always*).

b. Mean on 5-point Likert-type scale (1 = *very significantly*, 5 = *not at all*).

c. Scores range from 0 to 24. A score ≥7 suggests a clinically significant level of psychological distress.

d. These data include only web-based study respondents.

** $p < .05$; *** $p < .01$

of discriminatory practices but high engagement in mentoring experiences and restorative practices (self-care). More in-depth analyses reveal additional differences across groups by race/ethnicity and class.

## GENDER DIFFERENCES BY RACE AND ETHNICITY

Table 9.2 displays gender differences by race/ethnicity. Among African Americans, seven out of sixteen indicators reveal significant gender differences, with males less likely to report that inadequate mentoring negatively impacted their career. Among the occupational scales, vocational strain was the only significant factor that showed a difference, with females reporting higher levels of vocational strain than males. Mexican Americans show a similar profile to African Americans with the exception of higher self-care by females. Puerto Ricans show few significant gender differences, with males reporting higher levels of mentoring functions but both males and females reporting a similar impact from inadequate mentoring. With respect to coping strategies, females reported higher self-care activities, while males reported higher use of recreational activities. A distinct profile is revealed by the American Indian / Alaska Native group, whereby females reported the highest levels of perceived discrimination.

Differences by gender across groups reveal that Puerto Rican women were more likely to report class discrimination than the total sample. Mexican American and Puerto Rican women reported higher perceptions of gender and racial/ethnic discrimination than African American women. Mexican American men were least likely to report gender discrimination, while about one-fifth of Puerto Rican men reported gender discrimination. About two in five African American and Puerto Rican men reported racial/ethnic discrimination "often or always" by a superior or colleague. Particularly noteworthy is that American Indian / Alaska Native respondent sreported the highest percentages of class discrimination, followed by Puerto Ricans overall (52.0 percent and 32.4 percent, respectively). However, Mexican American participants reported the highest frequency of mothers with less than a high school diploma ($n = 51$, 38.9 percent). In separate analyses of the Mexican American sample, findings show that those with mothers who had high school completion plus compared to those whose parents had less than a high school education were more likely to spend less years in a doctorate program, 4.33 ($SD = 0.87$) versus 6.09 ($SD = 2.17$) years; reported higher discrimination scores with a mean score of 15.54 ($SD = 4.43$) compared to 13.39 ($SD = 4.47$); and were twice as likely to report that inadequate mentoring had a "very significant/great deal" of impact on their academic careers (28.6 percent vs. 14 percent). The findings show that those with Mexican American mothers with higher education were more likely to have access to social capital throughout their life course

TABLE 9.2   Mean scale scores by race/ethnicity and gender

| Variable | African American | | | Mexican American | | | Puerto Rican | | | American Indian / Alaska Native | | |
|---|---|---|---|---|---|---|---|---|---|---|---|---|
| | Total (N = 333) | Male (n = 126; 37.8%) | Female (n = 207; 62.2%) | Total (N = 133) | Male (n = 51; 38.3%) | Female (n = 82; 61.7%) | Total (N = 77) | Male (n = 36; 46.8%) | Female (n = 41; 53.2%) | Total (N = 25) | Male (n = 8; 68.0%) | Female (n = 17; 68.0%) |
| Mean of mentor facilitated activities | 1.31 (1.584) | 1.14 (1.553) | 1.41 (1.598) | 1.44 (1.5687) | 1.18 (1.506) | 1.61 (1.593) | 1.57 (1.8095) | 2.03** (1.993) | 1.17** (1.55) | 1.00 (1.5275) | 1.13 (2.232) | 0.94 (1.144) |
| Mean of frequency mentoring functioning[a] | 13.43 (5.973) | 12.95 (5.845) | 13.74 (6.047) | 13.19 (5.5320) | 13.00 (5.733) | 13.30 (5.455) | 12.63 (6.2309) | 13.39 (6.309) | 11.94 (6.180) | 11.68 (5.5753) | 10.71 (5.736) | 12.13 (5.643) |
| Impact of inadequate mentoring[b] | 3.24 (1.398) | 3.46** (1.358) | 3.12** (1.409) | 3.22 (1.398) | 3.48* (1.037) | 3.07* (3.22) | 3.30 (1.212) | 3.43 (1.168) | 3.19 (1.256) | 3.00 (1.382) | 3.14 (1.069) | 2.94 (1.526) |
| Mean discrimination scale | 14.34 (5.003) | 12.98*** (4.812) | 15.13*** (4.953) | 14.14 (4.556) | 11.83*** (4.042) | 15.55*** (4.293) | 14.25 (4.871) | 13.21 (4.858) | 15.19 (4.762) | 16.35 (5.236) | 12.86** (6.256) | 17.88** (4.048) |
| Role overload scale[c] | 31.56 (7.63) | 31.52 (7.743) | 31.59 (7.591) | 33.53 (8.10) | 32.19 (8.034) | 34.35 (8.080) | 33.98 (6.69) | 34.75 (6.269) | 33.31 (7.046) | 33.35 (8.38) | 33.00 (9.747) | 33.50 (8.050) |
| Social support scale | 40.95 (8.60) | 40.62 (8.969) | 41.14 (8.400) | 40.92 (7.76) | | | 42.74 (5.68) | 43.57 (4.392) | 42.03 (6.828) | 41.52 (7.23) | | |
| Role ambiguity scale | 22.40 (7.39) | 22.04 (7.156) | 22.61 (7.529) | 23.40 (7.07) | 22.93 (6.579) | 23.68 (7.377) | 21.33 (7.07) | 20.54 (6.920) | 22.00 (7.224) | 24.29 (7.44) | 24.43 (5.381) | 24.21 (8.478) |
| Vocational strain scale | 18.85 (5.795) | 17.73** (5.409) | 19.52** (5.926) | 18.89 (5.678) | 17.57* (5.320) | 19.71* (5.777) | 17.51 (5.140) | 17.04 (5.081) | 17.91 (5.234) | 18.32 (4.932) | 18.43 (5.381) | 18.27 (4.949) |
| Mean of physical symptoms index—doctor (individual went to see a doctor) | 0.51 (1.309) | 0.44 (1.062) | 0.56 (1.44) | 0.83 (1.820) | 0.67 (1.645) | 0.93 (1.923) | 0.69 (1.310) | 0.33** (0.676) | 1.00** (1.628) | 0.92 (2.308) | 1.75 (3.495) | 0.53 (1.463) |

(continued)

TABLE 9.2 Mean scale scores by race/ethnicity and gender (*continued*)

| Variable | African American | | | Mexican American | | | Puerto Rican | | | American Indian / Alaska Native | | |
|---|---|---|---|---|---|---|---|---|---|---|---|---|
| | Total (N = 333) | Male (n = 126; 37.8%) | Female (n = 207; 62.2%) | Total (N = 133) | Male (n = 51; 38.3%) | Female (n = 82; 61.7%) | Total (N = 77) | Male (n = 36; 46.8%) | Female (n = 41; 53.2%) | Total (N = 25) | Male (n = 8; 68.0%) | Female (n = 17; 68.0%) |
| Mean of physical symptoms index—other (individual did not go to see a doctor) | 3.37 (3.090) | 2.94** (2.856) | 3.63** (3.202) | 4.19 (3.269) | 4.00 (3.250) | 4.30 (3.295) | 3.78 (3.202) | 3.61 (3.017) | 3.93 (3.387) | 4.80 (4.500) | 4.25 (5.092) | 5.06 (4.337) |
| Mean of physical symptoms index—total | 3.88 (3.184) | 3.37** (2.922) | 4.18** (3.303) | 5.02 (3.479) | 4.67 (3.576) | 5.23 (3.422) | 4.47 (3.243) | 3.94 (2.937) | 4.93 (3.460) | 5.72 (4.345) | 6.00 (5.043) | 5.59 (4.139) |
| Mental health status scale (CES-D8)[d] | 4.15 (4.482) | 3.56* (4.155) | 4.48* (4.630) | 4.16 (4.797) | 3.55 (4.388) | 4.56 (5.038) | 3.93 (4.967) | 3.71 (5.021) | 4.13 (4.975) | 5.04 (5.256) | 4.13 (5.842) | 5.47 (5.088) |
| Self-care Scale | 28.92 (7.714) | 28.24 (7.076) | 29.32 (8.054) | 28.47 (7.097) | 26.83* (6.889) | 29.46* (7.085) | 29.33 (7.120) | 26.86** (6.759) | 31.42** (6.828) | 30.65 (6.678) | 28.14 (4.298) | 31.75 (7.335) |
| Rational cognitive coping scale | 28.82 (6.902) | 29.58 (6.379) | 28.37 (7.168) | 28.68 (6.451) | 27.74 (5.482) | 29.25 (6.952) | 30.17 (6.251) | 30.56 (6.079) | 29.84 (6.471) | 29.70 (7.824) | 32.29 (6.211) | 28.56 (8.358) |
| Recreation scale | 24.39 (8.121) | 24.94 (8.323) | 24.07 (8.004) | 22.92 (7.126) | 23.52 (6.062) | 22.55 (7.722) | 23.90 (7.953) | 25.75* (8.4818) | 22.33* (7.300) | 24.18 (7.048) | 23.43 (4.353) | 24.53 (8.123) |

NOTE: Values are means, with standard deviations in parentheses.

a. Mentoring scale that consists of five items with five response options. Scores range from 5 to 25, with higher scores indicating more activity (1 = *never*, 5 = *always*).

b. Mean on 5-point Likert-type scale (1 = *very significantly*, 5 = *not at all*).

c. These data include only web-based study respondents.

d. Scores range from 0 to 24. A score ≥7 suggests a clinically significant level of psychological distress.

* *p* < .1; ** *p* < .05; *** *p* < .01

and were more likely to confront perpetrators of discrimination and to assess quality of Mentoring (Zambrana et al., 2017a).

Within each of the four groups, variations in experiences along the intersections of race/ethnicity and gender are observed. Women had higher mean discrimination scores than their male counterparts, with Mexican American women having the highest mean score. Mexican American women (58 percent) and African American women (51 percent) were the most likely to report these incidents as "extremely/very upsetting." The least likely to report the incidents as upsetting were African American men (40 percent) and Mexican American men (39 percent), which suggests that for men these incidents could possibly represent a "normalizing" of daily microaggressive encounters or a hardening against racism (Priest et al., 2013).

For both Mexican American and American Indian / Alaska Native female respondents, gender differences are not as striking as for African Americans, except in discrimination, where Mexican American and American Indian / Alaska Native women reported higher levels of all forms of discrimination than their African American counterparts. These higher mean scores for race/ethnicity, gender, and class bias were less prominent among Puerto Rican and African American groups. These differences may be partly explained by Mexican American and American Indian / Alaska Native female respondents more likely to be first generation (maternal education less than high school), and report a greater sense of cultural obligation to their families and communities. Similar to other participants, but with significantly higher intensity, Mexican American and American Indian / Alaska Native respondents addressed the lack of respect for their values and culture and their perceived difference and isolation in their institutions.[4] As one participant commented, "I was socialized and raised and value having a close, tight-knit relationship with my entire extended family, and that has not felt compatible with academia" (Mexican American female). Another Mexican American female respondent reflected on her educational pathway and her torn loyalties to institution and family: "It's an infrastructure thing. I think it's the way that work is set up at least in academia; where there's this model that you go off somewhere far away to study, because all you care about is the knowledge and the research. And then you go off to somewhere else to go to graduate school to study that is a good fit for that research that you're pursuing, and then you're supposed to take a job anywhere and be grateful for it because you get to study what you want to study. And I just always felt like it was such a cultural violation of everything that I was socialized to value and to care."

Several respondents discussed mentorship during their undergraduate and graduate life course journey and reported that a mentor made a significant difference in their career path. One Mexican American male respondent explained what helped him move ahead: "When I was an undergraduate, my mentor . . .

worked at the university. And I'd sit with him and talk to him. I absolutely had almost no contact with academics. He said that just continue doing what you're doing. You're doing the right thing. Don't worry about the grades. What's important is that you're there. He said it's not necessary that all the janitors are Black and the gardeners are Mexican or Indian. I noticed that all the teachers are White and that you are one of great minority. I had learned that from what I had seen, but it also was [powerful] for him to tell me that."

These results show that the overall experiences of respondents with absent or inadequate mentoring hampered development of social capital essential to academic success. Specifically the majority of respondents reported difficulty in finding mentorship to publish and develop their navigational capital and encountered racial and ethnic discrimination in the workplace such as mis-identification, stereotype threat, and lowered expectations. For example, Mexican American respondents were the most likely to report the common presence of stereotypes in their workplace settings and reported their colleagues' and administrators' use of derogatory terms when referring to Mexicans. Mexican Americans are often deemed "second-class academics" and occupy marginalized positions in higher education (Garza, 1988, 1993; Núñez, Hurtado, & Galdeano, 2015).

Female respondents clearly articulated their perception that they were responsible for and expected to perform their duties of research, teaching, and service related to representing their people and in helping students and transforming institutional structures. They did so with no additional compensation and in addition to their other responsibilities. One Native American male respondent described the institutional racism and disrespect that permeates institutions with regard to adequate compensation for leadership roles and the teaching and service burden that disproportionately impacts the career path of URM faculty because the institutional racism, including the service burden, deprives them of time to engage in research production and contributes to majority faculty not having to engage in any diversity service. American Indian / Alaska Native faculty may especially encounter racism in the classroom and negative evaluations, particularly when interacting with students on multicultural issues.

## SAFETY IN WHITE SPACES: GENDER, (IN)VISIBILITY, AND IDENTITY ACCOMMODATION

The data show a set of patterns across race/ethnicity that are most striking with respect to gender differences within and across groups. Gender did not account for large differences as all respondents had relatively high mean scores for major study variables. For URM men and women, inadequate mentoring and discriminatory practices contribute to high levels of feeling upset and few resources to buffer the discriminatory incidents, particularly economic. Some explanations for men consistently reporting fewer mentoring activities included, as reflected in their narratives, senior mentors not reaching out and providing clear advice, feeling dismissed and not returning for advice, and lack of interest in topics being investigated. Women reported a higher number of mentor-facilitated activities and functions, which may suggest that they reach out to a larger circle of senior mentors and/or that majority-culture males are more responsive to URM women. Alternatively, females' higher mentoring interactions, jointly with engagement in higher institutional service activities, may account for greater exposure to racist incidents and discriminatory practices. In other words, women are in unsafe public spaces to a larger extent than their male counterparts and are witnesses to as well as targets of racist incidents. Mexican American females and Puerto Rican males were most likely to report racism, while Mexican American males were the least likely to report incidents of discrimination.

Mentoring is crucial to all professionals and is needed most by racial/ethnic groups who did not have mentors throughout their life course and struggled with whether they made the wrong career choice (Hernández-Avila, 2003; Stein, 1994; Tippeconnic & McKinney, 2003). An important question raised by these data is the quality of the mentoring relationship between URM males and institutional agents. Inadequate mentoring can derail a career path particularly if the individual has limited social capital to buttress the inadequacy of guidance and assistance. The conundrum is that in spite of women experiencing the highest burden of service obligations and strain, men are more likely to leave the academic career path. Future inquiry can more comprehensively explore in what ways the mentoring experience is not supporting and in turn retaining URM men in the academy. These data signal the loss of a crucial cohort in the academy, which requires remediation if we are to be inclusive of the next generation of young men and future scholars.

Vocational strain and physical and mental health outcomes were higher for females. These areas were fully explored in prior chapters. Prior work has suggested that the wealth gap, the flow of resources back to the family of origin, unwelcoming environments, and high levels of institutional service, especially among women, can be exceptionally burdensome. An African American female described the stress of teaching and the lack of respect experienced as part of fulfilling her role obligations:

> Along with teaching, I do feel that students—for me I think it has been until recently an intersection of race, gender, and perceived age, because there was a time when I taught here earlier where I think I had even a younger appearance and students—I just think they looked at those three factors. And challenged me a lot and questioned why I did things the way I did and argued with me over

grades and things like that. So I definitely think that students—my perception is that there are a lot of students who I have felt that or suspected that students, a lot of students will treat women and faculty of color with less respect.

However, we can speculate that the emotional and physical toll of performing the multiple roles of worker, daughter, partner, friend, and oftentimes caregiver without economic and social resources contributes to strain and stress for both men and women. The data suggest a high usage of emotional labor and racial battle fatigue in daily interactions with faculty and students with first-generation Mexican Americans and American Indian / Alaska Native respondentsreporting the highest perceptions of exclusion from majority-culture activities and high perceived disregard for the unique social and ethnic aspects of group obligations to family and community.

## MULTIPLE DISADVANTAGES IN INTERSECTIONAL GENDER STATUS

Challenges to White feminist thought have a bitter yet recalcitrant history. Although many women feel the omnipresent chill of sexism, URM women experience a unique double or triple minority status (racism, sexism, and elitism) that renders them invisible to the persistent challenges (e.g., everyday microaggressions, negative mentoring relationships) they confront due to their social status, such as ethnocentrism and patriarchy (Espino, 2016; Hernandez-Truyol, 1997). Many of the respondents observed that the focus on women did not include them. One African American male observed, "And so over the last ten years there have been a significant number of women who have been promoted, you know, with tenure in those particular areas, particularly in engineering and a lot of the natural mathematical sciences. So there is conversation and dialogue around issues of diversity but that diversity pretty much focuses on gender and very—relatively little bit in regard to race and ethnicity." An African American female midcareer participant spoke more directly to the issue of what she termed gender racism: "So I think there is some bias, but it's the gender racism combined bias versus the just gender bias because the White women seem to be thriving. . . . We have a female dean. Our president went from being a provost, a female and she's president of the university. . . . White women are doing well."

Important factors influence URM experiences such as colorism and political ideology. For example, subscribing to a White normative ideology and/or color blindness most likely contributes to more receptive conditions in institutional environments. Many faculty of all racial/ethnic groups avoid challenging existing normative structures to protect their jobs, because the institutional ideology and practice is already consistent with their views, or they enjoy the status of honorary Whites (Bonilla-Silva, 2006). Other factors that may inform group "fit" include an upper-middle-class family ancestry that has bestowed the privileges of dominant culture environments and social capital, such as professional networks and the confidence to navigate institutional spaces.[5] An important insight is that within URM groups, differences exist based on SES, colorism, reported multiraciality, and life course experiences such as being reared in White-dominant communities versus ethnically segregated neighborhoods. Yet mistreatment of racial/ethnic groups has been observed to disadvantage some groups more than others and is associated with above factors and region of the United States. An analysis of the data showed that American Indian / Alaska Natives reported the least institutional support resources and the most adverse physical and mental health profile. It was estimated in 2014 that only one in four American Indian / Alaska Native students between eighteen and twenty-four years old was enrolled in a degree-granting postsecondary institution. Unlike for all other URM groups, the percentage of enrollment of American Indian / Alaska Native students has failed to grow (Field, 2017). Similar to American Indian / Alaska Natives, "the majority of Chicano/a in faculty positions in major research universities are first-generation (first to graduate high school) academics" (Reyes, 1997, p. 18) and experience the "push-pull effect" between Chicanas' professional careers and cultural identity.

Although the majoritarian narrative tells individuals that upward mobility alleviates marginalization and discrimination, URM faculty and especially women continue to report unequal treatment by colleagues and students, which diminishes their ability to function at their highest levels of competence and research productivity. In effect, scholars widely agree that implicit bias is structurally embedded in institutional policies and practices that drive the power relations between dominant and subordinate groups, providing the privilege of authority and respect to some groups over others and some women over others. This is the paradox of institutions that employ color-blind racist practices (Evans & Moore, 2015; Embrick, 2015). These findings provide evidence for why research and policies must acknowledge the unique positionalities, experiences, and treatment of individuals of intersecting coconstituted identities and particularly how gender matters within groups and across racial/ethnic gender groups. Academia can be characterized as a colonizing force, insisting that URM faculty in general conform to Eurocentric standards, values, and scholarship to promote their success, resulting in experiences of devaluation and not belonging in these institutions of higher education.

# 10 · CREATING A SENSE OF BELONGING FOR URMS IN THE ACADEMY

No one will look at you and see the next great scientist. Don't expect to be recognized or noticed. Certainly, don't expect to be given the benefit of having unrealized potential. You will have to work twice as hard, you will have to give 200 percent, because you must repaint a portrait that they have already painted of you—stroke by stroke.

—Mexican American female

The rendering of the lived experiences of historically under-represented racial/ethnic groups has yielded multiple insights that make a difference in, and partly determine, life course outcomes. Traversing through many disciplinary and interdisciplinary fields of knowledge, including sociology, history of higher education, women's and gender studies, public health, racial/ethnic studies, and psychology, yielded a deep interpretive context that allowed a rich mapping of the multilevel factors that are silently associated with URM educational trajectories and professional pathways. Several troubling discoveries have emerged: as a nation we are in trouble on all fronts in terms of equity and equality; very modest progress has been accomplished in fifty years regarding inclusion and equity for these U.S. racial/ethnic minorities; available data on institutions of higher education tend to combine racial/ethnic international and immigrant groups to enhance the profile of progress; historically under-represented groups continue to experience severe underrepresentation in all professions including the professoriate; and euphemisms such as *diversity, people of color,* and *inclusion* masquerade as indicators of change but in reality represent temples of power to disguise privilege and exclusion. Equally important is the relative absence of empirical work on lived experiences of historically underrepresented minority faculty in mainstream journals that sustain the invisibility of limited progress. The celebration of fifty years of the *Chronicle of Higher Education* illustrates that the headlines in the 1970s were similar to those in contemporary editions, with underrepresented minorities noticeably absent from both. In fact, we may not be witnessing much progress at all but rather experiencing the power that language has to create illusions of progress.

In each chapter of this book, a narrative has been weaved portraying the life course experiences of URM faculty and their strategies to navigate difficult professional institutions and situations to achieve career success. These faculty experiences in predominantly White research universities demonstrate the ways in which historically exclusionary practices have served to create separate but unequal minority-serving colleges and universities. Unwelcoming climates in elite higher education institutions have continued to perpetuate forms of persistent and unrelenting unfair and unequal treatment (racism). These institutional practices adversely affect patterns of retention, tenure, and promotion and in turn have repercussions for URM physical and mental health outcomes. These outcomes are detrimental to institutions of higher education as a whole as institutional investments yield limited benefits for all of their students and contribute to significant harm to URM faculty.

To contextualize these data, this chapter draws on striking themes evoked by the narratives to inform how institutional structures are deeply embedded in the reproduction of exclusion and racism while simultaneously claiming the diversity discourse as a language of power to maintain the status quo; discusses select high-impact, solution-driven responses and effective institutional practices to increase recruitment and retention of URM; and ponders future challenges that are driven by the reality that the university is a state-driven institution implicated in broader systems of the reproduction of power relations and the maintenance of the status quo.

This book was written at a historical moment when individual opinion reigns regal on the entire spectrum of intellectual thought. From alt-right to progressive White scholars, a discourse exists. Many White scholars have joined URM scholars to express outrage at blatant inequity in our higher education system. Marybeth Gasman, professor at the University of Pennsylvania, incited the higher education community with her article in the *Washington Post* (September 26, 2016) titled "An Ivy League Professor on Why Colleges Don't Hire More Faculty of Color: 'We Don't Want Them.'" What has for so long been unspoken yet lingering in the shadows of intellectual discourses is that inequity is reproduced throughout the life course in the communities where many URMs live and attend school and later in their social networks and careers. Marcia Chatelain, professor of history at Georgetown University, in discussing slavery and other forms of exclusion, stated, "What institutions need to think about is historical impact, their exclusionary policies toward various communities, and the way that institutions are uniquely poised to do the critical work of racial reconciliation and healing." Yet healing cannot be accomplished without institutional change, accountability, and acknowledgment of past and current wrongs.

Only a small number of URM individuals have had the opportunity to enter elite academic institutions, and they unquestionably remain severely underrepresented with respect to their proportion in the U.S. population. However, the misappropriation of the word *underrepresented* for numerous non-URM groups clouds the struggle for proportional representation, a goal White women and underrepresented minorities have been arguing for since the early twentieth century. URM groups have distinct legacies of past and current treatment that shape their lived experiences in institutional White spaces. The three distinguishing characteristics of URM groups are (1) historicity of colonized and enslaved peoples, not voluntary immigrant or refugee subjects; (2) historic stereotypic representations that infuse the unconscious structure of our institutions and nurture implicit bias; and (3) persistent and unwavering policies and practices that historically and in the contemporary moment disfavor these groups and were the cornerstone of discriminatory practices such as Jim Crow laws. The focus of this book is on those nonimmigrant groups whose incorporation into the United States was involuntary and who experienced formal legal and informal exclusion from access to civil liberties in the country up to the middle of the twentieth century. Grappling with the preponderance of evidence (statistical data, narratives, autobiographies, and small studies since the early 1970s) on mistreatment and exclusion of URM faculty, the data reveal that the topic of equity and fairness is not novel (Aisenberg & Harrington, 1988; Higginbotham, 2009; Moses, 1989; Turner & Myers, 2000; Valverde, 1993). However, overwhelming gaps exist in critical race/ethnicity/class analyses of the intersection of an institutional narrative of fair and equitable practices and the lived experiences of underrepresentation and exclusion.

## SNAIL-LIKE PROGRESS: STRUCTURAL INEQUALITY VERSUS INDIVIDUAL DEFICITS

Social scientists, especially in sociology, education, and psychology, have weathered disciplinary and interdisciplinary tensions regarding the role of individual agency and the power of structure. Although the intellectual compromise is that each factor plays an important role in a person's ultimate outcome, in this case faculty retention and promotion, these data suggest otherwise. A burning question lurks within the higher education diversity discourse: is there a moral imperative to intentionally include historically URM groups? The first argument to be made is that the majority of URM faculty bring a range of intellectual and pedagogical diversity of thought. Their particular life course experiences often shape how they teach, what they study, and their ability to nurture and mentor and serve as role models to the next generation of all students. They are a valuable domestic talent pool yet have been overwhelmingly unwelcomed throughout the history of higher education. As chapter 2 has detailed, from their inception, U.S. colleges and universities have been a predominately White, male, and upper-class environment. Though URMs started to be included at more substantial rates during the mid-1970s, their numbers have remained relatively stagnant despite their increasing numbers in the U.S. population. A plethora of reports in recent years have argued convincingly on the importance of employing URM faculty. For example, between 1985 and 2013, the percentage of URM full-time instructional faculty at degree-granting institutions grew from 4.1 percent to 6.0 percent for Blacks and from 1.7 percent to 5.0 percent for Hispanics, and Native Americans have remained the same at 0.4 percent. The invisibility of the taxation experienced by URM faculty is unveiled outside the boundaries of mainstream literature in what is often referred to as the gray literature. All too often the body of work that examines URM adverse experiences in academia is published in nonmainstream journals and by peripheral presses, which suggests that mainstream publication outlets have limited interest in writings that challenge their privilege and power and that unmask processes of racism (Christian, 2012; Cooper & Stevens, 2002; McNeal, 2003).

Six major themes were pointedly evoked from the data collected for this book: academic isolation and torn/dual cultural identities, lack of institutional supports including access to effective mentoring and difficult interpersonal experiences, devalorization of research agenda and methodologies, racial/ethnic/cultural taxation of university service, encounters with discrimination and racism, and the adverse impact of these experiences on their physical and mental health. While this book discusses overarching themes that provide rich insight into the obstacles to successful career pathways that so stubbornly persist, the experiential themes are illustrated in four areas that engage institutional change: promoting a sense of belonging, transmission of social capital, diversity laborers, and the impact of vigilance and excessive workplace stress on physical and mental well-being.

The data show a profound consistency between workplace stressors, perceived lack of belonging, and intellectual research agenda. The narrative data provoke deep reflection and serve to guide possible explanations for the survey findings. For example, it has been empirically documented, but institutionally denied, that URM research agendas that tackle and uplift deep-rooted racial, ethnic, and gender inequality in research publications are not given the same weight, legitimacy, and acclaim.[1] Closely related to this conundrum is the traditional objection to the use of nonmainstream theoretical frameworks such as

CRT and intersectional theory that instigate analyses by examining power rela-tions, historic antecedents, and repeated patterns of inequity throughout the life course. Study participants described the rigorous challenges they confronted in navigating these elite academic White spaces, shining a light on structural inequality.

## PROMOTING A SPACE OF BELONGING: NAVIGATING THE HALLS OF THE IVORY TOWER

A principal overarching theme from the study data is that the majority of par-ticipants pursued the doctorate in elite research institutions to take their place in the professorial ranks because they possessed a deeply contested cognitive map embodied in the discourse on race/ethnicity that fueled their research agenda. They also reported a strong commitment and caring ethic about the world and their communities and expressed a desire to make a difference in all students' lives, uplift disadvantaged individuals and their communities, and train the next generation of leaders in ethical and equitable practices and policies. In spite of their deep social commitments to community, they reported a sense of unbe-longing in their work environments. For many of the participants, their path to the professoriate was not planned but came about due to life course experi-ences with parents, mentors, and role models who encouraged their intellectual growth via success in school and research experiences in college and provided practical guidance in how to continue to seek resources to develop a career. The participants were smart, admired, and talented in many ways. Nonetheless many had grown, developed, and resided among their own group and thus had less familiarity with Anglocentric ways of being and knowing and in turn had less access to the social networks needed to connect with the people and resources that are necessary to build a successful career.

While URMs were explicitly excluded from early U.S. colleges, the exclusion is implicit in research universities today. In particular, URMs continue to expe-rience the effects of institutionalized racism and normative value systems that permeate institutional culture as seen through implicit bias and stereotype (see chapter 5). These effects are made tangible through formal policies and proce-dures, including search committees and the scholars targeted, and are informal, such as how search committees evaluate candidates, specifically the value placed on various forms of scholarship as well as how candidates are perceived. The notion of the "fit," or the "quality of the mind," "is a particular enigma"; "Conse-quently, respondents reported witnessing or being subjected to statements on a regular basis that suggest that their racial/ethnic status—and that of other can-didates for faculty positions—marks them as distinct, different, and unable to fit or integrate fully into the institutional structure" (Zambrana, Wingfield, Lapey-rouse, Dávila, Hoagland, & Burciaga Valdez, 2017, p. 222).

URMs also feel these effects as they attempt to navigate the unwritten rules of their departments and universities (chapter 7). Without the appropriate social networks and informal knowledge, URMs often find themselves "out of the loop" on tenure and promotion guidelines, family leave protocol, and other important career-defining procedures (see chapters 6 and 7). Beyond these constraints, research on the roles of race/ethnicity in psychological functioning and stress offers important insights into the effects of implicit bias in academic institutional culture. Understanding how race operates psychologically, for example, the effects of implicit bias, highlights why this is important in under-standing public policy choices and the effectiveness of these policies (Godsil, 2015). URMs' sense of isolation or being "the only one," overt and covert racism and discrimination leading to a feeling of being "set up to fail," and the devaluing of their research and intellectual pursuits characterize the unwelcoming insti-tutional climates in which they find themselves (see chapter 5). Whereas many respondents reported that they became academics to address issues in marginal-ized communities like their own, they found their work dismissed or disregarded by colleagues. Additionally, they reflected on the high racial/ethnic tax or bur-den demanded of them for diversity service and group representation.

## SOCIAL CAPITAL IS NOT A MAGIC KEY
## BUT A KEY THAT OPENS DOORS

A second theme is the role of mentoring as a mechanism for the transmission of social capital and social support resources. Table 4.1 shows the different phases of support and building of social capital throughout the life course that enabled the participants to enter the halls of the ivory tower (see chapter 4). Mentorship is part of professional socialization and goes beyond training to include counsel, guidance, and facilitation of intellectual and career development. While the tra-ditional mentor-protégé relationship has been questioned (Hansman, 2002) and mentoring should not be considered a panacea for all of their challenges, atten-tion to faculty development and support through mentoring and other means are needed (Turner, González, & Wood, 2008). For instance, a one-size-fits-all mentorship model is problematic for URMs in elite PWIs, particularly when they view only White senior faculty and administrators in the ranks and do not see other faculty like themselves represented (Stanley, 2006, p. 713).

Cook and Gibbs (2009) recommend faculty development programs to increase retention and provide the educational and socialization experiences necessary to reduce gender and racial disparities in academic promotions. From a resilience framework, Cora-Bramble (2006) suggests supporting faculty to develop an "academic survival toolkit" that includes the personal and professional competencies (e.g., training on assertiveness, cross-ethnic power dynamics, negotiation, and networking skills) that have been found to be protective mechanisms or buffers mitigating the adverse effects of disparate treatment in academic promotion, inadequate mentorship, or unequal access to academic opportunities. Building a scholarly community at both the institutional and departmental levels through mentorship and other faculty development programs will help to increase retention and provide the educational and socialization experiences necessary to reduce gender and racial disparities in academic promotions (Cook & Gibbs, 2009; Turner et al., 2008). Although ideal mentors should possess a racial/ethnic/gender lens for understanding their mentees and promoting sensitivity to the particular issues that faculty face, they do not necessarily have to be of the same gender or racial/ethnic background as their mentees (Weems, 2003).

Mentoring is a crucial component of educational access, advancement, and success in faculty retention. Fair and ethical principles need to guide and be responsive to helpful mentoring based on mentees' needs. Strategies of good mentors include (1) showing deep respect for mentees' contributions, ideas, and intellect (Nakamura, Shernoff, & Hooker, 2009); (2) offering political guidance in the form of knowledge about institutional norms and the role of race and power relations in higher education institutions without demanding assimilation; (3) forging connections between mentees and interested and responsive faculty who have power and prestige; and (4) providing concrete scholarly opportunities along with offering moral support and encouragement in ways that promote mentees' autonomy and independent scholarship.

## DIVERSITY LABORERS: INSTITUTIONAL MASCOTS

A third theme is the participants' perceived functionality as diversity laborers or institutional servants propagating an institutional image of diversity and a reputation as inclusive. This is a paradox for the faculty because they perceive themselves as agents of change both within and outside of their workplace and the institution perceives them as institutional agents of service within the institution. This service labor force is a valuable resource for the institution for which they oftentimes receive neither monetary compensation nor reward in their system of career advancement. Thus the institution colludes with its own faculty to disregard and undervalue the central assets of this URM faculty group to demonstrate the illusion of change.

Many participants perceived that both their time and their research responsibilities were undermined. The majority of respondents reported being asked to represent their racial/ethnic group for special visitors or accrediting committees and for university and departmental hiring committees and were required to teach race/ethnicity and diversity courses regardless of their area of expertise. Although the unique focus of their research agenda and expertise was touted for visitors and in reports, it was not perceived as salient in the tenure and promotion process. All too often diversity work or what is referred to as identity and cultural taxation (Joseph & Hirshfield, 2011) was used in the interest of the university and to the detriment of the faculty member. University-related diversity work was time-consuming, involved tedious emotional labor, and oftentimes was disturbing to the participants because it involved pretense regarding the valuing of diversity to aspiring faculty applicants or external accreditation members. Several compelling narratives address the diversity rhetoric and the required performance (Chun & Evans, 2012; Gutierrez y Muhs, 2012; Harley, 2008). Chapters 5 and 6 detailed diversity faculty requirements as discrimination since generally majority-culture and many international faculty are not often asked to perform in this capacity.

An equitable solution to the additional diversity work is threefold: recognize and reward faculty who carry additional service or teaching burdens (e.g., URM, women) monetarily and/or by providing additional teaching assistants, take into account service obligations, and consider additional responsibilities in the promotion and tenure process (Brayboy, 2003; Eddy & Gaston-Gayles, 2008; Gallagher & Trower, 2009; Griffin & Reddick, 2011; Rodríguez, Campbell, Fogarty, & Williams, 2014; Stanley, 2006; Turner, 2002; Williams, Phillips, & Hall, 2014); ensure that faculty are not overinvolved in service-related activities (Stanley, 2006); and provide training for chairs and departmental faculty on the distinct needs and challenges of various pools of faculty groups, including URM, international, and differently abled faculty.

## VIGILANCE AND EMOTIONAL LABOR: EXCESSIVE WORKPLACE STRESS AND IMPACT ON HEALTH

Another major theme for participants is the anticipatory stress of racism and discrimination in blatant and subtle forms that have been embedded in lived experience throughout the life course (Zambrana, Wingfield, Lapeyrouse, Hoagland, & Burciaga Valdez, 2016). These deprivileging experiences are entrenched in institutional cultures and reproduced in the workplace environment. For example, institutional agents' perceptions of their research *as not scientific enough* jointly with lack of mentoring and support resources have been injurious to their career paths and well-being. Together, psychological vigilance coupled with perceived surveillance and hypervisibility contribute to presumed incompetence, lower productivity, and stress-related symptoms, which can take a toll on physical and mental well-being. Persistent interrogations of who they are, what their research interests are, and "where they came from" represent a pervasive and unrelenting source of stress. Unpleasant peer interactions and excessive institutional demands encourage fear and distance rather than a sense of community belonging. Incidents of discrimination in elite universities are racially stratified in large part because more senior faculty tend to come from White privileged backgrounds while URM faculty are often the first in their families to pursue academic careers. Furthermore, despite the relative upward mobility of URM faculty, they are still subject to the negative impact of life course and intergenerational effects of discrimination and wealth gaps.

Therefore, the chronic nature of race-based discrimination and the continuing microaggressions, reduced opportunities, and effects of major life events contribute to the adverse physiological effects (allostatic load) that can accelerate disease processes. Persistent undermining of one's competency and hypervigilance due to persistent chronic exposure to discrimination, perceived or anticipated, in the workplace and over the life course contribute to cumulative disadvantages for physical and mental health, which may help explain the lower rates of retention, promotion, and tenure of URM faculty and observed premature morbidity and mortality.

These findings provide insights into strategic actions that universities can employ to improve retention and nurture a more welcoming and responsive climate for URM faculty. Drawing from the work of Delgado and Stefancic (2001), Griffin and colleagues (2011a, 2001b), and Zambrana et al. (2016), elite universities can diminish discriminatory practices by looking beyond overt individual cases of racism and cultivating campus awareness that racism is endemic to higher education (Museus, Ledesma, & Parker, 2015).

The following section synthesizes literature reviews, institutional reports on policies and practices, and study narratives to identify strategies that support the premise that racial, ethnic, and gender inclusion of URM faculty is an asset not only to institutional diversity goals but also to innovative knowledge production, the transfer of diverse knowledge, and robust partnerships between universities and underserved communities. A faculty that is *more* connected to the campus, community, and social issues ensures the viability, vitality, and relevance of the academy.

## TRANSFORMING THE INSTITUTION: BUILDING URM REPRESENTATION VIA RESPONSIVE AND EFFECTIVE STRATEGIC ACTIONS AND PRACTICES

Institutional transformation requires a critical examination of the values and philosophy of the institution, and an incorporation of multiple faculty pools that capitalize on the talents, perspectives, and values each group has to offer. The landmark step is to engage majority-culture White faculty and international faculty in critical self-reflection regarding knowledge of other groups, implicit biases, prejudice (Robinson, 2014), and elitism. Ross (2011) advocates a transformation-based model of diversity competency training, where people come to "understand their own view of the world and to look outside of their view to see and understand the experiences and viewpoints of others," which is critical both for faculty and for the departmental and institutional leadership (Price et al., 2005). Institutional leaders should implement focused and specific initiatives to improve interactions between URM and White faculty. Four areas of import include institutional climate; recruitment, hiring, and retention; tenure and promotion; and work-family practice.

## Institutional Climate

Activities that support the development of an institutional culture that encourages faculty to openly express opinions, makes them feel valued, builds social connections and professional partnerships that bridge diversity lines, and incorporates faculty perspectives into the main mission and culture of the institution are important steps toward building an interpersonal culture that embraces equity and inclusion in diversity (Cook & Gibbs, 2009; Piercy et al., 2005). Three exemplars of fair, intentional, and equitable practice are proffered. Institutions need to embrace dedicated support within departments, profile work of URM faculty to the same extent as that of non-URM faculty, and encourage faculty to produce and contribute with more enthusiasm to the field and the institution (Bhopal & Jackson, 2013). Institutional leadership needs to embrace a broader and more inclusive definition of scholarship in the form of a statement that is disseminated from the provost's office (Career Leadership & University Excellence, 2012). Institutional supports including mentoring and transmission of knowledge by senior faculty and majority peers in the form of transparent and helpful advice and clarification of procedures serve a foundational role in helping to understand the "rules of the game" in academia. Deans and chairs play a particularly central role in facilitating knowledge of the normative institutional expectations and transmitting social capital such as access to career-enhancing networks to early career faculty and in promoting responsive practices among senior faculty. Annual meetings between department chairs and early career faculty can be planned to learn of their progress, to guide and assess research productivity, and to become informed of the roles that URM faculty play in diversity-related activities such as mentoring students. Moreover, implementing training modules for all faculty on supporting faculty and students from diverse ethnic and URM backgrounds can serve as an equity tool for workload (Bhopal & Jackson, 2013).

## Recruitment, Retention, and Promotion

There are many assumptions underlying the "promising" practices for diverse faculty hiring that, for the most part, are ineffective in actually changing the overall composition of the faculty (Kayes, 2006, p. 65). A common assumption is that if the president, provost, dean, chair, and onward down the line of key stakeholders all openly advocate for hiring URM faculty, it will be actualized during the search and hiring process. However, members of hiring committees are often not diverse themselves or not well informed about the mission to recruit URM faculty (American Federation of Teachers, 2010) and have implicit biases, such as eliminating candidates based on what graduate school they attended, with the highest-ranked candidates frequently having attended elite research-extensive institutions (Mickelson & Oliver, 1991). *Recruitment* of diverse faculty is not *retention*, so any initiatives to diversify faculty that fail to address hostile institutional climates will end up fueling the "revolving door" so common for URM faculty (Kayes, 2006, p. 65).

Chapter 7 highlighted that for early career faculty the recruitment and tenure and promotion processes are often unclear, and respondents perceive less fair and equitable treatment. Imprecise standards and guidelines for promotion and tenure lead some faculty to feel as though they are being set up to fail. As illustrated, respondents perceived that they were being evaluated and rewarded differently than their non-URM colleagues, and this began at the recruitment stage. Various scholars who have studied the factors that influence success of recruitment of URMs recommend proactive, ongoing, inclusive models of recruitment that include all faculty members, even those not on the search committee (Adams & Bargerhuff, 2005; Bilimoria & Buch, 2010). Rather than passive job postings or mass emails announcing a position, the institution should be actively cultivating relationships and supporting the growth and development of URM alumni and other scholars at nearby universities to increase the pool of candidates.

In addition, departmental and institutional procedures on tenure and promotion criteria need to be clear, transparent, and equitable to ensure that all faculty understand the expectations for achieving tenure (Turner et al., 2008; Weems, 2003) and that the relevant scholarly pursuits of a diverse faculty are recognized and rewarded and "not derailed through diversity service." Equitable tenure and promotion policies must be inclusive of new and interdisciplinary or alternative ways of thinking, teaching, and writing within a more diverse academy. Broadening the range of legitimate scholarly activity includes recognizing publications in peer-reviewed journals that embrace a wider range of interdisciplinary scholarship, recognizing and valuing teaching and service engagement on diversity and race/ethnicity/gender and class issues, supporting faculty engagement in socially relevant and engaged scholarship, and providing opportunity for authentic academic expression for a diverse academic faculty. Additionally, the inequitable distribution of service, mentoring, and advising responsibilities carried by URM faculty needs to be either redistributed or accorded appropriate recognition in the evaluation, tenure, and promotion process (Cook & Gibbs, 2009; Moore et al., 2010; Piercy et al., 2005; Turner et al., 2008; Weems, 2003). Strategic actions that can be implemented are interrelated and include promoting tenure clarity through making explicit how the institutional mission affects faculty work; setting weights or priorities for faculty work, including defined and explicated factors beyond excellence in teaching and research that matter for tenure; providing written and clear information to faculty about how tenure is achieved and how this interfaces with mentoring; giving annual feedback to early career faculty; and providing sample model dossiers and feedback letters.

While institutions are hurriedly implementing multiple approaches to enact the contemporary buzzwords of transparency, fairness, and equity, the racialized hierarchy in higher education, guided by what is referred to as the White racial frame (Bonilla-Silva, 2009; Feagin, 2013) or the power and privilege of those who lead, remains unchanged. For example, recent policy obligates candidates for tenure and promotion to sign a form that confirms the dossier documents provided to the tenure or promotion committee. All the documents are important. Yet the fact that documents are available does not address the mind-set and predetermined criteria of the faculty who are the peer evaluators. A supportive recommended practice in the tenure process is a collaborative process between the departmental unit head and the faculty member in selection of the chair and the members of their tenure or promotion committee. Moreover, many early career faculty, especially URM faculty, require the department chair to inform them of the nature and scope of research domains and publication outlets. The tenure and promotion committee chair must be prepared to teach how to prepare a "winning" personal statement and other documents to address any potential institutional perceived pitfalls in the dossier.

Alternatively, other evidence reveals that initiatives geared toward creating more hospitable environments for women have achieved important levels of success. For example, the National Science Foundation's ADVANCE program, which began in 2001 with the goal of increasing the representation and advancement of women in science and engineering, has funded projects at more than one hundred higher education institutions and STEM-related nonprofit organizations. Through these initiatives, higher education institutions have successfully increased the number of women faculty and administrators. These emerging institutional agents are now in a proactive position to evaluate and identify accountability measures to innovate and adapt new practices, policies (such as work-family policies), and strategies to continue to increase the representation of women in STEM-related academic careers and leadership roles (see National

Academy of Sciences, 2007). These national initiatives to increase representation of women at all levels and to promote successful career trajectories suggest that targeted programs can also be enacted effectively in higher education institutions to increase representation of URM men and women faculty.

## Work-Family Balance Practices

Chapter 6 discussed the struggles of respondents in maintaining a healthy work-family balance. A significant finding was that both men and women placed a high value on parenting and experienced barriers to balance. For example, several male respondents emphasized the role of "superdaddy" as a response to stereotypic perceptions of racial/ethnic men not being responsible fathers. Work-family balance involved the strains of perceived excessive work demands in an environment of discrimination and racism, albeit covert, among a legacy of family economic disadvantage. Study participants described a lack of information on how to access work-family policies, their fears of being regarded as a challenging faculty member, a lack of belongingness within their collegial network, a racial/ethnic tax characterized by feeling unvalued in their work roles, being marginalized and isolated on campus, and being burdened by expected service on diversity committees. These study findings provide rich insights into how these professionals view their career choices as sacrifices. These data fill a major gap in the family science and higher education literature on how their experiences may differ from those of their non-URM counterparts.

Given the evidence that it is more difficult for women with children to achieve tenure, universities themselves have designed and implemented policies to address these inequities. The effectiveness of these policies reveals differences by institutions in both access to and use of policies that are often inhibited by departmental culture and built-in limitations. Earlier studies identified structural reasons why there is resistance to encouraging women faculty to use family work policies or to develop more effective policies: administrators have cited financial costs, the limitations of flexibility, and perceptions of fairness (Quinn, Lange, & Olswang, 2004; Raabe, 1997; Sullivan, Hollenshead, & Smith, 2004; Varner, 2000; Ward & Wolf-Wendel, 2012; Young & Wright, 2001).[2] Another study compared faculty work-life policies among the top ten medical schools and rated each school across a variety of available policies and programs.[3] Findings showed that "accessibility to policy information is generally inconsistent and unclear, and only 39% of the policies were available to the public online" (Bristol, Abbuhl, Cappola, & Sonnad, 2008, p. 1313). Welch, Wiehe, Palmer-Smith, and Dankoski (2011) replicated this study with Big Ten medical schools and confirmed that policies differed extensively by institution based on length of time at university and part-time or full-time status.[4] Women faculty may be hesitant to employ university policies because of a larger culture that considers their use evidence that one does not "have what it takes" to become a full professor, yet policy effectiveness may be measured by the progress women have achieved in rates of increase in tenure and promotion (American Council on Education, 2015; Johnson, 2016). Furthermore, the menu of options available to a significant portion of women based on family of origin, partner profession, and homophily increases their strategies for managing multiple responsibilities such as taking extended leaves without pay, scaling back, outsourcing domestic labor, and/or "the gendered likelihood of quitting which reinforces the separate spheres of work and home" (Cha, 2010; Moen, Lam, Ammons, & Kelly, 2013).[5]

Nonetheless, the push to increase the representation of majority-culture women in all professional occupations, including medicine, law, and higher education, has been largely a success. The current climate has shown itself to be increasingly "friendly" to women as more women in positions of leadership promote women-friendly policies. In contrast, data show that for URM women and men, the coconstituted identity of race/ethnicity and gender doubles the burden of bias and the fears of using family leave policies for either parenting or other extended family caretaking. A limited body of work is available on URM use of family friendly policies with few exceptions (Castañeda et al., 2015; Castañeda & Isgro, 2013). Key recommendations that can diminish the fears and burdens of URM women and men faculty include training department chairs on how to implement family-responsive policies and manage with flexibility (UC Hastings College of the Law, n.d.) and transparent family-friendly support policies that minimize the power of academic gatekeepers who may not otherwise apply policies evenhandedly (Castañeda et al., 2015). Importantly, a greater awareness of the familial definitions among URM professionals is warranted. The definition of family needs to extend beyond nuclear family to include extended and intergenerational family members such as grandparents, aunts, and uncles who may serve as mother or father surrogates. Other important policies include dual-career employment positions for domestic partnerships, eliminating salary inequity and providing regular pay increases that are commensurate with market trends (Piercy et al., 2005), and diverse, affordable child care options that attend to the needs of all children of university employees whether through on-campus child care, child care subsidy grants, and/or dependent care travel grants (UC Hastings College of the Law, n.d.). The policies that include financial benefits and attention to facilitating the institutional experiences of these faculty would be responsive to their current reported needs.

More than 150 years ago, America's historically White colleges and universities began to extend the promise of higher education to women and racial/ethnic minorities (ACE & AAUP, 2000). As the preceding chapters have described, by any measure the numbers of underrepresented minority faculty in all professions are disproportionately low compared with the general population and all other demographic groups. This reality underscores a static historical record of exclusionary practices that continue to fuel a national crisis in higher education given the predicted shortage of URM faculty. Four major challenges confront institutions of higher education: how history has defined the present and drives the future, the limited presence of URM faculty in leadership positions, the shifting of the faculty role from intellectuals to entrepreneurs, and the unprecedented increase in international faculty to serve as nontenured faculty and to fulfill the illusion of diversity.

Four decades ago, leaders of the civil rights movement demanded institutional transformation to open up the higher education opportunity structure. Despite the force of various political and social movements, the intervening four decades have yielded modest progress, with successful and welcomed advancements geared to helping women overcome substantial challenges in accessing entrance into medical and law schools and employment in STEM fields. In contrast, URM women and men still lag considerably behind their White female counterparts. Structural responses such as federal legislation that sought to remedy gross inequities in higher education through affirmative action have been dismantled with few URM beneficiaries. Shifting demographics and funding challenges in the twenty-first century are affecting not only who enrolls in today's elite colleges and universities but also who is able to teach and conduct research. While colleges, universities, boards, and agencies have jumped on the diverse faculty bandwagon (see chapter 1), not only by issuing resolutions, policies, and mandates but also by inventing programs, initiatives, and strategies all intended to increase URM faculty, the pathways for faculty to advance through the ranks remain stagnant. One area of serious concern regarding these limited pathways to the professoriate and senior rank is the small number of senior faculty in leadership positions. Leaders serve three important institutional functions: bringing the voice of unrepresented faculty to the attention of institutional agents, advocating for transformational change, and serving as role models and mentors in successfully shepherding early career URM faculty through the university pipeline (Whittaker, Montgomery, & Acosta, 2015).

## Leadership Matters Sometimes

Senior university leadership is in a position to scrutinize the dynamics of institutional power that influence hiring practices, retention, and tenure and promotion of all faculty across the entire spectrum of higher education to increase inclusion of the domestic talent pool.[6] By facilitating social change at the highest level of the organization, colleges and universities can fulfill their mission of equity by developing, with intention and commitment, transformational and responsive policies and practices so as to more fully support the vital intellectual and social contributions of underrepresented minority faculty. Yet change usually comes about when leaders are exposed to different ways of thinking and/ or experiences that challenge their normative values and expectations, or equally important when they represent the groups who are most deeply affected by injurious institutional cultures, although not always.

Two outstanding issues are evident when examining the roles of URM leadership in higher education institutions. Study data and empirical scholarship describe a significant lack of senior URM administrators, and oftentimes early career faculty assume, prematurely, burdensome administrative and leadership positions as center directors or chairs of ethnic study departments. These positions often involve excessive work with little or no compensation or benefits toward career outcomes (Ballesteros, 2008; Biddix, 2011; León & Nevarez, 2007; Martinez, 1999). Current study participants disclosed parallel narratives that confirm the empirical research in reporting excessive diversity burdens and perceptions of resistant and unchanging institutions. For example, Valverde, in his 1993 book *Leaders of Color in Higher Education: Unrecognized Triumphs in Harsh Institutions*, described the experiences of faculty of color in leadership positions. He conducted interviews with four groups (African American, Hispanic Americans, Native Americans, and Asian American administrators). In the introduction, he states, "This book is written for persons who want to be agents of change, persons of color who will assume leadership roles in higher education, persons trying to grow better campuses, and persons whose fundamental purpose is to bring about equality for all in our social systems" (p. xvii). Each chapter elucidates what is referred to as a "harsh environment" by the study participants, and distinct differences for each group are observed. In other words, not all racial/ethnic minorities need the same resources. The last chapter in Valverde's book proffers pointed and effective lessons learned. Not unexpectedly, the author notes that the lack of mentors and sponsorship, perceived betrayal, severe consequences for mistakes with no second chances, perceptions that hiring is for "image purposes" (p. 143), double standards that turn prior experiences into risks rather than assets, a dearth of access to social capital in the power of negotiating roles, responsibilities and compensation, and the sagacious advice to "keep your guard up" were all factors that made life in the academy for historically underrepresented minorities complicated and paradoxical. As so well delineated in this book, URM faculty are asked and expected to report and compromise more than their White counterparts.

A more recent book, published two decades later, describes the experiences of faculty and nonfaculty administrators who represent a significant spectrum of diversity in administrative positions. Chun and Evans (2012) discuss a range of identities in academic administration, women, minority, and lesbian/ gay/bisexual/transgendered (LGBT) administrators in higher education and the barriers they confront on a daily basis. Through the lens of situational analysis, the authors provide firsthand accounts of White privilege influencing interactions, practices, and outcomes in the academic workplace. Furthermore, they examine the actual experiences of former faculty diversity officers to depict how budget cuts and reorganization adversely affect employment conditions for diverse administrators. All too often URM early career faculty are asked to engage in an administrative role whose reward may be, although not always, modest additional remuneration. Equally important, the leadership role in diversity work often is accompanied by few financial support resources as well as limited decision-making power (Nixon, 2017). All too often those who are assigned diversity roles have limited influence in swaying institutional policy to improve fairness, transparency, and transformation change. Although leadership presents an opportunity to use the power of position and authority as a tool for equity improvements and change, burnout is often the outcome. These positions require intense emotional labor to manage institutional demands embedded within dominant cultural norms—that is, institutions reflect a fragile moral compass defined by the ruling administration, diversity rhetoric, stakeholders, and donors. Balancing these multiple interests may obscure accountability to any single stakeholder.

The resistance of higher education, especially elite institutions, to leadership change has resulted in their support of efforts to reform and strengthen minority-serving institutions. These institutions, as discussed in chapter 2, were created to cement the exclusion of historically underrepresented students by maintaining essentially segregated systems of education with limited financial and social capital resources available to students who most needed them. The post–civil rights agenda intended to expand the social and economic opportunity structure and to increase access to PWIs where knowledge is produced and resources are abundant. The missing link in PWIs is equal opportunity and equity in access to faculty and leadership positions.

Due to few URMs in higher education, the available narratives suggest that the burden of leadership for many URM administrators is replete with countervailing pressures to their community-based, socially minded agenda. One of the most significant challenges is engaging with colleagues and other administrators surrounding initiatives, programs, and student and faculty selection that include the word *diversity*. In Beale, Chesler, and Ramus's (2014) study of the definitions of diversity, 66 faculty members made a total of 182 comments related to the meaning of diversity and 203 comments related to their approach to diversity and acts of advocacy (p. 173). The thematic content analyses revealed magnanimous themes: treating everyone equally/fairly, appreciating difference, and working toward social justice. Not surprisingly, the majority of faculty provided definitions and measured their actions by individual merit, not by historic legacies or group-framed themes. Few faculty took into account major group dimensions of inequality such as group identities marked by coconstituted history, race, ethnicity, and class (p. 175). These data suggest that engaging with a discourse on diversity of faculty or programs for leaders entails a relentless process of differing interpretations, interests, and priorities that defy a consensual outcome or equity-driven institutional change.

Multiple reports since the early 1990s coupled with a small body of work on URM leadership highlight the continued dilemmas that seem almost insurmountable. For example, Martinez (1999) articulated the importance of increasing URM leadership by arguing that they bring a democratizing view:

> It is not an accident, for instance, that Hispanics and other minorities are concerned with issues of social justice, or that white Americans continue to perceive affirmative action as reverse racism (e.g., a threat to their life worlds). Socially marginal views stemming from minority positions in society can offer great insights into democratic institutions and society in general. It can be argued that Hispanic leadership in higher education brings a socially marginalized experience that, by emphasizing social justice, can yield a broader, more inclusive view of democracy and of the role of higher education in a democratic society than can the experience of the dominant group. (p. 8)

Many leaders in higher education, both dominant culture and URM, are playing a valuable role in setting the agenda for addressing critical problems and establishing a vision for transformation through responsive and inclusionary policies that reflect new ways to grow the organizational culture and to include reward systems for implementing innovative inclusive institutional diversity practices that benefit everyone including URM faculty. All too often, leaders play a gatekeeper role to guard the interests of the institution and its relationship to external corporate partners, wealthy alumni, and normative, historically defined and perceived constructs of what constitutes the image of a professor and what defines excellence, science, and research. Without intentional inclusion and informed knowledge of the role of higher education as a democratizing institutional model, our domestic and historic talent pool will face a challenging entry into the academic opportunity structure. Rankings, generating dollars and status symbols, seem to take center stage rather than equity. Diversity becomes symbolic and intangible, as shown by 182 definitions of diversity by 66 faculty members (Beale et al., 2014). The clarion call for change post–civil rights has yielded a significant corpus of work on ways to be more inclusive and strive toward institutional equity and domestic workforce development. Yet the historical pull and weight of wealth accumulation, elite inclusion, and patterns of exclusion have become entrenched in higher education with its emphasis on academics as knowledge entrepreneurs.

## CLASH IN SOCIAL VERSUS ENTREPRENEURIAL AGENDA

For several decades now an accelerated process of academic corporatization or academic capitalism and entrepreneurship has been evolving. Many scholars, particularly in higher education, have expressed concerns over the trend to reproduce the links between political economy, business market practices, and the state (Cantwell & Kauppinen, 2014). Education that was envisioned as a right and equalizer of opportunity has been transformed into a commodity available to some groups but not others. This corporatization moves beyond the traditional conceptualization of the binary of knowledge for its own sake and/ or for profit versus knowledge to solve national, community, or social problems. It has emerged with the new developments in technology, innovation, and cost-cutting measures. Higher education systems have increased the percentage of adjuncts and part-time faculty, who now exceed the numbers of full-time tenured and tenure-track faculty. From fall 1993 to fall 2013, the number of full-time faculty at degree-granting postsecondary institutions increased by 45 percent, while the number of part-time faculty increased by 104 percent. As a result, the percentage of all faculty who were part-time increased from 40 to 49 percent during this period. Not unexpectedly, this has followed the trends of Silicon Valley as an example of the proliferation of new startups with a powerful focus on individual creativity and low capital investments that yield high returns on investment. In conjunction with neoliberalism that brings back into play current institutional approaches of laissez-faire and hegemony of the market (Roggero, 2011, p. 39), the production of knowledge has eluded the private-public dichotomy and can no longer be understood as a "simple intrusion of private capital into the academic world" (p. 26). The intersections of globalization, private capital driving the production of knowledge in predominantly elite universities, and a focus on professors as laborers or entrepreneurs in the service of the university and the state (which no longer wishes to support higher education) present a dismal future for the retention of tenure and the inclusion of historically underrepresented faculty.

In no way does this short missive seek to provide an erudite understanding of a multilayered set of processes that were set in motion perhaps fifty years ago. However, these analyses underscore that historically underrepresented groups have been excluded from the markets and financial sectors throughout the life course. As a result, they are less likely than majority Whites and other racial and ethnic groups, both native and foreign-born, to possess wealth, assets, and personal or family capital. Moreover, they have less access to social networks that possess wealth, including philanthropic foundations, foreign governments, private venture capitalists, and state and federal funding contacts. As Schrecker (2010) observes regarding capital-driven models, "Such a constricted model of the academic community would not only stunt careers and futures of students and teachers but also would undermine the very idea of the university as a place for intellectual growth and meaningful scholarship" (p. 233). Thus the limited social capital available to URMs places them at even further disadvantage in the context of the new and increasing entrepreneurial emphases of universities.

Equally important, the production of knowledge as a market commodity deemphasizes the solving of social problems and the helping of underserved populations and communities, a central research agenda of many URM faculty. Inevitably, the entrepreneurial agenda, historically predominant in STEM, medicine, and business, not only erodes the purposes of the university and the meaning of intellectual pursuits but also devalues the concerns and intellectual agendas of URM faculty. Entrepreneurship requires additional time and money, which are not readily available to URMs due to the wealth gap and outflow of resources to their families of origin. In contrast, the brain drain and the recruitment of elite faculty from universities throughout the world have contributed to a labor force in high / very high research universities in particular where an entrepreneurial spirit can thrive without a social justice interest. Moreover, these entrepreneurial fields are disciplines where URMs are least likely to be present.

## GLOBALIZATION OF FACULTY: NEW INVESTMENTS, NEW TRENDS

Colleges and universities in the United States have aggressively recruited international students and faculty and touted the advantages of creating a multicultural learning and social environment since the passage of the Hart-Celler Act in 1965 (Bazemore, Janda, Derlega, & Paulson, 2010; Kim, Wolf-Wendel, & Twombly, 2011). The coincidence that it was passed one year after the Civil Rights Act of 1964 is a noteworthy observation. The inclusion of foreign-born faculty in the reporting of faculty characteristics at colleges and universities requires closer examination. The presence of international faculty (citizen or noncitizen) on U.S. college campuses has been steadily increasing. During the 2006–2007 academic year, 98,239 international scholars with nonimmigrant visas were teaching or conducting research on U.S. campuses, an increase of 1.3 percent compared to the previous year (Mamiseishvili & Rosser, 2010). The "10-year stay rate" of foreign-born scholars is 58 percent (Stephan, 2010, p. 83), with many eventually returning to their home countries (Altbach, 2004).[7]

The increase in international faculty on U.S. campuses may seem advantageous in responding to calls for increasing faculty diversity (Mamiseishvili & Rosser, 2010). When higher education institutions report on the diversity of their faculty body, they often aggregate foreign-born faculty with U.S.-born URM faculty under racial/ethnic identifiers such as "Black" and "Hispanic" rather than

"African American" and "Mexican American." Yet there are significant differences between these groups associated with nativity, class, race/ethnicity, and political perceptions. For example, at research universities, the proportion of foreign-born faculty is larger than the proportion of URM faculty.[8] In a study of foreign-born and URM faculty at research universities, the sample consisted of 3 percent Black faculty and 6.8 percent Hispanic faculty. However, further disaggregation showed that the sample had 3.7 percent Black foreign-born faculty in contrast to 2.4 percent of U.S. Black faculty, and 9.7 percent Hispanic foreign-born faculty in contrast to 3.7 percent of U.S. Hispanic faculty (Mamiseishvili & Rosser, 2010). Several studies have demonstrated that foreign-born faculty members are more likely to be productive in research but spend less time on teaching and service (Corley & Sabharwal, 2007; Kim, Wolf-Wendel, & Twombly, 2011; Mamiseishvili & Rosser, 2010; Webber, 2012). Caution is warranted as data may be skewed and subsequent recommendations for policy and practice may reflect the needs of foreign-born faculty rather than those of URM faculty. While the inclusion of foreign-born scholars in the faculty ranks contributes to productivity and innovation, research universities need to address the slow rate of URM faculty inclusion and representation. The inclusion of foreign-born faculty without disaggregation masks the continued and unequal representation of URM faculty.

Globalization and international faculty will shape the internationalization of U.S. institutions and their research focus and agenda will generate new fields of knowledge in all major disciplines including the sciences, social sciences, and humanities. Foreign-born faculty represent a relatively high proportion of college and universities' faculty and students of color and account for up to 30 percent of faculty, which is higher than the proportion of foreign-born U.S. residents as a percentage of the total population (Lin, Pearce, & Wang, 2009; Webber, 2012).[9]

In addition, universities are recruiting and foreign governments are sending foreign-born graduate students at significant rates for economic gain and the training of global elites. These increases may decrease the prospects of developing a diverse domestic workforce of faculty who can train the next generation of URM students. An important question arises regarding the role of international faculty in training future citizens: will they be more or less successful in training the next generation of URM students? The retention of foreign-born faculty should be an important goal of universities and colleges since they are significant contributors to the scientific enterprise and their presence at universities can encourage foreign students to aspire to join academia (Corley & Sabharwal, 2007). However, this talent pool of faculty and graduate students cannot become the symbol of diversity and replace what should be a national, institutional commitment to equity and inclusion. For example, inclusion of foreign-born graduate students and faculty in U.S. universities call for increases in financial aid and fellowship resources. Universities need to ensure that these economic resources are also available for talented first-generation and economically disadvantaged students including URM.

Beyond the potential scientific contributions of international faculty, they bring a distinct positionality. Two distinguishing factors have been observed: they have limited U.S. collective historical memory and generally do not have a socially driven research agenda. Rather, many international students and faculty came to the United States for a better economic and social life, for freedom, and to participate in a democracy. Thus they may not be aware of and may inadvertently support the status quo and often advocate for services for international students that may exclude URM. In addition, foreign-born faculty may also assume or be placed in leadership and/or gatekeeper positions and/or on the least desirable point in the spectrum of work as fulfilling a diversity position due to the very absence of and institutional reluctance to place other domestic racial/ethnic faculty in leadership unless they are "star faculty." In contrast, a series of case studies revealed how predominantly White universities hire international faculty in order to meet diversity requirements only to later force them from their position once those diversity requirements have been officially met (Eskay, Onu, Obiyo, Igbo, & Udaya, 2012).

## SYMBOLIC VERSUS INTENTIONAL DIVERSITY: A PATH TOWARD MEANINGFUL INCORPORATION

The writing of this book has affirmed my own discomfort with the distorted use and application of diversity in elite and other universities over the past twenty years. Extensive works, opinion pieces, and essays have been written on diversity, what it means, and what it has accomplished. What have forty years of diversity yielded with respect to progress for socially and economically disadvantaged U.S. groups? The twenty-first century embraced an uncomfortable stance of the disadvantaged as inclusive of "women and minorities." Minorities are defined as any group in society distinguished numerically, phenotypically, and racially from, and less dominant than, the White male majority and include all non-Whites, Asians, immigrants, and historically underrepresented domestic U.S. populations, often homogenized as a category labeled *people of color*. This dichotomy is reminiscent of prior categorizations of the population into White and "others" and affirms a strong White supremacist power structure. It also belies the economic (income inequality and wealth gaps), social (significant negative stereotypic perceptions by majority society), and historical (forced incorporation) realities of underrepresented groups. More to the point, within these people of color categories, disadvantage is prescribed to one group while advantage is granted to another group in the form of what Bonilla-Silva defines as an honorary status of preferred or honorary Whites. Language, accent, or focus of work may be a deterrent to hire some groups but not others in the amorphous category of people of color. The ability to systematically exclude historically underrepresented groups and replace them with any nonmajority scholar has been facilitated by rhetoric of diversity that is undefined. Calls for underrepresented minority faculty to be provided access to the educational opportunity structure are not new and continue at an ever more pressing pace. For example, Gomez in 1973 outlined recommendations for changes in recruitment of, retention of, and commitment to Mexican Americans at the student, faculty, and administration levels of higher education. In the 1990s, student boycotts for more faculty diversity garnered national and media attention (see Zambrana et al., 2017b, on Mexican American faculty). Yet the increases in faculty are most representative of White men and more recently White women, Asian and Asian American, and international faculty.

Findings from this study and narratives of URM faculty voices paint a decidedly different picture (Kayes, 2006) from the unanimous claims in higher education of diversity among faculty and students and welcoming institutional climates. In fact, as Turner (2002) points out, "efforts to diversify the faculty continue to be amongst the least successful elements of campus commitments to diversity" (p. 14). A compounding factor is the increasingly disproportionate underrepresentation of URM faculty at higher senior professorial and administrative ranks, thus limiting the pool of potential mentors who are willing to successfully shepherd early career URM faculty through the university pipeline (Whittaker et al., 2015). Unwittingly perhaps, the construct of diversity has served to increase the competitive forces among varying global and elite groups to the exclusion of URM. Alternatively, diversity may be a powerful tool to abscond from the commitment to "level the playing field" or to engage in restitution of opportunity post–civil rights or to ensure the status quo by not allowing dissenters, if you will, into the existing social structure. Another result of this homogenizing discourse is to spin a story of a more universal nature, reflected in the writings of identity group narratives pondering injustice, oppression, discrimination, and racism. The new discourse on diversity increasingly inserts the term *underrepresented* to speak of varying populations or subpopulations including immigrant and refugee populations. The national framework of homogenizing and erasing differences under a meritocratic platform of "all Americans," underrepresented Americans, "women or minorities," and people of color has left little room for conversations on diversity, equity, and inclusion among historically underrepresented groups and differences among racial/ethnic groups. An inclusionary conversation requires the disruption of a homogenizing approach and surfaces the role of race and implicit bias in White spaces and its impact on the URM career path in academic settings. Unveiling the role of implicit bias that grants unearned privilege oftentimes to non-URM subjects and the erasure of the historicity of unequal treatment allows for a solution-driven conversation (Acosta-Belen & Bose, 2012).

However, incorporation of URM faculty means more than merely adding numbers; it requires power sharing and institutional change. This includes the integration of URM faculty into key roles in decision-making and formulating policies that address the needs of diverse university constituents. Incorporation itself then is also a mechanism for institutional transformation to intentional diversity and inclusion beyond appearance or tokenism. This means that the mere presence of URM faculty does not diminish the significant barriers discussed regarding their quest for success and job satisfaction. Alex-Assensoh (2003) focuses on five ways to move toward the meaningful incorporation of URM faculty: providing full access to institutional resources; ensuring representation in college and university administration; promoting active involvement in college-level policy making; implementing ethnically and racially egalitarian policies; and providing greater parity in terms of tenure, promotion, and salary outcomes. To achieve this, the administration must demonstrate an institution-wide commitment to specific targeted diversity pools, enacting decisions to support diversity, involving diverse faculty in decision-making, and valuing all departments and faculty members (Piercy et al., 2005). Intentional diversity goals require institutionalization, led by strong campus advocates inclusive of URM leadership, and must be incorporated into the research, teaching, and service missions of the institution at all levels (Adams & Bargerhuff, 2005; Brayboy, 2003; Turner et al., 2008; Weems, 2003).

As I have demonstrated in *Toxic Ivory Towers: The Consequences of Work Stress on Underrepresented Minority Faculty*, significant obstacles remain, ranging from a focus only on quantifiable research as legitimate science to color blindness and undefined views on diversity, which prevent an informed understanding of the structural constraints URM faculty confront, and persistent discriminatory practices and policies. However, throughout this research study, faculty alluded to and often explicitly proffered suggestions toward creating a more hospitable environment. Oftentimes these suggestions came as much from what they viewed as ideal practices to strive for as from their disheartening experiences in toxic institutional arrangements. Unquestionably, by translating these insights into tangible policies and practices, we can transform institutions of higher education into truly inclusive spaces for the next generation of civic and intellectual leaders.

The study data speak starkly to historic populations whose lives have been shaped by a life course trajectory and historic memory of subordination and discrimination that continues in varied economic, political, and social forms.

Concern has been expressed about universities losing their soul and intellectual honesty (Stricker, 1988). The study findings are proffered in the hope that these data will serve as a catalyst for institutional transformation, with the ultimate goal of producing a welcoming, supportive, and inclusive climate for URM participation as cocreators of future higher education cultures that fulfill the promise of equity for all. Apropos of this sentiment, I conclude with the voices of two URM early career scholars who want to survive and thrive in their ivory tower. A Mexican American female speaks to her commitment to make a difference in her community. "Ultimately I want my name to be known and I want when my life on this earth is over to have made a difference to my community and to have left a positive impact somewhere with my work." One African American male stated that he has stayed the course to assist the institution to retain other URM faculty: "I hope my endpoint will be moving toward an administrative role, so I can help directly to impact processes to assure they are done objectively so as to assure that underrepresented groups in academic are retained. They come, but they leave quickly."

In conclusion, without clear and recognizable intentional inclusivity and color braveness that informs the diversity conversation into equity, current institutional practices will prevail and continue to disallow the critical contributions and inclusion of URM scholars. Elite higher education institutions hold the power to produce knowledge and direct the allocation of resources to inform solutions to deeply embedded social injustices and to contribute to a broader historic and interdisciplinary education of future generations. URM scholars have sacrificed much to participate in elite institutions so as to contribute to a more well-rounded citizenry and to create a more just and equitable society. I have drawn three major lessons from the writing of this book: If we are to be responsive to promoting democratic ideals, we must be concerned about the future state of higher education as a mechanism to reach racial/ethnic equity. The knowledge that we create and the ways we teach to shape the types of citizens and change agents our students become fall on our shoulders as cocreators of a more just society. And by virtue of our privilege and power as academics, we must lead every day. As leaders, we need to embody the commitment to institutional change, equity, and full inclusion of all groups including URM faculty. New visions and innovative strategies are called for to shift human capital and financial resources. To be sure, these changes cannot unfold overnight without the full support of leadership and all faculty, administrators, and staff.

# APPENDIX A
## Self-Administered Web-Based Survey

## Variables and Measures

| Independent variables | Definition/measure |
|---|---|
| **Academic, social, and economic statuses** | |
| *Sociodemographic status (23 items)* | |
| Race/ethnicity (2 items) | Hispanic/Latino origin? Yes/no |
| | What is your race? |
| Country of birth (1 item) | United States / Puerto Rico/Mexico and other (open-ended response) |
| Employed at university/college (2 items) | Yes/no; if yes, identify university/college |
| | Coded as research university applying Carnegie classification of public or private, and geographic region |
| Employment position (3 items) | Rank/tenure/administrative position |
| Age (1 item) | Year born |
| Gender (1 item) | Male/female/other |
| Sexual orientation (1 item) | Heterosexual/homosexual/bisexual/something else (with a prefer not to answer option) |
| Marital status (1 item) | Never married; separated; married living with spouse; married not living with spouse; widowed; divorced; living with partner |
| Household size (1 item) | Total members in household including participant |
| Children (3 items) | Includes number of children, ages of children, and future plans for children |
| Assets (3 items) | Individual annual income; own home; total household net worth |
| Parents country of birth (2 items) | Father's/mother's country of birth |
| Parents educational attainment (2 items) | Highest level of education completed by parents/guardians |
| *Employment and educational background (15 items)* | |
| Appointment status (3 items) | Academic department appointment; joint appointment; yes/no response. Current position nine- or twelve-month appointment? Administrative position (yes/no) |
| Time at current institution (1 item) | Response: Years? Months? |

*(continued)*

## Variables and Measures (*continued*)

| Independent variables | Definition/measure |
|---|---|
| Hours worked per week (1 item) | Estimated number of hours dedicated to research; teaching; university service; and outside professional activities. Hours recoded into three to four categories |
| Doctoral/master's degree status (4 items) | Identify type of doctoral and master's degree and primary academic field number (discipline) |
| Discipline (1 item) | |
| Institution awarded (2 items) | |
| Postdoctoral training (3 items) | Yes/no option to postdoctoral training; number of years in training and institution name |

**Academic ambient stressors**

*Department/college/school diversity and colleagueship (3 items)*

| | |
|---|---|
| Faculty in department (2 items) | Number of total full-time faculty; number of URM faculty |
| Colleagueship opportunities (1 item) | Opportunities to collaborate with five-point Likert-type scale: *never* to *always* |

*Mentoring (13 items)[']*

| | |
|---|---|
| Participation in formal and/or informal mentoring program (3 items) | Yes/no; name of program and number of years in mentoring program |
| Demographic characteristics of mentor (6 items) | Yes/no; current mentor; mentor in last three years; number of current mentors; gender; race/ethnicity; location of mentor |
| Frequency of mentor facilitated activities[a] (3 items) | Six activities with yes/no response options; one item on mentor reviews annual progress; five-point Likert-type scale from *very significantly* to *not at all* |
| Cognitive appraisal on mentoring impact on career (1 item) | |

*Perceived gender, race/ethnicity, and class bias (7 items)*

| | |
|---|---|
| Perceptions of bias or discrimination in the workplace (6 items) | Responses were on a four-point scale from 1 = *never* to 4 = *always*, with scale scores ranging from 6 to 24, with higher scores indicating higher perceptions of bias and discrimination |
| Cognitive appraisal how upsetting the experience was (1 item) | five-point Likert-type scale from *extremely upsetting* to *not upsetting at all* |

*Family-personal work balance (5 items)*

| | |
|---|---|
| Caretaking (2 items) | Yes/no; caretaking on a regular basis |
| Satisfaction between balance (1 item) | Five-point scale: *very dissatisfied* to *very satisfied* |

| Independent variables | Definition/measure |
|---|---|
| Supervisory support (1 item) | Five-point scale: *rarely or never true* to *true most of the time* to measure supervisory respect toward balance |
| Intuitional policy support (1 item) | Five-point scale *rarely or never true* to *true most of the time* to measure institutional policies toward balance |

| **Occupational stressors** | |
|---|---|
| *Stress-inducing work roles (OSI-R; 30 items)[b]* | *All item scores ranged from 10 to 50, with higher scores indicating higher overload, ambiguity, vocational strain, etc. Seven scales were used in this study.* |
| Role ambiguity (10 items) | Measures the extent to which priorities, expectations, and evaluation criteria are clear to the individual using five-point response scale of *rarely or never true* to *true most of the time* |
| Vocational strain (10 items) | Measures the extent to which the individual is having problems in work quality or output. Attitudes toward work are measured using five-point response scale of *rarely or never true* to *true most of the time* |
| Role overload (10 items) | Measures the extent to which job demands exceed resources (personal and workplace) and the extent to which the individual is able to accomplish workloads using five-point response scale of 1 = *rarely or never true* to *true most of the time* |

| **Moderating resources (40 items)** | |
|---|---|
| Recreation (10 items) | Measures the extent to which the individual makes use of and derives pleasure and relaxation from regular recreational activities using five-point response scale of *rarely or never true* to *true most of the time* |
| Self-care (10 items) | Measures the extent to which the individual regularly engages in personal activities that reduce or alleviate chronic stress using five-point response scale of *rarely or never true* to *true most of the time* |
| Social support (10 items) | Measures the extent to which the individual feels support and help from those around him or her using five-point response scale of *rarely or never true* to *true most of the time* |
| Rational/cognitive coping (10 items) | Measures the extent to which the individual possesses and uses cognitive skills in the face of work-related stress using five-point response scale of *rarely or never true* to *true most of the time* |

| **Life events and social support (14 items)** | |
|---|---|
| Religious/spiritual support (2 items) | Measures identification of any religious traditions and importance of religion in coping with life and work |

(continued)

## Variables and Measures (*continued*)

| Independent variables | Definition/measure |
| --- | --- |
| Life event stress (12 items) | Measures stressful life events within the past year with four response options included (1 = *no*, 2 = *yes and it upset me not too much*, 3 = *yes and it upset me moderately*, and 4 = *yes and it upset me very much*) with scores ranging from 13 to 52, with higher scores indicating a higher number and intensity of upsetting life events[c] |

| Dependent variables | Definition/measure |
| --- | --- |
| *Outcomes (27 items)* | |
| Perceived physical health status (1 item) | Recoded items from the Medical Outcome Study SF-36 measure of self-reported physical health status. Respondents asked to rate their health from *excellent* to *poor* |
| Physical symptoms index (PSI; 18 items) | Physical symptom indicators were measured with the eighteen-item PSI.[d] PSI assesses physical and somatic health symptoms associated with psychological distress. Each is a condition/state about which a person would likely be aware (e.g., headache). Respondents are asked to indicate for each symptom if they didn't have it, had it, or saw a doctor for it in the past thirty days. Three scores are computed: the number of symptoms they had (have symptoms), the number for which they saw a doctor (doctor symptoms), and sum of both (total). Possible total scores range from 0 to 18. In text, physical symptoms and chronic conditions are noted. |
| Mental health status (CES-D; 8 items) | The eight-item Center for Epidemiologic Studies Depression Scale (CES-D)[e] measures major components of depression with an emphasis on affective components. Scoring is based on a Likert-type scale ranging from 0 (*rarely*) to 3 (*most days*), with scores ranging from 0 to 24. Higher scores indicate higher levels of distress. A score greater than or equal to 7 suggests a clinically significant level of psychological distress |

a. Robert Wood Johnson Foundation (1995).
b. Osipow (1998).
c. Berkman and Syme (1979).
d. Spector and Jex (1998).
e. Radloff (1977).

# APPENDIX B
## Sample Individual and Group Interview Questions

These are broad qualitative study questions that included subquestions and probes.

1. How did you come to choose an academic career?
2. Who or what have been the major sources of inspiration and support for you in this career path?
3. Who were the people that facilitated the successful completion of your graduate education?
4. Tell me about your first academic/first tenure-track position.
5. Describe your ideal mentoring relationship. Has mentoring made a difference in your career path?
6. Describe how your family (partner and/or children) and personal obligations and responsibilities have an effect on your career path.
7. What are the ways (strategies) you use to balance the competing demands of work and family/personal life?
8. Have you ever had experiences of racism and/or gender (male, female, LGBT) discrimination in the work environment?
9. Tell me about three to four institutional challenges that you have most hindered (facilitated) your career path and advancement.
10. In the last five years, have you ever been told by a doctor or other health care professional that you had/have a physical condition and/or psychological distress?
11. Describe your experience and/or plans for the tenure and promotion process (assistant professor). Describe your experience in the tenure and promotion process (associate professor).
12. What are your future academic dreams and aspirations?

# ACKNOWLEDGMENTS

In writing this book, like so many large scholarly projects, I have accrued significant debt to many colleagues, students, friends, publishing agents, and enthusiastic and supportive funders along the way. Our Faculty Advisory Board (FAB) was instrumental in providing critical feedback in our research design, the survey instruments, and the recruitment of URM faculty. FAB members included Professors Rosina Becerra (UCLA), Llewellyn J. Cornelius (Georgia State University), Sarah Fenstermaker (University of Michigan), Angela B. Ginorio (University of Washington), Elizabeth Higginbotham (Emeritus, University of Delaware), Kerry Ann Rockquemore (President and CEO of the National Center for Faculty Development & Diversity), Denise Segura (UC Santa Barbara), Abby Stewart (University of Michigan), Robert Valdez (University of New Mexico), and William Vega (University of Southern California). I wish to thank Dr. Lisa M. Lapeyrouse (Michigan State University) for the analysis of the survey data of qualitative respondents and acknowledge Todd Bartko, PhD (statistician) for his analyses of survey data and production of tables with utmost patience and responsiveness to the multiple challenges that were encountered and resolved with his assistance.

The next large group of people is the University of Maryland graduate and undergraduate students who searched the traditional and gray literature and wrote endless annotations to document the problem so the project would possess the necessary legitimacy to get funded. Students include Drs. Ana Perez, Tamyka Morant, Cristina Perez, Maria Velasquez, and Angel Miles; and Djuan Short, Anaya McMurray, Vanessa Lopes, Jennifer Eliason, Tangere Hoagland, Wendy M. Laybourne, Christie Moy, Emily Livingstone, Lauren Dammier, Melva Coles, Emily Dotterer, Alyssa Hill, and Brandi Samuel. The graduate student who has taken this book to the finish line is Lenora Knowles, who worked incessantly in 2016–2017 and learned more than she bargained for in the completion of this book. So important in this endeavor was the initial qualitative dedicated research team. Drs. Beth-Douthirt-Cohen, Cara Kennedy, Dr. Laura Logie, and Damien Waters showed intellectual acuity in their thematic coding and analysis. My colleague and dean of the University of Maryland, College of Arts and Humanities, Dr. Bonnie Thornton Dill, has been a supporter of this endeavor and conducted several of the initial interviews. I am deeply appreciative of her support. In addition, I acknowledge the support of the Department of Women's Studies, which has consistently shown enthusiasm for my research.

This type of critical race work was funded by the Robert Wood Johnson Foundation. I am especially grateful to our former program officer at RWJF, Dr. Debra Pérez, for her staunch support, political guidance, and unwavering enthusiasm about this study (Grant 68480), and the University of Maryland Tier 1 seed grants, Division of Research, Faculty Incentive Program. I am also grateful for the current funding support being provided by the Annie E. Casey Foundation (Grant 214.0277) and the enthusiastic support of Dr. Kantahyanee Murray. We are deeply indebted to the Robert Wood Johnson New Connections program project officer Dr. Cathy Malone and former staff at Equal Measure, Ms. Sharon Norris Shelton, who was instrumental in identifying study participants, disseminating the results through invitations to the participants, and supporting the early career faculty in responsive mentoring venues.

Strong supporters and champions of this book include the staff at the Consortium on Race, Gender and Ethnicity. This work could not have been completed without the commitment, persistence, expertise, patience, and management eye of Dr. Laura A. Logie, former assistant director. She ensured the coordination and integration of a decade of materials and dozens of research assistants. Ms. Wendy Hall, in addition to her office management tasks, skillfully engaged the details and requirements of manuscript preparation. I remain deeply appreciative of the steadfast work ethic and engagement with the mission of CRGE and the work we do. Finally, and most importantly, I wish to also extend a heartfelt expression of gratitude to the URM faculty across the United States, to whom this book is dedicated, who participated in the study and all those who thanked me and supported this work during its development and presentation.

The completion and final review of the book was a significant, often unending, task. Several esteemed faculty colleagues gave of their time, wisdom, and interdisciplinary talents to help me and support me in the last stages of manuscript completion. Drs. Maxine Baca-Zinn, Roberto O. Valdez, Lynn Weber, and Nelly Stromquist read the manuscript or chapters and provided feedback in multiple ways and strong encouragement at every step of the way. I am deeply grateful for their friendship and caring for me and the topic area. Other colleagues include Drs. Raymond L. Rodriguez and Rebecca Hernandez, who provided thoughtful conversation and inspiration and support along the way. The external reviewers of the manuscript exhibited high levels of deliberate and considered critique and simultaneously attended to the validation of the quality of the content in this work. I thank them for their intentional review and demonstrated empathy for the subjects of the study. I also wish to express deep appreciation to Kimberly Guinta of Rutgers University Press for her trust, confidence, and ongoing support throughout the process; to all the staff at Rutgers—too many to name—for their high levels of competence and attention to book production; and to editor Cecelia Cancellero for her thoughtful and intensive reviews of the work to ensure a high-quality and clear product.

# NOTES

## CHAPTER 1    WHERE IS THE DIVERSITY?

1. Diversity as a construct can be traced back to the 1980s, when demographic projections showed that by 2000, the United States would become more heterogeneous. Drawing on a business model of better managing organizations, diversity was conceptualized as a set of rare, valuable, and difficult to imitate resources (Zanoni, Janssens, Benschop, & Nkomo, 2010; Embrick, 2015).

2. For the purposes of this book, historically underrepresented minority (URM) refers to African Americans with a history of intergenerational slavery in the U.S., Mexican American, Puerto Rican, and American Indian / Alaska Native faculty who are part of the domestic talent pool and are defined as severely underrepresented due to their historic exclusion in institutions of higher education. These four groups represent small percentages of all faculty in the academy relative to their proportion in the general U.S. population. Notably, American Indian / Alaska Natives are historically underrepresented and share many of the same barriers and challenges as other URM but are distinct in their unique status as members of sovereign nations and their relationship as Tribal peoples to settler colonialism.

    Puerto Ricans in the United States, despite being U.S. citizens since 1917, have been excluded or disinvested in, first as a racially suspect and unskilled migrant population, and later as a group presumed to comprise a politically apathetic "underclass" (Thomas, 2015). These four groups are hereinafter referred to as historically underrepresented minorities (URM). The delineation URM does not include international faculty, Asian Americans, or other Latin American subgroups.

3. These data may represent an overestimation as many higher education institutions count faculty and students by self-reported race/ethnicity and do not identify by nativity and/or country of origin. These data often are a mix of U.S.- and foreign-born self-identified Blacks and other Hispanics from Europe and South America.

4. During the same historic period, an opening of the doors to America was realized through the Immigration and Naturalization Act of 1965, also known as the Hart-Celler Act. This act abolished an earlier quota system based on national origin and established a new immigration policy based on reuniting immigrant families and attracting skilled labor to the United States. Over the next four decades, the policies put into effect in 1965 would greatly change the demographic makeup of the American population, as immigrants entering the United States under the new legislation came increasingly from countries in Asia, Africa, and Latin America, as opposed to Europe.

5. *Regents of the University of California v. Bakke*, 438 U.S. 265 (1978), was a landmark decision by the U.S. Supreme Court. It upheld affirmative action, allowing race to be one of several factors in college admission policies. However, the court ruled that specific quotas, such as the sixteen of one hundred seats set aside for minority students by the university, were impermissible.

6. The Higher Education Act (HEA) is the federal law that governs the administration of federal student aid programs. The HEA was originally passed in 1965 and signed into law by President Johnson. To encourage growth and change, it must be reapproved, or "reauthorized," by

Congress approximately every five years. In addition to major reauthorization bills, Congress also considers many bills that may directly or indirectly impact the HEA.

7.  Some of these included (1) H.R.3180, a bill to amend the Higher Education Act of 1965 to provide students with increased flexibility in the use of Federal Pell Grants and for other purposes; (2) S.60–114th Congress (2015–2016), a bill to prohibit aliens who are not lawfully present in the United States from being eligible for postsecondary education benefits that are not available to all U.S. citizens and nationals; (3) S.687–114th Congress, a bill to authorize the establishment of American Dream Accounts; (4) S.729–114th Congress, the Fairness for Struggling Students Act of 2015; (5) S.793, the Bank on Students Emergency Loan Refinancing Act; and (6) S.796/H.R.1507, a bill to incentivize state support for postsecondary education and to promote increased access and affordability for higher education for students, including Dreamer students. Many of these policies are central in increasing the successful educational pathways of historically underrepresented young men and women so as to increase future faculty representation at all colleges and universities, particularly predominately White institutions (PWIs).

8.  One of the earliest uses of the term *person of color* was in a U.S. law from 1807 that prohibited the import of slaves into any port or area located within the boundaries of the United States. The law was applicable to "any negro, mulatto, or person of colour" (Malesky, 2014). According to Schaefer (2002), "People or person of color" has been predominantly circulated in contemporary popular, activist, and academic discourses in the United States. It is slowly replacing *racial and ethnic minorities* as it presumes a social relationship among non-White racial groupings. The employment of what is thought to be a more inclusive category further develops and contests traditional uses of race and national identities. Safire (1988) goes further to note the political solidarity evoked by the term. Loretta Ross, cofounder of SisterSong Women of Color Reproductive Justice Collective, notes how the term *women of color* emerged not as a "biological term" but as a "political term" that strategically brought together ethnic minority women across an inclusive agenda for women's reproductive rights (Makers, 2017). According to the Women of Color Network (2014), the term *women of color* developed to "unify all women experiencing multiple layers of marginalization with race and ethnicity as a common issue." While the collective recognizes the possible homogenizing nature of such a term, the network highlights its continued utility to unite women with shared experiences in relationship to Western and European-based cultures, ways of knowing, and ways of being. It is noteworthy that the definition of who is included in *people of color* varies considerably, which in turn complicates the meanings and interpretations of the term *diversity*. Moreover, as astutely observed by Villalpando and Delgado Bernal (2002), the aggregation of all minorities into a category of people of color fails to distinguish which groups have truly been included and which groups are disproportionately excluded compared to their representation in the U.S. population.

9.  Grounded in Black feminist scholarship and activism (e.g., Collins, 2000; Combahee River Collective, 1977) and formally coined in 1991 by Black legal scholar Kimberlé Williams Crenshaw, intersectionality has been used across a significant number of disciplines.

10.  The Black Feminist Movement grew out of, and in response to, the Black Liberation Movement and the Women's Movement. In an effort to meet the needs of Black women who felt they were being racially excluded in the Women's Movement and sexually oppressed in the Black Liberation Movement, the Black Feminist Movement marked its "birth" with the 1973 founding of the National Black Feminist Organization in New York (Hull, Scott, & Smith, 2003).

**11.** For this study, data were also collected for 108 other Hispanics, a group that includes a mix of South Americans, Central Americans, non–Puerto Rican Spanish-speaking Caribbeans, and Spanish Europeans. Among these respondents, 80 percent were foreign-born, which coincides with migration patterns of the 1970s to 1990s. It is estimated that foreign-born Hispanics represent 2.4 percent of the total 5.0 percent of Hispanic faculty (Hurtado, Eagan, Pryor, Whang, & Tran, 2012; U.S. Department of Education, 2013). Similar to many other non-URM foreign-born faculty, these groups are more likely to come from elite privileged classes in their country of origin, have White skin privilege, and have immigrated to access social, economic, and employment opportunities in the United States post-1965. These international faculty are not the focus of this study.

**12.** These data are limited by the cross-sectional study design, the voluntary nature of the participants, and potential selection bias, as many participants were identified by a network known to the author. Respondents were identified through professional listservs, networks such as RWJF New Connections, Brothers and Sisters of the Academy, Latina Research network, among others, and university websites. URM faculty who were not part of these networks and/or did not self-identify as URM might have been excluded. Moreover, those who either felt well-suited to academia or, by the same measure, totally dissatisfied might have elected not to participate. Participants might also have provided socially desirable responses because they feared the consequences of disclosure to the interviewers, who were senior faculty members. Other factors that may have influenced experiences include colorism and phenotype, philosophic and political orientation, higher socioeconomic status of family of origin, and geographic location. Further, these data are unable to capture any undisclosed or undiagnosed disability (physical or mental) that may be associated with career path and progression. Findings are representative neither of all college faculty nor of all URM faculty in research universities. These data may not be representative of the multiple issues that URM women confront. Lastly, nonrandom sampling procedures and sample size do not permit causal inferences. Thus advanced statistical tests of differences with few exceptions are avoided to prevent readers from erroneous inferences. Patterns and experiences of the sample are highlighted. These findings, nonetheless, fill an important gap in knowledge on workplace stress and health among URM professionals and provide insight into the perceived experiences of four racial/ethnic URM faculty at PWIs.

**13.** In the demographic survey items only, a sexual orientation question asked if individuals identified as heterosexual, homosexual, bisexual, something else, or prefer not to answer. Of the total study participants ($n = 676$) that included 108 other Hispanics, a separate subanalysis of 98 participants who identified as LGBQ is being conducted. These results are being reported elsewhere.

**14.** The growing body of knowledge on international faculty shows that they are predominantly in research universities, are less likely to teach, are less burdened with diversity responsibilities, and are more likely to be engaged in research activities (Corley & Sabharwal, 2007; Kim, Wolf-Wendel, & Twombly, 2011; Mamiseishvili & Rosser, 2010; Webber, 2012).

**15.** The U.S. Census Bureau has estimated the number of Asians in 2015 to be approximately 21 million, or 6.5 percent of the U.S. population. The number of individuals who reported Asian as their only race was approximately 18 million, representing 5.6 percent of the total population. About another 3 million reported their race as Asian and one or more other races. Among Asians, Chinese (excluding those of Taiwanese origin) were the largest group in the United States, with an estimated population of 4.8 million, or 22.8 percent of the Asian-alone or in-combination population. Asian Indians were the second largest group, with a population of 4 million, or 19 percent of the Asian-alone population. Filipinos were the third largest group, with a population of 3.9 million, or 18.6 percent of the population. These three groups—Chinese, Asian Indians, and Filipinos—accounted for about 60 percent of the Asian population. Other sizable populations included 2 million Vietnamese and 1.8 million Koreans. Nearly three-fourths of the Asian-alone population were U.S. citizens, either through birth (about 33 percent) or naturalization (about 39 percent). In 2015 more than about 54 percent of Asians twenty-five years or older had a bachelor's degree or higher (Ryan & Bauman, 2016). College education completions rates ranged from 72 percent for Indians to 18 percent for Cambodians. In a recent report, the data show an overall median household income of $73,060, with a range of $100,000 for Indians and $55,000 for Cambodians (Lopez, Ruiz, & Patten, 2018). Although both native- and foreign-born Asians have experienced historical forms of exclusion and contemporary forms of discrimination, an exploration of their experiences is beyond the scope of this book.

## CHAPTER 2    THE HISTORY AND IMPORTANCE OF THE INCLUSION OF HISTORICALLY UNDERREPRESENTED FACULTY IN THE ACADEMY

1. This chapter provides a very brief and incomplete overview of the history of American higher education to contextualize its institutional roots of privilege. My gratitude goes to Dr. Victoria Maria MacDonald, who contributed her expertise as an educational historian for this chapter and provided invaluable historical perspective.

2. By the early nineteenth century, colleges for White women were created, beginning in 1836 with Wesleyan Female College (formerly George Female College) in Macon, Georgia. These White-only antebellum southern colleges did not threaten southern White male patriarchy and provided baccalaureate-level curricula (Farnham, 1994; McCandless, 1999). The movement for higher education attainment for women in the Northeast was first justified as "republican motherhood," preparing women to guide the next generation of citizens and civic leaders (Kerber, 1986). Teacher training, first in normal schools and then in state-run teacher education colleges, allowed higher education access as an extension of women's nurturing roles as mothers to the role of teachers and furthermore as an inexpensive way of staffing the nation's expanding common school system (Hoffman, 1981; Ogren, 2005). Historians have recently emphasized evidence from academies offering more rigorous curricula beyond finishing school and "ornamental arts" (Beadie & Tolley, 2002; Nash; 2005; Tolley, 2003).

3. The Asian American and Native American Pacific Islander–serving institutions (AANA-PISI) program started in 2008 as a competitive federal grant for educational institutions with high concentrations of underserved AAPI students allocated over a five-year period. According to the U.S. Department of Education (2016), the program more specifically provides "discretionary grants" to help eligible schools "improve their academic quality, increase their self-sufficiency, and strengthen their capacity to make a substantial contribution to the higher education resources of the Nation." The 2014 report titled "Measuring the Impact of MSI-Funded Programs on Student Successes: Findings from the Evaluation of Asian American and Native American Pacific Islander-Serving Institutions" states that the program "encourages campuses that serve disproportionately high numbers of low-income AAPI students to pursue innovative and targeted strategies that respond to those students' unique needs" and "signals a national commitment to the AAPI community, rightfully acknowledging low-income AAPI students as a population that faces barriers similar to those of other minority groups" (Teranishi, Bordoloi Pazich, Alcantar, & Kim Nguyen, 2014, p. 8).

4. Education was systematically denied to Mexican Americans up until the 1960s. Uncovering the historical record of discriminatory and exclusionary practices that denied Mexican Americans educational opportunity based on linguistic differences and phenotype is central to understanding past and contemporary patterns of exclusion. As early as 1916, discriminatory educational policies across the country segregated Mexican American children from White classrooms and placed Spanish-speaking students and children with Spanish surnames in segregated schools (MacDonald, 2004), which dispossessed Mexican Americans of their culture and language (Delgado Bernal, 2000). The de facto exclusion of Mexican Americans from the educational pipeline up until the early 1960s was systematically enforced (MacDonald & Rivera, 2015). Seven years prior to the *Brown v. Board of Education* case that ended segregation in the United States, *Méndez v. Westminster* ended almost a hundred years of segregation that had remained a practice since the end of the U.S.-Mexico War of 1848. The war's completion gave rise to measures to segregate Mexicans and Mexican Americans from "White" public institutions such as swimming pools, eating establishments, parks, and schools.

5. Scholars have different perspectives on the role of minority-serving institutions as educational equalizers for African American, Latino, and American Indian/Native American college aspirants and future faculty. In a recent book, Conrad and Gasman (2015) present MSIs as the new hope for innovation and respect for students' identities and their abilities to honor their own communities. The authors state that MSIs "prepare individuals to thrive where they live" (p. 275). Other scholars poignantly illustrate the low availability of financial and research faculty resources in these institutions. For example, in a book on Hispanic-serving institutions, the authors observe that these institutions are relatively recent developments. They warn that it is too early to know how students will fare in coconstructing safe and inclusive learning environments in dominant-culture institutions that are now serving higher rates of Hispanic students (Núñez, Hurtado, & Galdeano, 2015; Turner, Cosme, & Dinehart, 2018). Equally important is that although MSIs are often important sites for cultivating a sense of belonging, doctoral degrees from MSIs are not viewed by PWIs (research-extensive institutions) as meeting the criteria of excellence for continued doctoral work or faculty employment. Caution must be exercised in proposing and advocating for solutions that segregate students in unequal spaces that are perceived as producing noncompetitive professionals. On the other hand, an extensive body of knowledge argues for the need for investments in under-resourced MSIs and transformational changes in overresourced PWIs that can train the next generation of URM scholars in caring environments.

6. The Hispanic Association for Colleges and Universities represents more than 470 colleges and universities committed to Hispanic higher education success in the United States, Puerto Rico, Latin America, and Spain. Although their member institutions in the United States represent only 10 percent of all higher education institutions nationwide, together they are home to more than two-thirds of all Hispanic college students. HACU is the only national educational association that represents Hispanic-serving institutions. For further information on HACU, see http://www.hacu.net/hacu/HACU_101.asp.

7. It was from the German research university that we obtained the concepts of *Lehrfreiheit* (the right to teach) and *Lernfreiheit* (the right to study and conduct research) that would later develop into the principle of academic freedom (Fuchs, 1963).

8. The world wars ushered in a new era of growth in America's research universities. Federally funded military and scientific research became a significant source of university funding during this era. In fact, the federal government played an important role as the first funder of the defense industry during World War I. However, the government soon discovered that it was more efficient to conduct research at universities. Post–World War II and Cold War

universities were then funded as sites of technological innovation not necessarily related to defense (Geiger, 2014).

9. There are 335 doctorate-granting institutions in the United States. Within this category, 108 are considered R1 "very high research activity" (RU/VH) and 98 are considered "high research activity" (RU/H) institutions (McCormick & Zhao, 2005). Our sample included faculty only from doctorate-granting institutions that are deemed RU/VH and RU/H (Indiana University Center for Postsecondary Research, 2016).

10. Data show that professionals who emigrated from South American countries such as Chile and Argentina from the 1970s to the 1990s have successfully acquired positions in higher education institutions under the umbrella category Hispanic/Latino.

11. Eduardo Bonilla-Silva (2006) extends the work on racial formations and Latinos and argues that symbolic racism has replaced biological racism, with more concern for moral character and traditions of individualism. With his focus on institutional practices and criteria for entry into White privilege ("Honorary Whites"), he convincingly argues that the hierarchy of racial formation in the United States buffers and maintains White privilege. The maintenance of a plural racial stratification system upholds the system of White privilege by creating separate groups with separate political, social, and cultural interests.

## CHAPTER 3    THE ACADEMY AS A SITE OF INTELLECTUAL DETERMINISM

1. The Collaborative on Academic Careers in Higher Education (COACHE) is a research-practice partnership bringing together faculty and academic leaders who believe that the search for best practices begins with sound data—data that make the recruitment and management of faculty talent and their own leadership more effective. COACHE, based at the Harvard Graduate School of Education, enrolled its first cohort of institutional partners in the 2005–2006 academic year.

2. The goals of the ADVANCE program are (1) to develop systemic approaches to increase the representation and advancement of women in academic STEM careers, (2) to develop innovative and sustainable ways to promote gender equity in the STEM academic workforce, and (3) to contribute to the development of a more diverse science and engineering workforce. ADVANCE aims to contribute to and inform the general knowledge base on gender equity in the academic STEM disciplines.

## CHAPTER 4    MENTORING

1. STEAM is an educational approach to learning that uses science, technology, engineering, the arts, and mathematics as access points for guiding student inquiry, dialogue, and critical thinking. The end results are students who take thoughtful risks, engage in experiential learning, persist in problem solving, embrace collaboration, and work through the creative process. These are the innovators, educators, leaders, and learners of the twenty-first century.

2. In 2015, the University of California, Davis ADVANCE program began its pilot LAUNCH committee mentoring program for new faculty members. Since its inauguration, thirty-four new faculty members have been trained by a committee made up of senior faculty of the new faculty member's department, the department chair, a senior faculty member from an outside

but related department, and an ADVANCE faculty member (see http://ucd-advance.ucdavis
.edu/post/our-launch-program-takes).

## CHAPTER 5    UNWELCOMING CLIMATES

1. According to Henderson and Herring (2013), "Critical diversity is the equal inclusion of
people from varied backgrounds on a parity basis throughout all ranks and divisions of an
organization. It especially refers to those who are considered to be different from the traditional members because of exclusionary practices" (p. 300).

## CHAPTER 6    WORK-FAMILY BALANCE

1. I acknowledge the contributions of Drs. Chavella Pittman and Rashawn Ray during the
initial stages of writing this chapter.
2. A limitation of this study is that data were not collected on the demographic characteristics of spouses of women participants. These data would be important to collect in future
studies to glean additional insights into URM family assets and economic strain and stressors.

## CHAPTER 7    THE INTERSECTION OF HIRING, APPOINTMENT, TENURE, AND PROMOTION

1. Dysconscious racism tacitly accepts dominant White culture norms and privileges.
2. In an earlier study, Cross (1994) found that Harvard recruits most of its tenure-track faculty from other institutions. However, this is not the case when recruiting Black faculty in
most disciplines or international faculty such as African-born or Caribbean-born Black scholars. In these instances, Harvard recruits from those teaching at universities in the United
Kingdom and other European nations. Current practices may have changed.

## CHAPTER 8    WORKPLACE STRESS

1. The John Henryism (JH) construct was developed by Sherman James and colleagues in
1983 to refer to the positive relationship between high-effort coping and elevated blood pressure. John Henry, also known as the "steel-driving man," was a railroad worker who died of
mental and physical exhaustion shortly after outworking a steam-powered drill (LaVeist &
Isaac, 2012).
2. All survey data were analyzed using SPSS, and only basic frequency statistics are reported.
Univariate and bivariate tests were applied to test differences by race and ethnicity as appropriate. The survey data are presented for selected scale items by race and ethnicity for the four
groups for the following measures: self-reported health conditions, life events, depression and
mental health, work stress scales (vocational strain and role overload), and coping resources.
Due to small sample sizes for some measures and nonresponses, tests of significance were not
conducted on all measures.
3. Methodologically, it was observed that if investigators use the mean for the scale of the
twelve life events, the overall mean will be low and not reflect the impact of the most significant life events. A varimax factor rotation was conducted and yielded one factor with three

life events: death or serious illness of a close friend or family member, money problems, and major conflict with colleagues.

## CHAPTER 9    DOES GENDER MATTER?

1. Williams, Phillips, and Hall (2014) conducted mixed-methods analyses using a sample from the Association for Women in Science that included Latinas, Asian Americans, and Black women in the qualitative data. The authors also included White women as a comparison group.

2. Examples of cultural taxation include serving on multiple committees; teaching diversity courses; helping local communities; mentoring students of color or female students, faculty of color, or students who want to do a diversity project; and educating White faculty, administrators, and students about diversity.

3. Trower and Bleak (2004) use the term *faculty of color* and include the following groups: African American, Hispanic, Asian American/Pacific Islander, American Indian / Alaska Native, and multiracial.

4. Discrimination and racism were keenly perceived. Hurtado, Eagan, Pryor, Whang, and Tran (2012) found that 39.7 percent of American Indian faculty reported that subtle discrimination at the workplace was a source of stress. Racism as already observed can take many forms, including American Indian / Alaska Native faculty being perceived as overidentified with their culture and advocating for their communities. Undermining their competency and commitments, they are often discouraged from conducting research on their own people by senior faculty as majority-culture faculty perceive it impossible to do objective scientific research on native populations (Stein, 1994). Their values of being connected to their history and culture, however, provide another source of motivation for teaching, strength, and resistance—to help others understand native culture (Jaime & Rios, 2006). These sources of strength and resistance in teaching, research, and service, on the other hand, are often devalued in the evaluations conducted by tenure and promotion committees (Fenelon, 2003; Hernández-Avila, 2003). Their contributions can often be criticized as being forms of activism, rather than scholarly research (Trucks-Bordeaux, 2003). A separate subanalysis of Native American/American Indian faculty is being reported elsewhere.

5. Nativity and place of birth are not designations of underrepresentation. In fact, foreign-born faculty compared to URM faculty are less likely to have a domestic social justice agenda. Foreign-born faculty often are advocates for increasing focus on globalization and internationalization.

## CHAPTER 10    CREATING A SENSE OF BELONGING FOR URMS IN THE ACADEMY

1. A recent example is the initial acclaim for Alice Goffman's 2014 book *On the run: Fugitive life in an American city*. See Lewis-Kraus (2016).

2. Sullivan, Hollingshead and Smith (2004) describe the following five characteristics of effective family-work places: (1) formalization—policies must be written and consistent; (2) educated faculty—potential users must be aware of and understand how to use the programs; (3) addressed barriers—those who develop policies must understand why faculty to whom the policies might be useful will resist using them, for example, departmental culture

or if unpaid leave would be difficult for that faculty member; (4) programs promoted with data—showing the importance of investing in the programs and showing their effectiveness in a concrete manner; and (5) collaboration between policies and relevant institutional committees—for example, the departmental tenure committee and the policy committee that develops an intervention.

3. The top ten medical schools were Harvard, Johns Hopkins, University of Pennsylvania, University of California San Francisco, Washington University, Duke, Stanford, University of Washington, Yale, and Baylor College of Medicine. The schools were listed by *U.S. News & World Report* and identified by visiting websites.

4. The Big Ten medical schools included Indiana, Michigan State, Northwestern, Ohio State, Penn State, Illinois, Iowa, Michigan, Minnesota, and Wisconsin. (Purdue was omitted due to its lack of a medical school.) Data were verified by human resources at eight of the ten schools.

5. Overall a substantial cost for women prevails in terms of trying to combine work and family. Women who are married with young children have 35 percent lower odds than men with young children to get a tenure-track position, 28 percent lower odds than married women with no kids, and 33 percent lower odds than single women with no kids (Mason, Goulden, & Frasch, 2009). In Wolfinger, Mason, and Goulden's 2009 study of women PhDs, women graduates were more likely to become adjunct faculty, which corresponds to Marschke, Laursen, Nielsen McCarl, and Rankin's 2007 analysis about how soon universities can expect to find numerical gender equity under current attempts to address concerns. In contrast, a study of academics in the United Kingdom in 1998 showed that women did experience more stress probably due to domestic responsibilities and were more willing to express the pressures but showed lower levels of burnout and may "actually be coping better with demands place on them" (p. 78). Marschke et al. (2007) write, "Reaching numerical equality (i.e., 50/50) with men is not possible if current hiring, retention and promotion practices continue" (p. 17) and racial and ethnic inequities are not addressed.

6. Today's typical college leader is a married White male with a doctorate in education. He is sixty-one years old, up from sixty in 2006, according to the American Council on Education's latest survey, "The American College President 2012." The survey, released at the association's annual meeting, indicates that racial and ethnic minorities, who represent 13 percent of college presidents, are slightly less prevalent than they were in 2006, when 14 percent of college leaders were members of minority groups. See http://www.chronicle.com/article/Who-Are-College-Presidents-/131138.

7. According to the Institute of International Education, the number of international scholars in the United States has increased from 115,098 in the 2009–2010 academic year to 124,861 in the 2014–2015 academic year. Nearly 75 percent are in the science, technology, engineering, and math (STEM) fields, with China, India, South Korea, and Germany being the top sending countries. See https://www.higheredjobs.com/Articles/articleDisplay.cfm?ID=1012.

8. The H-1B is a temporary (nonimmigrant) visa that allows employers to petition for highly educated foreign professionals to work in "specialty occupations" that require at least a bachelor's degree or the equivalent. Jobs in STEM fields often qualify. Typically, the initial duration of an H-1B visa classification is three years, and they may be extended for a maximum of six years. From the creation of the H-1B program in 1990 to 2010, H-1B-driven increases in STEM workers were associated with a significant increase in wages for college-educated U.S.-born workers in 219 U.S. cities. From 2009 to 2011, wage growth for U.S.-born workers with at least a bachelor's degree was nominal, but wage growth for workers in occupations with large numbers of H-1B petitions was substantially higher. On average, H-1B workers earn higher wages

than employed U.S.-born workers with bachelor's degrees: $76,356 compared to $67,301, including in areas like computer and information technology, engineering, health care, and postsecondary education. Sixty-five thousand H-1B visas are allocated every year, with an additional twenty thousand available (Advanced Degree Exemption) to foreign students who have completed graduate programs at a U.S. university. However, in 2015, 172,748 H-1B visas were issued, more than twice the combined caps. The explanation lies in the fact that there are some H-1B cap-exempt employers: institutions of higher education, nonprofits, nonprofit research organizations, and government research organizations. See http://globalriskinsights .com/2017/02/winners-and-losers-in-the-revision-of-the-us-non-immigrant-visa-policy/ and https://www.americanimmigrationcouncil.org/sites/default/files/research/the_h-1b _visa_program_a_primer_on_the_program_and_its_impact_on_jobs_wages_and_the _economy.pdf.

9.  Foreign-born faculty are less likely to be satisfied with their career and more likely to have lower salaries (Corley & Sabharwal, 2007; Mamiseishvili, 2013), although this may be applicable only to faculty from certain geographic areas, such as Asia and the Middle East (Wells, Seifert, Park, Reed, & Umbach, 2007). Possible reasons for this dissatisfaction have been found to be that they may encounter difficulties and stress associated with completing and maintaining immigration status paperwork, adjusting to different cultural values, U.S. racism, coping with loneliness and isolation and adjustment to classroom dynamics (Collins, 2009; Eskay, Onu, Obiyo, Igbo, & Udaya, 2012; Gahungu, 2011; Skachkova, 2007; Thomas & Johnson, 2004).

# REFERENCES

Acosta-Belen, E., & Bose, C. E. (2012). *Unfinished business: Latino and other faculty diversity in the SUNY system*. Albany, NY: Center for Latino, Latin American, and Caribbean Studies (CELAC) at the University at Albany, SUNY.

Adams, B. M., Aranda, M. P., Kemp, B. J., & Takagi, K. (2002). Ethnic and gender differences in appraisal, coping and social support: A comparison of White-American, African-American, Japanese-American and Mexican-American spousal caregivers of people with dementia. *Journal of Clinical Geropsychology, 8*, 279–301.

Adams, K., & Bargerhuff, M. E. (2005). Dialogue and action: Addressing recruitment of diverse faculty in one Midwestern university's college of education and human services. *Education, 125*, 539–545.

Agathangelou, A. M., & Ling, L. M. H. (2002). An unten(ur)able position. *International Feminist Journal of Politics, 4*(3), 368–398.

Aguirre, A. J. (2000). *Women and minority faculty in the academic workplace: Recruitment, retention, and academic culture*. San Francisco, CA: Jossey-Bass.

Aguirre, A. J., Martinez, R., & Hernandez, A. (1993). Majority and minority faculty perceptions in academe. *Research in Higher Education, 34*, 371–385.

Ahmed, S. (2012). *On being included: Racism and diversity in institutional life*. Durham, NC: Duke University Press.

Aisenberg, N., & Harrington, M. (1988). *Women of academe: Outsiders in the sacred grove*. Amherst, MA: University of Massachusetts Press.

Akinbami, L. J., Moorman, J. E., & Liu, X. (2011). *Asthma prevalence, health care use, and mortality: United States, 2005–2009*. Washington, DC: U.S. Department of Health and Human Services, Centers for Disease Control and Prevention, National Center for Health Statistics.

Alamilla, S. G., Kim, B. S., & Lam, N. A. (2010). Acculturation, enculturation, perceived racism, minority status stressors, and psychological symptomatology among Latino/as. *Hispanic Journal of Behavioral Sciences, 32*(1), 55–76.

Alexander-Snow, M., & Johnson, B. (1999). Perspectives from faculty of color. In R. J. Menges & Associates (Eds.), *Faculty in new jobs: A guide to settling in, becoming established, and building institutional support* (pp. 88–117). San Francisco, CA: Jossey-Bass.

Alex-Assensoh, Y. (2003). Race in the academy: Moving beyond diversity and toward the incorporation of faculty of color in predominately white colleges and universities. *Journal of Black Studies, 34*, 5–11.

Allen, W. R., Epps, E. G., Guillory, E. A., Suh, S. A., Bonus-Hammarth, M., & Stassen, M.L.A. (2002). Outsiders within: Race, gender, and faculty status in U.S. higher education. In W. Smith, P. G. Altbach, & K. Lomotey (Eds.), *The racial crisis in American higher education: Continuing challenges for the twenty-first century* (pp. 112–127). Albany, NY: State University of New York Press.

Allison, D. C. (2008). Free to be me?: Black professors, White institutions. *Journal of Black Studies, 38*(4), 641–662.

Almaguer, T. (1994). *Racial fault lines: The historical origins of White supremacy in California.* Berkeley, CA: University of California Press.

Altbach, P. (2004). Globalization and the university: Myths and realities in an unequal world. *Tertiary Education and Management, 10*(1), 3–25. doi:10.1023/B:TEAM.0000012239.55136.4b

Amatea, E. S., & Fong, M. L. (1991). The impact of role stressors and personal resources on the stress experience of professional women. *Psychology of Women Quarterly, 15,* 419–430.

Amato, P. (1998). More than money? Men's contribution to their children's lives. In A. Booth & A. Creuter (Eds.), *Men in families: When do they get involved? What difference does it make?* (pp. 241–278). Mahwah, NJ: Lawrence Erlbaum.

American Association of Universities. (2016). AAU history. Retrieved from http://www.aau.edu/about/default.aspx?id=16754

American Council on Education. (2013). ACE brief examines scarcity of Asian Pacific Islander American leaders in higher education. Retrieved from http://www.acenet.edu/news-room/Pages/ACE-Brief-Examines-Scarcity-of-Asian-Pacific-Islander-American-Leaders-in-Higher-Education.aspx

American Council on Education. (2015). Pipelines, pathways, and institutional leadership: An update on the status of women in higher education. Washington, DC: American Council on Education. Retrieved from http://www.acenet.edu/news-room/Documents/Higher-Ed-Spotlight-Pipelines-Pathways-and-Institutional-Leadership-Status-of-Women.pdf

American Council on Education & American Association of University Professors. (2000). *Does diversity make a difference? Three research studies on diversity in college classrooms.* Washington, DC: Authors.

American Federation of Teachers (AFT). (2010). *Promoting racial and ethnic diversity in the faculty: What higher education unions can do.* Washington, DC: AFT Higher Education.

American Psychological Association. (2004). *Public policy, work, and families: The report of the APA presidential initiative on work and families.* Washington, DC: Author. Retrieved from http://www.apa.org/work-family

Anderson, J. (1988). *The education of Blacks in the South, 1860–1935.* Chapel Hill, NC: University of North Carolina Press.

Anzaldúa, G. (2007). *Borderlands: The new mestiza = La frontera* (3rd ed.). San Francisco, CA: AuntLute Books.

Aranda, M. P., Castaneda, I., Lee, P.-J., & Sobel, E. (2001). Stress, social support, and coping as predictors of depressive symptoms: Gender differences among Mexican Americans. *Social Work Research, 24,* 37–48.

Araujo, B. Y., & Borrell, L. N. (2006). Understanding the link between discrimination, mental health outcomes, and life chances among Latinos. *Hispanic Journal of Behavioral Sciences, 28*(2), 245–266.

Arrellano-Morales, L., Roesch, S. C., Gallo, L. C., Emory, K. T., Molina, K. M., Gonzalez, P., Penedo, F. J., Navas-Nacher, E. L., Teng, Y., Deng, Y., Isasi, C. R., Schneiderman, N., & Brondolo, E. (2015). Prevalence and correlates of perceived ethnic discrimination in the Hispanic community health study/study of Latinos sociocultural ancillary study. *Journal of Latina/o Psychology, 3*(3), 160–176.

Arrington, P. (2008). *Stress at work: How do social workers cope? NASW Membership Workforce Study.* Washington, DC: National Association of Social Workers.

Astin, A. W. (1982). *Minorities in American higher education: Recent trends, current prospect, and recommendations.* San Francisco, CA: Jossey-Bass.

Baca Zinn, M., & Dill, Bonnie T. (1996). Theorizing difference from multicultural feminism. *Feminist Studies, 22*(2), 321–331.

Bacchus, D. N. (2008). Coping with work-related stress: A study of the use of coping resources among professional black women. *Journal of Ethnic & Cultural Diversity in Social Work, 17*(1), 60–81.

Back, L. (2004). Ivory towers? The academy and racism. In I. Law, D. Phillips, & L. Turney (Eds.), *Institutional racism in higher education* (pp. 1–6). Sterling, VA: Trentham Books.

Baez, B. (1998). *Negotiating and resisting racism: How faculty of color construct promotion and tenure.* Retrieved from ERIC (ED 430 420).

Baez, B. (2002). *Affirmative action, hate speech, and tenure: Narratives about race, law, and the academy.* New York, NY: RoutledgeFalmer.

Bailey, D., Wolfe, D., & Wolfe, C. R. (1996). The contextual impact of social support across race and gender: Implications of African American Women in the workplace. *Journal of Black Studies, 26*(3), 287–307.

Balderrama, M., Teixeira, M. T., & Valdez, E. (2004). Una lucha de fronteras (A struggle of borders): Women of color in the academy. *Race, Gender & Class, 11*, 135–154.

Ballesteros, D. (2008). Leadership always makes a difference. In L. A. Valverde (Ed.), *Latino change agents in higher education* (pp. 193–214). San Francisco, CA: Jossey-Bass.

Ballysingh, T. A., Zerquera, D. D., Turner, C. S., & Sáenz, V. B. (2018). Answering the call: Hispanic-serving institutions as leaders in the quest for access, excellence, and equity in American higher education. *Association of Mexican American Educators Journal, 11*(3), 6–28.

Barnes, L. B., Agago, M. O., & Coombs, W. T. (1998). Effects of job related stress on faculty intention to leave academia. *Research in Higher Education, 39*(4): 457–469.

Bazemore, S. D., Janda, L. H., Derlega, V. J., & Paulson, J. (2010). The role of rejection in mediating the effects of stigma consciousness among foreign-born university professors. *Journal of Diversity in Higher Education, 3*(2): 85–96.

Beach, J. M. (2010). *Gateway to opportunity? A history of the community college in the United States* (1st ed.). Sterling, VA: Stylus.

Beadie, N., & Tolley, K. (2002). *Chartered schools: Two hundred years of independent academies in the United States, 1727–1925.* New York, NY: RoutledgeFalmer.

Beale, R., Chesler, M. A., & Ramus, E. (2014). Advocates for diversity . . . or not: Faculty members as change-agents? In M. A. Chesler & A. A. Young Jr. (Eds.), *Faculty identities and the challenge of diversity: Reflections on teaching in higher education* (pp. 171–186). Boulder, CO: Paradigm.

Bell, S., Morrow, M., & Tatsogluol, E. (1999). Teaching in environments of resistance: Toward a critical, feminist and antiracist pedagogy. In M. Mayberry & E. Rose (Eds.), *Meeting the challenge: Innovative feminist pedagogies in action* (pp. 23–48). New York, NY: Routledge.

Berdahl, R. O., Altbach, P., & Gumport, P. (2005). *The contexts of American higher education.* Baltimore, MD: Johns Hopkins University Press.

Berkman, L. F., & Syme, L. F. (1979). Social networks, host resistance, and mortality: A nine-year follow-up study of Alameda County residents. *American Journal of Epidemiology, 109*(2), 186–204.

Bhopal, K., & Jackson, J. (2013, June). The experiences of Black and minority ethnic academics: Multiple identities and career progression. Retrieved from http://eprints.soton.ac.uk/id/eprint/350967

Bianchi, S. M., & Milkie, M. A. (2010). Work and family research in the first decade of the 21st century. *Journal of Marriage and Family, 72*, 705–725.

Biddix, J. P. (2011). "Stepping stones": Career paths to the SSAO for men and women at four year institutions. *Journal of Student Affairs Research and Practice, 48*(4), 443–461.

Bilimoria, D., & Buch, K. K. (2010). The search is on: Engendering faculty diversity through more effective search and recruitment. *Change, 42,* 27–32.

Blackburn, R. T. & Bentley, R. J. (1993). Faculty research productivity: Some moderators of stress. *Research in Higher Education, 34,* 725–745.

Blackwell, L. V., Snyder, L. A., & Mavriplis, C. (2009). Diverse faculty in STEM fields: Attitudes, performance and fair treatment. *Journal of Diversity in Higher Education, 2*(4), 195–205.

Blake-Beard, S. (2011). Matching by race and gender in mentoring relationships: Keeping our eyes on the prize. *Journal of Social Issues, 67*(3), 622–643.

Boice, R. (1999). *Advice for new faculty: Nihil nimus.* Boston, MA: Allyn & Bacon.

Bonilla-Silva, E. (1997). Rethinking racism: Toward a structural interpretation. *American Sociological Review, 62,* 465–480.

Bonilla-Silva, E. (2006). *Racism without racists: Colorblind racism and the persistence of racial inequality in the United States* (2nd ed.). Lanham, MD: Rowman & Littlefield.

Bonilla-Silva, E. (2009). *Racism without racists: Colorblind racism and the persistence of racial inequality in the United States* (3rd ed.). Lanham, MD: Rowman & Littlefield.

Bonilla-Silva, E. (2015). The structure of racism in color-blind, "post-racial" America. *American Behavioral Scientist, 59*(11), 1358–1376.

Bonilla-Silva, E., & Baiocchi, G. (2001). Anything but racism: How sociologists limit the significance of racism. *Race & Society, 4*(2), 117–131.

Bonilla-Silva, E., & Embrick, D. G. (2007). "Every place has a ghetto . . .": The significance of Whites' social and residential segregation. *Journal of Symbolic Interaction, 30*(3), 323–345.

Bourdieu, P. (1986). The forms of capital. In J. G. Richardson (Ed.), *Handbook of theory and research for sociology of education* (pp. 241–258). New York, NY: Greenwood Press.

Bowen, W. G., Kurzweil, M. A., & Tobin, E. M. (2005). *Equity and excellence in American higher education.* Charlottesville, VA: University of Virginia Press.

Bowen-Reid, T. L., & Harrell, J. P. (2002). Racist experiences and health outcomes: An examination of spirituality as a buffer. *Journal of Black Psychology, 28*(1), 18–36.

Bower, B. L. (2002). Campus life for faculty of color: Still strangers after all these years? *New Directions for Community Colleges, 118,* 79–88.

Bowleg, L. (2012). The problem with the phrase "women and minorities": Intersectionality, an important theoretical framework for public health. *American Journal of Public Health, 102*(7), 1267–1273.

Bowleg, L. P., Huang, J. M., Brooks, K., Black, A., & Burkholder, G. P. (2003). Triple jeopardy and beyond: Multiple minority stress and resilience among Black lesbians. *Journal of Lesbian Studies, 7*(4), 87–108.

Boyd, T., Cintrón, R., & Alexander-Snow, M. (2010). The experience of being a junior minority female faculty member. *Forum on Public Policy, 2010*(2), 1–23.

Boykin, S. D., Zambrana, R. E., Williams, K., Salas-Lopez, D., Sheppard, V., & Headley, A. (2003). Mentoring underrepresented minority female medical school faculty: Momentum to increase retention and promotion. *Journal of the Association for Academic Minority Physician, 14*(1), 15–18.

Bozeman, B., & Feeney, M. K. (2007). Toward a useful theory of mentoring: A conceptual analysis and critique. *Administration & Society, 39*(6), 719–739.

Brayboy, B. M. J. (2003). The implementation of diversity in predominately White colleges and universities. *Journal of Black Studies, 34*(1), 72–86.

Brint, S., & Karabel, J. (1991). *The diverted dream: Community colleges and the promise of educational opportunity in America, 1900–1985.* New York, NY: Oxford University Press.

Bristol, M. N., Abbuhl, S., Cappola, A. R., & Sonnad, S. S. (2008). Work-life policies for faculty at the top ten medical schools. *Journal of Women's Health, 17,* 1312–1320.

Brondolo, E., Brady ver Halen, N. B., Pencille, M., Beatty, D., & Contrada, R. J. (2009). Coping with racism: A selective review of the literature and a theoretical and methodological critique. *Journal of Behavioral Medicine, 32*(1), 64–88.

Brondolo, E., Libretti, M., Rivera, L., & Walsemann, K. M. (2012). Racism and social capital: The implications for social and physical well-being. *Journal of Social Issues, 68*(2), 358–384.

Brown, A. (2014). U.S. Hispanic and Asian populations growing, but for different reasons. Pew Research Center. Retrieved from http://www.pewresearch.org/fact-tank/2014/06/26/u-s-hispanic-and-asian-populations-growing-but-for-different-reasons/

Brown, M. C., Davis, G. L., & McClendon, S. A. (1999). Mentoring graduate underrepresented students of color: Myths, models, and modes. *Peabody Journal of Education, 74*(2), 105–118.

Brown, R. D., Bond, S., Gerndt, J., Krager, L., Krantz, B., Lukin, M., & Prentice, D. (1986). Stress on campus: An interactional perspective. *Research in Higher Education, 24*(1), 97–112.

Browne, I., & Misra, J. (2003). The intersection of gender and race in the labor market. *Annual Review of Sociology, 29,* 487–513.

Burgard, S. A., & Ailshire, J. A. (2009). Putting work to bed: Stressful experiences on the job and sleep quality. *Journal of Health and Social Behavior, 50*(4), 476–492.

Burgard, S. A., & Lin, K. Y. (2013). Bad jobs, bad health? How work and working conditions contribute to health disparities. *American Behavioral Scientist, 57*(8), 1105–1127.

Burton, L. M., Bonilla-Silva, E., Ray, V., Buckelew, R., & Freeman, E. H. (2010). Critical race theories, colorism, and the decade's research on families of color. *Journal of Marriage and Family, 72*(3), 440–459.

Cantu, C. (2009). Colegio Jacinto Traveno: The rise and fall of the first Chicano college. *South Texas Studies, 19,* 33–51.

Cantwell, B., & Kauppinen, I. (Eds.). (2014). *Academic capitalism in the age of globalization.* Baltimore, MD: Johns Hopkins University Press.

Carbado, D. W., & Gulati, M. (2013). *Acting white?: Rethinking race in post-racial America.* New York, NY: Oxford University Press.

Career Leadership & University Excellence. (2012). Planning group on promotion and tenure. Albany: University at Albany, State University of New York. Retrieved from http://www.albany.edu/academics/files/CLUE_PT_Full_Final_Report.pdf

Carnevale, A. P. (1999). *Education = success: Empowering Hispanic youth and adults.* Princeton, NJ: Educational Testing Service.

Carr, P. L., Palepu, A., Szalacha, L., Caswell, C., & Inui, T. (2007). "Flying below the radar": A qualitative study of minority experience and management of discrimination in academic medicine. *Medical Education, 41,* 601–609.

Castañeda, M., & Isgro, K. L. (2013). *Mothers in academia.* New York, NY: Columbia University Press.

Castañeda, M., Zambrana, R. E., Marsh, K., Vega, W., Becerra, R., & Pérez, D. J. (2015). Role of institutional climate on underrepresented faculty perceptions and decision-making in use of work-family policies. *Family Relations, 64*(5), 711–725.

Castellanos, J., Gloria, A. M., & Kamimura, M. (2006). *The Latina/o pathways to the Ph.D.* Sterling, VA: Stylus.

Castellanos, J., & Jones, L. (2003). *The majority in the minority: Expanding the representation of Latina/o faculty, administrators and students in higher education.* Sterling, VA: Stylus.

Castro, C. (2012). *Women of color navigating the academy: The discursive power of professionalism.* Unpublished doctoral dissertation, Temple University, Philadelphia, PA.

Cerecer, P., Elk, L., Alanis, I., & Murakami-Ramalho, E. (2011). Transformative resistance as agency: Chicanas/Latinas (re)creating academic spaces. *Journal of the Professoriate, 5*(1), 70–98.

Cha, Y. (2010). Reinforcing separate sphere: The effects of spousal overwork on men's and women's employment in dual-earner households. *American Sociological Review, 75*(2), 303–329.

Chadiha, L. A., Aranda, M. P., Biegel, D. E., & Chang, C.-W. (2014). The importance of mentoring faculty members of color in schools of social work. *Journal of Teaching in Social Work, 34*(4), 351–362.

Charles, C. Z. (2003). The dynamics of racial residential segregation. *Annual Review of Sociology, 29,* 167–207.

Chávez, M. (2011). *Everyday injustice: Latino professionals and racism.* Lanham, MD: Rowman & Littlefield.

Cheney, G., & Ashcraft, K. L. (2007). Considering "the professional" in communication studies: Implications for theory and research within and beyond the boundaries of organizational communication. *Communication Theory, 17*(2), 146–175.

Chesler, M. A., & Young, A. A. (2014). *Faculty identities and the challenge of diversity: Reflections on teaching in higher education.* Boulder, CO: Paradigm.

Childers, C. D., & Sage, J. A. (2003, August). Working women, work family and family work conflicts: A first look at differences in White women and women of color. Paper submitted to the American Sociological Association conference, Atlanta.

Christian, M. (2012). *Integrated but unequal: Black faculty in predominantly white space.* Trenton, NJ: Africa World Press.

*Chronicle of Higher Education.* (2012). Percentage of full-time faculty members by sex, rank, and racial and ethnic group, Fall 2009. Retrieved from http://chronicle.com.proxy-um.researchport.umd.edu/article/Percentage-of-Faculty-Members/128518/

*Chronicle of Higher Education.* (2015). Hiring in academe: Insights on diversity, equity, and inclusion. Washington, DC: Author.

Chun, E. B., & Evans, A. (2012). *Diverse administrators in peril: The indentured class in higher education.* Boulder, CO: Paradigm.

Churchill, C. J., & Levy, G. E. (2012). *The enigmatic academy: Class, bureaucracy, and religion in American education.* Philadelphia, PA: Temple University Press.

Clark, R., Anderson, N. B., Clark, V. R., & Williams, D. R. (1999). Racism as a stressor for African Americans: A biopsychosocial model. *American Psychologist, 54*(10), 805–816.

Clark, S. C. (2002). Employees' sense of community, sense of control, and work/family conflict in Native American organizations. *Journal of Vocational Behavior, 61,* 92–108.

Cobas, J., Duany, J., & Feagin, J. (Eds.). (2009). *How the United States racializes Latinos: At home and abroad.* Boulder, CO: Paradigm.

Coker, A. (2003). African-American female adult learners: Motivations, challenges and coping strategies. *Journal of Black Studies, 33,* 654–674.

Collaborative on Academic Careers in Higher Education (COACHE). (2007). *COACHE highlights report 2007.* Cambridge, MA: Author.

Collins, P. H. (1991). *Black feminist thought: Knowledge, consciousness, and the politics of empowerment.* New York, NY: Routledge.

Collins, P. H. (2000). *Black feminist thought: Knowledge, consciousness, and the politics of empowerment* (2nd ed.). New York, NY: Routledge.

Collins, P. H. (2009). Emerging intersections—Building knowledge and transforming institutions. In B. T. Dill and R. E. Zambrana (Eds.), *Emerging intersections: Race, class, and gender in theory, policy, and practice* (pp. vii–xvii). New Brunswick, NJ: Rutgers University Press.

Collins, P. H. (2015). Intersectionality's definitional dilemmas. *Annual Review of Sociology, 41*, 1–20.

Collins, P. H., & Bilge, S. (2016). *Intersectionality*. Malden, MA: Polity Press.

Comas-Díaz, L. (1997). Mental health needs of Latinos with professional status. In J. G. Garcia & M. C. Zea (Eds.), *Psychological interventions and research with Latino populations* (pp. 142–165). Needham Heights, MA: Allyn & Bacon.

Combahee River Collective. (1977). *Combahee River Collective statement: Black feminist organizing in the seventies and eighties*. Latham, NY: Kitchen Table/Women of Color Press.

Conrad, C., & Gasman, M. (2015). *Educating a diverse nation: Lessons from minority-serving institutions*. Cambridge, MA: Harvard University Press.

Conway, C. (2016). Interview with Junot Díaz. LinkedIn.

Cook, B. J., & Cordova, D. I. (2007). *Minorities in higher education. 22nd annual status report: 2007 supplement*. Washington, DC: American Council on Education.

Cook, E. D., & Gibbs, H. R. (2009). Diverse academic faculty: A precious resource for innovative institutions. In T. R. Cole, T. J. Goodrich, & E. R. Gritz (Eds.), *Faculty health in academic medicine* (pp. 93–111). Totowa, NJ: Humana Press.

Cook-Lynn, E. (1996). *Why I can't read Wallace Stenger, and other essays*. Madison, WI: University of Wisconsin Press.

Cooper, J. E., & Stevens, D. D. (Eds.). (2002). *Tenure in the sacred grove: Issues and strategies for women and minority faculty*. Albany, NY: State University of New York Press.

Cora-Bramble, D. (2006). Minority faculty recruitment, retention and advancement: Applications of a resilience-based theoretical framework. *Journal of Health Care for the Poor and Underserved, 17*, 251–255.

Corley, E. A., & Sabharwal, M. (2007). Foreign-born academic scientists and engineers: Producing more and getting less than their U.S.-born peers? *Research in Higher Education, 48*(8), 909–940.

Cowin, K. M., Cohen, L. M., Ciechanowski, K. M., & Orozco, R. A. (2011). Portraits of mentor-junior faculty relationships: From power dynamics to collaboration. *Journal of Education, 192*(1), 37–47.

Cox, A. (2008). *Women of color faculty at the University of Michigan: Recruitment, retention, and campus climate*. Unpublished manuscript, University of Michigan, Ann Arbor.

Crawford, I., Suarez-Balcazar, Y., Reich, J., Figert, A., & Nyde, P. (1996). The use of research participation for mentoring prospective minority graduate students. *Teaching Sociology, 24*(3), 256–263.

Crenshaw, K. (1991). Mapping the margins: Intersectionality, identity politics, and violence against women of color. *Stanford Law Review, 43*(6), 1241–1299. doi:10.2307/1229039

Crisp, G., & Cruz, I. (2009). Mentoring college students: A critical review of the literature between 1990 and 2007. *Research in Higher Education, 50*(6), 525–545.

Cross, T. (1994). Black faculty at Harvard: Does the pipeline defense hold water? *Journal of Blacks in Higher Education, 4*, 42–46.

Cross, T., & Slater, R. (2002). A short list of colleges and universities that are taking measures to increase their number of Black faculty. *Journal of Blacks in Higher Education, 36*, 99–103.

Cueva, B. (2014). Institutional academic violence: Racial and gendered microaggressions in higher education. *Chicana/Latina Studies, 13*(2), 142–168.

Daley, S., Wingard, D. L., & Reznik, V. (2006). Improving the retention of underrepresented minority faculty in academic medicine. *Journal of the National Medical Association, 98,* 1435–1440.

Damiano-Teixeira, K. M. (2006). Managing conflicting roles: A qualitative study with female faculty members. *Journal of Family and Economic Issues, 27*(2), 310–334.

Dancy, D. E., & Brown, M. C. (2011). The mentoring and induction of educators of color: Addressing the imposter syndrome in academe. *Journal of School Leadership, 21*(4), 607–634.

Davies, P. G., Spencer, S. J., & Steele, C. M. (2005). Clearing the air: Identity safety moderates the effects of stereotype threat on women's leadership aspirations. *Journal of Personality and Social Psychology, 88*(2), 276–287.

Dayton, B., Gonzalez-Vasquez, N., Martinez, C. R., & Plum, C. (2004). Hispanic-serving institutions through the eyes of students and administrators. *New Directions for Student Services, 105,* 29–40.

DeCastro, R., Griffith, K. A., Ubel, P. A., Stewart, A., & Jagsi, R. (2014). Mentoring and the career satisfaction of male and female academic medical faculty. *Academic Medicine, 89*(2), 301–311. doi:10.1097/ACM.0000000000000109

Dedovic, K., Wadiwalla, M., Engert, V., & Pruessner, J. C. (2009). The role of sex and gender socialization in stress reactivity. *Developmental Psychology, 45*(1), 45–55.

DeJesus, G. H., & Rice, D. W. (2002). The N-word and academia: The psychology of employing an epithet. *Black Issues in Higher Education, 19*(3), 52.

Delgado, R. (1989). Storytelling for oppositionists and others: A plea for narrative. *Michigan Law Review, 87,* 2401–2441.

Delgado, R. (2007). The myth of upward mobility. *University of Pittsburg Law Review, 68,* 835–913.

Delgado, R., & Stefancic, J. (2001). *Critical race theory: An introduction.* New York, NY: New York University Press.

Delgado, R., & Stefancic, J. (2013). *Critical race theory: The cutting edge* (3rd ed.). Philadelphia, PA: Temple University Press.

Delgado Bernal, D. (2000). Historical struggles for educational equity: Setting the context for Chicana/o schooling today. In C. Tejeda, C. Martinez, & Z. Cantwellardo (Eds.), *Charting new terrains of Chicana(o)/Latina(o) education* (pp. 67–90). Cresskill, NJ: Hampton.

Delgado Bernal, D., & Villalpando, O. (2002). An apartheid of knowledge in academia: The struggle over the "legitimate" knowledge of faculty of color. *Equity & Excellence in Education, 35*(2), 169–180.

Diggs, G. A., Garrison-Wade, D. F., Estrada, D., & Galindo, R. (2009). Smiling faces and colored spaces: The experiences of faculty of color pursing tenure in the academy. *Urban Review, 41*(4), 312–333.

Dill, Bonnie T. (2009). Intersections, identities, and inequalities in higher education. In Bonnie T. Dill & Ruth E. Zambrana (Eds.), *Emerging intersections: Race, class, and gender in theory, policy, and practice* (pp. 229–253). New Brunswick, NJ: Rutgers University Press.

Dill, B. T., & Kohlman, M. H. (2012). Intersectionality: A transformative paradigm in feminist theory and social justice. In S. N. Hesse-Biber (Ed.), *Handbook of feminist research: Theory and praxis* (2nd ed., pp. 154–174). Thousand Oaks, CA: SAGE.

Dill, B. T., & Zambrana, R. E. (2009). Critical thinking about inequality: An emerging lens. In B. T. Dill & R. E. Zambrana (Eds.), *Emerging intersections: Race, class, and gender in theory, policy, and practice* (pp. 1–21). New Brunswick, NJ: Rutgers University Press.

Dinwiddie, G. Y., Zambrana, R. E., Doamekpor, L. A., & Lopez, L. (2016). The impact of educational attainment on observed race/ethnic disparities in inflammatory risk in the 2001–2008 National Health and Nutrition Examination Survey. *International Journal of Environmental Research and Public Health, 13*(1), 42.

Dinwiddie, G. Y., Zambrana, R. E., & Garza, M. A. (2014). Exploring risk factors in Latino cardiovascular disease: The role of education, nativity and gender. *American Journal of Public Health, 104,* 1742–1750.

Dixon-Reeves, R. (2003). Mentoring as a precursor to incorporation: An assessment of the mentoring experience of recently minted Ph.D.s. *Journal of Black Studies, 34,* 12–27.

Dixson, A. D., & Rousseau, C. K. (2005). And we are still not saved: Critical race theory in education ten years later. *Race Ethnicity and Education, 8*(1), 7–27.

Dougal, A. L., & Baum, A. (2001). Stress, health, and illness. In A. Baum, T. Revenson, & J. Singer (Eds.), *Handbook of health psychology* (pp. 321–337). Mahwah, NJ: Lawrence Erlbaum.

Douglass, J. A. (2005). *The Carnegie commission and council: A retrospective.* Berkeley, CA: Center for Studies in Higher Education.

Du Bois, W. E. B. (1903). The talented tenth. In B. T. Washington, W. E. B. Du Bois, & P. Laurence, *The Negro problem: A series of articles by representative Negroes of to-day* (pp. 31–75). New York, NY: James Pott.

Dunbar, E. (2014, December 2). Who really burns: Quitting a dean's job in the age of Mike Brown. *Jezebel.* Retrieved from http://jezebel.com/who-really-burns-quitting-a-deans-job-in-the-age-of-mi-1665631269

Duquette, A., Kérouac, S., Sandhu, B. K., Ducharme, F., & Saulnier, P. (1995). Psychosocial determinants of burnout in geriatric nursing. *International Journal of Nursing Studies, 5,* 443–456.

Ecklund, E. H., & Lincoln, A. E. (2011). Scientists want more children. *PLOS ONE, 6*(8), e22590.

Eddy, P., & Gaston-Gayles, J. (2008). New faculty on the block: Issues of stress and support. *Journal of Human Behavior in the Social Environment, 17*(1–2), 89–106.

Edmondson Bell, E. L., & Nkomo, S. M. (2003). Our separate ways: Black and white women and the struggle for professional identity. *The Diversity Factor, 11*(1), 11–15.

Eisenmann, L. (2006). *Higher education for women in postwar America, 1945–1965.* Baltimore, MD: Johns Hopkins University Press.

Ek, L. D., Cerecer, P. D. Q., Alanis, I., & Rodríguez, M. A. (2010). "I don't belong here": Chicanas/Latinas at a Hispanic serving institution creating community through Muxerista mentoring. *Equity & Excellence in Education, 43*(4), 539–553.

Elligan, D., & Utsey, S. (1999). Utility of an African-centered support group for African American men confronting societal racism and oppression. *Cultural Diversity and Ethnic Minority Psychology, 41*(3), 295–313.

Elliot, M. (2003). Work and family role strain among university employees. *Journal of Family and Economic Issues, 24*(2), 157–181.

Elliot, M. (2008). Gender differences in the causes of work and family strain among academic faculty. *Journal of Human Behavior in the Social Environment, 17*(1–2), 157–173.

Ellison, C. G., & Taylor, R. J. (1996). Turning to prayer: Social and situational antecedents of religious coping among African Americans. *Review of Religious Research, 38,* 111–131.

Embrick, D. G. (2011). The diversity ideology in the business world: A new oppression for a new age. *Critical sociology, 37*(5), 541–556.

Eskay, M. K., Onu, V. C., Obiyo, N. O., Igbo, J. N., & Udaya, J. (2012). Surviving as foreign born immigrants in America's higher education: Eight exemplary cases. *US-China Education Review, 2*, 236–243.

Espino, M. M. (2016). "Get an education in case he leaves you": Consejos for Mexican American women PhDs. *Harvard Educational Review, 86*(2), 183–205.

Espino, M., & Zambrana, R. E. (Forthcoming 2019). "How do you advance here? How do you survive?" An exploration of under-represented minority faculty perceptions of mentoring modalities. *Review of Higher Education.*

Essien, V. (2003). Visible and invisible barriers to the incorporation of faculty of color in predominantly White law schools. *Journal of Black Studies, 34*, 63–71.

Evans, E., & Grant, C. (2008). *Mama, PhD: Women write about motherhood and academic life.* New Brunswick, NJ: Rutgers University Press.

Evans, L., & Moore, W. L. (2015). Impossible burdens: White institutions, emotional labor, and micro-resistance. *Social Problems, 62*(3), 439–454. doi:10.1093/socpro/spv009

Evans, S. Y. (2007). Women of color in American higher education. *NEA Higher Education Journal,* 131–138.

Farmbry, K. (2007). Expanding the pipeline: Explorations on diversifying the professoriate. *Journal of Public Affairs Education, 13*(1), 115–132.

Farnham, C. A. (1994). *The education of the southern belle: Higher education and student socialization in the antebellum South.* New York, NY: New York University Press.

Fasching-Varner, K. J., & Albert, K. (Eds.). (2015). *Racial battle fatigue in higher education: Exposing the myth of post-racial America.* Lanham, MD: Rowman & Littlefield.

Feagin, J. R. (1991). The continuing significance of race. *American Sociological Review, 56*, 101–116.

Feagin, J. R. (2006). *Systemic racism: A theory of oppression.* New York, NY: Routledge.

Feagin, J. R. (2010). *Racist America: Roots, current realities, and future reparations* (2nd ed.). New York, NY: Routledge.

Feagin, J. R. (2013). *The White racial frame: Centuries of racial framing and counter-framing* (2nd ed.). New York, NY: Routledge.

Feagin, J. R., & McKinney, K. D. (2003). *The many costs of racism.* Lanham, MD: Rowman & Littlefield.

Felder, P. (2010). On doctoral student development: Exploring faculty mentoring in the shaping of African American doctoral student success. *Qualitative Report, 15*(2), 455–474.

Fenelon, J. (2003). Race, research, and tenure: Institutional credibility and the incorporation of African, Latino, and American Indian faculty. *Journal of Black Studies, 87, 34*, 87–100.

Feskanich, D., Hastrup, J. L., Marshall, J. R., Coldritz, G. A., Stampfer, M. J., Willett, W. C., & Kawachi, I. (2002). Stress and suicide in the Nurses' Health Study. *Journal of Epidemiology and Community Health, 56*, 95–98.

Fiegener, M. K. (2009). *Numbers of U.S. doctorates awarded rise for sixth year, but growth slower.* InfoBrief. NSF 10-308. National Science Foundation. Retrieved from https://eric.ed.gov/?id=ED507250

Fiegener, M. K. (2015). *Doctorate recipients from U.S. universities: 2014.* National Center for Science and Engineering Statistics. Retrieved from http://www.nsf.gov/statistics/2016/nsf16300

Field, K. (2017). Fighting long odds. *Chronicle of Higher Education, 63*(19).

Fine, M. (1991). *Framing dropouts: Notes on the politics of an urban public high school.* Albany, NY: State University of New York Press.

Flaherty, C. (2015). Demanding 10 percent. *Inside Higher Ed.* Retrieved from https://www.insidehighered.com/news/2015/11/30/student-activists-want-more-black-faculty-members-how-realistic-are-some-their-goals?utm_source=Inside+Higher+Ed&utm_campaign=a4aa6bbc5a-DNU20151130&utm_medium=email&utm_term=0_1fcbc04421-a4aa6bbc5a-198459893

Fletcher, S., & Mullen, C. A. (Eds.). (2012). *The SAGE handbook of mentoring and coaching in education.* London: Sage.

Flores, G. M. (2011). Racialized tokens: Latina teachers negotiating, surviving, and thriving in a White women's profession. *Qualitative Sociology, 34,* 313–335.

Fong, B. (2000). Toto, I think we're still in Kansas: Supporting and mentoring faculty of color and administrators. *Liberal Education, 86*(4), 56–60.

Ford, K. A. (2014). Race, gender, and bodily (mis)recognitions: Women of color faculty experiences with White students. In M. A. Chesler & A. A. Young (Eds.), *Faculty identities and the challenge of diversity* (pp. 117–133). Boulder, CO: Paradigm.

Fouad, N. A., & Carter, R. T. (1992). Gender and racial issues for new counseling psychologists in academia. *Counseling Psychologist, 20*(1), 123–140.

Frone, M. R., Russell, M., & Barnes, G. M. (1996). Work family conflict, gender, and health outcomes. *Journal of Occupational Health Psychology, 1*(1), 57–69.

Fuchs, R. F. (1963). Academic freedom—its basic philosophy, function, and history. *Law and Contemporary Problems, 28*(3), 431–446.

Gahungu, A. (2011). Integration of foreign-born faculty in academia: Foreignness as an asset. *International Journal of Educational Leadership Preparation, 6*(1), 1–22.

Gallagher, A., & Trower, C. A. (2009). The demand for diversity. *Chronicle of Higher Education.* Retrieved from http://www.chronicle.com/article/The-Demand-for-Diversity/44849

Garcia, A. (2005). Counter stories of race and gender: Situating experiences of Latina in the academy. *Latino Studies, 3,* 261–273.

García-López, G., & Segura, D. A. (2008). They are testing you all the time: Negotiating dual femininities among Chicana attorneys. *Feminist Studies, 34,* 229–258.

Garza, H. (1988). The "barrioization" of Hispanic faculty. *Educational Record, 68*(4), 122–124.

Garza, H. (1993). Second-class academics: Chicano/Latino faculty in U.S. universities. In J. Gainen & R. Boice (Eds.), *Building a diverse faculty* (pp. 33–41). San Francisco, CA: Jossey-Bass.

Gasman, M. (2016, September 26). An Ivy League professor on why colleges don't hire more faculty of color: "We don't want them." *Washington Post.* Retrieved from https://www.washingtonpost.com/news/grade-point/wp/2016/09/26/an-ivy-league-professor-on-why-colleges-dont-hire-more-faculty-of-color-we-dont-want-them/?utm_term=.ccb12c18829e

Gasman, M., & Conrad, C. F. (2011). *Minority serving institutions: Educating all students.* Philadelphia: University of Pennsylvania, Center for MSIs.

Gasman, M., Kim, J., & Nguyen, T.-H. (2011). Effectively recruiting faculty of color at highly selective institutions: A school of education case study. *Journal of Diversity in High Education, 4*(4), 212–222. doi:10.1037/a0028130

Gasman, M., Lundy-Wagner, V., Ransom, T., & Bowman, N. (2010). *Unearthing promise and potential: Our nation's historically Black colleges and universities.* San Francisco, CA: Jossey-Bass.

Gasman, M., Nguyen, T., & Conrad, C. F. (2015). Lives intertwined: A primer on the history and emergence of minority serving institutions. *Journal of Diversity in Higher Education, 8*(2), 120–138.

Gee, G., & Walsemann, K. (2009). Does health predict the reporting of racial discrimination or do reports of discrimination predict health? Findings from the National Longitudinal Study of Youth. *Social Science & Medicine, 68,* 1676–1684.

Geiger, R. L. (1986). *To advance knowledge: The growth of American research universities, 1900–1940.* New York, NY: Oxford University Press.

Geiger, R. L. (1993). *Research and relevant knowledge: American research universities since World War II.* New York, NY: Oxford University Press.

Geiger, R. L. (2000). The era of multipurpose colleges in American higher education, 1850–1890. In R. L. Geiger (Ed.), *The American college in the nineteenth century* (pp. 127–152). Nashville, TN: Vanderbilt University Press.

Geiger, R. L. (2014). *The history of American higher education: Learning and culture from the founding to World War II.* Princeton, NJ: Princeton University Press.

Geiger, R. L., & Sá, C. M. (2008). *Tapping the riches of science: Universities and the promise of economic growth.* Cambridge, MA: Harvard University Press.

Gerson, K. (2010). *The unfinished revolution: Coming of age in a new era of gender, work, and family.* New York, NY: Oxford University Press.

Gillespie, N. A., Walsh, M., Winefield, A. H., Dua, J., & Stough, C. (2001). Occupational stress in universities: Staff perceptions of the causes, consequences and moderators of stress. *Work & Stress, 15*(1), 53–72.

Gilman, D. C. (1885). *The benefits which society derives from universities.* Baltimore, MD: Johns Hopkins University Press.

Ginther, D. K., Schaffer, W. T., Schnell, J., Masimore, B., Liu, F., Haak, L. L., & Kington, R. (2011). Race, ethnicity, and NIH research awards. *Science, 333,* 1015–1019.

Giroux, H. A. (1983). Theories of reproduction and resistance in the new sociology of education: A critical analysis. *Harvard Educational Review, 53,* 257–293.

Gleason, P. (1995). *Contending with modernity: Catholic higher education in the twentieth century.* New York, NY: Oxford University Press.

Godsil, R. D. (2015). Breaking the cycle: Implicit bias, racial anxiety, and stereotype threat. *Poverty & Race, 24*(1), 1–10.

Godsil, R. D., Tropp, L. R., Atiba Goff, P., & Powell, J. A. (2014, November). The science of equality, volume 1: Addressing implicit bias, racial anxiety, and stereotype threat in education and health care. Perception Institute in association with the Haas Institute for a Fair and Inclusive Society at UC Berkeley and the Center for Policing Equity at UCLA. Retrieved from http://perception.org/wp-content/uploads/2014/11/Science-of-Equality.pdf

Golden, L. (2001). Flexible work hours: Which workers get them? *American Behavioral Scientist, 44,* 1152–1178.

Goldin, C., & Katz, L. F. (1999). The shaping of higher education: The formative years in the United States, 1890–1940. *Journal of Economic Perspectives, 13*(1), 37–62.

Goldin, C. D., & Katz, L. F. (2008). *The race between education and technology.* Cambridge, MA: Belknap.

Gomez, A. I. (1973). *Mexican Americans in higher education.* Paper presented at the Society for Applied Anthropology's Symposium on Mexican American Education, April 12–14, Tucson, Arizona. Retrieved from http://files.eric.ed.gov/fulltext/ED077618.pdf

Gonzáles, L. D., Murukami, E., & Núñez, A. M. (2013). Latina faculty in the labyrinth: Constructing and contesting legitimacy in Hispanic Serving Institutions. *Journal of Educational Foundations, 27*(1/2), 65.

González, J. C. (2007). Surviving the doctorate and thriving as faculty: Latina junior faculty reflecting on their doctoral studies experiences. *Equity & Excellence in Education, 40,* 291–300.

Green, A. (2016, January 16). The cost of balancing academia and racism. *Atlantic.* Retrieved from http://www.theatlantic.com/education/archive/2016/01/balancing-academia -racism/424887/

Gregory, S. T. (2001). Black faculty women in the academy: History, status, and future. *Journal of Negro Education, 70,* 124–138.

Griffin, K. A., Bennett, J. C., & Harris, J. (2011). Analyzing gender differences in Black faculty marginalization through a sequential mixed-methods design. *New Directions for Institutional Research, 151,* 45–61.

Griffin, K. A., Pifer, M. J., Humphrey, J. R., & Hazelwood, A. M. (2011). (Re)defining departure: Exploring Black professors' experiences with and responses to racism and racial climate. *American Journal of Education, 117,* 495–526.

Griffin, K. A., & Reddick, R. J. (2011). Gender differences in the mentoring patterns of Black professors at predominantly White research universities. *American Educational Research Journal, 48*(5), 1032–1057.

Grzywacz, J. G., Almeida, D. M., & McDonald, D. A. (2002). Work-family spillover and daily reports of work and family stress in the adult labor-force. *Family Relations, 51,* 28–36.

Guillory, J., & Ward, K. (2007). Tribal colleges and universities: Identity, invisibility, and current issues. In M. Gasman, B. Baez, & C. S. V. Turner (Eds.), *Understanding minority serving institutions* (pp. 91–110). Albany, NY: State University of New York Press.

Guinier, L. (2015). *The tyranny of the meritocracy: Democratizing higher education in America.* Boston, MA: Beacon Press.

Gutiérrez y Muhs, G., Niemann, Y. F., González, C. G., & Harris, A. P. (Eds.). (2012). *Presumed incompetent: The intersections of race and class for women in academia.* Boulder, CO: University Press of Colorado.

Guzman, F., Trevino, J., Lubuguin, F., & Aryan, B. (2010). Microaggressions and the pipeline for scholars of color. In D. W. Sue (Ed.), *Microaggressions and marginality: Manifestation, dynamics, and impact* (pp. 145–167). Hoboken, NJ: John Wiley & Sons.

Hall, S. S., & MacDermid, S. M. (2009). A quantitative typology of dual-earner couples: Unanswered questions about circumstance, motivations, and outcomes. *Journal of Family and Economic Issues, 30,* 215–225.

Hamilton, A. (2011). School girls and college women: Female education in the 19th and early 20th centuries. In C. Deluzio & P. C. Mancall (Eds.), *Women's rights: People and perspectives* (pp. 79–93). Santa Barbara, CA: ABC-CLIO.

Hammer, L. B., Kossek, E. E., Anger, W. K., Bodner, T., & Zimmerman, K. L. (2011). Clarifying work-family intervention processes: The roles of work-family conflict and family supportive supervisor behaviors. *Journal of Applied Psychology, 96*(1), 134–150.

Hancock, A.-M. (2016). *Intersectionality: An intellectual history.* New York, NY: Oxford University Press.

Hansman, C. A. (2002). Diversity and power in mentoring relationships. In C. A. Hansman (Ed.), *Critical perspectives on mentoring: Trends and issues* (pp. 39–48). Columbus, OH: ERIC.

Harding, R. C., Hudson, M., Erickson, L., Taualii, M., & Freeman, B. (2015). First Nations, Maori, American Indians, and Native Hawaiians as sovereigns: EAP with indigenous nations within nations. *Journal of Workplace Behavioral Health, 30*(1–2), 14–31. doi:10.1080/15555240.2015.998969

Harley, D. A. (2008). Maids of academe: African American women faculty at predominately White institutions. *Journal of African American Studies, 12,* 19–36. doi:10.1007/s12111-007-9030-5

Harley, S., & the Black Women and Work Collective (Eds.). (2002). *Sister circle: Black women and work*. New Brunswick, NJ: Rutgers University Press.

Harlow, R. (2003). "Race doesn't matter, but . . .": The effect of race on professors' experiences and emotion management in the undergraduate college classroom. *Social Psychology Quarterly, 66*(4), 348–363.

Harper, S. R. (2012). Race without racism: How higher education researchers minimize racist institutional norms. *Review of Higher Education, 36*(1), 9–29.

Harrell, S. P. (2000). A multidimensional conceptualization of racism-related stress: Implications for the well-being of people of color. *American Journal of Orthopsychiatry, 70*(1), 42–57.

Harrington, M. (1962). *The other America: Poverty in the United States*. New York: Macmillan.

Hart, J., & Cress, C. M. (2008). Are women faculty just "worrywarts"? Accounting for gender differences in self-reported stress. *Journal of Human Behavior in the Social Environment, 17*(1–2), 175–193.

Harwarth, I., Maline, M., & DeBra, E. (1997). *Women's colleges in the United States: History, issues and challenges*. Collingdale, PA: Diane Publishing.

Hassouneh, D., Lutz, K. F., Beckett, A. K., Junkins, E. P., & Horton, L. L. (2014). The experiences of underrepresented minority faculty in schools of medicine. *Medical Education Online, 19*, 247–268.

Heckman, D. R., Johnson, S., Foo, M. D., & Yang, W. (2017). Does diversity-valuing behavior result in diminished performance ratings for non-White and female leaders? *Academy of Management Journal, 60*, 771–797. doi:10.5465/amj.2014.0538

Heflin, C., & Pattillo, M. (2006). Poverty in the family: Race, siblings, and socioeconomic heterogeneity. *Social Science Research, 35*, 804–822.

Hendel, D. D., & Horn, A. S. (2008). The relationship between academic life conditions and perceived sources of faculty stress over time. *Journal of Human Behavior in the Social Environment, 17*(1–2), 61–88.

Henderson, L., & Herring, C. (2013). Does critical diversity pay in higher education? Race, gender, and departmental ranking in research universities. *Politics, Groups, and Identities, 1*(3), 299–310.

Hendrix, K. G. (Ed.). (2007). *Neither White nor male: Female faculty of color*. San Francisco, CA: Jossey-Bass.

Herd, P., Goesling, B., & House, J. S. (2007). Socioeconomic position and health: The differential effects of education versus income on the onset versus progression of health problems. *Journal of Health and Social Behavior, 48*(3), 223–238.

Hernandez, T. J., & Morales, N. E. (1999). Career, culture, and compromise: Career development experiences of Latinas working in higher education. *Career Development Quarterly, 48*(1), 45–58.

Hernández-Avila, I. (2003). Thoughts on surviving as native scholars in the academy. *American Indian Quarterly, 27*(1–2), 240–248.

Hernandez-Truyol, B. E. (1997). Borders (en) gendered: Normativities, Latinas, and a LatCrit paradigm. *New York University Law Review, 72*, 882–927.

Higginbotham, E. (1990). Designing an inclusive curriculum: Bringing all women into the core. *Women's Studies Quarterly, 1–2*, 8–23.

Higginbotham, E. (2001). *Too much to ask: Black women in the era of integration*. Chapel Hill, NC: University of North Carolina Press.

Higginbotham, E. (2009). Entering a profession: Race, gender, and class in the lives of Black women attorneys. In B. T. Dill & R. E. Zambrana (Eds.), *Emerging intersections: Race, class, and gender in theory, policy, and practice* (pp. 22–49). New Brunswick, NJ: Rutgers University Press.

Higginbotham, E., & Cannon, L. W. (1992). Moving up with kin and community: Upward social mobility for Black and White women. *Gender & Society, 6,* 416–440.

Higgins, C., Duxbury, L., & Lee, C. (1994). Impact of life-cycle stage and gender on the ability to balance work and family responsibilities. *Family Relations, 43*(2), 144–150.

Hoffman, N. (1981). *Woman's "true" profession: Voices from the history of teaching.* Old Westbury, NY: Feminist Press.

Hogan, J., Carlson, J., & Dua, J. (2002). Stressors and stress reactions among university personnel. *International Journal of Stress Management, 9*(4), 289–294.

Holder, J. C., & Vaux, A. (1998). African American professionals: Coping with occupational stress in predominantly white work environments. *Journal of Vocational Behavior, 53*(3), 315–333.

Hoover, E. (2015, July 21). 7 myths about campus diversity. *Chronicle of Higher Education.* Retrieved from http://chronicle.com/article/article-content/231797/

Hull, A., Scott, P., & Smith, B. (2003). *All the women are White, all the Blacks are men, but some of us are brave.* Old Westbury, NY: Feminist Press.

Hurtado, A. (1996). *The color of privilege: Three blasphemies on race and feminism.* Critical perspectives on women and gender. Ann Arbor: University of Michigan Press.

Hurtado, S. (1992). The campus racial climate: Contexts of conflict. *Journal of Higher Education, 63*(5), 539–569.

Hurtado, S. (2007). Linking diversity with the educational and civic missions of higher education. *Review of Higher Education, 30,* 185–196.

Hurtado, S., Eagan, K., Pryor, J. H., Whang, H., & Tran, S. (2012). Undergraduate teaching faculty: The 2010–2011 HERI Faculty Survey. Los Angeles, CA: Higher Education Research Institute at UCLA. Retrieved from http://www.heri.ucla.edu/monographs/HERI-FAC2011-Monograph.pdf

Hurtado, S., Milem, J., Clayton-Pedersen, A., & Allen, W. (1999). *Enacting diverse learning environments: Improving the climate for racial/ethnic diversity in higher education* (Rep. No. 26-8). Washington, DC: George Washington University, School of Education & Human Development.

Indiana University Center for Postsecondary Research. (2016). *The Carnegie Classification of institutions of higher education* (2015 ed.). Bloomington, IN: Author.

Israel, B. A., Baker, E. A., Goldenhar, L. M., Heaney, C. A., & Schurman, S. J. (1996). Occupational stress, safety, and health: Conceptual framework and principles for effective prevention interventions. *Journal of Occupational Health Psychology, 1*(3), 261–286.

Jacobi, M. (1991). Mentoring and undergraduate academic success: A literature review. *Review of Educational Research, 61*(4), 505–532.

Jacobs, J. (2004). The faculty time divide. *Sociological Forum, 19*(1), 3–27.

Jacobs, J. A., & Winslow, S. E. (2004). Overworked faculty: Job stresses and family demands. *Annals of the American Academy, 596,* 104–129.

Jaime, A., & Rios, F. (2006). Negotiation and resistance amid the overwhelming presence of whiteness: A Native American faculty and student perspective. *Taboo: The Journal of Culture & Education, 10*(2), 37–54.

James, K., Lovato, C., & Khoo, G. (1994). Social identity correlates of minority workers' health. *Academy of Management Journal, 37*(2), 383–396.

James, S., Hartnett, S., & Kalsbeek, W. (1983). John Henryism and blood pressure differences among black men. *Journal of Behavioral Medicine, 6,* 259–278.

Jarmon, B. (2001). Unwritten rules of the game. In R. O. Mabokela & A. L. Green (Eds.), *Sisters of the academy: African American women scholars in higher education* (pp. 175–182). Sterling, VA: Stylus.

Jayakumar, U., Howard, T., Allen, W., & Han, J. C. (2009). Racial privilege in the professoriate: An exploration of campus climate, retention, and satisfaction. *Journal of Higher Education, 80*(5), 538–563.

Johnson, B. J., & Harvey, W. (2002). The socialization of black college faculty: Implications for policy and practice. *Review of Higher Education, 25*(3), 297–314.

Johnson, H. L. (2016). *Pipelines, pathways, and institutional leadership: An update on the status of women in higher education.* Washington, DC: American Council on Education.

Johnsrud, L. K. (1993). Women and minority faculty experiences: Defining and responding to diverse realities. In J. Gainen & R. Boice (Eds.), *Building a diverse faculty* (pp. 33–41). San Francisco, CA: Jossey-Bass.

Johnsrud, L. K., & Sadao, K. C. (1998). The common experience of "otherness": Ethnic and racial minority faculty. *Review of Higher Education, 21*(4), 315–342.

Jones, C., & Shorter-Gooden, K. (2003). *Shifting: The double lives of Black women in America* (1st ed.). New York, NY: HarperCollins.

Joseph, T. D., & Hirshfield, L. E. (2011). "Why don't you get somebody new to do it?" Race and cultural taxation in the academy. *Ethnic and Racial Studies, 34*(1), 121–141.

Judge, T. A., & Colquitt, J. A. (2004). Organizational justice and stress: The mediating role of work-family conflict. *Journal of Applied Psychology, 89*(3), 395–404.

Kachchaf, R., Ko, L., Hodari, A., & Ong, M. (2015). Career-life balance for women of color: Experiences in science and engineering academia. *Journal of Diversity in Higher Education, 8*(3), 175–191.

Kanter, R. M. (1977a). *Men and women of the corporation.* New York, NY: Basic Books.

Kanter, R. M. (1977b). Some effects of proportions on group life: Skewed sex ratios and responses to token women. *American Journal of Sociology, 82*(5), 965–990.

Kay, F. M., Hagan, J., & Parker, P. (2009). Principals in practice: The importance of mentorship in the early stages of career development. *Law and Policy, 31*(1), 69–110.

Kayes, P. E. (2006). New paradigms for diversifying faculty and staff in higher education: Uncovering cultural biases in the search and hiring process. *Multicultural Education, 14,* 65–69.

Keene, J. R., & Quadagno, J. (2004). Predictors of perceived work-family balance: Gender difference or gender similarity? *Sociological Perspectives, 47*(1), 1–24.

Keith, V. M., Lincoln, K. D., Taylor, R. J., & Jackson, J. S. (2010). Discriminatory experiences and depressive symptoms among African American women: Do skin tone and mastery matter? *Sex Roles, 62,* 48–59.

Kelly, E. L., Moen, P., & Tranby, E. (2011). Changing workplaces to reduce work-family conflict: Schedule control in a White-collar organization. *American Sociological Review, 76*(2), 265–290.

Kena, G., Musu-Gillette, L., Robinson, J., Wang, X., Rathbun, A., Zhang, J., Wilkinson-Flicker, S., Barmer, A., & Dunlop Velez, E. (2015). The condition of education 2015 (NCES 2015-144). Washington, DC: U.S. Department of Education, National Center for Education Statistics. Retrieved from http://nces.ed.gov/pubsearch

Kerber, L. K. (1986). *Women of the republic: Intellect and ideology in revolutionary America.* New York, NY: Norton.

Kessler, R. C., Mickelson, K. D., & Williams, D. R. (1999). The prevalence, distribution, and mental health correlates of perceived discrimination in the United States. *Journal of Health and Social Behavior, 40,* 208–230.

Kim, D., Wolf-Wendel, L., & Twombly, S. (2011). International faculty: Experience of academic life and productivity in U.S. universities. *Journal of Higher Education, 82*(2), 720–747.

Kirschbaum, C., Bartussek, D., & Strasburger, C. J. (1992). Cortisol responses to psychological stress and correlations with personality traits. *Personality and Individual Differences, 13*(12), 1353–1357.

Kivimäki, M., Nyberg, S. T., Fransson, E. I., Heikkilä, K., Alfredsson, L., Casini, A., Clays, E., & Batty, G. D. (2013). Associations of job strain and lifestyle risk factors with risk of coronary artery disease: A meta-analysis of individual participant data. *Canadian Medical Association Journal, 185*(9), 763–769. doi:10.1503/cmaj.121735

Knowles, M. F., & Harleston, B. W. (1997). *Achieving diversity in the professoriate: Challenges and opportunities.* Washington, DC: American Council on Education.

Krieger, N. (1990). Racial and gender discrimination: Risk factors for high blood pressure? *Social Science & Medicine, 30*, 1273–1281.

Krieger, N. (2012). Methods for the study of discrimination and health: An ecosocial approach. *American Journal of Public Health, 102*(5), 936–945.

Lacy, K. R. (2007). *Blue-chip black: Race, class, and status in the new Black middle class.* Berkeley, CA: University of California Press.

Lacy, K. R. (2012). All's fair? The foreclosure crisis and middle-class Black (in)stability. *American Behavioral Scientist, 56*, 1565–1580.

Laden, B. V., & Hagedorn, L. S. (2000). Job satisfaction among faculty of color in academe: Individual survivors or institutional transformers? *New Directions for Institutional Research, 105*(1), 57–66.

Lagemann, E. C. (1983). *Private power for the public good: A history of the Carnegie Foundation for the Advancement of Teaching* (1st ed.). Middletown, CT: Wesleyan University Press.

Lagemann, E. C. (1989). *The politics of knowledge: The Carnegie Corporation, philanthropy, and public policy* (1st ed.). Middletown, CT: Wesleyan University Press.

Lamont, M. (2009). *How professors think: Inside the curious world of academic judgment.* Cambridge, MA: Harvard University Press.

Landry, B., & Marsh, K. (2011). The evolution of the new Black middle class. *Annual Review of Sociology, 37*, 373–394.

Lareau, A. (2002). Invisible inequality: Social class and child rearing in Black families and White families. *American Sociological Review, 67*, 747–776.

Lareau, A. (2011). *Unequal childhoods: Class, race, and family life.* Berkeley, CA: University of California Press.

Lareau, A. (2014). Schools, housing, and the reproduction of inequality. In A. Lareau & K. Goyette (Eds.), *Choosing homes, choosing schools: Residential segregation and the search for a good school* (pp. 169–206). New York, NY: Russell Sage Foundation.

Lautenberger, D., Moses, A., & Castillo-Page, L. (2016). *An overview of women full-time medical school faculty of color.* Washington, DC: Association of American Medical Colleges.

LaVeist, T. A., & Isaac, L. A. (Eds.). (2012). *Race, ethnicity, and health: A public health reader.* San Francisco, CA: John Wiley & Sons.

Lawson, E. J., Rodgers-Rose, L. F., & Rajaram, S. (1999). The psychosocial context of Black women's health. *Heath Care of Women International, 20*(3), 279–289.

Laymon, K. (2014, November 29). My Vassar College faculty ID makes everything OK. *Gawker.* Retrieved from http://gawker.com/my-vassar-college-faculty-id-makes-everything-ok-1664133077

Lazarus, R. S., & Folkman, S. (1984). *Stress, appraisal and coping.* New York, NY: Springer.

Lease, S. H. (1999). Occupational role stressors, coping, support, and hardiness as predictors of strain in academic faculty: An emphasis on new and female faculty. *Research in Higher Education, 40*(3), 285–307.

Lee, J. M., & Keys, S. W. (2013). *Land-grant but unequal: State one-to-one match funding for 1890 land-grant universities* (APLU Office of Access and Success Pub. No. 3000-PB1). Washington, DC: Association of Public and Land-grant Universities.

Lee, S. M. (2002). Do Asian American faculty face a glass ceiling in higher education? *American Educational Research Journal, 39*(3), 695–724.

León, D. J., & Nevarez, C. (2007). Models of leadership institutes for increasing the number of top Latino administrators in higher education. *Journal of Hispanic Higher Education, 6*(4), 356–377.

Lepore, S. J., Revenson, T. A., Weinberger, S. L., Weston, P., et al. (2006). Effects of social stressors on cardiovascular reactivity in Black and White women. *Society of Behavioral Medicine, 31*(2), 120–127.

Lewis, T. T., Cogburn, C. D., & Williams, D. R. (2015). Self-reported experiences of discrimination and health: Scientific advances, ongoing controversies, and emerging issues. *Annual Review of Clinical Psychology, 11*, 407–440.

Lewis-Kraus, G. (2016, January 12). The trials of Alice Goffman. *New York Times Magazine.* Retrieved from https://www.nytimes.com/2016/01/17/magazine/the-trials-of-alice -goffman.html

Light, P. (1994). Not like us: Removing the barriers to recruiting minority faculty. *Journal of Policy Analysis and Management, 13*, 164–180.

Lin, Z., Pearce, R., & Wang, W. (2009). Imported talents: Demographic characteristics, achievement and job satisfaction of foreign born full time faculty in four year American colleges. *Higher Education, 57*(6), 703–721.

Lindholm, J. A., & Szelenyi, K. (2008). Faculty time stress: Correlates within and across academic disciplines. *Journal of Human Behavior in the Social Environment, 17*(1–2), 19–40.

Lucas, C. J. (2006). *American higher education: A history* (2nd ed.). New York, NY: Palgrave Macmillan.

MacDonald, V. M. (2004). *Latino education in the United States: A narrated history from 1513–2000* (1st ed.). New York, NY: Palgrave Macmillan.

MacDonald, V. M. (2013). Demanding their rights: The Latino struggle for educational access and equity. In National Park Service (Ed.), *American Latinos and the making of the United States: A theme study* (p. 25). Washington, DC: U.S. Department of Interior.

MacDonald, V. M., Botti, J. M., & Clark, L. H. (2007). From visibility to autonomy: Latinos and higher education in the U.S., 1965–2005. *Harvard Educational Review, 77*(4), 474–504.

MacDonald, V. M., & Garcia, T. (2003). Latino higher education: Historical pathways to access. In L. Jones & J. Castellanos (Eds.), *The majority in the minority: Retaining Latina/o faculty, administrators, and students in the 21st century* (pp. 15–43). Sterling, VA: Stylus Press.

MacDonald, V. M., & Hoffman, B. P. (2012). "Compromising la causa?" The Ford Foundation and Chicano intellectual nationalism in the creation of Chicano history. *History of Education Quarterly, 52*(3), 251–281.

MacDonald, V. M., & Rivera, J. (2015). History's prism in education: A spectrum of legacies across centuries of Mexican American agency; experience and activism 1600s–2000s. In R. E. Zambrana & S. Hurtado (Eds.), *The magic key: The educational journey of Mexican*

*Americans from K–12 to college and beyond* (pp. 25–53). Austin, TX: University of Texas Press.

Makers. (2017). History of women of color. Retrieved from http://www.makers.com/moments/history-term-women-color

Malesky, K. (2014). The journey from "colored" to minorities to "people of color." *NPR*. Retrieved from http://www.npr.org/sections/codeswitch/2014/03/30/295931070/thejourney-from-coloredto-minorities-to-people-of-color

Mamiseishvili, K. (2013). Contributions of foreign-born faculty to doctoral education and research. *New Directions for Higher Education, 163*(Fall), 89–98.

Mamiseishvili, K., & Rosser, V. J. (2010). International and citizen faculty in the United States: An examination of their productivity at research universities. *Research in Higher Education, 51,* 88–107.

Manuelito, K. (2005). The role of education in American Indian self-determination: Lessons from the Ramah Navajo Community School. *Anthropology & Education Quarterly, 36*(1), 73–87.

Margolis, E., & Romero, M. (1998). "The department is very male, very white, very old, and very conservative": The functioning of the hidden curriculum in graduate sociology departments. *Harvard Educational Review, 68*(1), 1–33.

Marmot, M. (2006). Status syndrome: A challenge to medicine. *JAMA, 295*(11), 1304–1307.

Marotte, M. R., Reynolds, P. M., & Savarese, R. J. (Eds.). (2011). *Papa PhD: Essays on fatherhood by men in the academy.* New Brunswick, NJ: Rutgers University Press.

Marschke, R., Laursen, S., Nielsen McCarl, J., & Rankin, P. (2007). Demographic inertia revisited: An immodest proposal to achieve equitable gender representation among faculty in higher education. *Journal of Higher Education, 78*(1), 1–26.

Martinengo, G., Jacob, J. I., & Hill, E. J. (2010). Gender and the work-family interface: Exploring differences across the family life course. *Journal of Family Issues, 31*(10), 1363–1390.

Martinez, R. (1999). *Hispanic leadership in American higher education.* San Antonio, TX: Hispanic Association of Colleges and Universities.

Martínez Alemán, A. M. (1995). Actuando: A Latina professor in Iowa. In R. V. Padilla & R. Chávez (Eds.), *The leaning ivory tower: Latino professors in American universities* (pp. 67–76). Albany, NY: State University of New York Press.

Martínez Alemán, A. M., & Renn, K. A. (Eds.). (2002). *Women in higher education: An encyclopedia.* Santa Barbara, CA: ABC-CLIO.

Mason, M. A., & Goulden, M. (2002). *Do babies matter (Part I & II)? The effect of family formation on the lifelong careers of academic men and women.* Washington, DC: American Association of University Professors.

Mason, M. A., Goulden, M., & Frasch, K. (2009). Why graduate students reject the fast track. *Academe, 95,* 11–16.

Mason, M. A., Wolfinger, N. H., & Goulden, M. (2013). *Do babies matter? Gender and family in the ivory tower.* New Brunswick, NJ: Rutgers University Press.

Matsuda, M. J., Lawrence, C. R., Delgado, R., & Crenshaw, K. W. (Eds.). (1993). *Words that wound: Critical race theory, assaultive speech, and the first amendment.* Boulder, CO: Westview.

Mattingly, M. J., & Sayer, L. C. (2006). Under pressure: Gender differences in the relationship between free time and feeling rushed. *Journal of Marriage and Family, 68,* 205–221.

Mays, V. M., Cochran, S. D., & Barnes, N. W. (2007). Race, race-based discrimination, and health outcomes among Blacks. *Annual Review of Psychology, 58,* 201–225.

Mays, V. M., & Ghavami, N. (2017). History, aspirations, and transformations of intersectionality: Focusing on gender. In C. Travis & J. White (Eds.), *American Psychological Association handbook of the psychology of women* (Vol. 1, pp. 541–566). Washington, DC: American Psychological Association.

McCandless, A. T. (1999). *The past in the present: Women's higher education in the twentieth-century American South.* Tuscaloosa, AL: University of Alabama Press.

McCormick, A. C., & Zhao, C. (2005). Rethinking and reframing the Carnegie Classification. *Change, 37*(5), 51–57.

McDonald, K. B., & Wingfield, A. M. H. (2008). (In)visibility blues: The paradox on institutional racism. *Sociological Spectrum, 29*, 28–50.

McDonald, L. M., & Korabik, K. (1991). Sources of stress and ways of coping among male and female managers. *Journal of Social Behavior and Personality, 6*, 185–198.

McEwen, B., & Kalia, M. (2010). The role of corticosteroids and stress in chronic pain conditions. *Metabolism Clinical and Experimental, 59*(Suppl. 1), S9–S15.

McEwen, B., & Lasley, E. N. (2003). Allostatic load: When protection gives way to damage. *Advances in Mind-Body Medicine, 19*(1), 28–33.

McGrath, J. E. (1976). Stress and behavioral organizations. In M. Dunnette (Ed.), *Handbook of industrial and organizational psychology* (pp. 1351–1395). Chicago, IL: Rand McNally.

McNeal, G. (2003). African American nurse faculty satisfaction and scholarly productivity at predominantly White and historically Black colleges and universities. *ABNF Journal, 14*, 4–12.

Medina, C., & Luna, G. (2000). Narratives from Latina professors in higher education. *Anthropology & Education Quarterly, 31*, 47–66.

Melchior, M., Caspi, A., Milne, B. J., Danese, A., Poulton, R., & Moffitt, T. E. (2007). Work stress precipitates depression and anxiety in young, working women and men. *Psychological Medicine, 37*, 1119–1129.

Menges, R. J., & Associates. (1999). *Faculty in new jobs: A guide to settling in, becoming established, and building institutional support.* San Francisco, CA: Jossey-Bass.

Mickelson, R. A., & Oliver, M. L. (1991). Making the short list: Black candidates and the faculty recruitment process. In P. A. Altbach & K. Lomotey (Eds.), *The racial crisis in American higher education* (pp. 149–166). Albany, NY: State University of New York Press.

Mihesuah, D. A. (1993). *Cultivating the rosebuds: The education of women at the Cherokee Female Seminary, 1851–1909.* Urbana, IL: University of Illinois Press.

Milkie, M., Raley, S., & Bianchi, S. M. (2009). Taking on the second shift: Time allocations and time pressures of U.S. mothers and fathers with preschoolers. *Social Forces, 88*, 487–517.

Miller, G. E., Buckholdt, D. R., & Shaw, B. (2008). Perspectives on stress and work. *Journal of Human Behavior in the Social Environment, 17*(1–2), 1–18.

Minow, M. (1990). *Making all the difference: Inclusion, exclusion, and American law.* Ithaca, NY: Cornell University Press.

Mirowsky, J., & Ross, C. E. (2007). Creative work and health. *Journal of Health and Social Behavior, 48*(4), 385–403.

Moen, P., Kelly, E. L., Tranby, E., & Huang, Q. (2011). Changing work, changing health: Can real work-time flexibility promote health behaviors and well-being? *Journal of Health and Social Behavior, 52*(4), 404–429.

Moen, P., Lam, J., Ammons, S., & Kelly, E. L. (2013). Time work by overworked professionals: Strategies in response to the stress of higher status. *Work and Occupations, 40*(2), 79–114.

Montero-Sieburth, M. (1996). Beyond affirmative action: An inquiry into the experiences on Latinas in academia. *New England Journal of Public Policy, 2*, 65–98.

Moore, H. A., Acosta, K., Perry, G., & Edwards, C. (2010). Splitting the academy: The emotions of intersectionality at work. *Sociological Quarterly, 51*, 179–204.

Moore, W. L. (2008). *Reproducing racism: White space, elite law schools, and racial inequality.* Lanham, MD: Rowman & Littlefield.

Moraga, C., & Anzaldúa, G. (2015). *This bridge called my back: Writings by radical women of color* (4th ed.). Albany, NY: State University of New York Press.

Moreno, J. F., Smith, D. G., Clayton-Pedersen, A. R., Parker, S., & Teraguchi, D. H. (2006). *The revolving door for underrepresented minority faculty in higher education: An analysis from the campus diversity initiative.* Washington, DC: Association of American Colleges and Universities.

Moses, Y. T. (1989). *Black women in academe: Issues and strategies.* Washington, DC: Association of American Colleges and Universities.

Museus, S. D., Ledesma, M. C., & Parker, T. L. (2015). Racism and racial equity in higher education. *ASHE Higher Education Report, 42*(1), 1–112.

Nadal, K. L., Mazzula, S. L., Rivera, D. P., & Fujii-Doe, W. (2014). Microaggressions and Latina/o Americans: An analysis of nativity, gender, and ethnicity. *Journal of Latino/a Psychology, 2*(2), 67–78.

Nakamura, J., Shernoff, D. J., & Hooker, C. H. (2009). *Good mentoring: Fostering excellent practice in higher education.* San Francisco, CA: John Wiley & Sons.

Nash, M. A. (2005). *Women's education in the United States, 1780–1840* (1st ed.). New York, NY: Palgrave Macmillan.

National Academy of Sciences, National Academy of Engineering, and Institute of Medicine. (2007). *Beyond bias and barriers: Fulfilling the potential of women in academic science and engineering.* Washington, DC: National Academies Press. doi:10.17226/11741

National Institute of Occupational Safety and Health (NIOSH). (1997). *Musculoskeletal disorders and workplace factors: A critical review of epidemiologic evidence for work-related musculoskeletal disorders of the neck, upper extremity, and low back* (NIOSH Pub. No. 97-141). Retrieved from https://www.cdc.gov/niosh/docs/97-141/

NIOSH. (1999). *Stress at work* (NIOSH Pub. No. 99-101). Retrieved from http://www.cdc.gov/niosh/docs/99-101/

NIOSH. (2001). *Women's health and safety issues at work* (NIOSH Pub. No. 2001-123). Retrieved from http://www.cdc.gov/niosh/topics/women/

National Research Council. (2004). *Understanding racial and ethnic differences in health in later life: A research agenda.* Washington, DC: National Academies Press.

National Research Council. (2010). *Gender differences at critical transitions in the careers of science, engineering, and mathematics faculty.* Washington, DC: National Academies Press.

Newman, K. S., & Massengill, R. P. (2006). The texture of hardship: Qualitative sociology of poverty, 1995–2005. *Annual Review of Sociology, 32*, 423–446.

Niemann, Y. F. (1999). The making of a token: A case study of stereotype threat, stigma, racism, and tokenism in academia. *Frontiers, 20*, 111–126.

Niemann, Y. F. (2012). The making of a token: A case study of stereotype threat, stigma, racism, and tokenism in academe. In G. Gutiérrez y Muhs, Y. F. Niemann, C. G. Gonzalez, & A. P. Harris (Eds.), *Presumed incompetent: The intersections of race and class for women in academia* (pp. 336–355). Logan, UT: Utah State University Press.

Niemann, Y. F., & Dovidio, J. F. (1998). Relationship of solo status, academic rank, and perceived distinctiveness to job satisfaction of racial/ethnic minorities. *Journal of Applied Psychology, 83*(1), 55–71.

Nieves-Squires, S. (1991). *Hispanic women: Making their presence on campus less tenuous.* Washington, DC: Association of American Colleges and Universities.

Nixon, M. (2017). Experiences of women of color university chief diversity officers. *Journal of Diversity in Higher Education, 10,* 310–317. doi:10.1037/dhe0000043

Nomaguchi, K. M. (2009). Change in work-family conflict among employed parents between 1977 and 1997. *Journal of Marriage and Family, 71,* 15–32.

Northridge, M. E., Holtzman, D., Bergeron, C. D., Zambrana, R. E., & Greenberg, M. R. (2015). Mentoring for publication in the American Journal of Public Health. *American Journal of Public Health, 105*(Suppl. 1), S14–S16.

Noy, S., & Ray, R. (2011). Graduate students' perspectives of their advisors: Is there systematic disadvantage in mentorship? *Journal of Higher Education, 10*(10), 1–39.

Núñez, A. M., Hurtado, S., & Galdeano, E. C. (2015). *Hispanic-serving institutions: Advancing research and transformative practice.* New York, NY: Routledge.

Nyberg, S. T., Fransson, E. I., Heikkilä, K., Alfredsson, L., Casini, A., Clays, E., & Kivimäki, M. (2013). Job strain and cardiovascular disease risk factors: Meta-analysis of individual participant data from 47,000 men and women. *PLOS ONE, 8,* e67323. doi:10.137/journal.pone.0067323

Nzinga-Johnson, S. (2013). *Laboring positions: Black women, mothering and the academy.* Toronto, Canada: Demeter Press.

O'Brien, E. M., & Zudak, C. (1998). Minority-serving institutions: An overview. In J. P. Merisotis & C. T. O'Brien (Eds.), *Minority-serving institutions: Distinct purposes, common goals* (pp. 5–15). San Francisco, CA: Jossey-Bass.

Offer, S., & Schneider, S. (2011). Revisiting the gender gap in time-use patterns: Multitasking and well-being among mothers and fathers in dual-earner families. *American Sociological Review, 76*(6), 809–833.

Ogbu, J. U. (1978). *Minority education and caste: The American system in cross-cultural perspective.* San Diego, CA: Academic Press. Retrieved from http://ed-share.educ.msu.edu/scan/te/danagnos/te9202c.pdf

Ogbu, J. U., & Simons, H. D. (1998). Voluntary and involuntary minorities: A cultural-ecological theory of school performance with some implications for education. *Anthropology & Education Quarterly, 29*(2), 155–188.

Ogren, C. A. (2005). *The American state normal school: An instrument of great good.* New York, NY: Palgrave Macmillan.

Okazaki, S. (2009). Impact of racism on ethnic minority mental health. *Perspectives on Psychological Science, 4*(1), 103–107.

O'Laughlin, E. M., & Bischoff, L. G. (2005). Balancing parenthood and academic: Work/family stress as influence by gender and tenure status. *Journal of Family Issues, 26*(1), 76–106.

Olivas, M. A. (1989). Indian, Chicano, and Puerto Rican colleges: Status and issues. *Bilingual Review, 9*(1), 36–58.

Oliver, M. L., & Shapiro, T. M. (1995). *Black wealth/White wealth: A new perspective on racial inequality.* New York, NY: Routledge.

O'Meara, K., & Braskamp, L. (2005). Aligning faculty reward systems and development to promote faculty and student growth. *NASPA Journal, 42*(2), 223–240.

O'Neil, R., & Greenberger, E. (1994). Patterns of commitment to work and parenting: Implications for role strain. *Journal of Marriage and Family, 56,* 101–118.

Orbuch, T. L., & Custer, L. (1995). The social context of married women's work and its impact on Black husbands and White husbands. *Journal of Marriage and Family, 57,* 333–345.

Osipow, S. (1998). *Workplace Stress Inventory Revised Edition (OSI-R) Professional Manual.* Lutz, FL: Psychological Assessment Resources.

Otieno, T., Lutz, P. M., & Schoolmaster, F. A. (2010). Enhancing recruitment, professional development, and socialization of junior faculty through formal mentoring programs. *Metropolitan Universities, 21*(2), 77–91.

Palmieri, P. A. (1995). *In Adamless Eden: The community of women faculty at Wellesley.* New Haven, CT: Yale University Press.

Paradies, Y., Ben, J., Denson, N., Elias, A., Priet, N., Pieterse, A., Gupta, A., Kelaher, M., & Gee, G. (2015). Racism as a determinant of health: A systematic review and meta-analysis. *PLOS ONE, 10*(9), e0138511.

Patitu, C. L., & Hinton, K. G. (2003). The experience of African American women faculty and administrators in higher education: Has anything changed? *New Directions for Student Services, 104,* 79–93.

Pattillo-McCoy, M. (1999). *Black picket fences: Privilege and peril among the Black middle class.* Chicago, IL: University of Chicago Press.

Patton, T. O. (2004). Reflections of a Black woman professor: Racism and sexism in academia. *Howard Journal of Communications, 15*(3), 185–200.

Pearlin, L. I. (1989). The sociological study of stress. *Journal of Health and Social Behavior, 30,* 241–256.

Pearlin, L. I., Schieman, S., Fazio, E. M., & Meersman, S. C. (2005). Stress, health, and the life course: Some conceptual perspectives. *Journal of Health and Social Behavior, 46*(2), 274–288.

Penner, A. M., & Saperstein, A. (2013). Engendering racial perceptions: An intersectional analysis of how social status shapes race. *Gender & Society, 27*(3), 319–344.

Perna, L. W. (2001a). The relationship between family responsibilities and employment status among college and university faculty. *Journal of Higher Education, 72*(5), 584–611.

Perna, L. W. (2001b). Sex and race differences in faculty tenure and promotion. *Research in Higher Education, 42*(5), 541–567.

Perry, B. (2002). American Indian victims of campus ethnoviolence. *Journal of American Indian Education, 41,* 35–55.

Perry, G., Moore, H., Acosta, K., Frey, C., & Edwards, C. (2009). Maintaining credibility and authority as an instructor of color in diversity-education classrooms: A qualitative inquiry. *Journal of Higher Education, 80,* 80–105.

Peterson, N. B., Friedman, R. H., Ash, A. S., Franco, S., & Carr, P. L. (2004). Faculty self-reported experience with racial and ethnic discrimination in academic medicine. *Journal of General Internal Medicine, 19,* 259–265.

Pew Research Center. (2013). The rise of Asian Americans. Retrieved from http://www.pewsocialtrends.org/2012/06/19/the-rise-of-asian-americans/

Picca, L., & Feagin, J. (2007). *Two-face racism: Whites in the backstage and frontstage.* New York, NY: Routledge.

Pierce, J. L. (1995). *Gender trials: Emotional lives in contemporary law firms.* Berkeley, CA: University of California Press.

Piercy, F., Giddings, V., Allen, K., Dixon, B., Meszaros, P., & Joest, K. (2005). Improving campus climate to support faculty diversity and retention: A pilot program for new faculty. *Innovative Higher Education, 30*(1), 53–66.

Pifer, M. J., & Baker, V. L. (2013). Managing the process: The intradepartmental networks of early-career academics. *Innovations in Higher Education, 38,* 323–337.

Pinto, K. M., & Coltrane, S. (2009). Divisions of labor in Mexican origin and Anglo families: Structure and culture. *Sex Roles, 60,* 482–495.

Pittman, C. T. (2010). Exploring how African American faculty cope with classroom racial stressors. *Journal of Negro Education, 79*(1), 66–78.

Plummer, D. L., & Slane, S. (1996). Patterns of coping in racially stressful situations. *Journal of Black Psychology, 22,* 302–315.

Pollard, L. A. (1977). *Women on college and university faculties.* New York, NY: Arno Press.

Ponjuan, L. (2005). *Understanding the work lives of faculty of color: Job satisfaction, perception of climate, and intention to leave.* Unpublished doctoral dissertation, University of Michigan, Ann Arbor.

Price, E. G., Gozu, A., Kern, D. E., Power, N. R., Wand, G. S., Golden, S., & Cooper, L. A. (2005). The role of cultural diversity climate in recruitment, promotion, and retention of faculty in academic medicine. *Journal of General Internal Medicine, 20,* 565–571.

Price, E. G., Powe, N. R., Kern, D. E., Hill Golden, S., Wand, G. S., & Cooper, L. A. (2009). Improving the diversity climate in academic medicine: Faculty perceptions as a catalyst for change. *Academic Medicine, 84*(1), 95–105.

Priest, N., Yin, P., Trenerry, B., Truong, M., Karlsen, S., & Kelly, Y. (2013). A systematic review of studies examining the relationship between reported racism and health and wellbeing for children and young people. *Social Science & Medicine, 95,* 115–127.

Quinn, K., Lange, S. E., & Olswang, S. G. (2004). *Family-friendly policies and the research university.* Washington, DC: American Association of University Professors.

Raabe, P. (1997). Work-family policies for faculty: How "career-and family-friendly" is academe. In M. A. Ferber & J. W. Loeb (Eds.), *Academic couples: Problems and promises* (pp. 208–225). Urbana, IL: University of Illinois Press.

Radloff, L. S. (1977). A self-report depression scale for research in the general population. *Applied Psychological Measurement, 1*(3), 385–401.

Rainie, S. C., Jorgensen, M., Cornell, S., & Arsenault, J. (2015). The changing landscape of health care provisions to American Indian nations. *American Indian Culture and Research Journal, 39*(1), 1–23. doi:10.17953/aicr.39.1.j1u030g668113403

Ramirez, E. (2011). "No one taught me the steps": Latinos' experiences applying to graduate school. *Journal of Latinos and Education, 10*(3), 204–222.

Ramirez, E. (2013). Examining Latinos/as' graduate school choice process: An intersectionality perspective. *Journal of Hispanic Higher Education, 12*(1), 23–36.

Reddick, R. J., & Saenz, V. B. (2012). Coming home: "Hermanos academicos" reflect on past and present realities as professors at their alma mater. *Harvard Educational Review, 82*(3), 353–380.

Reevy, G. M., & Deason, G. (2014). Predictors of depression, stress, and anxiety among non-tenure track faculty. *Frontiers in Psychology, 5,* 1–17.

Reybold, L. E. (2014). The irony of ethics: (De)coding the lived experience of women and minority faculty. *International Journal of Higher Education, 3,* 92–105. doi:10.5430/ijhe.v3n2p92

Reyes, A. X. (2005). Dissonance in the academy: Reflections of a Latina professor. *Latino Studies, 3*(2), 274–279. doi:10.1057/palgrave.lst.8600137

Reyes, M. L. (1997). Chicanas in academe: An endangered species. In S. de Castell & M. Bryson (Eds.), *Radical interventions: Identity, politics, and difference/s in educational praxis* (pp. 15–38). Albany, NY: State University of New York Press.

Rice, R. E., Sorcinelli, M. D., & Austin, A. E. (Eds.). (2000). *Heeding new voices: Academic careers for a new generation* (New pathways: Faculty careers and employment for the 21st century, Inquiry 7). Washington, DC: American Association for Higher Education.

Richard, G. V., & Krieshok, Thomas S. (1989). Occupational stress, strain, and coping in university faculty. *Journal of Vocational Behavior, 34* (1), 117–132.

Ridgeway, C. L. (2014). Why status matters for inequality. *American Sociological Review, 79*, 1–16.

Riesman, D. (1956). *The academic procession: Constraint and variety in American higher education.* Lincoln, NE: University of Nebraska Press.

Rivera, D. P., Forquer, E. E., & Rangel, R. (2010). Microaggressions and the life experience of Latina/o Americans. In D. W. Sue (Ed.), *Microaggressions and marginality: Manifestation, dynamics, and impact* (pp. 59–84). Hoboken, NJ: John Wiley.

Roberts, R. K., Swanson, N. G., & Murphy, L. R. (2004). Discrimination and occupational mental health. *Journal of Mental Health, 13*(2), 129–142.

Robert Wood Johnson Foundation. (1995). *National Faculty Survey.* Princeton, NJ: Author.

Robinson, C. C., & Clardy, P. (Eds.). (2010). *Tedious journeys: Autoethnography by women of color in academe.* New York, NY: Peter Lang.

Robinson, O. V. (2014). Characteristics of racism and the health consequences experienced by Black nursing faculty. *Association of Black Nursing Faculty, 25*(4), 110–115.

Rockquemore, K. A., & Laszloffy, T. (2008). *The Black academic's guide to winning tenure without losing your soul.* Boulder, CO: Lynne Rienner.

Rodríguez, J., Campbell, K. M., Fogarty, J. P., & Williams, R. L. (2014). Underrepresented minority faculty in academic medicine: A systematic review of URM faculty development. *Family Medicine, 46*(2), 100–104.

Rodriguez-Calcagno, M., & Brewer, E. W. (2005). Job stress among Hispanic professionals. *Hispanic Journal of Behavioral Sciences, 27*, 504–516.

Roehling, P. V., Jarvis, L., & Swope, H. E. (2005). Variations in negative work-family spillover among White, Black, and Hispanic American men and women: Does ethnicity matter? *Journal of Family Issues, 26*, 840–865.

Roggero, G. (2011). *The production of living knowledge.* Philadelphia, PA: Temple University Press.

Romero, M. (1997). Class-based, gendered and racialized institutions of higher education: Everyday life of academia from the view of Chicana faculty. *Race, Gender & Class, 4*(2), 151–173.

Rosenberg, L., Palmer, J. R., Adams-Campbell, L. L., & Rao, R. S. (1999). Obesity and hypertension among college-educated black women in the United States. *Journal of Human Hypertension, 13*(4), 237–241.

Rosengren, A., Orth-Gomer, K., Wedel, H., & Wilhelmsen, L. (1993). Stressful life events, social support, and mortality in men born in 1933. *British Medical Journal, 307*, 1102–1105.

Ross, H. J. (2011). *Reinventing diversity: Transforming organizational community to strengthen people, purpose, and performance.* Lanham, MD: Rowman & Littlefield.

Rosser, V. J. (2004). Faculty members' intentions to leave: A national study on their work life and satisfaction. *Research in Higher Education, 45*(3), 285–309.

Rossiter, M. W. (1982). *Women scientists in America: Struggles and strategies to 1940.* Baltimore, MD: Johns Hopkins University Press.

Rossiter, M. W. (1995). *Women scientists in America: Before affirmative action, 1940–1972.* Baltimore, MD: Johns Hopkins University Press.

Rothwell, D. W., & Han, C. K. (2010). Exploring the relationship between assets and family stress among low-income families. *Family Relations, 59*, 396–407.

Rozanski, A., Blumenthal, J., & Kaplan, J. (1999). Impact of psychological factors on the pathogenesis of cardiovascular disease and implications for therapy. *Circulation, 99*, 2192–2217.

Rudd, E., Morrison, E., Nerad, M., Sadrozinski, R., & Cerny, J. (2008). Equality and illusion: Gender and tenure in art history careers. *Journal of Marriage and Family, 70*, 228–238.

Rury, J. L., & Hill, S. A. (2011). *The African American struggle for secondary schooling, 1940–1980: Closing the graduation gap.* New York, NY: Teachers College Press.

Ryan, C., & Bauman, K. (2016). Educational attainment in the United States: 2015. U.S. Census Bureau. Retrieved from https://www.census.gov/content/dam/Census/library/publications/2016/demo/p20-578.pdf

Safire, W. (1988, November 20). On language: People of color. *New York Times.* Retrieved from https://www.nytimes.com/1988/11/20/magazine/on-language-people-of-color.html

Saint Onge, J. M., & Krueger, P. M. (2011). Education and racial-ethnic differences in types of exercise in the United States. *Journal of Health and Social Behavior, 52*(2), 197–211.

Salazar, C. F. (2009). Strategies to survive and thrive in academia: The collective voices of counseling faculty of color. *International Journal for the Advancement of Counseling, 31*(3), 181–198.

Sampaio, A. (2006). Women of color teaching political science: Examining the intersections of race, gender, and course material in the classroom. *Political Science and Politics, 39,* 917–922.

Sanchez, J. L., & Brock, P. (1996). Outcomes of perceived discrimination among Hispanic employees: Is diversity management a luxury or a necessity? *Academy of Management Journal, 39,* 704–719.

Sandoval, C. (2000). *Methodology of the oppressed* (Theory out of bounds, Vol. 18). Minneapolis, MN: University of Minnesota Press.

Sauter, S., Hurrell, J., Murphy, L., & Levi, L. (1997). Psychosocial and organizational factors. In J. Stellman (Ed.), *Encyclopedia of occupational health and safety* (Vol. 1, pp. 34.1–34.77). Geneva, Switzerland: International Labor Office.

Sawyer, P. J., Major, B., Casad, B. J., Townsend, S., & Mendes, W. B. (2012). Discrimination and the stress response: Psychological and physiological consequences of anticipating prejudice in interethnic interactions. *American Journal of Public Health, 102*(5), 1020–1026.

Sax, L. J., Hagedorn, L. S., Arredondo, M., & Dicrisi, F. A., III. (2002). Faculty research productivity: Exploring the role of gender and family-related stress. *Research in Higher Education, 43*(4), 423–446.

Sayer, L. C., England, P., Bittman, M., & Bianchi, S. M. (2009). How long is the second (plus first) shift? Gender differences in paid, unpaid, and total work time in Australia and the United States. *Journal of Comparative Family Studies, 40,* 523–544.

Schaefer, R. T. (2002). *Sociology: A brief introduction.* Boston, MA: McGraw Hill.

Schieman, S., Whitestone, Y. K., & Van Gundy, K. (2006). The nature of work and the stress of higher status. *Journal of Health and Social Behavior, 47*(3), 242–257.

Schneider, B., Grebner, K., Schnabel, A., Hampel, H., Georgi, K., & Seidler, A. (2011). Impact of employment status and work-related factors on risk of completed suicide: A case control psychological autopsy study. *Psychiatry Research, 190*(2–3), 265–270. doi:10.1016/j.psychres.2011.07.037

Schneiderman, N., Liabre, M., Cowle, C., Barnhart, J., Carmethon, M., Gallo, L., Gaiachell, A., Heiss, G., Kaplan, R., LaVange, L., Teng, Y., Villa-Caballero, L., & Aviles-Santa, M. (2014). Prevalence of diabetes among Hispanics/Latinos from diverse backgrounds: The Hispanic Community Health Study/Study of Latinos (HCHS/SOL). *Diabetes Care, 37*(8), 2233–2239.

Schrecker, E. (2010). *The lost soul of higher education: Corporatization, the assault on academic freedom and the end of the American university.* New York, NY: New Press.

Schulz, R., & Beach, S. R. (1999). Caregiving as a risk factor for mortality: The Caregiver Health Effects Study. *Journal of the American Medical Association, 282*(23), 2215–2219.

Schuster, J. H., & Finkelstein, M. J. (2006). *The American faculty: The restructuring of academic work and careers.* Baltimore, MD: Johns Hopkins University Press.

Segura, D. (1989). Chicana and Mexican immigrant women at work: The impact of class, race, and gender on occupational mobility. *Gender & Society, 3,* 37–52.

Segura, D. A. (1992). Chicanas in white collar jobs: "You have to prove yourself more." *Sociological Perspectives, 35*(1), 163–182.

Segura, D. A. (2003). Navigating between two worlds: The labyrinth of Chicana intellectual production in the academy. *Journal of Black Studies, 34*(1), 28–51.

Segura, D. A., Brooks, S., Shin, J. H., & Romo, L. (2012). *Review of recommendations from the Committee on the Status of Racial and Ethnic Minorities (action item).* American Sociological Association.

Sellers, R. M., Caldwell, C. H., Schmeelk-Cone, K. H., & Zimmerman, M. A. (2003). Racial identity, racial discrimination, perceived stress, and psychological distress among African American young adults. *Journal of Health and Social Behavior, 43,* 302–317.

Sellers, S. L., & Neighbors, H. W. (2008). Effects of goal-striving stress on the mental health of black Americans. *Journal of Health and Social Behavior, 49*(1), 92-103.

Shapiro, T. M. (2004). *The hidden cost of being African-American: How wealth perpetuates inequality.* New York, NY: Oxford University Press.

Shapiro, T. M. (2017). *Toxic inequality: How America's wealth gap destroys mobility, deepens the racial divide, & threatens our future.* New York, NY: Basic Books.

Shaw, C. (2014, May 8). Overworked and isolated—Work pressure fuels mental illness in academia. *Guardian.* Retrieved from https://www.theguardian.com/higher-education -network/blog/2014/may/08/work-pressure-fuels-academic-mental-illness-guardian -study-health

Shollen, S. L., Bland, C. J., Finstad, D. A., & Taylor, A. L. (2009). Organizational climate and family life: How these factors affect the status of women faculty at one medical school. *Academic Medicine, 84*(1), 87–94.

Shollen, S. L., Bland, C. J., Taylor, A. L., Weber-Main, A. M., & Mulcahy, P. A. (2008). Establishing effective mentoring relationships for faculty, especially across gender and ethnicity. *American Academic, 4,* 131–156.

Shorter-Gooden, K. (2004). Multiple resistance strategies: How African American women cope with racism and sexism. *Journal of Black Psychology, 30,* 406–425.

Siemieńska, R., & Zimmer, A. (2007). *Gendered career trajectories in academia in cross-national perspective.* Poland: Wydawnicto Naukowe Scholar.

Simon, R. W. (1995). Gender, multiple roles, role meaning, and mental health. *Journal of Health and Social Behavior, 36,* 182–194.

Skachkova, P. (2007). Academic careers of immigrant women professors in the U.S. *Higher Education, 53,* 697–738.

Sloan, M. M., Evenson Newhouse, R. J., & Thompson, A. B. (2013). Counting on coworkers: Race, social support, and emotional experiences on the job. *Social Psychology Quarterly, 76*(4), 343–372.

Smith, D. G., Turner, C. S. V., Osefi-Kofi, N., & Richards, S. (2004). Interrupting the usual: Successful strategies for hiring diverse faculty. *Journal of Higher Education, 75,* 133–160.

Smith, J. W., & Calasanti, T. (2005). The influences of gender, race and ethnicity on workplace experiences of institutional and social isolation: An exploratory study of university faculty. *Sociological Spectrum, 25,* 307–334.

Smith, M. T. (2013). *Fact sheet: The state of Asian American women in the United States.* Washington, DC: Center for American Progress.

Smith, W. A., Allen, Allen, W. R., & Danley, L. L. (2007). "Assume the position . . . you fit the description": Psychosocial experiences and racial battle fatigue among African American male college students. *American Behavioral Scientist, 51*(4), 551–578.

Smith, W. A., Yosso, T. J., & Solórzano, D. G. (2007). Racial primes and Black misandry on historically White campuses: Toward critical race accountability in educational administration. *Educational Administration Quarterly, 43*(5), 559–585.

Solomon, B. M. (1985). *In the company of educated women and higher education in America.* New Haven, CT: Yale University Press.

Solórzano, D. G., Ceja, M., & Yosso, T. (2000). Critical race theory, racial microaggressions, and campus racial climate: The experiences of African American college students. *Journal of Negro Education, 69,* 60–73.

Sorcinelli, M. D. (2000). Principles of good practice: Supporting early career faculty: Guidance for deans, department chairs, and other academic leaders. In R. E. Rice, M. D. Sorcinelli, & A. E. Austin (Eds.), *Heeding new voices: Academic careers for a new generation* (New pathways: Faculty careers and employment for the 21st century, Inquiry 7). Washington, DC: American Association for Higher Education.

Spain, D., & Bianchi, S. M. (1996). *Balancing act: Motherhood, marriage, and employment among American women.* New York, NY: Russell Sage Foundation.

Spalter-Roth, R., Mayorova, O. V., Shin, J. H., & White, P. (2011). The impact of cross-race mentoring for "ideal" and "alternative" careers in sociology. Retrieved from http://www .asanet.org/images/research/docs/pdf/Impact_of_Crossrace_Mentoring_Report _2011.pdf

Spector, P. E., & Jex, S. M. (1998). Development of four self-report measures of job stressors and strain: Interpersonal conflict at work scale, organizational constraints scale, quantitative workload inventory, and physical symptoms inventory. *Journal of Occupational Health Psychology, 2*(4), 356–367.

Stack, C. (1974). *All our kin: Strategies for survival in a Black community.* New York, NY: Harper & Row.

Stanley, C. (2006). Coloring the academic landscape: Faculty of color breaking the silence in predominately White colleges and universities. *American Educational Research Journal, 43*(4), 701–736.

Stansfeld, S., Fuhrer, R., Shipley, M. J., & Marmot, M. G. (1999). Work characteristics predict psychiatric disorders: Prospective results from the Whitehall II Study. *Occupational and Environmental Medicine, 56,* 440–461.

Stein, W. J. (1992). *Tribally controlled colleges: Making good medicine.* New York, NY: Peter Lang.

Stein, W. J. (1994). The survival of American Indian faculty: Thought and action. *National Education Association Higher Education Journal, 10,* 101–114.

Stephan, P. E. (2010). The "I"s have it: Immigration and innovation, the perspective from academe. *Innovation Policy and the Economy, 10*(1), 83–127.

Sternthal, M. J., Slopen, N., & Williams, D. R. (2011). Racial disparities in health: How much does stress really matter? *Du Bois Review, 8,* 95–113.

St. John, E. (1999). United we stand: NAFEO, HACU, and AIHEC have formed a new alliance to improve support for students of color. *Black Issues in Higher Education, 16,* 16–17.

St. Pierre, N., & Stein, W. J. (1997). *Tribally controlled colleges: Facts in brief.* Bozeman, MT: Montana State University Press.

Stricker, F. (1988). American professors in the progressive era: Income, aspirations, and professionalism. *Journal of Interdisciplinary History, 19*(2), 231–257.

Stroman, C. A., & Seltzer, R. (1991). Racial differences in coping with job stress: A research note. *Journal of Social Behavior and Personality, 6*(7), 309–318.

Sue, D. W. (2004). Whiteness and ethnocentric monoculturalism: Making the invisible visible. *American Psychologist, 59*(8), 761–769.

Sue, D. W. (2010). *Microaggressions in everyday life: Race, gender, and sexual orientation.* Hoboken, NJ: John Wiley & Sons.

Sue, D. W., Capodilupo, C. M., Torino, G. C., Bucceri, J. M., Holder, A. M., Nadal, K. L., & Esquilin, M. (2007). Racial micro-aggressions in everyday life: Implications for clinical practice. *American Psychologist, 62*(4), 271–286.

Sue, D. W., Nadal, K. L., Capodilupo, C. M., Lin, A. I., Torino, G. C., & Rivera, D. P. (2008). Racial microaggressions against Black Americans: Implications for counseling. *Journal of Counseling & Development, 86*(3), 330–338.

Sullivan, B., Hollenshead, C., & Smith, G. (2004). Developing and implementing work-family policies for faculty. *Academe, 90*(6), 24–27.

Swim, J. K., Hyers, L. L., Cohen, L. L., Fitzgerald, D. C., & Byslma, W. H. (2003). African American college students' experiences with everyday racism: Characteristics of and responses to these incidents. *Journal of Black Psychology, 29*(1), 38–67.

Taylor, P., Kochhar, R., Fry, R., Velasco, G., & Motel, S. (2011). *Wealth gap rises to record highs between Whites, Blacks and Hispanics.* Washington, DC: Pew Research Center.

Telles, E. E., & Ortiz, V. (2009). *Generations of exclusion: Mexican Americans, assimilation, and race.* New York, NY: Russell Sage Foundation.

Tennant, C. (2001). Work-related stress and depressive disorders. *Journal of Psychosomatic Research, 51*, 697–704.

Teranishi, R., Martin, M., Pazich, L. B., Alcantar, C. M., & Nguyen, T. L. K. (2014). *Measuring the impact of MSI-funded programs on student success: Findings from the evaluation of Asian American and Native American Pacific Islander-serving institutions.* Los Angeles, CA: National Commission on Asian American and Pacific Islander Research in Education.

Thelin, J. R. (2011). *A history of American higher education* (2nd ed.). Baltimore, MD: Johns Hopkins University Press.

Thoits, P. A. (2011). Mechanisms linking social ties and support to physical and mental health. *Journal of Health and Social Behavior, 52*(2), 145–161.

Thomas, G. D., & Hollenshead, C. (2001). Resisting from the margins: The coping strategies of Black women and other women of color faculty members at a research university. *Journal of Negro Education, 70*, 166–175.

Thomas, J. M., & Johnson, B. J. (2004). Perspectives of international faculty members: Their experiences and stories. *Education and Society, 22*(3), 47–64.

Thomas, L. (2015). Puerto Ricans in the United States. In *Oxford research encyclopedias: American history.* Retrieved from http://americanhistory.oxfordre.com/view/10.1093/acrefore/9780199329175.001.0001/acrefore-9780199329175-e-32

Thompson, C. J., & Dey, E. L. (1998). Pushed to the margins: Sources of stress for African American college and university faculty. *Journal of Higher Education, 69*(3), 324–345.

Thompson, G. L., & Louque, A. C. (2005). *Exposing the "culture of arrogance" in the academy: A blueprint for increasing Black faculty satisfaction in higher education.* Sterling, VA: Stylus.

Thornton, A., & Young-DeMarco, L. (2001). Four decades of trends in attitudes toward family issues in the United States: The 1960s through the 1990s. *Journal of Marriage and Family, 63*, 1009–1037.

Tippeconnic, J. W., III, & McKinney, S. (2003). Native faculty: Scholarship and development. In M. K. P. Ah Nee-Benham & W. J. Stein (Eds.), *The renaissance of American Indian higher education: Capturing the dream* (pp. 241–256). Mahwah, NJ: Lawrence Erlbaum.

Tippeconnic Fox, M. J. (2005). Voices from within: Native American faculty and staff in campus. *New Directions for Student Services, 2005*(109), 49–59.

Tix, A. P., & Frazier, P. A. (1998). The use of religious coping during stressful life events: Main effects, moderation, and mediation. *Journal of Consulting and Clinical Psychology, 66*(2), 411–422.

Tolley, K. (2003). *The science education of American girls: A historical perspective.* New York, NY: RoutledgeFalmer.

Trethewey, A. (1999). Disciplined bodies: Women's embodied identities at work. *Organization Studies, 20*(3), 423–450.

Trower, C. A. (2003). Leveling the field. *Academic Workplace, 14*(2).

Trower, C. A. (2009). Toward a greater understanding of the tenure track for minorities. *Change, 41*(5), 38–44.

Trower, C. A., & Bleak, J. L. (2004). *Study of new scholars: Tenure-Track Faculty Job Satisfaction Survey. Race: Statistical report [Universities].* Cambridge, MA: Harvard School of Education.

Trower, C. A., & Chait, R. P. (2002). Faculty diversity: Too little for too long. *Harvard Magazine, 104*(4), 33–37.

Trucks-Bordeaux, T. (2003). Academic massacres. *American Indian Quarterly, 27*(1/2), 416–419.

Tsui, L. (2007). Effective strategies to increase diversity in STEM fields: A review of the research. *Journal of Negro Education, 76*(4), 555–581.

Tuitt, F. A., & Carter, D. J. (2008). Negotiating atmospheric threats and racial assaults in predominantly White institutions. *Journal of Public Management & Social Policy, 14*(2), 51–68.

Tuitt, F., Hanna, M., Martinez, L. M., Salazar, M., & Griffin, R. (2009). Teaching in the line of fire: Faculty of color in the academy. *NEA Higher Education Journal, 16*, 65–74.

Turner, C. S. V. (2002). *Diversifying the faculty: A guidebook for search committees.* Washington, DC: Association of American Colleges & Universities.

Turner, C. S. V. (2003). Incorporation and marginalization in the academy: From border toward center for faculty of color? *Journal of Black Studies, 34*, 112–125.

Turner, C. S. V. (2015). Lessons from the field: Cultivating nurturing environments in higher education. *Review of Higher Education, 38*(3), 333–358.

Turner, C. S. V., Cosmé, P. X., Dinehart, L., Martí, R., McDonald, D., Ramirez, M., . . . & Zamora, J. (2018). Hispanic-serving institution scholars and administrators on improving Latina/Latino/Latinx/Hispanic teacher pipelines: Critical junctures along career pathways. *Association of Mexican American Educators Journal, 11*(3), 251–275.

Turner, C. S., & González, J. C. (Eds.). (2014). *Modeling mentoring across race/ethnicity and gender: Practices to cultivate the next generation of diverse faculty.* Sterling, VA: Stylus.

Turner, C. S. V., González, J. C., & Wood, J. L. (2008). Faculty of color in academe: What 20 years of literature tells us. *Journal of Diversity in Higher Education, 1*(3), 139–168.

Turner, C. S. V., & Myers, S. L. (2000). *Faculty of color in academe: Bittersweet success.* Boston, MA: Allyn & Bacon.

UC Hastings College of the Law. (n.d.). Effective policies and programs for retention and advancement of women in academia. *Work Life Law.*

Umbach, P. (2007). How effective are they? Exploring the impact of contingent faculty on undergraduate education. *Review of Higher Education, 30*(2), 91–123.

U.S. Department of Education. (1988, 1993, 1998, 2000, 2004, 2010). *National study of postsecondary faculty. Integrated Postsecondary Education Data System*. Washington, DC: National Center for Education Statistics.

U.S. Department of Education. (1991). *Historically Black colleges and universities and higher education desegregation*. Washington, DC: Office of Civil Rights. Retrieved from http://www2.ed.gov/about/offices/list/ocr/docs/hq9511.html

U.S. Department of Education. (2012). *The condition of education 2012* (NCES 2012-045). Washington, DC: National Center for Education Statistics.

U.S. Department of Education. (2013). *Integrated Postsecondary Education Data System*. Washington, DC: National Center for Education Statistics.

U.S. Department of Education. (2015a). *The condition of education 2015: Characteristics of postsecondary faculty* (NCES 2015-144). Washington, DC: National Center for Education Statistics.

U.S. Department of Education. (2015b). *2013 annual report to the president on the results of the participation of historically Black colleges and universities in federal programs*. Washington, DC: White House Initiative on Historically Black Colleges and Universities.

U.S. Department of Education. (2016). *The condition of education 2016: Characteristics of postsecondary faculty* (NCES 2016-144). Washington, DC: National Center for Education Statistics. Retrieved from https://nces.ed.gov/fastfacts/display.asp?id=61

U.S. Department of the Interior, Bureau of Education. (1917). *A study of the private and higher schools for colored people in the United States*. Washington, DC: Government Printing Office.

Valdez, Z. (2015). *The new entrepreneurs: How race, class, and gender shape American enterprise*. Stanford, CA: Stanford University Press.

Vallejo, J. A. (2009). Latina spaces: Middle-class ethnic capital and professional associations in the Latino community. *City & Community, 8*(2), 129–154.

Vallejo, J. A. (2012). *Barriers to burbs: The making of the Mexican American middle class*. Stanford, CA: Stanford University Press.

Valverde, L. A. (1993). *Leaders of color in higher education: Unrecognized triumphs in harsh institutions*. Walnut Creek, CA: Rowman & Littlefield.

Valverde, L. A. (2002). *Leaders of color in higher education: Unrecognized triumphs in harsh institutions*. Walnut Creek, CA: AltaMira Press.

Varner, A. (2000). *The consequences and costs of delaying attempted childbirth for women faculty*. University Park: Pennsylvania State University, Department of Labor Studies and Industrial Relations.

Vasquez, M. J. T., Lott, B., García-Vásquez, E., Grant, S. K., Iwamasa, G. Y., Molina, L. E., Ragsdale, B. L., & Vestal-Dowdy, E. (2006). Personal reflections: Barriers and strategies in increasing diversity in psychology. *American Psychologist, 61*, 157–172.

Veysey, L. R. (1965). *The emergence of the American university*. Chicago, IL: University of Chicago Press.

Villalpando, O., & Delgado Bernal, D. (2002). A critical race theory analysis of barriers that impede the success of faculty of color. In W. A. Smith, P. G. Altbach, & K. Lomotey (Eds.), *The racial crisis in American higher education: Continuing challenges for the twenty-first century* (rev. ed., pp. 243–270). Albany, NY: State University of New York Press.

Wallenstein, P. (2008). *Higher education and the civil rights movement: White supremacy, black southerners, and college campuses*. Gainesville, FL: University Press of Florida.

Wang, H., Leineweber, C., Kirkeeide, R., Svane, B., Schenck-Gustafsson, K., Theorell, T., & Orth-Gomér, K. (2007). Psychosocial stress and atherosclerosis: Family and work stress accelerate progression of coronary heart disease in women. *Journal of Internal Medicine*, *261*(3), 245–254.

Ward, K., & Wolf-Wendel, L. (2004). *Fear factor: How safe is it to make time for family?* Washington, DC: American Association of University Professors.

Ward, K., & Wolf-Wendel, L. (2012). *Academic motherhood: How faculty manage work and family.* New Brunswick, NJ: Rutgers University Press.

Ward, R. A. (2010). What does racism look like? An autoethnographical examination of the culture of racism in higher education. In C. C. Robinson & P. Clardy (Eds.), *Tedious journeys: Autoethnography by women of color in academe* (pp. 119–148). New York, NY: Peter Lang.

Webb, M., & Gonzalez, L. (2006). The burden of hypertension: Mental representations of African American women. *Issues in Mental Health Nursing*, *27*, 249–271.

Webber, K. L. (2012). Research productivity of foreign- and US-born faculty: Differences by time on task. *Higher Education*, *64*, 709–729.

Weber, L. (2013). *Understanding race, class, gender, and sexuality: A conceptual framework* (2nd ed.). Oxford: Oxford University Press.

Weber, L., Hancock, T., & Higginbotham, E. (1997). Women, power, and mental health. In S. Ruzek, V. Olesen, & A. Clark (Eds.), *Women's health: Complexities and differences* (pp. 380–396). Columbus, OH: Ohio State University Press.

Weber, L., & Higginbotham, E. (1997). Black and white professional-managerial women's perceptions of racism and sexism in the workplace. In E. Higginbotham & M. Romero (Eds.), *Women and work: Exploring race, ethnicity, and class* (pp. 153–175). Thousand Oaks, CA: SAGE.

Weems, R. E. (2003). The incorporation of Black faculty at predominantly White institutions: A historical and contemporary perspective. *Journal of Black Studies*, *34*(1), 101–111.

Weigt, J. M., & Solomon Richards, C. (2008). Work-family management among low-wage service workers and assistant professors in the USA: A comparative intersectional analysis. *Gender, Work and Organization*, *15*(6), 621–649.

Welch, J. L., Wiehe, S. E., Palmer-Smith, V., & Dankoski, M. E. (2011). Flexibility in faculty work-life policies at medical school in the Big Ten Conference. *Journal of Women's Health*, *20*(5), 725–732.

Wells, R., Seifert, T., Park, S., Reed, E., & Umbach, P. D. (2007). Job satisfaction of international faculty in U.S. higher education. *Journal of the Professoriate*, *2*, 5–32.

Whittaker, J. A., Montgomery, B. L., & Acosta, V. M. (2015). Retention of underrepresented minority faculty: Strategic initiatives for institutional value proposition based on perspectives from a range of academic institutions. *Journal of Undergraduate Neuroscience Education*, *13*(3), A136–A145.

Wight, V. R., Bianchi, S. M., & Hunt, B. R. (2013). Explaining racial/ethnic variation in partnered women's and men's housework: Does one size fit all? *Journal of Family Issues*, *34*, 394–427.

Williams, D. R. (2012). Miles to go before we sleep: Racial inequities in health. *Journal of Health and Social Behavior*, *53*(3), 279–295.

Williams, D. R., Neighbors, H. W., & Jackson, J. S. (2003). Racial/ethnic discrimination and health: Findings from community studies. *American Journal of Public Health*, *93*(2), 411–447.

Williams, D. R., & Williams-Morris, R. (2000). Racism and mental health: The African American experience. *Ethnicity & Health*, *5*, 243–268.

Williams, J. A. (2015). The invisible labor of minority professors. *Chronicle of Higher Education*, November 8. Retrieved from http://chronicle.com/article/The-Invisible-Labor-of/ 234098

Williams, J. C., Phillips, K. W., & Hall, E. V. (2014). *Double jeopardy? Gender bias against women of color in science.* San Francisco, CA: Work Life Law, UC Hastings College of Law.

Williams, R. A. (Ed.). (2014). *Men of color in higher education: New foundations for developing models for success.* Sterling, VA: Stylus.

Williams, W. M., & Ceci, S. J. (2012). When scientists choose motherhood. *American Scientist, 100*(2), 138–145.

Wilson, R. (1995). *Affirmative action: Yesterday, today, and beyond.* Washington, DC: American Council on Education.

Wingfield, A. H. (2010). Are some emotions marked Whites only: Racialized feelings rules in professional workplaces. *Social Problems, 57*(2), 251–268.

Wingfield, A. H. (2013). *No more invisible man: Race and gender in men's work.* Philadelphia, PA: Temple University Press.

Wingfield, A. H., & Alston, R. S. (2014). Maintaining hierarchies in predominantly White organizations: A theory of racial tasks. *American Behavioral Scientist, 58,* 274–287.

Wingfield, A. H., & Feagin, J. (2012). The racial dialectic: President Barack Obama and the White racial frame. *Qualitative Sociology, 35*(2), 143–162.

Wolfinger, N. H., Mason, M., & Goulden, M. (2009). "Stay in the game": Gender, family formation, and alternative trajectories in the academic life course. *Social Forces, 87,* 1591–1621.

Women of Color Network. (2014). History. Retrieved from http://www.wocninc.org/about -wocn/history/

Wong, E., Bigby, J., Kleinpeter, M., Mitchell, J., Camacho, D., Dan, A., & Sarto, G. (2001). Promoting the advancement of minority women faculty in academic medicine: The National Centers for Excellence in Women's Health. *Journal of Women's Health & Gender-Based Medicine, 10*(6), 1524.

Wood, F. B., & Budden, C. (2006). Strategic stress intervention in the academic environment. *Journal of College Teaching and Learning, 3*(2), 13–18.

Xie, Y., & Shauman, K. A. (1998). Sex differences in research productivity: New evidence about an old puzzle. *American Sociological Review, 63*(6), 847–870.

Yosso, T. (2005). Whose culture has capital? A critical race theory discussion of community cultural wealth. *Race Ethnicity and Education, 8*(1), 69–91.

Young, A. A., Furhman, M., & Chesler, M. A. (2014). How race and gender shape perceived challenges to classroom authority and expertise. In M. A. Chesler & A. A. Young (Eds.), *Faculty identities and the challenge of diversity* (pp. 45–63). Boulder, CO: Paradigm.

Young, C., & Wright, J. (2001). Mentoring: The components for success. *Journal of Instructional Psychology, 28*(3), 202–206.

Zambrana, R. E., Dávila, B. A., Espino, M. M., Lapeyrouse, L. M., Valdez, R. B., & Segura, D. (2017). Mexican American faculty in research universities: Can the next generation beat the odds? *Sociology of Race and Ethnicity, 3*(4), 458–473.

Zambrana, R. E., Dejesus, A. D., & Davila, B. A. (2015). Examining the influence of K–12 school experiences on the higher education pathway. In R. E. Zambrana & S. Hurtado (Eds.), *The magic key: The educational journey of Mexican Americans from K–12 to college and beyond* (pp. 122–144). Austin, TX: University of Texas Press.

Zambrana, R. E., Dorrington, C., & Alonzo Bell, S. (1997). Mexican American women in higher education: A comparative study. *Race, Gender & Class, 4*(2), 127–149.

Zambrana, R. E., & Frith, S. (1988). Mexican American professional women: Role satisfaction differences in single and multiple role lifestyles. *Journal of Social Behavior and Personality, 3*(4), 347–361.

Zambrana, R. E., & Hurtado, S. (Eds.). (2015). *The magic key: The educational journey of Mexican Americans from K–12 to college and beyond.* Austin, TX: University of Texas Press.

Zambrana, R. E., & MacDonald, V. (2009). Staggered inequalities in access to higher education by gender, race, and ethnicity. In B. T. Dill & R. E. Zambrana (Eds.), *Emerging intersections: Race, class, and gender in theory, policy, and practice* (pp. 73–100). New Brunswick, NJ: Rutgers University Press.

Zambrana, R. E., Ray, R., Espino, M. M., Castro, C., Cohen, B. D., & Eliason, J. (2015). "Don't leave us behind": The importance of mentoring for underrepresented minority faculty. *American Educational Research Journal, 52*(1), 40–72.

Zambrana, R. E., Wingfield, A. H., Lapeyrouse, L. M., Hoagland, T. L., & Burciaga Valdez, R. (2017b). Blatant, subtle, and insidious: URM faculty perceptions of discriminatory practices in predominantly white institutions. *Sociological Inquiry, 87*(2), 207–232.

Zanoni, P., Janssens, M., Benschop, Y., & Nkomo, S. (2010). Unpacking diversity, grasping inequality: Rethinking difference through critical perspectives. *Organization, 17*(1), 9–29.

Zellers, D. F., Howard, V. M., & Barcic, M. A. (2008). Faculty mentoring programs: Reenvisioning rather than reinventing the wheel. *Review of Educational Research, 78*(3), 552–558.

Zuberi, T., & Bonilla-Silva, E. (Eds.). (2008). *White logic, white methods: Racism and methodology.* Lanham, MD: Rowman & Littlefield.

# INDEX

Page numbers followed by *f* and *t* refer to figures and tables, respectively.